D1531600

Course	Retailing
Course Number	**MKTG 4033**
	UNIV OF CINCINNATI
	MARKETING

http://create.mheducation.com

ISBN-10: 1308486375   ISBN-13: 9781308486376

Contents

Credits

Introduction to the World of Retailing

EXECUTIVE BRIEFING
Mindy Grossman,
Chief Executive Officer, HSN Inc.

When I was a senior in college, I had a revelation about my life and the direction in which I was heading. I immediately called my parents and told them that I was not going to marry my high school boyfriend and go to law school like I had planned. I was going to follow my passion and head to New York to work in the fashion industry. Needless to say, they were surprised.

When I received my first VP position at 26, my parents finally stopped asking when I was going to go back and get my law degree. I've been on an exciting ride since then and have been fortunate enough to hold esteemed positions at great companies, such as the SVP of menswear at Warnaco, VP of new business development at Polo Ralph Lauren, president of Chaps Ralph Lauren, president and CEO of Polo Jeans Company, and global VP for Nike.

Then I received a call one day to meet with Barry Diller, who was the president of IAC, which owned HSN at the time. After discussing my ideas with him, I discovered I had the ability to make an impact on this company and transform HSN into a lifestyle network. My friends and colleagues were shocked when I announced that I was leaving Nike and going to HSN. They had gone through eight CEOs in 10 years and I would be the first female CEO of the company. I saw the company's potential and was excited to take on the challenge.

Over the last seven years, we have transformed HSN into a dynamic, interactive, multichannel retailer that offers a curated assortment of exclusive products from top lifestyle brands and engages our customers wherever and whenever they would like to shop. As a matter fact, close to 40 percent of our HSN sales come from our digital platform—online, tablet, mobile, and social media.

Our product offering is diverse with 79,000 unique products, 70 percent of which are proprietary to HSN. Widely respected celebrities and designers, such as Queen Latifah, India Hicks, Badgley Mischka, Naeem Khan, and New York fashion icon, Iris Apfel, have come to our campus in St. Petersburg, Florida to promote their products. We also have had Mary J. Blige, Mariah Carey, and P. Diddy sell their fragrances on HSN.

CHAPTER 1

LEARNING OBJECTIVES

LO1 Identify retailing activities.

LO2 Realize the importance of retailing in the U.S. and world economies.

LO3 Analyze the changing retail industry.

LO4 Recognize the opportunities in retailing for you.

LO5 Understand the strategic retail management decision process.

Our ability to entertain and inspire versus just selling a product is really how retail is evolving. We bring content, community, and commerce to life through our strategic partnerships with the entertainment community across film, music, and live events. We were Universal's partner for the launch of *Snow White and the Huntsman* and our 24-hour event featured 25 designers and brands that created over 220 unique products inspired by the film, including the launch of Oscar-winning costume designer Colleen Atwood's first consumer collection. Our HSN Live concert series provides our customers with a live music experience featuring some of the music industry's biggest stars. Lionel Richie held a concert at HSN's studios to kick off the release of *Tuskegee,* his first best-selling album in more than 25 years. The power of appearing on HSN is unparalleled.

When I met with Lady Gaga about potentially developing a line for HSN, she said, "You have the coolest job." Think of all the amazing things she has done in her career, and here she was telling me I had a cool job. And you know what? She's absolutely right.

Retailing is such a common part of our everyday lives that we often take it for granted. For most people, retailers simply are places to buy things. At a very young age, children know what stores have the things they want, and they expect to find the products they want when they visit a store or website. Sometimes consumers talk to a sales associate when they visit a store, and other times the only retail employees they interact with are cashiers collecting the money for purchases. Some college students work part-time or over the holidays for retailers and have a somewhat deeper insight into what retailers do. But these limited exposures to retailing are just the tip of the iceberg. Behind the stores, website, sales associates, and cashiers are an army of managers responsible for making sure that the products and services that people want are available when

EXHIBIT 1–1
Quiz on What You
Know about Retailing

1. Which of the following companies is *not* a retailer:
   (a) McDonald's
   (b) Holiday Inn
   (c) Macy's
   (d) eBay
   (e) All are retailers

2. What is the annual compensation (salary plus bonus) of a typical Walmart Supercenter 30-something store manager?
   (a) Under $49,999
   (b) $50,000 to $89,999
   (c) $90,000 to $149,999
   (d) over $150,000

3. Which of the following products/concepts was initiated or developed by retailer buyers?
   (a) tea bags
   (b) panty hose
   (c) Rudolph the Red-Nosed Reindeer
   (d) establishing Thanksgiving on the third Thursday of November
   (e) All of these products/concepts were developed/initiated by retailers.

4. What is the largest company in the world in terms of number of employees?
   (a) Walmart
   (b) General Electric
   (c) IBM
   (d) ExxonMobil
   (e) Mitsubishi

5. Which of the following retailers is owned by a company headquartered outside the United States?
   (a) Food Lion
   (b) Ben & Jerry's Ice Cream
   (c) 7-Eleven
   (d) A&P supermarkets
   (e) All of these are owned by foreign companies.

6. What country has the most efficient retail structure (lowest cost to move merchandise from a manufacturer's factory to a retail stores)?
   (a) Japan
   (b) United States
   (c) South Korea
   (d) France
   (e) Germany

7. What percentage of total retailer sales in the United States are made over the Internet?
   (a) 30 percent
   (b) 20 percent
   (c) 14 percent
   (d) 8 percent
   (e) 3 percent

8. What percent of the U.S. workforce is employed by retailers or firms selling products or providing services to retailers?
   (a) 10 percent
   (b) 17 percent
   (c) 25 percent
   (d) 43 percent
   (e) 62 percent

they want them, where they want them, and at a fair price. Take the quiz in Exhibit 1–1 to check out the accuracy of your views about the retail industry and career opportunities the industry offers. The answers are at the end of the chapter.

To illustrate what is below the tip of the iceberg, consider Macy's. Macy's stocks and sells more than 100,000 different sizes, colors, and brands of products. Managers at Macy's need to determine what subset of these 100,000 items they are going to offer from the millions of potential products Macy's could sell. Then managers negotiate with more than 3,000 suppliers the price they will pay the supplier for the products and the prices they will charge their customers. Managers decide which of the 100,000 products will be sold at each of Macy's 840 stores and how they will be displayed. Managers select, train, and motivate the 150,000 store employees to make sure the merchandise is attractively displayed and customers get the service they expect. And, perhaps most importantly, Macy's managers develop strategies to guide these decisions and provide a good return to its stockholders while facing intense competition.[1]

Working in this highly competitive, rapidly changing retail environment is both challenging and exciting, and it offers significant financial rewards. This book describes the world of retailing and offers key principles for effectively managing retail businesses. Knowledge of retailing principles and practices will help you develop management skills for many business contexts. For example, retailers are the customers for most business-to-consumer (B-to-C) companies such as Procter & Gamble and Hewlett-Packard. Thus, brand managers in B-to-C companies need to have a thorough understanding of how retailers operate and make money so that they can encourage retailers to offer and promote their products. Financial and health care institutions use retail principles to develop their offerings; improve customer service; and provide convenient, easy access to their customers. Thus, any student interested in professional B-to-C selling, marketing management, or finance should find this book useful.

WHAT IS RETAILING?

Retailing is the set of business activities that adds value to products and services sold to consumers for their personal or family use. Often, people think of retailing only as the sale of products in stores, but retailing also involves the sale of services such as overnight lodging in a motel, a doctor's exam, a haircut, or a home-delivered pizza. Not all retailing is done in stores. Examples of nonstore retailing include ordering a T-shirt on your mobile phone app, buying cosmetics from an Avon salesperson, ordering hiking boots from an L.L. Bean catalog, and renting a Blu-Ray from a Redbox kiosk.

LO1
Identify retailing activities.

REFACT
The word *retail* is derived from the French word *retailer,* meaning to cut a piece off or break bulk.[2]

The Retailer's Role in a Supply Chain

A **retailer** is a business that sells products and/or services to consumers for their personal or family use. Retailers are a key component in a supply chain that links manufacturers to consumers. A **supply chain** is a set of firms that make and deliver goods and services to consumers. Exhibit 1–2 shows the retailer's position within a supply chain.

Retailers typically buy products from wholesalers and/or manufacturers and resell them to consumers. Why are retailers needed? Wouldn't it be easier and cheaper for consumers to cut out the middlemen, the wholesalers and retailers, and buy directly from manufacturers? The answer, generally, is no, because retailers add value and are more efficient at adding this value than manufacturers or wholesalers.

Retailers Create Value

The value-creating activities undertaken by retailers include (1) providing an assortment of products and services, (2) breaking bulk, (3) holding inventory, and (4) providing services.

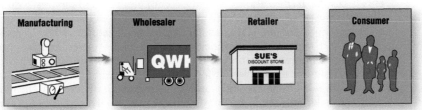

EXHIBIT 1–2
Example of a Supply Chain

Providing Assortments Conventional supermarkets typically carry about 30,000 different items made by more than 500 companies. Offering an assortment enables their customers to choose from a wide selection of products, brands, sizes, and prices at one location. Manufacturers specialize in producing specific types of products. For example, Frito-Lay makes snacks, Yoplait makes yogurt, Skippy makes peanut butter, and Heinz makes ketchup. If each of these manufacturers had its own stores that sold only its own products, consumers would have to go to many different stores to buy the groceries needed to prepare a single meal.

Breaking Bulk To reduce transportation costs, manufacturers and wholesalers typically ship cases of frozen dinners or cartons of blouses to retailers. Retailers then offer the products in smaller quantities tailored to individual consumers' and households' consumption patterns—an activity called **breaking bulk**. Breaking bulk is important to both manufacturers and consumers. It allows manufacturers to efficiently make and ship merchandise in larger quantities at one time and enables consumers to purchase merchandise in smaller, more useful quantities.

Holding Inventory A major value-providing activity performed by retailers is **holding inventory** so that products will be available when consumers want them. Thus, consumers can keep a smaller inventory of products at home because they know local retailers will have the products available when they need more. This activity is particularly important to consumers with limited storage space, such as families living in small apartments.

Retailers add value by providing an assortment of products that customers can buy at one location when they want them.

Providing Services Retailers provide services that make it easier for customers to buy and use products. For example, retailers offer credit so that consumers can have a product now and pay for it later. They display products so that consumers can see and test them before buying. Some retailers employ salespeople in stores or maintain Web sites to answer questions and provide additional information about the products they sell.

Costs of Channel Activities

While the value-creating activities undertaken by channel members provide benefits to customers, they also increase the cost of products and services. Exhibit 1–3 illustrates the supply chain costs of getting a T-shirt from the manufacturer to the consumer. In this example, it costs the T-shirt manufacturer $10.00 to make and market the T-shirt. These costs include the design, raw materials, labor, production equipment, transportation to the wholesaler, and so on. The manufacturer sells the T-shirt to the wholesaler for $11.00 and makes $1.00 profit. The wholesaler incurs $2.00 to handle and store the T-shirt and transport it to the retailers. The wholesaler sells the T-shirt to the retailers for $14.00, making a $1.00 profit.

Channel Member			Profit as a Percentage of Sales
Manufacturer	Cost	$10.00	
	Profit	$1.00	9.10%
	Selling price to wholesaler	$11.00	
Wholesaler	Price paid to manufacturer	$11.00	
	Cost to add value	$2.00	
	Profit	$1.00	8.00%
	Selling price to retailer	$14.00	
Retailer	Price paid to distributor	$14.00	
	Cost to add value	$4.00	
	Profit	$1.95	
	Selling price to customer	$19.95	9.77%

EXHIBIT 1–3

Costs Incurred to Undertake Value-Added Activities in the Distribution Channel for a T-Shirt

The retailer then incurs costs to fold the shirt, put price tags on it, store it, employ sales associates, light and air condition the store, and so on. The retailer sells the shirt to a customer for $19.95, making a profit of $1.95.

Note that the costs in the supply chain, $8.95 ($19.95 − $11.00), are almost as much as the cost to make the product. These costs are justified by the considerable value added by the wholesaler and retailers to the product. By providing assortments, breaking bulk, holding inventory, and providing services, retailers increase the benefits that consumers receive from their products and services.

Consider a T-shirt in a shipping crate in an Iowa manufacturer's warehouse. The T-shirt will not satisfy the needs of a student who wants to have something to wear at the basketball game tonight. The student finds the T-shirt more valuable and will pay more for it if it is available from a nearby department store that also sells pants, belts, and other items complementing the T-shirt and provides sales associates who can help the student find what he likes. If retailers did not provide these benefits, wholesalers or manufacturers would have to provide them, and they would typically not be as efficient as retailers in providing these benefits.

Retailers Perform Wholesaling and Production Activities

Wholesalers buy and store merchandise in large quantities from manufacturers and then resell the merchandise (usually in smaller quantities) to retailers. When manufacturers like Apple and Nike sell directly to consumers, they are performing the production, wholesaling, and retail business activities. Some large retailers, like Costco and Home Depot, function as both retailers and wholesalers: They perform retailing activities when they sell to consumers, but they engage in wholesaling activities when they sell to other businesses, such as restaurants or building contractors.

In some supply chains, the manufacturing, wholesaling, and retailing activities are performed by independent firms, but most supply chains feature some vertical integration. **Vertical integration** means that a firm performs more than one set of activities in the channel, as occurs when a retailer engages in wholesaling activities by operating its own distribution centers to supply its stores. **Backward integration** arises when a retailer performs some wholesaling and manufacturing activities, such as operating warehouses or designing private-label merchandise. **Forward integration** occurs when a manufacturer undertakes retailing and wholesaling activities, such as Apple operating its own retail stores.

Most large retailers such as Safeway, Walmart, and Lowe's manage their own distribution centers and perform activities undertaken by wholesalers. They buy directly from manufacturers, have merchandise shipped to their warehouses, and then distribute the merchandise to their stores. Other retailers, such as J. Crew and Victoria's Secret, are even more vertically integrated. They design the merchandise they sell and then contract with manufacturers to produce it exclusively for them.

Apple is a vertically integrated company because it performs the manufacturing, distribution, and retailing activities in its supply chain.

Differences in Distribution Channels around the World

Some critical differences among the retailing and distribution systems in the United States, European Union, China, and India are summarized in Exhibit 1–4. As this exhibit suggests, the U.S. retail industry has the greatest retail density (retail stores per person) and concentration of large retail firms. Real estate in the United States is relatively inexpensive, and most consumers own automobiles. Thus, retailers often operate large stores in lightly populated areas. Many U.S. retailers have stores with more than 20,000 square feet. Due to their size, they have the scale economies to operate their own warehouses, eliminating the need for wholesalers. This combination of large stores and large firms in the United States results in a very efficient distribution system.

In contrast, the Indian distribution system is characterized by small stores operated by relatively small firms and a large independent wholesale industry. To make the daily deliveries to these small retailers efficiently, the merchandise often passes through several different wholesalers. In addition, the infrastructure to support modern retailing, especially the transportation and communication systems, is not as well developed in India as it is in more developed economies. These efficiency

EXHIBIT 1–4   Comparison of Retailing and Distribution across the World

	United States	Northern Europe	India	China
Concentration (percent of sales made by large retailers)	Highest	High	Lowest	Low
Retail density (square feet of retail space per person)	Highest	Modest	Lowest	Low
Average store size	Highest	Modest	Lowest	Modest
Role of wholesalers	Minimal	Modest	Extensive	Extensive
Infrastructure supporting efficient supply chain	Best	Good	Weakest	Weak
Restrictions on retail locations, store size, and ownership	Minimal	Extensive	Extensive	Modest

The retail industry in India is dominated by small, local retailers with few modern national chains.

differences mean that a much larger percentage of the Indian labor force is employed in distribution and retailing than is the case in the United States, and the supply chain costs in India are higher.[3]

China's retail industry is highly fragmented like the retail industry in India. It is composed of many small and medium-sized firms. The number of national and even regional chains is limited. However, China's retail distribution system is going through a period of rapid development. This development is spurred by the government's shifting interest from focusing on exports and satisfying basic consumer needs that provide a higher quality of life. In China, the government removed most restrictions on direct foreign investments, and global retailers flocked to this huge and growing market. Now, Walmart operates 370 stores in China, and Carrefour, the second largest retailer in the world, operates 204. However, there is great disparity between the distribution system in the first-tier, eastern coastal cities—Beijing, Shanghai, and Guangdong—and the smaller western cities. The retail offering in the first-tier cities is very similar to the urban retail environment in U.S. cities such as New York and Chicago. In contrast, retailing in the smaller western cities is more similar to retailing in India.[4]

The European distribution system falls between the American and Indian systems on this continuum of efficiency and scale. In northern Europe, retailing is similar to that in the United States, with high concentration levels in some national markets. For example, 80 percent or more of sales in sectors such as food and home improvements are made by five or fewer firms. Southern European retailing is more fragmented across all sectors. For example, traditional farmers' market retailing remains important in some sectors, operating alongside large "big-box" formats.[5]

Social and political objectives have created some of these differences in distribution systems in countries. An important priority of the Indian and European economic policies is to reduce unemployment by protecting small businesses such as independent neighborhood retailers.[6] Some countries have passed laws prohibiting large stores, as well as strict zoning laws to preserve green spaces, protect town centers, and inhibit the development of large-scale retailing in the suburbs.

Finally, retail productivity is reduced when countries restrict the hours that stores can operate. For example, in France, many stores close at 7 p.m. on weeknights. Labor unions in France and elsewhere in Europe are opposed to U.S.-style 24/7 shopping because of the strains it could put on store employees.[7]

SOCIAL AND ECONOMIC SIGNIFICANCE OF RETAILING

Role in Developed Economies

LO2

Realize the importance of retailing in the U.S. and world economies.

Retail sales (excluding automobile and automotive parts sales) in 2011 were $4.3 trillion. More than 8 percent of the total U.S. gross domestic product comes from retailing, almost as much as the contribution of the entire U.S. manufacturing industry sector.[8] But this sales level underestimates the impact of retailing on the U.S. economy because it does not include the sales and employment of many firms providing consumer services such as entertainment, home repairs, and health care.

Consumer spending plays a critical role in the economies of the United States and other developed countries. When consumers spend more money buying goods and services from retailers, a country's economy flourishes. Merchandise flies off the shelves, and retailers place orders for replacement merchandise. Manufacturers hire more employees, place orders for raw materials, and make more products. However, if consumers feel uncertain about their financial future and decide to refrain from buying new refrigerators or blue jeans, the economy slows down.

The retail sector plays a key role in developed economies, not only because consumer demand is an indication of a vibrant financial system, but also because retailers are large employers. More than 14 million people were employed in retailing in 2012—approximately 11 percent of the U.S. workforce—and an additional 15 percent work for companies that either provide services to and/or sell products through retailers.[9]

Corporate Social Responsibility

In addition to providing the benefit to their customers outlined in the previous section and a fair return for their stockholders, most retailers engage in socially responsible activities. **Corporate social responsibility (CSR)** involves an organization voluntarily engaging in business practices that meet or exceed the ethical and legal expectations of its stakeholders—its employees, customers, community, and society in general.

Many retailers now go the extra mile to support their communities, environment, and social causes. Examples include reducing their use of energy, supporting local schools, and working with national organizations such as the American Red Cross and Habitat for Humanity. These corporate social responsibility activities promote a positive image to customers, build employee morale, and save money—a win–win scenario for both the companies and their stakeholders.[10]

For example, community philanthropy is the cornerstone of Target's CSR activities. Store managers have a budget for donations they can make to local events. Since 1946, Target has given 5 percent of its income to support local activities in the communities in which it has stores, such as company-sponsored youth leagues or a special exhibit at the local zoo. Target has been innovative in using social media to support its CSR program. Target's "Bullseye Gives" program asked its million Facebook fans to vote on how the company should allocate $3 million among 10 nonprofits.[11]

Many retailers are building LEED-certified stores. The Leadership in Energy and Environmental Design (LEED) certification is based on an assessment of the store's impact on human and environmental health, sustainable site development, water savings, energy efficiency, materials selection, and indoor environmental

REFACT

Shoppers in the United Kingdom are more likely to buy goods on the basis of environmental, animal welfare, or fair trade claims than their counterparts in continental Europe. About 41 percent of British consumers have bought ethically produced products, compared with 34 percent in Germany, 31 percent in France, and 12 percent in Spain.[12]

Home Depot employees' involvement with Habitat for Humanity helps the local community and builds company morale.

quality. Some features in a prototype LEED-certified McDonald's restaurant are its permeable pavement that cleans rainwater; a cistern buried behind the restaurant that collects rainwater, which is used to water the landscaping; a roof garden that insulates the restaurant; the use of less-toxic cleaners and of paints and resins that do not emit chemical odors; and the installation of low-flow toilets and urinals that use less water than standard low-flow toilets. Walmart's new stores have fuel cells that supply half of the electricity. Holes are punched in the roof for skylights that provide 70 percent of the store's lighting needs during the day. To help keep the scorching sun at bay and cool the building naturally, roofs are painted white.[13]

The production of apparel has adverse effects on the environment because it involves the use of dyes, solvents, and huge amounts of water and petroleum for transportation. An industry group called the Sustainable Apparel Coalition has developed an index to rate the relative sustainability of apparel. Some members of the coalition are Walmart, Target, Kohl's, Nordstrom, and Patagonia. Environmentalists anticipate that the index will be used by consumers when selecting products and by retail buyers when they select the assortments of products to offer. The index considers the entire life of a product—from raw materials to disposal. Brands can get higher scores by asking consumers to wash items in cold, rather than hot, water. Some buyers are rewarded for the design of products with high index levels. A new Nike "Flyknit" running shoe worn by U.S., Kenyan, and other marathoners at the London Olympics was designed based on the index. The shoe is knit from polyester, eliminating the waste of shoes sewn from cut textiles.[14]

Companies typically go through several stages before they fully integrate CSR into their strategy. Companies in the first stage engage only in CSR activities required by law. In this stage, companies are not actually convinced of the importance of CSR actions. In the second stage, companies go beyond activities required by law to engage in CSR activities that also provide a short-term financial benefit to the

The Nike Flyknit receives a high Sustainable Apparel Coalition index because its construction reduces waste by an average of 80 percent when compared to typical Nike running footwear.

company. For example, a retailer might reduce the energy consumption of its stores just because doing so reduces its costs. In the third stage, companies operate responsibly because they believe this is the "right thing" to do. Companies in the fourth and final stage engage in socially and environmentally responsible actions because they believe these activities must be done for the "well-being" of everyone. These companies have truly incorporated the concept of CSR into their business strategy.[15]

Role in Developing Economies— The Bottom of the Pyramid

Retailers need to also focus on opportunities available by serving the needs of the 4 billion people (25 percent of the world's population) at the lowest end of the income distribution. Serving these customers also provides an important social benefit: reducing worldwide poverty.[16] Consumers in this low income consumer segment, referred to as the **base of the pyramid** or **bottom of the pyramid (BoP)**, have a potential spending power of more than $5 trillion. The sheer size and growth of the BoP markets, especially in the countries with emerging economies such as China, India, and Brazil, and maturation of consumer goods and retail markets in developed economies is motivating firms to enter the BoP market.

Undertaking retailing activities to the BoP market is challenging. It is difficult to communicate and complete transactions with people in the BoP market because they are more likely to lack access to mass media, the Internet, mobile phones, or credit cards than more affluent markets. Most people in BoP markets live in rural areas—remote villages that are not connected to the outside world through adequate roads. Limited local demand combined with the high cost of transporting goods to and from remote villages results in higher costs and prices for consumer goods. Thus, engagement at the BoP markets requires innovative approaches for doing business. Retrofitting business models used in the more developed markets will not work.[17] Retailing View 1.1 describes how Grupo Elektra has improved the lifestyle of Latin America's working poor.

THE GROWING IMPORTANCE OF RETAILING AND RETAILERS

Evolution of the Retail Industry

LO3

Analyze the changing retail industry.

REFACT

James Cash Penney opened the first JCPenney store, called Golden Rule, in Kemmerer, Wyoming, in 1902.[18]

From a consumer's perspective, retailers are local businesses. Even though many consumers collect information and make purchases using the Internet or a mobile device, more than 90 percent of all retail sales are made in stores—usually stores that are less than a 15-minute drive from the consumer's home or workplace. Thus, retail stores predominately compete against other stores that are located nearby.

There has been a dramatic change in the structure of the retail industry over the past 50 years. Fifty years ago, Sears and JCPenney were the only retail firms that had chains of stores across the United States. The retail industry consisted of the small, independent, local retailers competing against other small, independent retailers in the same community. Walmart, Home Depot, Staples, and Best Buy did not exist or were small companies with a few stores. Now, the retail industry is dominated by large, national, and even international retail firms. While there are more than 1 million retailers in the United States, over 40 percent of U.S. retail sales are made by companies with more than 10,000 employees. Home improvement centers are the most concentrated sector in the retail industry, with the four largest firms accounting for 92.7 percent of U.S. annual sales in the sector. The top four department store chains account for 73.2 percent of annual U.S. sales in that sector, and the top four drug store chains account for 63.0 percent in that sector. On the other hand, the least concentrated sectors are food service and drinking, where only 5.8 percent of sales are represented by the top four firms in the sector, and furniture stores where only 13.9 percent of sales are represented by the top four firms in the sector.[19]

The largest retailers in the world are shown in Exhibit 1–5. Nine of the top 20 retailers are headquartered in the United States; while Germany has five. Of these top 20 retailers, the U.S. retailers have fewer global operations than the non-U.S. based retailers. The average number of countries that these U.S.-based retailers operate in is five, compared to the non-U.S.-headquartered retailers, who operate in an average of 16 countries. Five of the largest U.S.-based retailers operate in only one or two countries. Only four of the 11 non-U.S-based retailers operate stores in the United States, the largest retail market in the world.

The development of information systems is one the forces facilitating the growth of large retail firms—the shift from an industry dominated by small, local retailers to large multinational chains. Prior to the development of these systems, it was difficult for someone other than the local store manager to track

REFACT

Walmart's annual sales are five times greater than the sales of Procter & Gamble, the largest consumer product producer.[20]

RETAILING VIEW Grupo Elektra Improves the Lifestyle of Latin America's Working Poor   1.1

Grupo Elektra, with headquarters in Mexico City, owns and operates more than 2,600 specialty stores in Mexico, Brazil, Argentina, Guatemala, El Salvador, Honduras, Panama, and Peru. Its stores sell consumer electronics and appliances to Latin America's working poor. It is quite a challenge to sell consumer durable goods to families earning less than $400 per month and spend 90 percent of their income on basic necessities, such as food and housing. In addition, these BoP consumers often do not have formal jobs or bank accounts. But Grupo Elektra, and its banking affiliate, Banco Azteca, have been increasing sales and profits during one of the worst economic recessions in decades by servicing these low-income consumers. For the past five years, revenues and operating profits have grown at a double-digit rate.

Rather than wait for low-income consumers to open their own bank accounts so they can afford to buy its products, Elektra launched its own banks inside its network of specialty retail shops. These banks make small "micro-loans" to Elektra's customers so they can afford to buy its appliances. It determines how much money its new customers can really afford to borrow—and then pay back. Within 24 hours, the bank approves or denies a client's loan application using the information gathered by the credit officer at the branch. The officer visits the customers' houses to determine their income and expenses. The bank then establishes weekly installment payments that match the borrowing capacity of each customer. More than 5,000 loan officers travel by motorcycles to the applicants' homes to assess their creditworthiness and, when necessary, to collect payments from customers. Usually, however, cash payments are made once a week at an Electra store.

This approach has enabled thousands of low-income consumers to acquire durables that have long been inaccessible to them because they lacked the opportunity to use credit. Traditionally, these low-income people—the taxi drivers, mango vendors, and cleaning ladies of Latin

Grupo Elektra has developed a successful strategy for selling products and providing micro-loans to its customers at the base of the pyramid.

America—put their money in a cookie jar or below their mattresses. Now, they can establish a bank account for a minimum of only US $5 and have access to a debit card.

Sources: Erin Carlyle, "Billionaire Ricardo Salinas: Mexico's Credit Card," *Forbes*, May 7, 2012, p.100; Erin Carlyle, "Mexican Billionaire Buys Advance America, Largest Payday Lender In U.S.," *Forbes*, April 23, 2012, p. 102; and "Grupo Elektra: Will Selling in Brazil Prove to Be the Retailer's Next 'Growth Moment?" *Knowledge @ Wharton*, April 07, 2010.

DISCUSSION QUESTION

The typical interest rate charged by Grupo Elektra is 50 percent, a rate that would be illegal in most U.S. states. Is Elektra providing a benefit to its customers or taking advantage of its customers' lack of knowledge about these financial contracts?

EXHIBIT 1–5   The 20 Largest Retailers in the World

Rank	Name	Headquarters Location	Number of Countries	Stores in U.S.	Sales ($ millions)	Primary Format
1	Walmart	U.S.	16	Yes	418,993	Supercenter
2	Carrefour	France	33	No	119,652	Supercenter
3	Tesco	UK	13	Yes	92,171	Supercenter
4	Metro	Germany	33	No	86,931	Warehouse club
5	Kroger	U.S.	1	Yes	82,189	Supermarket
6	Schwarz Untematmens Trauhard	Germany	26	No	79,119	Discount store
7	Costco	U.S.	9	Yes	76,225	Warehouse club
8	Home Depot	U.S.	5	Yes	67,997	Home improvement
9	Walgreens	U.S.	2	Yes	67,420	Drug store
10	Aldi Einkauf	Germany	18	Yes	67,112	Discount store
11	Target	U.S.	1	Yes	65,786	Discount store
12	Rewe	Germany	13	No	61,134	Supermarket
13	CVS	U.S.	2	Yes	57,345	Drug store
14	Seven & Holding	Japan	18	Yes	57,055	Convenience store
15	Groupe Auchan	France	13	No	55,212	Supercenter
16	Edeka Zentrale	Germany	1	No	54,074	Supermarket
17	Aeon	Japan	8	No	53,458	Supercenter
18	Woolworth	Australia	2	No	51,171	Supermarket
19	Best Buy	U.S.	15	Yes	50,272	Electronics category specialist
20	Lowe's	U.S.	3	Yes	48,815	Home improvement

Source: "2011 Global 250 Retailers," *Stores Magazine,* January 2012.

REFACT

Walmart processes more than 100 million transactions per hour through its POS terminals in stores around the world.[21]

REFACT

Walmart has a data warehouse with more than 2.5 petabytes (2,500 terrabytes) of information—the equivalent of 167 times more than all of the books in America's Library of Congress.[22]

how the merchandise in the store was selling—whether it was selling above plan and needed to be reordered or was selling below plan and needed to have its price reduced. It was also difficult to collect and consolidate the plans from a number of different stores so that a buyer could place large orders with vendors to get price discounts. Thus, before the availability of modern information systems, it was difficult for retailers to lower costs through scale economies, and larger retailers had limited advantages over small local or regional retailers.

Most consumers shopping in their local stores don't realize the sophisticated information systems used by retailers today to manage these large, complex supply chain systems. To illustrate the complexity of these systems, consider the following example. You go to Best Buy and find a tablet you are going to buy. When you decide to buy a tablet in a store, the point-of-sale (POS) terminal transmits data about the transaction to the retailer's distribution center and then on to the manufacturer. Data about your purchase are incorporated into a sophisticated inventory management system. When the in-store inventory level drops below a prespecified level, an electronic notice is automatically transmitted, authorizing the shipment of more units to the retailer's distribution center and then to the store. The retail buyer or a computer program analyzes the sales data to determine how many and which tablet models will be stocked in the retailer's stores and what price will be charged.

To add even another layer of complexity, most large retailers contract with factories around the world to have merchandise made for them. Thus, for example, nearly 1,500 employees, working in both quality-control and full-service buying centers, help Target ensure that any factory worldwide that produces products with the Target name meet Target's own standards for product quality, without violating ethical labor standards.[23]

Role of Information Systems

Now, retailers are inundated with data about the thousands of transactions that take place each day. The challenge for retailers is to convert this raw data into information that managers can use to make better decisions. Many retailers now use the data they have on their customers to identify their best customers and target customized promotions to them, place products close to each other when they find that many customers are buying the same products at the same time, and tailor the assortment of products in each store to better match the needs of the store's local market.

In addition to playing an important role in society in general, retailing provides personal opportunities to work for a company in an exciting, challenging environment or to start an entrepreneurial venture. These opportunities are discussed in the next section.

Sophisticated supply chains have facilitated the economies of scale that large retailers have been able to achieve.

MANAGEMENT AND ENTREPRENEURIAL OPPORTUNITIES

Management Opportunities

To exploit these new technologies and systems and gain advantage in a highly competitive and challenging environment, retailers need to hire and promote the best and brightest. Sherry Hollack, a former vice president of talent development at Macy's, emphasized this point: "One of the biggest challenges facing Macy's, and most other retail chains, is hiring and retaining managers to lead our company in the coming years. The changing demographics are working against us. Over the next ten years, a lot of our senior managers, members of the Baby Boomer generation, will be retiring. So we are going to be competing with other retailers and firms in other industries for a smaller pool of available managers in the generations behind the Boomers. In addition, retailing is becoming a much more sophisticated business. Our managers need to be comfortable with new technologies, information and supply chain management systems, and international business as well as managing a diverse workforce and buying merchandise."[24]

Students often view retailing as part of marketing because managing distribution (place) is one of the 4 Ps of marketing. But retailers are businesses and, like manufacturers, undertake all the traditional business activities. Retailers raise capital from financial institutions; purchase goods and services; use accounting and

LO4

Recognize the opportunities in retailing for you.

management information systems to control their operations; manage warehouses and distribution systems; design and develop new products; and undertake marketing activities such as advertising, promotion, sales force management, and market research. Thus, retailers employ people with expertise and interests in finance, accounting, human resource management, supply chain management, and computer systems, as well as management and marketing.

Retail managers are often given considerable responsibility early in their careers. Retail management is also financially rewarding. Starting salaries are typically between $35,000 and $65,000 for college graduates entering management trainee positions. After completing a management training program, retail managers can

1.2   RETAILING VIEW   Sam Walton, Founder of Walmart (1918–1992)

Like Henry Ford with his Model T, Sam Walton revolutionized the retail industry. After graduating from the University of Missouri in 1940, Walton began working at a JCPenney store in Des Moines, Iowa. He served in the army during World War II and then purchased a Ben Franklin variety store franchise in Newport, Arkansas. He boosted sales by finding suppliers that would sell him merchandise at lower prices than his cost to buy from Ben Franklin.

Walton lost his store, however, in 1950 when the landlord refused to renew his lease. He then moved to Bentonville, Arkansas, where he and a younger brother franchised another Ben Franklin store. Walton employed a new self-service system that he had discovered at two Ben Franklin stores in Minnesota. He placed the checkout registers and clerks at the front of the store rather than scattering them throughout. By 1960, Walton had 15 stores in Arkansas and Missouri that laid the foundation for Walmart.

By the early 1960s, some retailers in large, urban, eastern cities had developed the discount store concept, incorporating self-service, shallow but broad assortments, low overhead costs, and large parking lots. In 1962, Walton brought this format to small southern towns, opening his first Walmart Discount City in Rogers, Arkansas.

Walton often visited his stores, dropping in unannounced to check the merchandise presentation or financial performance and talk to his "associates." He prided himself on a profit-sharing program and a friendly, open, supportive atmosphere—business practices he had learned when working for JCPenney. He often led his workers in the Walmart cheer: "Give me a W! Give me an A! Give me an L! Give me a Squiggly! (Here, everybody sort of does the twist. As part of Walmart's campaign to modernize its image, in 1998, it dropped the squiggly from its trademark.) Give me an M! Give me an A! Give me an R! Give me a T! What's that spell? Walmart! What's that spell? Walmart! Who's number one? THE CUSTOMER!"

He offered his own formula for how a large company should operate: "Think one store at a time. That sounds easy enough, but it's something we've constantly had to

REFACT

With 2.2 million employees, Walmart is the largest company in the world in terms of number of employees.[25]

Sam Walton believed in "management by walking around."

stay on top of. Communicate, communicate, communicate: What good is figuring out a better way to sell beach towels if you aren't going to tell everybody in your company about it? Keep your ear to the ground: A computer is not—and will never be—a substitute for getting out in your stores and learning what's going on."

In 1991, due to the success of his concept and management practices, Walton became America's wealthiest person; however, he maintained his simple, unassuming lifestyle. Whenever he traveled on business, he rented the same compact economy cars and stayed in the same inexpensive hotels as his employees did. He died of leukemia in 1992. Walmart is now the world's largest corporation.

Sources: Michael Bergdahl, *The Retail Revolution: How Wal-Mart Created a Brave New World of Business* (New York: Metropolitan Books, 2009); and Michael Bergdahl, *The 10 Rules of Sam Walton: Success Secrets for Remarkable Results* (Hoboken, NJ: Wiley, 2006).

DISCUSSION QUESTION

What were the key factors that led to Walmart's phenomenal growth and dominance of the retail industry?

double their starting salary in three to five years if they perform well. Senior buyers and others in higher managerial positions and store managers make between $120,000 and $300,000. (See Appendix 1A at the end of this chapter.)

Entrepreneurial Opportunities

Retailing also provides opportunities for people who wish to start their own business. Some of the world's most successful people are retailing entrepreneurs. Many are well known because their names appear over stores' doors; others you may not recognize. Retailing View 1.2 examines the life of one of the world's greatest entrepreneurs, Sam Walton. Some other innovative retail entrepreneurs include Jeff Bezos, Do Won and Jin Sook Chang, Ingvar Kamprad, and Howard Schultz. These entrepreneurs came from humble backgrounds and changed the way retailing is done.

Jeff Bezos (Amazon.com)   After his research uncovered that Internet usage was growing at a 2,300 percent annual rate in 1994, Jeffrey Bezos, the 30-year-old son of a Cuban refugee, quit his job on Wall Street and left behind a hefty bonus to start an Internet business. While his wife MacKenzie was driving their car across country, Jeff pecked out his business plan on a laptop computer. By the time they reached Seattle, he had rounded up the investment capital to launch the first Internet book retailer. The company, Amazon.com, is named after the river that carries the greatest amount of water, symbolizing Bezos's objective of achieving the greatest volume of Internet sales. Under his leadership, Amazon developed technologies to make shopping on the Internet faster, easier, and more personal than shopping in stores by offering personalized recommendations and home pages. Amazon.com has become more than a bookstore. It is now the largest on-line retailer, with annual sales greater than $48 billion. Amazon also provides virtual stores and fulfillment services for many other retailers.[26]

Do Won and Jin Sook Chang (Forever 21)   Do Won and Jin Sook Chang are self-made billionaires. In 1984, they cofounded the "fast fashion" retail chain Forever 21. The pair emigrated from South Korea in 1981 and became naturalized

Forever 21 founder Do Won and his daughter Linda Chang (senior marketing manager) visiting their flagship store in Times Square.

American citizens. The couple opened their first store in 1984, focused on trendy, exciting clothing options. That year, sales grew from $35,000 to $700,000. Forever 21 has continued to experience explosive growth, as evidenced by recent store openings, like a flagship Las Vegas attraction with 127,000 square feet, a massive 45,000-square-foot store in Los Angeles, and two new megastores in New York of 86,000 and 91,000 square feet. Today, it operates more than 500 stores worldwide with more than 35,000 employees and projected sales of greater than $3.5 billion. Forever 21 is a family operation with Do Won at the helm, Jin Sook in charge of merchandising, eldest daughter Linda running marketing, and daughter Esther managing visuals.[27]

Ingvar Kamprad (IKEA)   Ingvar Kamprad, the founder of the Swedish-based home furnishing retailer chain IKEA, was always an entrepreneur. His first business was selling matches to neighbors from his bicycle. He discovered he could make a good profit by buying matches in bulk and selling them individually at a low price. He then expanded to selling fish, Christmas tree decorations, seeds, ballpoint pens, and pencils. By the time he was 17 years of age, he had earned a reward for succeeding in school. His father gave him the money to establish what is now IKEA. Like Sam Walton, the founder of Walmart, Kamprad is known for his frugality. He drives an old Volvo, flies economy class, and encourages IKEA employees to write on both sides of a sheet of paper. This thriftiness has translated into a corporate philosophy of cost cutting throughout IKEA so that the chain can offer quality furniture with innovative designs at low prices. According to *Forbes* magazine, Kamprad is the richest person in Europe and the fourth-richest person in the world, with an estimated net worth of around $33 billion.[29]

Howard Schulz (Starbucks)   In 1982, Howard Schultz, a salesperson for a plastic manufacturer, was hired as the new head of marketing for Starbucks, a coffee roaster with six cafés. Shortly after he was hired, he went Verona, Italy, to attend an international housewares show. He had his first latte in Verona, but he saw something more important than the coffee. The café patrons were enjoying themselves while sipping their coffees in the elegant surroundings. He had a vision of recreating the Old World magic and romance behind the Italian coffee bar. The owner wanted to focus on his plan to sell roasted whole beans, and eventually Schultz acquired Starbucks and began the company's march across the world. Schultz's father struggled at low-paying jobs with little to show for it when he died. "He was beaten down, he wasn't respected," Schultz said. "He had no health insurance, and he had no workers' compensation when he got hurt on the job." So with Starbucks, Schultz "wanted to build the kind of company that my father never got a chance to work for, in which people were respected." Due to this childhood experience, Schultz initiated practices at Starbucks that are still uncommon in retailing, such as providing comprehensive health care for all employees working at least 20 hours a week, including coverage for unmarried spouses, and offering an employee stock-option plan. In 2012, Starbucks' sales were greater than $11 billion from the 17,000 stores it operates in 40 countries.[31]

In the next section, we discuss the decisions that retailers make to design and implement their retail strategy. This book is organized around this strategic decision-making process.

THE RETAIL MANAGEMENT DECISION PROCESS

LO5

Understand the strategic retail management decision process.

This book is organized around the management decisions that retailers make to provide value to their customers and develop an advantage over their competitors. Exhibit 1–6 identifies the chapters in this book associated with each type of decision.

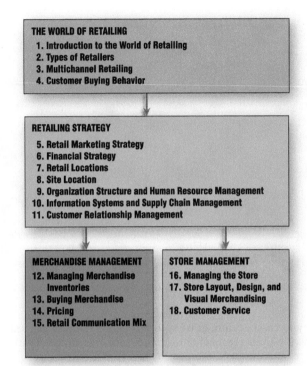

EXHIBIT 1–6
Retail Management
Decision Process

Understanding the World of Retailing—Section I

The first step in the retail management decision process, as Exhibit 1–6 shows, is understanding the world of retailing. Retail managers need to know the environment in which they operate before they can develop and implement effective strategies. The first section of this book therefore provides a general overview of the retailing industry and its customers.

The critical environmental factors in the world of retailing are (1) the macroenvironment and (2) the microenvironment. The impacts of the macroenvironment—including technological, social, and ethical/legal/political factors—on retailing are discussed throughout this book. For example, the influence of technology on the rise of multichannel retailing is reviewed in Chapter 3, the use of new information and supply chain technologies are examined in Chapter 10, customer relationship management systems are reviewed in Chapter 11, and new communication technologies are discussed in Chapter 15.

Competitors   The retailer's microenvironment focuses specifically on its competitors and customers. At first glance, identifying competitors appears easy: A retailer's primary competitors are other retailers that use the same retail approach. Thus, department stores compete against other department stores, and supermarkets compete with other supermarkets. This competition between the same type of retailers is called **intratype competition**.

Yet to appeal to a broader group of consumers, many retailers are increasing the variety of merchandise they offer. By offering greater variety, retailers satisfy the needs of customers seeking a one-stop shopping experience. For example, Walgreens has added jewelry, accessories, and apparel to its already extensive health and beauty categories to meet the lifestyle needs of its customers. Amazon seems to offer any product you might ever want to buy or rent. When retailers offer merchandise not typically associated with their type of store, such as clothing in a drugstore, the result is **scrambled merchandising**. Scrambled merchandising increases

Scrambled merchandise increases the level of intertype competition.

intertype competition, or competition among retailers that sell similar merchandise using different types of retail outlets, such as drug and department stores.

Increasing intertype competition makes it harder for retailers to identify and monitor their competition. In one sense, all retailers compete against one another for the dollars that consumers spend on goods and services. But the intensity of competition is greatest among retailers whose offerings are viewed as very similar.

Management's view of competition also may differ depending on the manager's position within the retail firm. For example, the manager of the Saks Fifth Avenue women's sportswear department in Bergen County, New Jersey, views the other women's sportswear specialty stores in the Riverside Square mall as her major competitors. But the Saks store manager views the Bloomingdale's store in a nearby mall as her strongest competitor. These differences in perspective arise because the department sales manager is primarily concerned with customers for a specific category of merchandise, whereas the store manager is concerned with customers seeking the entire selection of all merchandise and services offered by a department store. The chief executive officer (CEO) of a retail chain, in contrast, views competition from a much broader perspective. For example, Nordstrom might identify its strongest competitor as Saks, Neiman Marcus, Bloomingdale's, and even Bluefly.com.

Chapter 2 discusses various types of retailers and their competitive strategies, and Chapter 3 concentrates on different types of channels that retailers use to complete transactions with their customers.

Customers   The second factor in the microenvironment is customers. Retailers must respond to broad demographic and lifestyle trends in our society, such as the growth in the senior and minority segments of the U.S. population or the importance of shopping convenience to the increasing number of two-income families. To develop and implement an effective strategy, retailers must understand why customers shop, how they select a store, and how they select among that store's merchandise—the information found in Chapter 4.

Developing a Retail Strategy—Section II

The next stages in the retail management decision-making process, formulating and implementing a retail strategy, are based on an understanding of the macro- and microenvironments developed in the first section of this book. Section II

Toys R Us focuses on toys and apparel for children, while Walmart's strategic focus is much broader.

focuses on decisions related to developing a retail strategy, whereas Sections III and IV pertain to decisions surrounding the implementation of the strategy and building a long-term competitive advantage. The decisions discussed in Sections III and IV are more tactical.

Retail Strategy   The **retail strategy** identifies (1) the target market, or markets, toward which the retailer will direct its efforts; (2) the nature of the merchandise and services the retailer will offer to satisfy the needs of the target market; and (3) how the retailer will develop unique assets that enable it to achieve long-term advantage over its competitors.

The nature of a retail strategy can be illustrated by comparing the strategies of Walmart and Toys R Us. Initially, Walmart identified its target market as small towns (fewer than 35,000 in population) in Arkansas, Texas, and Oklahoma. It offered name-brand merchandise at low prices in a broad array of categories, ranging from laundry detergent to girls' dresses, but offerings in each category were limited. Today, even as Walmart stores have expanded across the world, the selection in each category remains limited. A Walmart store might have only 3 models of flat-screen television sets, while an electronic category specialist like Best Buy might carry 30 models.

In contrast to Walmart, Toys R Us defines its primary target as consumers living in suburban areas of large cities. Rather than carrying many merchandise categories, Toys R Us stores specialize in toys and children's apparel and carry most types and brands currently available in the market. Walmart emphasizes self-service: Customers select their merchandise, bring it to the checkout line, and then carry it to their cars. But Toys R Us provides more customer service. It has salespeople to assist customers with certain types of merchandise.

Because Walmart and Toys R Us both emphasize competitive prices, they have made strategic decisions to sustain their low prices by developing a cost advantage over their competitors. Both firms have sophisticated distribution and management information systems to manage inventory. Their strong relationships with their suppliers enable them to buy merchandise at low prices.

Strategic Decision Areas   The key strategic decisions a retailer makes are defining its target market and its financial objectives. Chapter 5 discusses how the selection of a retail market strategy requires analyzing the environment and the firm's strengths and weaknesses. When major environmental changes occur, the current strategy and the reasoning behind it must be reexamined. The retailer then decides what, if any, strategy changes are needed to take advantage of new opportunities or avoid new threats in the environment. The retailer's market strategy must be consistent with the firm's financial objectives. Chapter 6 reviews how financial variables, such as return on investment, inventory turnover, and profit margin, can be used to evaluate the market strategy and its implementation.

The next set of strategic decisions involves the development of critical assets that enable retailers to build strategic advantages. These strategic assets are location, human resource, information and supply chain systems, supply chain organization, and customer loyalty.

Decisions regarding location (reviewed in Chapters 7 and 8) are important because location is typically consumers' top consideration when selecting a store. Generally, consumers buy gas at the closest service station and patronize the shopping mall that's most convenient to their home or office. In addition, location offers an opportunity to gain a long-term advantage over the competition. When a retailer has the best location, a competing retailer must settle for the second-best location.

Retailing is a very labor-intensive industry. Employees play a critical role in providing the services customers seek when patronizing a retailer. Chapter 9 outlines how retailers coordinate the activities of buyers, store managers, and sales associates in the implementation of the retailing strategy.

Retail information and supply chain management systems also offer a significant opportunity for retailers to gain strategic advantage. Chapter 10 reviews how retailers are developing sophisticated computer and distribution technologies to monitor flows of information and merchandise from vendors to retail distribution centers to retail stores. These technologies are part of an overall inventory management system that enables retailers to (1) make sure desired merchandise is available when customers want it and (2) minimize the retailer's inventory investment.

Retailers, like most businesses, want to develop repeat purchases and loyalty in their best customers. Chapter 11 examines the process that retailers use to identify, design programs for, increase the share of wallet of, provide more value to, and build loyalty among their best customers. The implementation decisions are discussed in the next two sections.

Implementing the Retail Strategy—Sections III and IV

To implement a retail strategy, retailers develop a retail mix that satisfies the needs of its target market better than that of its competitors. The **retail mix** is a set of decisions retailers make to satisfy customer needs and influence their purchase decisions. Elements in the retail mix (Exhibit 1–7) include the types of merchandise and services offered, merchandise pricing, advertising and promotional

EXHIBIT 1–7
The Retail Mix

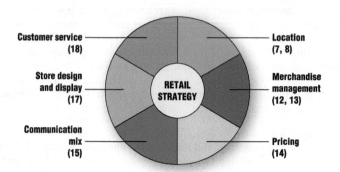

programs, store design, merchandise display, assistance to customers provided by salespeople, and convenience of the store's location. Section III reviews the implementation decisions made by buyers, and Section IV focuses on decisions made by store managers.

Managers in the merchandise management area decide how much and what types of merchandise to buy (Chapter 12), what vendors to use and how to interact with them (Chapter 13), the retail prices to set (Chapter 14), and how to advertise and promote merchandise (Chapter 15). Store managers must determine how to recruit, select, and motivate sales associates (Chapter 16); where and how merchandise will be displayed (Chapter 17); and the nature of services to provide for customers (Chapter 18). Whole Foods Market is one of the fastest growing and most profitable supermarket chains. In the next section, we illustrate the strategic and more tactical decisions Whole Foods has made and continues to make to achieve and sustain its success. The background of its founder and CEO, John Mackey, is described in Retailing View 1.3.

Whole Foods Market: An Organic and Natural Food Supermarket Chain

Retail Strategy   In the 1960s, natural, organic foods were available only in farmers' markets or small specialty stores catering to counterculture consumers. Consumers who patronized these health food stores felt that eating organic food would liberate them from the grasp of big agribusiness and food processors that were destroying the land with chemical pesticides, mistreating migrant farmworkers, and encouraging people to consume unhealthy processed foods. Whole Foods' strategy is to target health-conscious, environmentally conscious, middle-class consumers by using a modern supermarket format, rather than small, specialty health food stores. Its mission is to promote the vitality and well-being of all individuals by supplying the highest quality, most wholesome foods available.

Strategic Advantages   Some of the strategic assets Whole Foods has developed over the years to provide long-term advantages are a strong brand image that builds customer loyalty; committed employees who provide excellent customer service; good relationships with organic food suppliers that ensures a supply of organic food, even as demand for organic food grows faster than supply; an efficient supply chain connecting local growers to a national store network; and extensive information about its customers that it uses to develop assortments and target promotions.

Merchandise Management   In terms of merchandise, Whole Foods stores offer the array of food categories typically found in a supermarket. However, the assortment emphasizes organic and natural products that are fresh, nutritious, and safe to eat. Products are free of artificial preservatives, colors, flavors, and sweeteners, as well as hydrogenated fats and other unacceptable ingredients. In addition, Whole Foods seeks out and supports local producers whose fruits and vegetables meet its standards, particularly those who farm organically and are dedicated to environmentally friendly, sustainable agriculture.

Whole Foods offers seven lines of private-label products. Buyers work with artisan food producers and organic farmers to attain products sold under the super-premium Authentic Food Artisan brand. Its core private brands are called Whole Brands (department-specific products), Whole Foods (premium products), and Whole Kids Organic (organic products for children). The 365 Day Everyday Value and 365 Day Organic Everyday Value line provide natural products at value prices.

Whole Foods communicates the benefits of its offering through its website and social media. Its website has extensive information about natural and organic

1.3   RETAILING VIEW   Whole Foods: The Birth of the Organic Supermarket

John Mackey had a relatively conventional, middle-class, suburban upbringing. But it was the 1970s, so Mackey quit college and embraced an alternative lifestyle (e.g., long beard, wild hair). After having worked for a time in a vegetarian collective, he solicited money from family and friends so that he could open a new sort of co-op in 1978: organic food store on the first floor, restaurant on the second floor, and living quarters on the top of the old Victorian house he had found.

REFACT

Whole Foods has a rule that no employee can have a salary greater than 19 times the average salary of store employees. On average, a U.S. CEO makes 319 times the compensation of a production worker in their companies.[32]

A couple of years later, Mackey went further and opened the first Whole Foods store in a 10,000-square-foot space that had once been a nightclub. In keeping with its history, Mackey made sure his natural food store was no stodgy, boring site with just granola. He stocked beer, meat, and wine, and he "loved it. I loved retail. I loved being around food. I loved natural foods. I loved organic foods. I loved the whole idea of it. And a thought entered into my mind that maybe this is what I could do."

But being a grocer was not a particularly popular aspiration with his family. His mother, a former teacher, strongly discouraged his interest in Whole Foods. According to Mackey's account, on her deathbed in 1987, she asked him to promise to return to school to get his college degree; when he demurred, she complained, "I wish you'd just give up that stupid health-food store. Your father and I gave you a fine mind, and you're wasting it being a grocer."

He never did give up on his "stupid" store, though. Instead, as the concept spread across the United States, Mackey adopted and adapted his ideas to fit local tastes. Through decentralized decision-making units, Whole Foods stores could choose to stock items specific to the preferences of the local markets, like live lobsters in Portland, Maine, or a kombucha bar in Venice, California. Through acquisitions, Whole Foods gained additional knowledge, too. In buying Wellspring Grocery, it learned about private-label options. The purchase of Mrs. Gooch's provided Whole Foods with insights into diet supplements. When it purchased

Whole Foods founder and CEO, John Mackey

Bread & Circus, it gained access to the Boston chain's famed seafood procurement expertise.

Sources: www.wholefoodsmarket.com/company-info/whole-foods-market-history; and Nick Paumgarten, "Food Fighter," *New Yorker*, January 4, 2010.

DISCUSSION QUESTION

What factors in Whole Foods' macro- and microenvironment contributed to its success?

Employees at Whole Foods participate in decision making through self-managed teams.

foods. Its iPhone app provides not just the location information about the nearest Whole Foods store (by zip code) but also approximately 2,000 recipes, searchable by various criteria, including diet restrictions, ingredients, budgets, or family appeal. The "On Hand" option allows users to input the items on their pantry shelves and receive recommendations for some meal options. Moreover, the app offers special deals for each store, right next to a map that shows customers how to get there.[33]

Whole Foods also uses social media extensively. A global manager and community manager assigned at every store are responsible for customer engagement. A single Global Online Community Manager runs the company's central Twitter link, @Whole Foods. Most of the tweets in this realm come from individual customers with questions, complaints, or suggestions. The manager makes sure to respond almost immediately, to ensure that no customers get the sense Whole Foods is uninterested or ignoring their concerns. Then, in each community, another manager attends to local needs, including special deal postings, charity opportunities, and upcoming events. A Los Angeles store located on Third Street owns the Twitter handle @WholeFoods3rdSt; a Mount Washington location, near Baltimore, tweets from the @WholeFoodsMTW account.[34]

Store Management   All Whole Foods employees are organized into self-managed teams that meet regularly to discuss issues and solve problems. Almost all team members have stock options in the firm. They also receive a 20 percent discount in stores. Their personal wellness accounts help them cover health care expenses, both for themselves and their domestic partners. To select the benefits package, the entire company takes a vote every three years. Whole Foods thus has been on *Fortune* magazine's "100 Best Companies to Work For" list for 13 consecutive years.[35]

Whole Foods' decisions on visual merchandising and store design reinforce its strategy.[36] Its stores are designed to make grocery shopping fun—to transform a supermarket into an interactive theater with corporate staff serving as the producer and store management as the director. Sections of its newer stores are designed with self-contained architecture that curves inward, creating a feeling of intimacy that encourages shoppers to linger. The warm feeling of the store is enhanced by signs made of an eco-friendly, woodlike material rather than plastic. Art gallery–type lighting focuses attention on produce.

Finally, Whole Foods' store management provides excellent customer service. Curious about the life of a chicken in the display case? It comes with a 16-page booklet and an invitation to visit the live chickens at the company's Pennsylvania farm. Want to know the name of the farmer who grew those organic tomatoes? That information, along with some personal details, is readily available. Curious about the fish you're getting dressed at the free filleting station? The employee can offer not just ideas for cooking it but also the identity of the Whole Foods boat and the captain who caught it for you.[37]

Ethical and Legal Considerations

When making the decisions discussed previously, managers need to consider the ethical and legal implications of their decisions, in addition to the effects that those decisions have on the profitability of their firms and the satisfaction of their customers. **Ethics** are the principles governing individuals and companies that establish appropriate behavior and indicate what is right and wrong. Defining the term is easy, but determining what the principles are is difficult. What one person thinks is ethical, another may consider unethical.

What is ethical can vary from country to country and from industry to industry. For example, offering bribes to overcome bureaucratic roadblocks is an accepted practice in Middle Eastern countries but is considered unethical, and even illegal, in the United States. Ethical principles also can change over time. For example, some years ago, doctors and lawyers who advertised their services were considered unethical. Today, such advertising is accepted as common practice.

Examples of difficult situations that retail managers face include the following:

- Should a retailer sell merchandise that it suspects was made using child labor?
- Should a retailer advertise that its prices are the lowest available in the market, even though some are not?
- Should a retail buyer accept an expensive gift from a vendor?
- Should a retailer charge a supplier a fee for getting a new item in its store?
- Should retail salespeople use a high-pressure sales approach when they know the product is not the best for the customer's needs?
- Should a retailer disclose product information that may affect whether or not it is purchased?
- Should a retailer promote a product as being "on sale" if it never sold at a higher, nonsale price?
- Should a retailer offer credit at a higher interest rate or sell products at higher prices in stores patronized mostly by low-income customers?

Laws dictate which activities society has deemed to be clearly wrong, those activities for which retailers and their employees will be punished through the federal or state legal systems. However, most business decisions are not regulated by laws. Often retail managers have to rely on their firms' and industries' codes of ethics and/or their own codes of ethics to determine the right thing to do.

Many companies have codes of ethics to provide guidelines for their employees in making their ethical decisions. These ethical policies provide a clear sense of right and wrong so that companies and their customers can depend on their employees when questionable situations arise. However, in many situations, retail managers need to rely on their personal code of ethics—their personal sense of what is right or wrong.

Exhibit 1–8 lists some questions you can ask yourself to determine whether a behavior or activity is unethical. The questions emphasize that ethical behavior is determined by widely accepted views of what is right and wrong. Thus, you should engage only in activities about which you would be proud to tell your family, friends, employer, and customers. If the answer to any of these questions is yes, the behavior or activity is probably unethical, and you should not do it.

1. Would I be embarrassed if a customer found out about this behavior?
2. Would my supervisor disapprove of this behavior?
3. Would most coworkers feel that this behavior is unusual?
4. Am I about to do this because I think I can get away with it?
5. Would I be upset if a company did this to me?
6. Would my family or friends think less of me if I told them about engaging in this activity?
7. Am I concerned about the possible consequences of this behavior?
8. Would I be upset if this behavior or activity was publicized in a newspaper article?
9. Would society be worse off if everyone engaged in this behavior or activity?

EXHIBIT 1–8
Checklist for Making Ethical Decisions

Your firm can strongly affect the ethical choices you will have to make. When you view your firm's policies or requests as improper, you have three choices:

1. *Ignore your personal values, and do what your company asks you to do.* Self-respect suffers when you have to compromise your principles to please an employer. If you take this path, you will probably feel guilty and be dissatisfied with your job in the long run.

2. *Take a stand, and tell your employer what you think.* Try to influence the decisions and policies of your company and supervisors.

3. *Refuse to compromise your principles.* Taking this path may mean you will get fired or be forced to quit.

You should not take a job with a company whose products, policies, and conduct conflict with your standards. Before taking a job, investigate the company's procedures and selling approach to see whether they conflict with your personal ethical standards. Throughout this text, we will highlight the legal and ethical issues associated with the retail decisions made by managers.

SUMMARY

LO1 Identify retailing activities.

Retailing is defined as a set of business activities that add value to the products and services sold to consumers for their personal or family use. These value-added activities include providing assortments, breaking bulk, holding inventory, and providing services.

LO2 Realize the importance of retailing in the U.S. and world economies.

Retailing plays an important role in the U.S. economy. One out of four workers in the United States works for a retailer or for a company selling products to a retailer, and the U.S. retail sector accounts for about the same percentage of the U.S. GDP as the entire manufacturing sector. Retailing also plays an important role in developing economies. Some business scholars feel that there is need for modern retail methods to be used to serve consumers at the bottom of the pyramid.

LO3 Analyze the changing retail industry.

The retail industry has changed dramatically over the last 50 years. Many well-known national and international retailers were small startup companies 50 years ago. Now the industry is dominated by large firms. The development of information systems is one of the forces facilitating the growth of large retailers.

Before the availability of modern information systems, it was difficult for retailers to lower costs through economies of scale, and larger retailers had limited advantages over small local or regional retailers. With these information systems, retailers are able to efficiently and effectively manage millions of customer transactions with thousands of stores and suppliers across the globe.

LO4 Recognize the opportunities in retailing for you.

Retailing offers opportunities for exciting, challenging careers, either by working for a retail firm or starting your own business. Aspects of retail careers are discussed in Appendix 1A. Suggestions about starting your own business appear in Appendix A at the end of the book.

LO5 Understand the strategic retail management decision process.

The retail management decision process involves developing a strategy for creating a competitive advantage in the marketplace and then developing a retail mix to implement that strategy. The strategic decisions, discussed in the first section of this textbook, involve selecting a target market; defining the nature of the retailer's offering; and building a competitive advantage through locations, human resource management, information and supply chain management systems, and customer relationship management programs.

The merchandise and store management decisions for implementing the strategy, discussed in the second half of this textbook, involve selecting a merchandise assortment, buying merchandise, setting prices, communicating with customers, managing the store, presenting merchandise in stores, and providing customer service. Large retail chains use sophisticated information systems to analyze business opportunities and make these decisions about how to operate their businesses in multiple countries.

Answers to the Quiz in Exhibit 1–1

1. (d)	**3.** (e)	**5.** (e)	**7.** (d)
2. (d)	**4.** (a)	**6.** (b)	**8.** (b)

KEY TERMS

backward integration, *9*
base of the pyramid, *14*
bottom of the pyramid (BoP), *14*
breaking bulk, *8*
corporate social responsibility (CSR), *12*
ethics, *28*

forward integration, *9*
holding inventory, *8*
intertype competition, *22*
intratype competition, *21*
retailer, *7*
retailing, *7*

retail mix, *24*
retail strategy, *23*
scrambled merchandising, *21*
supply chain, *7*
vertical integration, *9*
wholesalers, *9*

GET OUT AND DO IT!

1. **CONTINUING CASE ASSIGNMENT** In most chapters of this textbook, there will be a GET OUT AND DO IT! assignment that will give you an opportunity to examine the strategy and tactics of one retailer. Your first assignment is to select a retailer and prepare a report on the retailer's history, including when it was founded and how it has evolved over time. To ensure that you can get information about the retailer for subsequent Continuing Case Assignments, the retailer you select should:
   - *Be a publicly held company so that you can access its financial statements and annual reports.* Do not select a retailer that is owned by another company. For example, Bath & Body Works is owned by Limited Brands, so you can get financial information about only the holding company and not the individual companies it owns, such as Victoria's Secret and White Barn Candle.
   - *Focus on one type of retailing.* For example, Abercrombie & Fitch operates just one type of specialty store and thus would be a good choice. However, Walmart operates discount stores, warehouse club stores, and supercenters and thus would not be a good choice.
   - *Be easy to visit and collect information about.* Some retailers and store managers may not allow you to interview them about the store, take pictures of the store, talk with sales associates, or analyze the merchandise assortment in the store. Try to pick a retailer with a local store manager who can help you complete the assignments.

   Some examples of retailers that meet the first two criteria are Whole Foods Market, Dress Barn, Burlington Coat Factory, Ross Stores, Ann Taylor, Cato, Finish Line, Foot Locker, Brookstone, Claire's, Walgreens, Staples, Office Depot, American Eagle Outfitter, Pacific Sunwear, Abercrombie & Fitch, Tiffany & Co., Zales, Autozone, Pep Boys, Hot Topic, Wet Seal, Best Buy, Family Dollar, Dollar General, Michaels, PetSmart, Dillard's, Pier 1 Imports, Home Depot, Lowe's, Bed Bath & Beyond, Men's Wearhouse, Kroger, Kohl's, Radio Shack, Safeway, and Target.

2. **GO SHOPPING** Visit a local retail store, and describe each of the elements in its retail mix.

3. **INTERNET EXERCISE** Data on U.S. retail sales are available at the U.S. Bureau of the Census Internet site at www.census.gov/retail/#ecommerce. Look at "Estimates of Monthly Retail and Food Services Sales by Kind of Business" for the most recent year. In which months are sales the highest? Which kinds of businesses experience the greatest fluctuations in monthly sales? List reasons that help explain your findings.

4. **INTERNET EXERCISE** Go to the home pages of Macy's, Target, Walmart, Toys R Us, and the National Retail Federation Retail Careers Center (www.nrf.com/RetailCareers/) to find information about retail careers with these organizations. Review the information about the different positions described. In which positions would you be interested? Which positions are not of interest to you? Which employer would interest you? Why?

5. **INTERNET EXERCISE** Choose one of the top 20 retailers (Exhibit 1–5). Go to the company's website, and find out how the company started and how it has changed over time.

6. **INTERNET EXERCISE** Go online and find an example of a retailer involved in corporate social responsibility. In a brief paragraph, describe how this retailer is taking steps to contribute to a social or ethical cause.

DISCUSSION QUESTIONS AND PROBLEMS

1. How do retailers add value to the products bought by consumers?

2. What is your favorite retailer? Why do you like this retailer? What would a competitive retailer have to do to get your patronage?

3. What are the benefits and limitations of purchasing a home entertainment system directly from a number of component manufacturers rather than from a retailer?

4. What retailers would be considered intratype competitors for a convenience store chain such as 7-Eleven? What firms would be intertype competitors?

5. How does Walmart contribute and/or detract from the communities in which it operates stores?

6. The same brand and style of men's suits are sold at different prices at a department store like Macy's and at a specialty store like Men's Wearhouse. Why would a customer choose to buy the suit from one store rather than the other?

7. Compare and contrast the retail mixes of department stores and full-line discount stores. Use bullet points or a table to list the similarities and differences.

8. An entrepreneur approaches you about how to sell her new writing pens to consumers. The pens have a unique benefit—they are more comfortable to use than traditional pens. The entrepreneur is concerned the retailers she has approached want to buy the pens from her at $10.00 a piece and then sell the pens in their stores at $18.00 to consumers. The entrepreneur is dismayed at the extra $8.00 the retailers are getting and has decided to sell the product directly to consumers for $10.00. She wants to know your opinion. What do you think? Why?

9. From a personal perspective, how does retailing rate as a potential career compared with others you are considering? Why?

10. In this chapter, some socially responsible activities engaged in by retailers are described. Take the perspective of a stockholder in one of these companies. What effect will these activities have on the value of its stock? Why might they have a positive or negative effect?

SUGGESTED READINGS

"2012 Global Retail Industry Trends." *Stores Magazine*, January 2012.

Ferrell, O.C., John Fraedrich, and Linda Ferrell. *Business Ethics: Ethical Decision Making & Cases*, 9th ed., Impendence, KY: Southwestern, 2012.

Fisher, Marshall L., and Ananth Raman. *The New Science of Retailing: How Analytics Are Improving Performance*. Boston: Harvard Business Press, 2010.

"Global Powers of Retailing Top 250." *Stores Magazine*, January 2012.

Lee, Min-young, Ann Fairhurst, and Scarlett Wesley. "Corporate Social Responsibility: A Review of the Top 100 US Retailers." *Corporate Reputation Review* (London) 12 (Summer 2009), pp. 140–159.

Mantrala, Murali K., and Manfred Krafft (Eds). *Retailing in the 21st Century: Current and Future Trends*, 2nd ed. Berlin: Springer, 2010.

Ortinau, David J., Barry J. Babin, and Jean-Charles Chebat, "Retailing Evolution Research: Introduction to the Special Section on Retailing Research," *Journal of Business Research*, 64, no. 6 (June 2011), pp. 541–542.

Plunkett, Jack (Ed). *Plunkett's Retail Industry Almanac 2012*. Houston: Plunkett Research, 2012.

Roberts, Bryan. *Walmart: Key Insights and Practical Lessons from the World's Largest Retailer*. Philadelphia: Kogan Page, 2012.

APPENDIX 1A Careers in Retailing

Retailing offers exciting and challenging career opportunities. Few other industries grant as many responsibilities to young managers. When students asked Dave Fuente, former CEO of Office Depot, what they needed to become a CEO someday, he responded, "You need to have profit and loss responsibility and the experience of managing people early in your career." Entry-level retail jobs for college graduates offer both these opportunities. Most college graduates begin their retail careers as assistant buyers, merchandise planners, or department managers in stores. In these positions, they are responsible for the profitability of a line of merchandise or an area of the store, and they manage people who work for them.

Even if you work for a large company, retailing provides an opportunity for you to do your own thing and be rewarded. You can come with an idea, execute it almost immediately, and see how well it is doing by reviewing the sales data at the end of the day.

Retailing offers a variety of career paths, such as buying, store management, sales promotion and advertising, personnel, operations/distribution, real estate, loss prevention, and finance. In addition, retailing offers almost immediate accountability for talented people, so they can reach key management positions fairly quickly. Starting salaries are competitive, and the compensation of top management ranks among the highest in any industry.

CAREER OPPORTUNITIES

In retail firms, career opportunities are in merchandising/buying, store management, and corporate staff functions. Corporate positions are in accounting, finance, real estate, promotions and advertising, computer and distribution systems, and human resources.

The primary entry-level opportunities for a retailing career are in the areas of buying and store management. Buying positions are more numbers-oriented, whereas store management positions are more people-oriented. Entry-level positions on the corporate staff are limited. Retailers typically want all of their employees to understand their customers and their merchandise. Therefore, most executives and corporate staff managers begin their careers in merchandise or store management.

Store Management

Successful store managers must have the ability to lead and motivate employees. They also need to be sensitive to customers' needs by making sure that merchandise is available and neatly displayed.

Store management involves all the discipline necessary to run a successful business: sales planning and goal setting, overall store image and merchandise presentation, budgets and expense control, customer service and sales supervision, personnel administration and development, and community relations.

Because store managers work in stores, they are often at quite a distance from the home office, which means they have limited direct supervision. Their hours generally mirror those of their store and can therefore include some weekends and evenings. In addition, they spend time during nonoperating hours tending to administrative responsibilities.

The typical entry-level store management position is a department manager with responsibility for merchandise presentation, customer service, and inventory control for an area of the store. The next level is an area or group manager with responsibility for executing merchandising plans and achieving sales goals for several areas, as well as supervising, training, and developing department managers. Beyond these positions, you might be promoted to store manager, then to district manager responsible for a group of stores, and then to regional manager responsible for a group of districts.

Merchandise Management

Merchandise management attracts people with strong analytical capabilities, an ability to predict what merchandise will appeal to their target markets, and a skill for negotiating with vendors as well as store management to get things done. Many retailers have broken the merchandising management activities into two different yet parallel career paths: buying and merchandise planning.

Retail merchandise buyers are similar to financial portfolio managers. They invest in a portfolio of merchandise; monitor the performance (sales) of the merchandise; and on the basis of the sales, either decide to buy more merchandise that is selling well or get rid of (discount) merchandise that is selling poorly. Buyers are responsible for selecting the type and amount of merchandise to buy, negotiating the wholesale price and payment terms with suppliers, setting the initial retail price for the merchandise, monitoring merchandise sales, and making appropriate retail price adjustments. Thus buyers need to have good financial planning skills, knowledge of their customers' needs and wants and competitive activities, and the ability to develop good working relationships with vendors. To develop a better understanding of their customers, buyers typically stay in contact with their stores by visiting them, talking to sales associates and managers, and monitoring the sales data available through their merchandise management systems.

Planners have an even more analytical role than buyers. Their primary responsibility is to determine the assortment of merchandise sent to each store—how many styles, colors, sizes, and individual items. Once the merchandise is in the stores, planners closely monitor sales and work with buyers on decisions such as how much additional merchandise to purchase if the merchandise is doing well or when to mark down the merchandise if sales are below expectations.

The typical entry-level position of college graduates interested in merchandise management is either assistant buyer or assistant planner in a merchandise category such as men's athletic shoes or consumer electronics. In these positions, you will do the sales analysis needed to support the decisions eventually made by the planner or buyer for whom you work. From this entry-level position, you could be promoted to buyer and then divisional merchandise manager, responsible for a number of merchandise categories. Most retailers believe that merchandise management skills are not category-specific. Thus, as you are promoted in the buying organization, you will probably work in various merchandise categories.

Corporate Staff

The corporate staff positions in retail firms involve activities and require knowledge, skills, and abilities similar to those in comparable positions in nonretail firms. Thus, many managers in these positions identify with their profession rather than the retail industry. For example, accountants in retail firms view themselves as accountant, not retailers.

Management Information Systems (MISs)   Employees in this area are involved with applications for capturing data and developing and maintaining inventory, as well as the design of store systems such as POS terminals, self-checkout systems, and in-store kiosks.

Operations/Distribution   Operations employees are responsible for operating and maintaining the store's physical plant; providing various customer services; overseeing the receipt, ticketing, warehousing, and distribution of a store's inventory; and buying and maintaining store supplies and operating equipment. Students in operations and MIS typically major in production, operations, or computer information systems.

Promotions/Advertising   Promotion's many aspects include public relations, advertising, visual merchandising, and special events. This department attempts to build the retail firm's brand image and encourage customers to visit the retailer's stores and/or website. Managers in this area typically major in marketing or mass communications.

Loss Prevention Loss prevention employees are responsible for protecting the retailer's assets. They develop systems and procedures to minimize employee theft and shoplifting. Managers in this area often major in sociology or criminology, although, as we discuss in Chapters 9 and 16, loss prevention is beginning to be viewed as a human resource management issue.

Finance/Accounting Many retailers are large businesses involved in complicated corporate structures. Most retailers also operate with a tight net profit margin. With such a fine line between success and failure, retailers continue to require financial experts. The finance/accounting division is responsible for the financial health of the company. Employees in this division prepare financial reports for all aspects of the business, including long-range forecasting and planning, economic trend analysis and budgeting, shortage control and internal audits, gross and net profit, accounts payable to vendors, and accounts receivable from charge customers. In addition, they manage the retailer's relationship with the financial community. Students interested in this area often major in finance or accounting.

Real Estate Employees in the real estate division are responsible for selecting locations for stores, negotiating leases and land purchases, and managing the leasehold costs. Students entering this area typically major in real estate or finance.

Store Design Employees working in this area are responsible for designing the store and presenting merchandise and fixtures in the store. Talented, creative students in business, architecture, art, and other related fields will have innumerable opportunities for growth in the area of retail store design.

Human Resource Management Human resource management is responsible for the effective selection, training, placement, advancement, and welfare of employees. Because there are seasonal peaks in retailing (such as Christmas, when many extra people must be hired), human resource personnel must be flexible and highly efficient.

ATTRACTIVENESS OF RETAILING CAREERS

Immediate Responsibility

Management trainees in retailing are given more responsibility more quickly than their counterparts in other industries. Buyers are responsible for choosing, promoting, pricing, distributing, and selling millions of dollars' worth of merchandise each season. The department manager, generally the first position after a training program, is often responsible for merchandising one or more departments, as well as managing 20 or more full- and part-time sales associates.

Many students and their parents think that people working in retailing have jobs as sales clerks and cashiers. They hold this view because, as customers in retail stores,

they typically interact only with sales associates, not their managers. But as we have discussed in this chapter, retail firms are large, sophisticated corporations that employ managers with a wide variety of knowledge, skills, and abilities. Entry-level positions for college are typically management trainees in the buying or store organization, not sales associates.

While some employees are promoted on the basis of their retail experience, a college degree is needed for most retail management positions, ranging from store manager to CEO. More than 150 colleges and universities in the United States offer programs of study and degrees or majors in retailing.

Financial Rewards

Starting salaries for management trainees with a college degree range from $30,000 to $60,000 a year, and the compensation of top management ranks with the highest in any industry. For example, store managers with only a few years of experience can earn up to $100,000 or more, depending on their performance bonuses. A senior buyer for a department store earns from $50,000 to $90,000 or more. A big-box store manager can earn from $50,000 to $150,000; a discount store manager makes from $70,000 to $100,000 or more; and a specialty store manager earns from $35,000 to $60,000 or more.

Compensation varies according to the amount of responsibility. Specialty store managers are generally paid less than department store managers because their annual sales volume is lower. But advancements in this area can be faster. Aggressive specialty store managers often are promoted to district managers and run 8 to 15 units after a few years, so they quickly move into higher pay brackets.

Because information systems enable retailers to assess the sales and profit performance of each manager, and even each sales associate, the compensation of retail managers is closely linked to objective measures of their performance. As a result, in addition to their salaries, retail managers are generally given strong monetary incentives based on the sales they create.

A compensation package consists of more than salary alone. In retailing, the benefits package is often substantial and may include a profit-sharing plan, savings plan, stock options, medical and dental insurance, life insurance, long-term disability protection and income protection plans, and paid vacations and holidays. Two additional benefits of retailing careers are that most retailers offer employees valuable discounts on the merchandise they sell, and some buying positions include extensive foreign travel.

Opportunities for Advancement

While the growth rate of retail parallels the growth rate of the overall economy, many opportunities for rapid advancement exist simply because of the sheer size of the retail industry. With so many retail firms, there is always a large number of firms that are experiencing a high growth rate, opening many new stores, and needing store managers and support staff positions.

Types of Retailers

EXECUTIVE BRIEFING
Debbie Ferree, Vice Chairman and
Chief Merchant, DSW Inc.

Math was always my favorite subject in school and came quite naturally to me, so it was no surprise that I entered college with the goal to become a college math professor, but my passion for fashion and love for business and retail caused me to change my career aspirations and transfer to the college of business.

Before joining DSW (Designer Shoe Warehouse), I worked in senior management positions for a variety of retailers, which gave me broad experience in different channels of distribution and business models: May Company and Burdines/Federated Department Stores—department stores; Ross Dress for Less— discount stores; and Harris Company—specialty retail.

In 1997, I joined DSW, a true off-price retailer, offering customers an assortment of end-of-season, closeout merchandise at deeply discounted prices. The department store landscape was changing rapidly and dramatically, where point-of-service discounting was the norm and customers were confused about the price they paid for a product. This created an opportunity in DSW to architect a new "hybrid" business model that would provide a very different shopping experience for the customer: an assortment of current, on-trend, in-season, fashion merchandise from well-known national brands at fair, everyday value (EDV) in an open-sell, attractive environment. This would define a new direction for the future in

retail. In 2004, I was promoted to president and chief merchandising officer of DSW and we took the company public in 2005.

To implement this new concept, we developed strategic partnerships with the leading designer brands in footwear. These vendors were focused on selling their brands through the department store channel and were initially skeptical about the new business model. The new model had many advantages and financial benefits: when they sold to DSW, there would be no extra charges such as advertising allowances or vendor chargebacks, and no renegotiations on prices at the end of the season or merchandise returns. Through collaboration and the development of financial and strategic plans that would support mutually profitable growth for both parties, we aligned on a plan that today generates over $2 billion in sales revenue in over 375 stores, an e-commerce business, and provides a long-term plan for continued growth.

The pillars of our success are a breathtaking assortment of on-trend merchandise, simple convenience, and irresistible value. We are using social media to create a community of shoe lovers who are loyal to our offerings, and regularly inform their friends about the new additions to our assortment and about their shopping experience in our stores

LEARNING OBJECTIVES

LO1 List the different characteristics that define retailers.

LO2 Categorize the various types of food retailers.

LO3 Identify the various types of general merchandise retailers.

LO4 Explain the differences between service and merchandise retailers.

LO5 Illustrate the types of ownership for retail firms.

and on our website. Our fan page is a place where shoe lovers can hang out and talk about shoes. We stimulate interaction between our over two million followers by presenting what our followers think of new styles, thanking them for their suggestions, answering their questions promptly, and running fun trivia contests with free pairs of shoes as prizes.

DSW's aspiration is to become "America's Favorite Place for Shoes" and "America's Favorite Place to Work." We have a strong culture that incorporates our core values—humility, accountability, collaboration, and passion—into a fun environment that stretches talent, supports individual development, and provides a rewarding career experience!

You want to have a good cup of coffee in the morning, not instant, but you don't want to bother with grinding coffee beans, boiling water, pouring it through ground coffee in a filter, and waiting. Think of all the different retailers that could help you satisfy this need. You could get your cup of brewed coffee from the drive-through window at the local Starbucks, or you could decide to buy an automatic coffeemaker with a timer so that your coffee will be ready when you wake up. You could purchase the coffeemaker at a discount store like Walmart or Target, a department store such as Macy's, a drugstore like CVS, or a category specialist such as Best Buy. If you want to buy the coffeemaker without taking the time to visit a store, you could visit www.thefind.com, search for "coffee and espresso maker," and review the details about 83,392 products sold by 5,485 retailers, ranging from Bed Bath & Beyond to Sur La Table to Newegg.

All these retailers are competing against one another to satisfy your need for a hassle-free, good cup of coffee. Many are selling the same brands, but they offer different services, prices, environments, and convenience. For example, if you want to buy a low-priced, basic coffeemaker, you can go to a discount store. But if you are interested in a coffeemaker with more features and want to have someone explain the different features, you can visit a department store or a category specialist.

To develop and implement a retail strategy, retailers need to understand the nature of competition in the retail marketplace. This chapter describes the different types of retailers and how they compete against one another by offering different benefits to consumers. These benefits are reflected in the nature of the retail mixes used by the retailers to satisfy customer needs: the types of merchandise and services offered, the degree to which their offerings emphasize services versus merchandise, and the prices charged.

RETAILER CHARACTERISTICS

LO1

List the different characteristics that define retailers.

The 1.1 million[1] retailers in the United States range from individual street vendors selling hot dogs to multichannel retailers that offer thousands of products in their stores and through catalog and Internet channels. The different types of retailers offer unique benefits. The type of retailer a consumer chooses to patronize depends on the benefits the consumer is seeking. For example, if you are shopping for a gift, you might value the convenience of buying a shirt from a retailer's Internet channel so the retailer will ship it to a friend in another city. Alternatively, you might prefer to buy a shirt from a local store when making a purchase for yourself so that you can try it on. You might go to a discount store to buy an inexpensive shirt for a camping trip or a sporting goods specialty store to buy a shirt with the insignia of your favorite football team.

All these retailers survive and prosper because they satisfy a group of consumers' needs more effectively than their competitors, and thus consumers patronize different retail types when they have different needs. As consumer needs and competition change, new retail formats are created and existing formats evolve.

Many retailers also are broadening their assortments, which means that their offerings overlap and competition increases. At eBay Motors, for example, consumers can buy cars and motorcycles from thousands of individual sellers and established dealers. The eBay sellers compete with traditional automobile dealers that sell cars and motorcycles through conventional dealerships. In another example, office supply stores compete with warehouse clubs, supercenters, supermarkets, and convenience stores because they sell many of the same products.

The most basic characteristic used to describe the different types of retailers is their retail mix, or the elements retailers use to satisfy their customers' needs. Four elements of the retail mix are particularly useful for classifying retailers: the type of merchandise and/or services offered, the variety and assortment of merchandise offered, the level of customer service, and the price of the merchandise.

Type of Merchandise

The United States, Canada, and Mexico have developed a classification scheme, called the **North American Industry Classification System (NAICS),** to collect data on business activity in each country. Every business is assigned a hierarchical, six-digit code based on the type of products and services it sells. The first two digits identify the firm's business sector, and the remaining four digits identify various subsectors.

The classifications for retailers selling merchandise, based largely on the type of merchandise sold, are illustrated in Exhibit 2–1. Merchandise retailers are in sectors 44 and 45. The next three digits provide a finer classification of merchandise retailers. For example, retailers selling clothing and clothing accessories are classified as 448, clothing stores as 4481, and men's clothing stores as 44811. The sixth digit, not illustrated in Exhibit 2–1, captures differences between the North American countries using the classification scheme.

NAICS Codes for Retailers   **EXHIBIT 2–1**

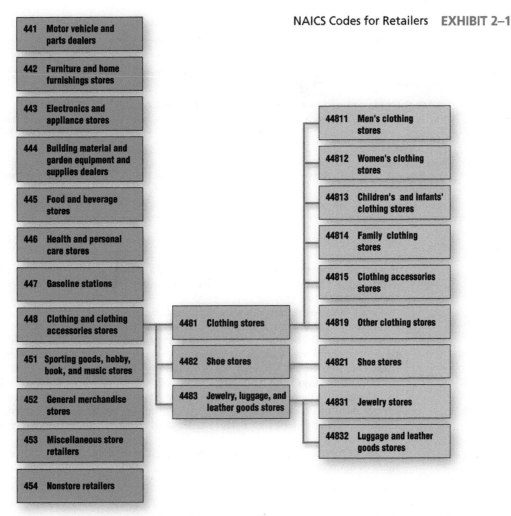

441	Motor vehicle and parts dealers
442	Furniture and home furnishings stores
443	Electronics and appliance stores
444	Building material and garden equipment and supplies dealers
445	Food and beverage stores
446	Health and personal care stores
447	Gasoline stations
448	Clothing and clothing accessories stores
451	Sporting goods, hobby, book, and music stores
452	General merchandise stores
453	Miscellaneous store retailers
454	Nonstore retailers

4481	Clothing stores
4482	Shoe stores
4483	Jewelry, luggage, and leather goods stores

44811	Men's clothing stores
44812	Women's clothing stores
44813	Children's and infants' clothing stores
44814	Family clothing stores
44815	Clothing accessories stores
44819	Other clothing stores
44821	Shoe stores
44831	Jewelry stores
44832	Luggage and leather goods stores

SOURCE: "North American Industry Classification System (NAICS)," U.S. Census Bureau, www.census.gov/epcd/www/naics.html.

Most services retailers are classified in sectors 71 (arts, entertainment, and recreation) and 72 (accommodation and food services). For example, food services and drinking places are in category 722, which is subdivided into full-service restaurants (7221) and limited-service eating places like fast-food restaurants (7222).

Variety and Assortment

Retailers can offer the same merchandise but differ in the variety and assortment of merchandise offered. **Variety** is the number of merchandise categories a retailer offers. **Assortment** is the number of different items offered in a merchandise category. Variety is often referred to as the **breadth of merchandise,** and assortment is referred to as the **depth of merchandise.** Each different item of merchandise is called a **stock-keeping unit (SKU).** Some examples of SKUs include an original scent, 33-ounce box of Tide laundry detergent with bleach or a blue, long-sleeve, button-down-collar Ralph Lauren shirt, size medium.

Warehouse clubs, discount stores, and toy stores all sell toys, but warehouse clubs and full-line discount stores sell many other categories of merchandise in addition to toys (i.e., they have greater variety). Stores specializing in toys stock

EXHIBIT 2–2   Variety and Assortment of Bicycles in Different Retail Outlets

	Adult Road	Adult Hybrid	Mountain	Child
Wheelworks	Bianci, Colnago, Peter Mooney, Serotta, Trek 150 SKUs $419.99–$7,999.99	Bianchi, Specialized, Trek 96 SKUs $349.99–$1,899.99	Salsa, Santa Cruz, Specialized, Trek 122 SKUs $299.99–$1,899.99	Electra, Gary Fisher, Haro, Kettler, Trek 56 SKUs $159.99–$429.99
Toys R Us	Mobo Triton Pro 3 SKUs $299.99–$359.99	—	Cycle Force, Huffy, Schwinn 4 SKUs $79.98–$135.99	Avigo, Cycle Force, Huffy, Mongoose, Pacific Cycle 228 SKUs $45.99–$499.99
Walmart	Cycle Force, Genesis, Kent, Mongoose 26 SKUs $99.97–$499.00	Cycle Force, Genesis, Schwinn, Tour de France 9 SKUs $179.00–$349.00	Havoc, Genesis, Schwinn, NEXT, Roadmaster 63 SKUs $88.00–$379.00	Huffy, Koxx, Micargi, Schwinn, Tour De France 195 SKUs $28.13–$675.00

more types of toys (more SKUs) and thus offer a greater assortment (i.e., greater depth in the form of more models, sizes, and brands) than the full-line discount stores or warehouse clubs.

Variety and assortment can also be applied to a specific merchandise category rather than an entire store. Exhibit 2–2 shows the breadth and depth of bicycles, as well as the different price points and brands carried by three very different types of stores: Wheelworks, a bicycle specialty retailer with one store in Belmont, Massachusetts; Toys R Us, a toy big-box category killer; and Walmart, a full-line discount store. Toys R Us has a large variety of merchandise besides bicycles, but its bicycle assortment is narrow. Wheelworks has the smallest variety because it carries only bicycles, parts, and accessories; but its assortment is very deep. Walmart, trying to cater to a wide target market, has a moderate variety and assortment.

One of the most interesting retailers that sells an amazing variety and assortment of merchandise is Amazon, which is highlighted in Retailing View 2.1.

How does Wheelworks' variety and assortment compare with Toys R Us and Walmart?

Why do the three retailers' assortments differ from each other?

Services Offered

Retailers also differ in the services they offer customers. Customers expect almost all retailers to provide certain services: displaying merchandise, accepting credit cards, providing parking, and being open at convenient hours. Some retailers charge customers for other services, such as home delivery and gift wrapping. However, retailers may differ on other services. For example, Wheelworks offers assistance in selecting the appropriate bicycle, as well as repairs. Walmart does not provide these services.

Prices and the Cost of Offering Breadth and Depth of Merchandise and Services

Stocking a deep and broad assortment, like the one Wheelworks offers in bicycles, is appealing to customers but costly for retailers. When a retailer offers many SKUs, its inventory investment increases because the retailer must have backup stock for each and every SKU.

Similarly, services attract customers to the retailer, but they also are costly. More staff must be paid to provide information and assist customers, alter products to meet customers' needs, and demonstrate merchandise. Child care facilities, restrooms, dressing rooms, and coat check rooms take up valuable store space that could be used to stock and display merchandise. Offering delayed billing, credit, or installment payments requires a financial investment that could be otherwise used to buy more merchandise.

To make a profit, retailers that offer broader variety, deeper assortments, and/or additional services need to charge higher prices. For example, department stores have higher prices than discount stores partially because of their higher costs. Department stores stock more fashionable merchandise and have to reduce prices when they make a mistake in guessing what the popular styles will be. They also provide more personal sales service and have more expensive mall locations. In contrast, discount stores appeal to customers who are looking for lower prices. These consumers are less interested in the costly services provided by department stores. Thus, a critical retail decision involves the trade-off between the costs and benefits of maintaining additional inventory or providing additional services. Chapters 6 and 12 address the considerations required in making this trade-off. In the next sections, we discuss the different types of food and general merchandise retailers.

40   SECTION I   The World of Retailing

2.1   RETAILING VIEW   Amazon: The Jack of All (Retail) Trades and Master of Many

When it started out in 1994, Amazon simply promised more books than anyone else. It took a few years for the online retailer to grow large enough to threaten the big names—Borders, Barnes & Noble, and so on. But today, its competitive threat spreads far beyond bookstores to take on virtually any type of retailer you might find.

Consider, for example, evidence showing that Walmart is losing sales to Amazon. Now that Amazon stocks items such as baby formula, clothing, and electronic goods,

Amazon offers the largest variety and assortment of any retailer in the world.

often at lower prices than even the low-price master, people see little reason to fight with traffic or search for parking at the world's largest retailer. Instead, they sit at home and wait for the items to arrive. Won't be home during the day to receive your delivery? No problem—Amazon is testing an option to ship deliveries to local 7-Eleven convenience stores, then e-mail customers with bar codes that identify them, and their package, to the convenience store clerks.

As we know though, retail isn't simply about physical goods. It also includes services, and on that front, Amazon is also taking on a wide spread of competitors. It offers textbook rentals through its Kindle products to college students. The Kindle Lending Library allows Amazon Prime members to receive free books each month. It provides authors an easy route to self-publishing their work. Its cloud computing services are free for the first year— and its cloud offers enough storage for every person on the planet to store 82 books. With the Amazon Flow Powered app, shoppers in stores also can scan barcodes and find Amazon's (usually competitive) price immediately. And of course, for Prime customers, Amazon always offers free shipping.

But its influence is not all threat. For small-business owners, the opportunity to sell through Amazon provides unparalleled exposure. Amazon actively seeks small retailers with interesting products but insufficient resources to distribute those offerings widely. To them, Amazon is less a threat and more a golden opportunity.

Sources: Chantal Tode, "Amazon Makes Play for Greater Influence Over In-Store Shoppers," *Mobile Commerce Daily*, July 3, 2012; Brad Tuttle, "Today's Value Shopper Heads to Amazon, Not Walmart," *Time*, April 10, 2012; Greg Bensinger, "Amazon's Tough Call," *The Wall Street Journal*, July 11, 2012; Molly McHugh, "Saving Cash on College Textbooks," *Digital Trends*, July 18, 2011; Maggie Shader, "Amazon Tests After-Hours Package Pickup at 7-Eleven Locations," *Consumer Reports*, September 8, 2011; James Kendrick, "Amazon Debits Kindle Owner Lending Library," *ZDNet*, November 3, 2011; Vanchi Govind, "Amazon.com Offers Cloud Computing Services for Free," *InfoTech*, November 3, 2010; Jeffrey A. Trachtenberg, "Secret of Self-Publishing: Success," *The Wall Street Journal*, October 31, 2011; and Zoe Fox, "How Amazon Became the World's Largest Retailer," *Mashable*, November 17, 2011.

DISCUSSION QUESTIONS

What categories is Amazon competing in? Which retailers are they competing against?

FOOD RETAILERS

LO2

Categorize the various types of food retailers.

The food retailing landscape is changing dramatically. Twenty years ago, consumers purchased food primarily at conventional supermarkets. Now conventional supermarkets only account for slightly more than 60 percent of food sales (not including restaurants).[3] Not only do full-line discount stores like Walmart and Target now offer a full assortment of grocery items in their superstores, but traditional supermarkets also are carrying more nonfood items. Many supermarkets

EXHIBIT 2–3
Sales and Growth Rate
for Retail Sectors

	Estimated Sales, 2013 ($ millions)	Estimated Sales Growth 2008–2013 (%)
Food Retailers		
Conventional supermarkets	$622,896	3.3
Supercenters	354,905	7.1
Warehouse clubs	159,075	6.7
Convenience stores	748,186	3.0
General Merchandise Retailers		
Department stores	73,291	−0.9
Apparel and accessory specialty stores	210,236	4.5
Jewelry stores	36,848	3.4
Shoe stores	29,606	1.8
Furniture stores	66,262	2.2
Home furnishing stores	59,465	2.8
Office supply stores	26,404	2.2
Sporting goods stores	49,717	5.3
Bookstores	19,101	2.1
Building material, hardware, and garden supply stores	393,254	3.6
Consumer electronics and appliance stores	141,800	4.4
Drugstores	250,172	4.2
Full-line discount stores	126,385	0.0
Extreme-value stores	52,454	3.1
Nonstore Retailers		
Nonstore retailing	340,421	9.0
E-commerce	282,055	15.0

Sources: *Economic Forecast: Outlook to 2013 Food, Drug, Mass* (Columbus, OH: Retail Forward, November 2008); *Economic Forecast: Outlook to 2013 Homegoods* (Columbus, OH.: Retail Forward, November 2008); *Economic Forecast: Outlook to 2013 Softgoods* (Columbus, OH: Retail Forward, November 2008).

offer pharmacies, health care clinics, banks, and cafés. Exhibit 2–3 contains information about the size and growth rates for each of these retail sectors.

The world's largest food retailer, Walmart, attains more than $443 billion in sales of supermarket-type merchandise. On this measure, it is followed by Carrefour (France), Tesco (United Kingdom), Metro Group (Germany), Schwartz Group (Germany), and Kroger (United States).[4] In North America specifically, the largest supermarket chains in order are Walmart, Kroger, Costco, Target, Safeway, Supervalu, Loblaw, Publix, and Ahold US.[5]

Kroger is the largest supermarket chain in the United States.

EXHIBIT 2–4
Characteristics of Food Retailers

	Conventional Supermarket	Limited-Assortment Supermarket	Supercenter	Warehouse Club	Convenience Store
Percentage food	70–80	80–90	30–40	60	90
Size (000 sq. ft.)	35–40	7–10	160–200	100–150	3–5
SKUs (000)	30–40	1–1.5	100–150	20	2–3
Variety	Average	Narrow	Broad	Broad	Narrow
Assortment	Average	Shallow	Deep	Shallow	Shallow
Ambience	Pleasant	Minimal	Average	Minimal	Average
Service	Modest	Limited	Limited	Limited	Limited
Prices	Average	Lowest	Low	Low	High
Gross margin (%)	20–22	10–12	15–18	12–15	25–30

Despite their similarly large sizes, most of Walmart's food sales are generated from its supercenter format, whereas Carrefour garners most of its sales using the hypermarket format that it developed. The remaining larger food retailers primarily sell through conventional supermarkets. Exhibit 2–4 shows the retail mixes for different types of food retailers.

Supermarkets

A **conventional supermarket** is a large, self-service retail food store offering groceries, meat, and produce, as well as some nonfood items, such as health and beauty aids and general merchandise.[7] Perishables, including meat, produce, baked goods, and dairy products, account for 30 percent of supermarket sales and typically have higher margins than packaged goods.[8]

Whereas conventional supermarkets carry about 30,000 SKUs, **limited-assortment supermarkets,** or **extreme-value food retailers,** only stock about 1,500 SKUs.[10] The two largest limited-assortment supermarket chains in the United States are Save-A-Lot and ALDI.

Rather than carrying 20 brands of laundry detergent, limited-assortment supermarkets offer one or two brands and sizes, one of which is a store brand. Stores are designed to maximize efficiency and reduce costs. For example, merchandise is shipped in cartons on crates that can serve as displays so that no unloading is needed. Some costly services that consumers take for granted, such as free bags and paying with credit cards, are not provided. Stores are typically located in second- or third-tier shopping centers with low rents. By trimming costs, limited-assortment supermarkets can offer merchandise at prices 40 percent lower than those at conventional supermarkets.[11] These features have supported the substantial growth of such retailers, which appeal strongly to customers who are not loyal to national brands and more willing to try a store brand, especially if it means they pay lower prices.[12]

Trends in Supermarket Retailing Although conventional supermarkets still sell the majority of food merchandise, they are under substantial competitive pressure on multiple sides: from supercenters, warehouse clubs, extreme-value retailers, convenience stores, and even drug stores.[13] All these types of retailers have increased the amount of space they devote to consumables. Family Dollar, which previously offered only discounted store brands, has expanded its assortment by about 20 percent, to include national brands such as Pepsi.[14]

Because consumers typically make three trips a week to buy food, but less than one trip a week to buy nonfood items, these competing retailers typically offer food merchandise to build the traffic in their stores and increase the sales of more profitable nonfood merchandise. They also have superior operating efficiencies and bargaining power with vendors that enable them to achieve low costs and offer low prices. These competing retailers have invested heavily in state-of-the-art supply chains, assortment planning, and pricing systems that reduce their inventories while increasing their sales and margins. These activities are discussed in more detail in Chapters 10 and 12.

To compete successfully against intrusions by other food retailing formats, conventional supermarkets are differentiating their offerings by (1) emphasizing fresh perishables, (2) targeting green and ethnic consumers, (3) providing better value with private-label merchandise, and (4) providing a better shopping experience.

Fresh Merchandise   Fresh-merchandise categories are located in the areas around the outer walls of a supermarket, known as the **"power perimeter,"** and include the dairy, bakery, meat, florist, produce, deli, and coffee bar. These departments attract consumers and are very profitable. Conventional supermarkets are building on their strength in these categories and devoting more space and attention to them. They are promoting fresh merchandise with cooking exhibitions and "action" stations, such as store-made sushi and freshly grilled meat. In response to this consumer desire for more and better fresh merchandise, food retailers such as Fresh Fare (Kroger) and Fresh Market are opening food stores focusing on the power perimeter merchandise.

Another example of the emphasis on "fresh" is the meal solutions offered to time-pressured consumers. A recent survey found that 64 percent of adult consumers have purchased ready-to-eat or heat-and-eat food from a grocery in the past month.[16] The choices in the stores are as varied as the stores themselves. Market District offers smoothies; Buehler's Fresh Food sells crab cakes and beef burgundy on a rotating "Dinner for 2" menu; Safeway's Lifestyle stores have sandwich and sushi stations. The ready-to-eat meals at a Publix store in Florida take up 4,500 square feet of space and include more than 80 entrees, such as cedar-plank salmon and Kung Pao scallops.[17]

Green Merchandise   Conventional supermarkets are offering more fair trade, natural, organic, and locally sourced foods for the growing segment of consumers who are health- and environmentally conscious. **Fair trade** is the practice of purchasing from factories that pay workers a living wage, considerably more than the prevailing minimum wage, and offer other benefits such as onsite medical treatment. Organic food purchases have jumped in recent years, with sales increasing by nearly 20 percent annually. Consumers also are buying a wider range of organic products, including staple items such as milk, eggs, and vegetables, as well as more fun options, such as ice cream and hair care products.[19]

Traditional supermarket chains also are opening smaller-format stores such as GreenWise Market (Publix) targeting health-conscious consumers who patronize Whole Foods. In a related food retailing trend, they offer locally grown products, a trend brought about in response to environmental concerns and the increasing financial costs (e.g., fuel) of transporting food long distances. The **locavore movement** focuses on reducing the carbon footprint caused by the

Health-conscious and environmentally conscious consumers are demanding organic and locally produced foods from food retailers.

REFACT

A recent survey found that one in three people have switched grocery stores. The top reasons for changing were as follows: 43 percent cited cost; 25 percent complained of long lines, poor selection, and low quality; 17% noted rude employees; and 14 percent disliked crowded stores.[15]

REFACT

Almost 70 percent of U.S. shoppers bought something organic over a recent three-month period.[18]

transportation of food throughout the world. Food miles are calculated using the distance that foods travel from the farm to the plate. Many Americans appreciate the idea of supporting local businesses, but they also want the variety of products they can find everyday in their grocery store. It is difficult to maintain a balance between buying locally and maintaining such variety.

Ethnic Merchandise   Hispanics, who now constitute 15 percent of the U.S. population, have significantly different shopping and eating patterns from those of the general population.[20] They are more likely to prepare meals from scratch, spend more on groceries, prefer stores with bilingual staff and signage, and place importance on fresh food. In addition to adding more ethnic merchandise in conventional supermarkets, retailers are opening supermarkets targeting Hispanic consumers.

For example, Northgate markets in California cater to just Hispanic consumers. Their 36 stores, each approximately 50,000 square feet, feature both domestic and imported Latin American grocery items. Furthermore, they contain a dedicated tortilleria, prepared foods, and a well-stocked and staffed meat department.[21]

Supercenters offer a vast assortments under one roof.

Private-Label Merchandise   Conventional supermarket chains are leveraging their quality reputation to offer more private-label merchandise. Private-label brands (discussed in Chapter 13) benefit both customers and retailers. The benefits to customers include having more choices and finding the same ingredients and quality as in national brands at a lower price or higher quality at a similar price to the national brands. The benefits of private-label brands to retailers include increased store loyalty, the ability to differentiate themselves from the competition, lower promotional costs, and higher gross margins compared with national brands.

Improving the Shopping Experience   Creating an enjoyable shopping experience through better store ambience and customer service is another approach that supermarket chains use to differentiate themselves from low-cost, low-price competitors. Supermarkets are increasingly incorporating "food as theater" concepts, such as in-store restaurants, open-air market designs, cooking and nutrition classes, demonstrations, baby-sitting services, and food and wine tasting. To appeal to on-the-go consumers, other supermarkets are offering self-service kiosks that are both fun and convenient. Among the offerings, in place at both conventional supermarkets and limited-assortment stores, are Coinstar, a change counting machine; Redbox, a movie rental kiosk; and Starbucks kiosks selling freshly ground and brewed cups of its subbranded Seattle's Best Coffee.[22]

Supercenters

Supercenters are large stores (160,000 to 200,000 square feet) that combine a supermarket with a full-line discount store. Walmart operates more than 3,000 supercenters in the United States. Its leading competitors include Meijer, SuperTarget (Target),

Fred Meyer (Kroger), and Super Kmart Center (Sears Holding). By offering broad assortments of grocery and general merchandise products under one roof, supercenters provide a one-stop shopping experience.

General merchandise (nonfood) items are often purchased on impulse when customers' primary reason for coming to the supercenter is to buy groceries. General merchandise has higher margins, enabling the supercenters to price food items more aggressively. However, supercenters are very large, so some customers find them inconvenient because it can take a long time to find the items they want.

Hypermarkets are also large (160,000 to 200,000 square feet), combination food (60 to 70 percent) and general merchandise (30 to 40 percent) stores. The world's second-largest retailer, Carrefour, operates hypermarkets. Hypermarkets typically stock fewer SKUs than do supercenters—between 40,000 and 60,000 items, ranging from groceries, hardware, and sports equipment to furniture and appliances to computers and electronics.

Hypermarkets were created in France after World War II. By building large stores on the outskirts of metropolitan areas, French retailers could attract customers and not violate strict land-use laws. They have spread throughout Europe and become popular in some South American countries such as Argentina and Brazil.

Hypermarkets are not common in the United States, though they are similar to supercenters. Both hypermarkets and supercenters are large, carry grocery and general merchandise categories, offer self-service, and are located in warehouse-type structures with large parking facilities. However, hypermarkets carry a larger proportion of food items than do supercenters and have a greater emphasis on perishables—produce, meat, fish, and bakery items. Supercenters, in contrast, have a larger percentage of nonfood items and focus more on dry groceries, such as breakfast cereal and canned goods, instead of fresh items.

Both supercenters and hypermarkets face challenges in finding locations for new **big-box** (large, limited-service) **stores.** Although Brazil and China are promising emerging markets, many others are shrinking.[23] In Europe and Japan, land for building large stores is limited and expensive. New supercenters and hypermarkets in these areas often have to be multistory, which increases operating costs and reduces shopper convenience. Furthermore, some countries place restrictions on the size of new retail outlets. In the United States, there has been a backlash against large retail stores, particularly Walmart outlets. These opposing sentiments are based on local views that big-box stores drive local retailers out of business, offer low wages, provide nonunion jobs, have unfair labor practices, threaten U.S. workers through their purchase of imported merchandise, and cause excessive automobile and delivery truck traffic.

Warehouse Clubs

Warehouse clubs are retailers that offer a limited and irregular assortment of food and general merchandise with little service at low prices for ultimate consumers and small businesses. The largest warehouse club chains are Costco, Sam's Club (Walmart), and BJ's Wholesale Club (operating only on the East Coast of the United States). Customers are attracted to these stores because they

People go to warehouse clubs such as Costco to search for treasures like computers at prices lower than those of competitors.

can stock up on large packs of basics like paper towels, large-size packaged groceries like a quart of ketchup, best-selling books and CDs, fresh meat and produce, and an unpredictable assortment of upscale merchandise and services at low prices. For example, at Costco you can buy a 5-carat diamond ring for $99,999.99 with an appraised value of $153,450. Heavy food sampling adds to the shopping experience. Sam's Club focuses more on small businesses, providing services such as group health insurance as well as products. BJ's has beefed up its assortment of fresh meat and produce in recent years. Although package sizes are large compared to those in conventional grocery stores, BJ's provides convenient individual packaging—an attribute that is particularly appealing to its more upscale customers.

Warehouse clubs are large (100,000 to 150,000 square feet) and typically located in low-rent districts. They have simple interiors and concrete floors. Aisles are wide so that forklifts can pick up pallets of merchandise and arrange them on the selling floor. Little service is offered. Warehouse clubs can offer low prices because they use low-cost locations, have inexpensive store designs, and offer little customer service; they further keep inventory holding costs low by carrying a limited assortment of fast-selling items. In addition, they buy merchandise opportunistically. For example, if Hewlett-Packard is introducing new models of its printers, warehouse clubs will buy the inventory of the older models at a significant discount and then offer them for sale until the inventory is depleted.

Most warehouse clubs have two types of members: wholesale members who own small businesses and individual members who purchase for their own use. For example, many small restaurants are wholesale customers that buy their supplies, food ingredients, and desserts from a warehouse club rather than from food distributors. To cater to their business customers, warehouse clubs sell food items in very large containers and packages—sizes that also appeal to larger families. Typically, members pay an annual fee of around $50, which amounts to significant additional income for the chains.

Convenience Stores

Convenience stores provide a limited variety and assortment of merchandise at a convenient location in 3,000- to 5,000-square-foot stores with speedy checkout. Convenience stores enable consumers to make purchases quickly, without having to search through a large store and wait in a long checkout line. More than half the items bought are consumed within 30 minutes of purchase.

Convenience stores generally charge higher prices than supermarkets for similar products like milk, eggs, and bread. These products once represented the majority of their sales, but now the majority of sales come from lower profit products, such as gasoline and cigarettes, putting a strain on their profits.

Convenience stores also face increased competition from other formats. Supercenter and supermarket chains are attempting to appeal to customers by offering gasoline and tying gasoline sales to their frequent shopper programs. For example, shoppers who spend at least $50 and swipe their Giant Eagle Advantage Card at any

At convenience stores you can jump out of your car and pick up a Coke and some chewing gum while getting gas.
© BP p.l.c.

GetGo, Market District, Giant Eagle, or Giant Eagle Express location receive a 10-cent discount per gallon on their next fill-up.[25] Drugstores and full-line discount stores also have easily accessible areas of their stores filled with convenience store merchandise.

In response to these competitive pressures, convenience stores are taking steps to decrease their dependency on gasoline sales, tailor assortments to local markets, offer more fresh options, and make their stores even more convenient to shop. For example, to get gasoline customers to spend more on other merchandise and services, convenience stores are offering more food options that appeal to on-the-go consumers, especially women and young adults.[26] Finally, convenience stores are adding new services, such as financial service kiosks that give customers the opportunity to cash checks, pay bills, and buy prepaid telephone minutes, theater tickets, and gift cards.

To increase convenience, convenience stores are opening smaller stores close to where consumers shop and work. For example, 7-Eleven has stores in airports, office buildings, and schools. Easy access, storefront parking, and quick in-and-out access are key benefits offered by convenience stores. They also are exploring the use of technology to increase shopping convenience. Sheetz, a Pennsylvania-based convenience store chain, has touch-screen "Made-to-Order" kiosks at which customers can order customized deli sandwiches, wraps, salads, subs, and nachos while pumping gasoline.[28] Retailing View 2.2 describes the difference between convenience stores in the United States and Japan.

REFACT

Gasoline sales at combination gas station–convenience stores contribute 71 percent of the store's sales. Cigarette and tobacco products contribute 38 percent of in-store merchandise sales.[27]

RETAILING VIEW   Convenience Stores in Japan Are Different   2.2

Japanese corporations might own several U.S. convenience store chains (e.g., 7-Eleven, Circle K), but convenience stores (*konbinis*) in Japan and in the United States have little in common. Whereas shoppers in the United States depend heavily on their cars, most Japanese consumers commute using public transportation and work very long hours. To be convenient, the convenience stores thus locate in central business districts and train and subway stations. Rather than gasoline, *konbinis* sell a broad assortment of services, in addition to their extensive food options, including concert and amusement park tickets. Shoppers can pay their bills or make copies, as well as pick up some fashionable clothing. In turn, Japanese consumers visit convenience stores for approximately 30 percent of their food purchases, whereas in the United States, convenience stores only account for 5 to 10 percent of this market.

Part of the reason for this greater share is the quality of food available in *konbinis*. Whereas late night U.S. snackers might embrace microwaveable burritos, *konbinis* often offer pasta dishes, fresh vegetables, fruit, and prepared meals of restaurant quality. Although they traditionally catered to male customers, more Japanese women in the workforce have led the *konbinis* to adjust their assortments accordingly. A traditional bento box

REFACT

Convenience store operator 7-Eleven has replaced McDonald's as the world's largest chain in terms of number of outlets. As of July 2012, 7-Eleven had a total of 46,000 stores in 16 countries, compared with 33,510 McDonald's outlets.[29]

might contain rice with grilled fish or fatty meat—a meal not particularly appealing to female customers. Instead, today's chains prepare healthier food in nicer looking packages, such as *pho* Vietnamese-style noodles; soup in bowls; and elaborate, high-quality desserts.

With their relatively small sizes—around 300 to 600 square feet—and limited storage space, Japanese convenience stores need stellar information and supply chain management capabilities to succeed. That is, they must precisely match store-specific demand with just-in-time supply provisions. The most successful store operators gather customer information during every checkout: automatically, with a system that specifies the time of purchase, product barcode, and price, and manually, when the cashier notes the customer's approximate age and gender. An efficient data analysis system then determines when, how, and what to send to restock each *konbini*. Some stores even might receive up to seven restocking deliveries per day.

Sources: Kazuaki Nagata, "Convenience Store Chains Go With Flow, Grow," *The Japan Times,* May 8, 2012; and Stephanie Strom, "7-Eleven Shifts Focus to Healthier Food Options," *The New York Times,* December, 2012, p. B.1.

DISCUSSION QUESTION

Would Japanese-style convenience stores be successful in the United States? Why or why not?

48

GENERAL MERCHANDISE RETAILERS

LO3

Identify the various types of general merchandise retailers.

The major types of general merchandise retailers are department stores, full-line discount stores, specialty stores, drugstores, category specialists, extreme-value retailers, off-price retailers, and outlet stores. Exhibit 2–5 summarizes the characteristics of general merchandise retailers that sell through stores.

Department Stores

REFACT

T. Stewart was the first U.S. department store, opening in 1847 in New York.[31]

Department stores are retailers that carry a broad variety and deep assortment, offer customer services, and organize their stores into distinct departments for displaying merchandise. The largest department store chains in the United States are Sears, Macy's, Kohl's, JCPenney, Nordstrom, and Dillards.[30]

Traditionally, department stores attracted customers by offering a pleasing ambience, attentive service, and a wide variety of merchandise under one roof. They sold both **soft goods** (nondurable or consumable goods), which have a shorter lifespan such as cosmetics, clothing, and bedding) and **hard goods,** also known as **durable goods,** which are manufactured items that are expected to last several years, such as appliances, furniture, and consumer electronics. But now, most department stores focus almost exclusively on soft goods. The major departments are women's, men's, and children's apparel; home furnishings; cosmetics; kitchenware; and small appliances. Each department within the store has a specific selling space allocated to it, as well as salespeople to assist customers. The department store often resembles a collection of specialty shops.

Department store chains can be categorized into three tiers. The first tier includes upscale, high-fashion chains with exclusive designer merchandise and excellent customer service, such as Neiman Marcus, Bloomingdale's (part of Macy's Inc.), Nordstrom, and Saks Fifth Avenue (part of Saks Inc.). Macy's and Dillards are in the second tier of traditional department stores, in which retailers sell more modestly priced merchandise with less customer service. The value-oriented third tier—Sears, JCPenney, and Kohl's—caters to more price-conscious consumers.

Department stores account for some of retailing's most cherished traditions—special events and parades (Macy's Thanksgiving parade in New York City), Santa Claus lands, and holiday decorations. But many consumers question the benefits and costs of shopping at department stores. Department stores are not

EXHIBIT 2–5   Characteristics of General Merchandise Retailers

Type	Variety	Assortment	Service	Prices	Size (000 sq. ft.)	SKUs (000)	Location
Department stores	Broad	Deep to average	Average to high	Average to high	100–200	100	Regional malls
Discount stores	Broad	Average to shallow	Low	Low	60–80	30	Stand alone, power strip centers
Category specialists	Narrow	Very deep	Low to high	Low	50–100	20–40	Stand alone, power strip centers
Specialty stores	Narrow	Deep	High	High	4–12	5	Regional malls
Home improvement centers	Narrow	Very deep	Low to high	Low	80–120	20–40	Stand alone, power strip centers
Drugstores	Narrow	Very deep	Average	Average to high	3–15	10–20	Stand alone, strip centers
Off-price stores	Average	Deep but varying	Low	Low	20–30	50	Outlet malls
Extreme-value retailers	Average	Average and varying	Low	Low	7–15	3–4	Urban, strip

Macy's is a very popular department store known for great sales.

as convenient as discount stores, such as Target, because they are located in large regional malls rather than local neighborhoods. JCPenney and Sears thus are following Kohl's by opening stores in nonmall locations. Customer service has diminished in the second- and third-tier stores because of the retailers' desire to increase profits by reducing labor costs.[32]

To deal with their eroding market share, department stores are (1) increasing the amount of exclusive merchandise they sell, (2) increasing their use of private-label merchandise, (3) expanding their multichannel presence.

- *Increase exclusive merchandise.* To differentiate their merchandise offerings and strengthen their image, department stores are aggressively seeking **exclusive brands** in which national brand vendors sell them merchandise that is not available elsewhere. Jennifer Lopez has a clothing line at Kohl's. Ralph Lauren designed a line of casual apparel exclusively for JCPenney called American Living. Furthermore, clothing is not the only category with exclusive lines: Customers looking for exclusive dinnerware collections can go to Macy's and get the Rachel Bilson line or else find the Kardashian Kollection at Sears.[33]

- *Increase private-label merchandise.* Department stores are placing more emphasis on developing their own **private-label brands,** or **store brands.** These items are developed and marketed by the retailer, available only in its stores. Macy's has been very successful in developing a strong image for its brands, including Alfani (women's fashion), Hotel Collection (luxury fabrics), and Tools of the Trade (housewares).[35]

- *Expand multichannel and social media presence.* Finally, like most retailers, most department stores have become active participants in multichannel retailing. At Macy's and Nordstrom, customers can buy or reserve products online and then pick them up at the store. Customers can also return online purchases to stores. At Macy's and JCPenney, sales associates can order out-of-stock merchandise online via their point-of-sale (POS) terminals and have it delivered directly to the customer. As Retailing View 2.3 describes, Nordstrom may be one of the most connected companies in the world.

REFACT

Almost 50 percent of JCPenney sales involve exclusive lines. Kohl's sells approximately 48 percent, and Macy's level is 40 percent of total sales.[34]

2.3 RETAILING VIEW Going Where the Customers Are

For Nordstrom, electronic offerings, such as a Facebook site or allowing customers to order online and pick up their purchases in stores, are old news. Its forward-looking, aggressive approach to social and mobile retailing has earned Nordstrom widespread recognition as a leader in terms of its connectivity—as well as a strong competitive advantage as retail continues to go virtual.

Back in 2010, Nordstrom introduced free wi-fi availability in its stores. This move exemplifies its superior recognition of how modern customers shop. Nearly all its in-store merchandise is available on its website. Furthermore, sales personnel are equipped with iPod Touch and iPad devices so that they can help a customer check out immediately, track inventory levels, and get suggestions for various departments. Staff members also are encouraged to interact with customers through social media, following Nordstrom's detailed guidelines. Such efforts reflect its goal to achieve seamless integration in its customer engagement, whether online, through mobile devices, or in stores.

Continuing its cutting-edge approach, social media for Nordstrom goes far beyond the basics of Facebook, Twitter, and YouTube. It also makes it presence felt on Pinterest, the online bulletin board; Instagram, Facebook's photo-sharing site; and the fashionista meeting place Polyvore. As a Nordstrom representative asserted, "Some people look at it as, 'If you have a Facebook site,

then you've got a social media strategy.' I think that's shortsighted."

To expand its online reach, Nordstrom has turned to an acquisitions strategy, purchasing shares in the flash sale site HauteLook, the children's clothing retailer Peek, the Sole Society shoe club, and the rapidly growing Bonobos menswear site. It also purchased advertising space in places with widespread reach, like in the massively popular Words with Friends game application.

Its efforts have paid off, not only in its image as a connected retailer, but also in the bottom line. It has attracted more than 1 million followers on Twitter. And the retailer's Internet sales grew by 30 percent in 2011. This result has prompted it to invest even more in its e-commerce efforts, up to $140 million in 2012.

Sources: David Hatch, "Nordstrom in Fashion with Social Media, Mobile Tech," *U.S. News and World Report,* May 15, 2012; Rimma Kats, "Nordstrom Put Focus on Social with New Media Initiative," *Mobile Marketer,* June 11, 2012; Sherilynn Macale, "This Retailer's Social-Powered Santa Claus Puts the Christmas Spirit Back in Gift Giving," *The Next Web,* November 25, 2011; and "Social Networking Guidelines," http://shop.nordstrom.com/c/social-networking-guidelines.

DISCUSSION QUESTION

How is social media helping Nordstrom stay connected with its customer base?

Full-Line Discount Stores

Full-line discount stores are retailers that offer a broad variety of merchandise, limited service, and low prices. Discount stores offer both private labels and national brands. The largest full-line discount store chains are Walmart, Target, and Kmart (Sears Holding). However, these full-line discount stores confront intense competition from category specialists that focus on a single category of merchandise, such as Staples, Best Buy, Bed Bath & Beyond, Sports Authority, and Lowe's.

In response, Walmart has taken a couple of routes. First, it has converted many of its discount stores into supercenters,[36] which are more efficient than traditional discount stores because of the economies of scale that result from the high traffic generated by the food offering. Second, it is expanding into more urban locations, using smaller storefronts that can be located in existing buildings, and appealing to price-oriented markets.[37]

Target has experienced considerable growth in the last decade because its stores offer fashionable merchandise at low prices in a pleasant shopping environment. It has developed an image of "cheap chic," continuously offering limited-edition exclusive apparel and cosmetic lines. In its GO International campaign, the retailer has teamed with such well-known designers as Missoni, Stefani, Harajuku Mini, Albertus Swanepoel, and Josie Natori.[38]

In contrast, Sears—and its Kmart brand—has struggled a bit in recent years and therefore is attempting an innovative and unusual solution. It will lease retail space in its stores to independent merchants. For example, in a huge Sears store in California, Western Athletic has leased approximately one-quarter of the space to insert a health club.[40]

REFACT

Hudson's Bay Company, the oldest retailer in North America, conquered the Canadian wilderness by trading furs more than 300 years ago. Today, it is one of the largest retailers in Canada, operating chains of discount, department, and home stores.[39]

EXHIBIT 2–6
Category Specialists

Apparel/Shoe/ Accessories	Furniture	Sporting Goods	Office Supply
Mens Wearhouse	IKEA	Bass Pro Shops Outdoor World	Office Depot
DSW	Pier 1	Cabela's	Staples
	Sofa Express	Dick's Sporting Goods	Office Max
Books	**Home**	L.L. Bean	**Pet Supplies**
Barnes & Noble	Bed Bath & Beyond	Golfsmith	PetSmart
Consumer Electronics	The Container Store	REI	PETCO
Best Buy	World Market	Sports Authority	**Musical Instruments**
Crafts	**Home Improvement**	**Toys**	Guitar Center
Michaels	Home Depot	Toys "R" Us	
	Lowe's		

EXHIBIT 2–6
Category Specialists

Category Specialists

Category specialists are big-box stores that offer a narrow but deep assortment of merchandise. Exhibit 2–6 lists some of the largest category specialists in the United States.

Most category specialists predominantly use a self-service approach, but they offer assistance to customers in some areas of the stores. For example, Staples stores have a warehouse atmosphere, with cartons of copy paper stacked on pallets, plus equipment in boxes on shelves. But in some departments, such as computers and other high-tech products, it provides salespeople in the display area to answer questions and make suggestions. Bass Pro Shops Outdoor World is a category specialist offering merchandise for outdoor recreational activities. The stores offer everything a person needs for hunting and fishing—from 27-cent plastic bait to boats and recreational vehicles costing $45,000. Sales associates are knowledgeable outdoors people. Each is hired for a particular department that matches that person's expertise. All private-branded products are field-tested by Bass Pro Shops' professional teams: the Redhead Pro Hunting Team and Tracker Pro Fishing Team.

By offering a complete assortment in a category, category specialists can "kill" a category of merchandise for other retailers and thus are frequently called **category killers.** Using their category dominance and buying power, they buy products at low prices and are ensured of supply when items are scarce. Department stores and full-line discount stores located near category specialists often have to reduce their offerings in the category because consumers are drawn to the deep assortment and competitive prices at the category killer.

Although category specialists compete with other types of retailers, competition between them is intense. Competing category specialists such as Lowe's and Home Depot, or Staples and Office Depot, have difficulty differentiating themselves on most of the elements of their retail mixes. They all provide similar assortments because they have similar access to national brands, and they all provide a similar level of service. Primarily then, they compete on price and location. Some category specialists are also experiencing intense competition from warehouse clubs like Sam's Club and Costco.[42]

Category specialists, like Staples, offer a deep assortment of merchandise at low prices.

Therefore, many of them are attempting to differentiate themselves with customer service. For example, Home Depot and Lowe's hire experienced builders as sales associates to help customers with electrical and plumbing repairs. They also provide classes to train home owners in tiling, painting, and other tasks to give shoppers the confidence to tackle their do-it-yourself (DIY) projects on their own. Home Depot offers an integrated line of Martha Stewart brand products, with different themes marked by unique icons, such that a customer can create a professional-looking decorated space simply by choosing products with matching icons.[44] Besides beefing up its sales associates' training to help customers purchase high-tech products like computers and printers, Staples has implemented "Easy Tech" in its stores to help people with computer and related problems and has installed Staples Copy and Print shops to compete with FedEx Office.

Specialty Stores

Specialty stores concentrate on a limited number of complementary merchandise categories and provide a high level of service. Exhibit 2–7 lists some of the largest specialty store chains.

Specialty stores tailor their retail strategy toward very specific market segments by offering deep but narrow assortments and sales associate expertise. Victoria's Secret is the leading specialty retailer of lingerie and beauty products in the United States. Using a multipronged location strategy that includes malls, lifestyle centers, and central business districts, the company conveys its message using supermodels and world-famous runway shows.[45]

Sephora, France's leading perfume and cosmetic chain—a division of luxury-goods conglomerate LVMH (Louis Vuitton-Moet Hennessy)—is another example of an innovative specialty store concept. Sephora provides a cosmetic and perfume specialty store offering a deep assortment in a self-service format. It also maintains separate stores-within-stores at JCPenney. The approximately 15,000 SKUs and 200 brands, including its own private-label brand, are grouped by product category instead of by brand like in department stores, with brands displayed alphabetically so customers can locate them easily. Customers are free to shop and experiment on their own. Sampling is encouraged. Knowledgeable salespeople are available to assist customers. The low-key environment results in customers' spending more time shopping.

Specialty retailers have such great appeal that they rank among the most profitable and fastest growing firms in the world. Apple stores sell a remarkable

EXHIBIT 2–7
Specialty Store Retailers

Apparel	Electronics/Software	Jewelry	GNC
Abercrombie & Fitch	Ascend Acoustics	Blue Nile	Kiehl's
Brooks Brothers	Apple	Tiffany & Co.	M.A.C.
The Buckle	Brookstone	Zales	MakeupMania.com
Forever 21	Crutchfield		
The Gap	GameStop	**Optical**	Sephora
H&M	Newegg	1-800 Contacts	**Shoes**
Indochino.com	Radio Shack	LensCrafters	ALDO
Ralph Lauren	Tiger Direct	Pearle Vision	Allen Edmonds
J. Crew		Sunglass Hut	FootLocker
Threadless	**Housewares**		Nine West
Urban Outfitters	Crate & Barrel	**Health/Beauty**	Steve Madden
Victoria's Secret	Pottery Barn	Aveda	The Walking Company
Zara	Sur la Table	Bath & Body Works	
	Williams Sonoma	The Body Shop	Zappos

$5,647 per square foot on average, and its stock price jumped more than 25 percent in 2011. Lululemon's specialty is far less technical, involving yoga-inspired apparel and accessories, but it keeps opening its specialty stores at a remarkable rate of several per month. These stores earn an average of $1,800 per square foot.[46]

Charming Charlie stores are not quite as well known as the preceding brands, but the small company's success confirms the appeal of specialty retailers. In just seven years, the accessories and jewelry chain has grown to 178 stores, spread over 33 states. Its rapid growth is well matched by its influence: It was one of the first retailers to group merchandise by color instead of category. Furthermore, it works to maintain affordable prices ranging from less than $5 to no more than $50. That is, this specialty store specializes in helping customers update their wardrobes with new pieces, rather than forcing them to start all over again.[47]

Sephora is an innovative specialty store selling perfume and cosmetics.

In addition, many manufacturers have opened their own specialty stores. Consider, for instance, Levi's (jeans and casual apparel), Godiva (chocolate), Cole Haan (shoes and accessories), Lacoste (apparel), Coach (purses and leather accessories), Tumi (luggage), Wolford (intimate apparel), Lucky brand (jeans and casual apparel), Samsonite (luggage), and Polo/Ralph Lauren (apparel and home). Tired of being at the mercy of retailers to purchase and merchandise their products, these manufacturers and specialty retailers can control their own destiny by operating their own stores.

Another growing specialty store sector is the resale store. Resale stores are retailers that sell secondhand or used merchandise. A special type of resale store is the **thrift store,** where merchandise is donated and proceeds go to charity. Another type of resale store is the **consignment shop,** a store that accepts used merchandise from people and pays them after it is sold. Resale stores earn national revenues of more than $13 billion. They also have enjoyed double-digit growth rates in the past few years.[49] Although the ambiance of resale stores traditionally was less appealing than that of other clothing or housewares retailers, the remarkable prices for used merchandise drew in customers.

Today, many resale stores also have increased their value by making their shopping space more pleasant and increasing levels of service.[50] With their lower expenses (in that they pay a discounted price to people selling their used apparel), resale stores are moving into storefronts in higher-end locations that have been abandoned by traditional retailers.[51]

Perhaps the best known and most widely expanded thrift shop is Goodwill Industries. In addition to its retail outlets, Goodwill runs an extensive job training and placement division, such that customers shopping at these outlets get a warm glow from knowing that their purchases help others. Unlike most other resale stores, Goodwill accepts all goods. The old stereotype of a cluttered, dark, odd-smelling Goodwill store has changed. The company has revamped and updated stores nationwide. Local stores seek to meet local needs, such that the New England–area Goodwill stores host annual bridal dress sales, and the Suncoast division in Florida maintains a catering department.[52]

Drugstores

Drugstores are specialty stores that concentrate on health and beauty care (HBC) products. Many drug stores have steadily increased the space devoted to cosmetics. Prescription pharmaceuticals often represent almost 65 percent of drugstore sales.[53]

The largest drugstore chains in the United States are Walgreens, CVS, and Rite Aid, which together run more than 36,000 stores, or 60 percent of the drug stores in the United States.[54] Much of this increased concentration has occurred through mergers and acquisitions. For instance, CVS acquired Longs, Sav-On, and Osco (as well as Caremark, which manages the prescription drug aspect for many insurance plans); Rite Aid acquired Brooks and Eckerd.

Drugstores face competition from pharmacies in discount stores and from pressure to reduce health care costs. In response, the major drugstore chains are offering a wider assortment of merchandise, including more frequently purchased food items, as well as new services, such as the convenience of drive-through windows for picking up prescriptions, in-store medical clinics, and even makeovers and spa treatments.[55]

In the Duane Reade store on Wall Street, near the New York Stock Exchange, customers find a vast array of offerings, such as $10 manicures, a hair salon staffed by a dedicated beauty consultant, a juice bar, and sushi chefs, next to typical drugstore products. Medical questions can be answered by the doctor who works there. In this store, the top sellers are now sushi, fresh juice, and bananas—though customers have not changed completely, so rounding out the top five sellers are coffee and Marlboro cigarettes.[56]

Walgreens hosts a café in its Chicago flagship store, where customers waiting to pick up a prescription can enjoy fresh coffee, breads, and pastries; munch on sushi or sandwiches; or visit the juice bar for a healthy smoothie or a nostalgic chocolate malted milkshake. But if they stop by later in the day, shoppers might prefer to browse the store's stock of 700 fine wines, artisanal cheeses, and gourmet chocolates.[57]

Although drugstores thus offer major advantages, especially in terms of convenience, they suffer from a price comparison when it comes to their grocery merchandise. A recent study indicated that the same selection of goods that cost $75.60 at a supermarket would run customers $102.94 at a nearby drug store.[58]

REFACT

Walgreens' merger/ acquisition of Alliance Boots has resulted in the largest pharmaceutical distribution network with more than 11,000 stores in 12 countries.[59]

Extreme-Value Retailers

Extreme-value retailers, also called **dollar stores,** are small discount stores that offer a broad variety but shallow assortment of household goods, health and beauty care (HBC) products, and groceries. The largest extreme-value retailers are Dollar General and Family Dollar.[60] As noted in the discussion of trends in food retailing, these stores have been expanding their assortments to include more private-label options, food, tobacco, and impulse buys such as candy, magazines, and gift cards.[61] Some extreme-value retailers, such as Dollar General, are adding refrigerated coolers and expanding their food offerings so that they can be known as the best destination store for a greater variety of household necessities. As a result, this retail model continues to attract significantly increasing numbers of shopper visits.[62]

Extreme-value retailers primarily target low-income consumers. These customers want well-known brands but cannot afford to buy the large-size packages offered by full-line discount stores or warehouse clubs. Vendors such as Procter & Gamble often create special, smaller packages for extreme-value retailers. Because these stores appeal to low-income consumers, are located where they live, and have expanded their assortments while keeping their unit prices low, they have cut into other retailers' businesses, including Walmart. Always ready for a good competitive battle, Walmart is opening smaller stores called Walmart Express in urban locations and creating smaller and less expensive packages to better compete.[63]

What you can still get for a dollar?

Despite some of these chains' names, few just sell merchandise for a dollar. The two largest—Dollar General and Family Dollar—do not employ a strict dollar limit and sell merchandise for up to $20. The names imply a good value but do not limit customers to the arbitrary dollar price point. Dollar Tree experimented with selling merchandise for more than a dollar, but it is back to being a dollar purist.[65]

Off-Price Retailers

Off-price retailers offer an inconsistent assortment of brand-name merchandise at a significant discount off the manufacturers' suggested retail price (MSRP). America's largest off-price retail chains are TJX Companies (which operates TJ Maxx, Marshalls, Winners, HomeGoods, TKMaxx, AJWright, and HomeSense), Ross Stores, Burlington Coat Factory, and Big Lots. Overstock.com and Bluefly.com are the largest Internet off-price retailers.

Off-price retailers are able to sell brand-name and even designer-label merchandise at 20 to 60 percent lower than the manufacturer's suggested retail price because of their unique buying and merchandising practices. Much of the merchandise is bought opportunistically from manufacturers that have overruns, canceled orders, forecasting mistakes causing excess inventory, closeouts, and irregulars. They also buy excess inventory from other retailers. **Closeouts** are end-of-season merchandise that will not be used in following seasons. **Irregulars** are merchandise with minor mistakes in construction. Off-price retailers can buy at low prices because they do not ask suppliers for advertising allowances, return privileges, markdown adjustments, or delayed payments. (These terms and conditions for buying merchandise are detailed in Chapter 13.)

Due to this opportunistic buying, customers cannot be confident that the same type of merchandise will be in stock each time they visit the store. Different bargains will be available on each visit. For many off-price shoppers, inconsistency is exactly why they like to go there. They enjoy hunting for hidden treasures. To improve their offerings' consistency, some off-price retailers complement their opportunistically bought merchandise with merchandise purchased at regular wholesale prices. Although not well known because few vendors to off-price retailers want to advertise their presence, the CEO of TJX asserts that the vast majority

Luxury merchandise at great prices.

of merchandise in its stores is same-season items, purchased directly from manufacturers.[66] She also claims less than 5 percent of TJX merchandise is irregular.

An online twist to off-price retailing are flash-sale sights such as Gilt Groupe, Rue La La, and HauteLook. They are called **flash sales** because each day at the same time, members receive an e-mail that announces the deals available. Each deal lasts for a specific and limited time, and the sales are first-come, first-served. A shopper who misses out on a great deal is far more likely to buy the next time around. These sites often require members to register.

A special type of off-price retailer is the outlet store. **Outlet stores** are off-price retailers owned by manufacturers or retailers. Those owned by manufacturers are also referred to as **factory outlets.** Manufacturers view outlet stores as an opportunity to improve their revenues from irregulars, production overruns, and merchandise returned by retailers. Others view it as simply another channel in which to sell their merchandise. Retailers with strong brand names such as Saks Fifth Avenue (Saks Fifth Avenue's Off 5th) and Williams-Sonoma operate outlet stores too. By selling excess merchandise in outlet stores rather than at markdown prices in their primary stores, these department and specialty store chains can maintain an image of offering desirable merchandise at full price.[67] For some retailers, their outlet stores are the wave of the future. Nordstrom expects that sometime soon, it will have more Nordstrom Rack stores than regular Nordstrom department stores.[68]

Outlet stores can have an adverse effect on profits, however, because they shift sales from full-price retailers to the lower-priced outlets. Additionally, outlet stores are becoming more promotional to compete with increased activity at other outlet stores within the same mall and with traditional off-price stores.[69]

SERVICE RETAILING

LO4

Explain the differences between service and merchandise retailers.

The retail firms discussed in the previous sections sell products to consumers. However, **service retailers,** or firms that primarily sell services rather than merchandise, are a large and growing part of the retail industry. Consider a typical Saturday: After a bagel and cup of coffee at a nearby Einstein Bros. Bagels, you go to the laundromat to wash and dry your clothes, drop a suit off at a dry cleaner, leave your computer to be serviced by the Geek Squad at Best Buy, and make your way to Jiffy Lube to have your car's oil changed. In a hurry, you drive through a Taco Bell so that you can eat lunch quickly and not be late for your 1:00 p.m. haircut. By midafternoon, you're ready for a workout at your health club. After stopping at home for a change of clothes, you're off to dinner, a movie, and finally clubbing with a friend. You end your day having interacted with 10 different services retailers throughout the day.

Several trends suggest considerable future growth in service retailing. For example, the aging population will increase demand for health care services. Younger people are also spending more time and money on health and fitness. Busy parents in two-income families are willing to pay to have their homes cleaned, lawns maintained, clothes washed and pressed, and meals prepared so that they can spend more time with their families.

Exhibit 2–8 shows the wide variety of services, along with some national companies that provide these services. These companies are retailers because they sell

Type of Service	Service Retail Firms
Airlines	American, Southwest, British Airways, JetBlue
Automobile maintenance and repair	Jiffy Lube, Midas, AAMCO
Automobile rental	Hertz, Avis, Budget, Enterprise
Banks	Citi, Wachovia, Bank of America
Child care centers	Kindercare, Gymboree
Dry cleaners	Zoots
Education	Babson College, University of Florida, Princeton Review
Entertainment	Disney World, Six Flags, Chuck E. Cheese, Dave & Busters
Express package delivery	FedEx, UPS, U.S. Postal Service
Fast food	Wendy's, McDonald's, Starbucks
Financial services	Merrill Lynch, Morgan Stanley, American Express, VISA
Fitness	Jazzercise, Bally's, Gold's Gym
Health care	Humana, HCA, Kaiser
Home maintenance	Chemlawn, Mini Maid, Roto-Rooter
Hotels and motels	Hyatt, Sheraton, Marriott, Days Inn
Income tax preparation	H&R Block
Insurance	Allstate, State Farm, Geico
Internet access/electronic information	Google, Internet Explorer, Mozilla Firefox, Safari
Movie theaters	AMC, Odeon/Cineplex
QSR	Panera Bread, Red Mango, Pinkberry
Real estate	Century 21, Coldwell Banker
Restaurants	Applebees's, Cheesecake Factory
Truck rentals	U-Haul, Ryder
Weight loss	Weight Watchers, Jenny Craig, Curves
Video rental	Blockbuster
Vision centers	LensCrafters, Pearle

EXHIBIT 2–8
Services Retailers

goods and services to consumers. However, some are not just retailers. For example, airlines, banks, hotels, and insurance and express mail companies sell their services to businesses as well as consumers.

Organizations such as banks, hospitals, health spas, legal clinics, entertainment firms, and universities that offer services to consumers traditionally have not considered themselves retailers. Yet due to increased competition, these organizations are adopting retailing principles to attract customers and satisfy their needs. For example, Zoots is a dry-cleaning chain in the Boston area.[70] Founded by a former Staples executive, Zoots has adopted many retailing best practices: It has convenient locations, and it offers pickup and delivery service. Zoots stores also provide extended hours, are open on weekends, and offer a drop-off option for those who cannot get to the store during operating hours. The stores are bright and clean. Customers can check their order status, schedule a pickup, and provide special instructions using the online MY ZOOTS service. Clerks are taught to welcome customers and acknowledge their presence, especially if there is a line.

Most retailers provide both merchandise and services for their customers. However, the emphasis placed on the merchandise versus the service differs across retail formats, as Exhibit 2–9 shows. On the left side of the exhibit

Going to Zoots to pick up laundry and dry cleaning is as easy as going to an ATM machine.

EXHIBIT 2–9   Continuum of Merchandise and Services Retailers

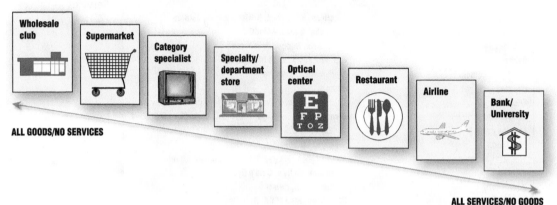

are supermarkets and warehouse clubs. These retail formats consist of self-service stores that offer very few services, except perhaps cashing checks and assisting customers at checkout.

Moving along the continuum from left to right, department and specialty stores provide higher levels of service. In addition to providing assistance from sales associates, they offer services such as gift wrapping, bridal registries, and alterations. Optical centers and restaurants lie somewhere in the middle of the merchandise-service continuum. In addition to selling frames, eyeglasses, and contact lenses, optical centers provide important services like eye examinations and eyeglass fittings. Similarly, restaurants offer food plus a place to eat, music in the background, a pleasant ambience, and table service.

As we move to the right end of the continuum, we encounter retailers whose offerings are primarily services. However, even these retailers have some products associated with the services offered, such as a meal on an airplane or a checkbook at a bank.

Differences between Service and Merchandise Retailers

Four important differences in the nature of the offerings provided by services and merchandise retailers are (1) intangibility, (2) simultaneous production and consumption, (3) perishability, and (4) inconsistency of the offering to customers.

Intangibility   Services are less tangible than products—customers cannot see or touch them. They are performances or actions rather than objects. For example, health care services cannot be seen or touched by a patient. Intangibility introduces several challenges for services retailers. Because customers cannot touch and feel services, it is difficult for them to evaluate services before they buy them or even after they buy and consume them. Due to the intangibility of their offerings, services retailers often use tangible symbols to inform customers about the quality of their services. For example, lawyers frequently have elegant, carpeted offices with expensive antique furniture. Services retailers also have difficulty evaluating the quality of services they are providing. For example, it can be hard for a law firm to evaluate how well its lawyers are performing their jobs. To determine the quality of their offerings, services retailers often solicit customer evaluations and scrutinize complaints. In addition, online evaluation systems such as Angie's List and Yelp compile reviews from other consumers. The summary reviews give a sense of how well the service provider performs, according to people who have already purchased the service.

Simultaneous Production and Consumption   Products are typically made in a factory, stored and sold by a retailer, and then used by consumers in their homes. Service providers, however, create and deliver the service as the customer is consuming it. For example, when you eat at a restaurant, the meal is prepared and consumed almost at the same time. The simultaneity of production and consumption also creates some special problems for services retailers. First, the customers are present when the service is produced, may even have an opportunity to see it produced, and in some cases may be part of the production process. For example, customers at Build-A-Bear Workshop make their own teddy bears. Second, other customers consuming the service at the same time can affect the quality of the service provided. For example, an obnoxious passenger next to you on an airplane can make the flight very unpleasant. Third, services retailers often do not get a second chance to satisfy the needs of their customers. Whereas customers can return damaged merchandise to a store, customers who are dissatisfied with services have limited recourse. Thus, it is critical for services retailers to get it right the first time.

Because services are produced and consumed at the same time, it is difficult to reduce costs through mass production. For this reason, most services retailers are small, local firms. Some national services retailers are able to reduce costs by "industrializing" the services they offer. They make substantial investments in equipment and training to provide a uniform service.

Perishability   Services are perishable. They cannot be saved, stored, or resold. Once an airplane takes off with an empty seat, the sale is lost forever. In contrast, merchandise can be held in inventory until a customer is ready to buy it. Due to the perishability of services, services retailing must match supply and demand. Most services retailers have a capacity constraint, and their capacity cannot be changed easily. There are a fixed number of tables in a restaurant, seats in a classroom, beds in a hospital, and electricity that can be generated by a power plant. To increase capacity, services retailers need to make major investments, such as buying more airplanes or building an addition to increase the size of the hospital or restaurant. In addition, demand for service varies considerably over time. Consumers are most likely to fly on airplanes during holidays and the summer, eat in restaurants at lunch- and dinnertime, and use electricity in the evening rather than earlier in the day.

Services retailers use a variety of programs to match demand and supply. For example, airlines and hotels set lower prices on weekends, when they have excess capacity because businesspeople are not traveling. To achieve more capacity flexibility, health clinics stay open longer during flu season and tax preparation services are open on weekends during March and April. Restaurants increase staffing on weekends, may not open until dinnertime, and use a reservation system to guarantee service delivery at a specific time. Finally, services retailers attempt to make customers' waiting time more enjoyable. For example, videos and park employees entertain customers while they wait in line at Disney theme parks.

Inconsistency   Products can be produced by machines with very tight quality control, so customers are reasonably assured that all boxes of Cheerios will be identical. But because services are performances produced by people (employees and customers), no two services will be identical. For example, tax accountants can have different knowledge and skills for preparing tax returns. The waiter at the Olive Garden can be in a bad mood and make your dining experience a disaster. Thus, an important challenge for services retailers is to provide consistent high-quality services. Many factors that determine service quality are beyond the control of retailers; however, services retailers expend considerable time and effort selecting, training, managing, and motivating their service providers.

TYPES OF OWNERSHIP

LO5

Explain the types of ownership for retail firms.

Previous sections of this chapter discussed how retailers may be classified in terms of their retail mix and the merchandise and services they sell. Another way to classify retailers is by their ownership. The major classifications of retail ownership are (1) independent, single-store establishments; (2) corporate chains; and (3) franchises.

Independent, Single-Store Establishments

Retailing is one of the few sectors in most countries in which entrepreneurial activity is extensive. Many retail start-ups are owner-managed, which means management has direct contact with customers and can respond quickly to their needs. Small retailers are also very flexible and can react quickly to market changes and customer needs. They are not bound by the bureaucracies inherent in large retail organizations.[71]

For example, after more than a decade working for other UK fashion firms, Deryane Todd decided to open her own shop and, since then has expanded multiple times. The secret to the success of The Dressing Room is Todd's strong attention to determining and then providing exactly what her customers want. Despite the long hours and seven-day workweek, Todd expresses her love for her job because of the options it provides her. Todd hires her staff, trains them in her own way, determines the layout of the store, and designs the website.[72]

Whereas single-store retailers can tailor their offerings to their customers' needs, corporate chains can more effectively negotiate lower prices for merchandise and advertising because of their larger size. Corporate chains can and do invest in sophisticated analytical systems to help them buy and price merchandise. In addition, corporate chains have a broader management base, with people who specialize in specific retail activities. Single-store retailers typically must rely on their owner-managers' capabilities to make the broad range of necessary retail decisions.

To compete against corporate chains, some independent retailers join a **wholesale-sponsored voluntary cooperative group,** which is an organization operated by a wholesaler offering a merchandising program to small, independent

The secret of success to The Dressing Room in the United Kingdom is the owner's attention to understanding what her customers want.

retailers on a voluntary basis. The Independent Grocers Alliance (IGA), Tru Serv (supplier to True Value Hardware), and Ace Hardware are wholesale-sponsored voluntary cooperative groups. In addition to engaging in buying, warehousing, and distribution, these groups offer members services such as advice on store design and layout, site selection, bookkeeping and inventory management systems, and employee training programs.

Corporate Retail Chains

A **retail chain** is a company that operates multiple retail units under common ownership and usually has centralized decision making for defining and implementing its strategy. Retail chains can range in size from a drugstore with two stores to retailers with thousands of stores, such as Kroger, Walmart, Best Buy, and Macy's. Some retail chains are divisions of larger corporations or holding companies. For example, the Williams Sonoma corporation actually consists of four brands, Williams Sonoma, Pottery Barn, west elm, and Rejuvenation. Furthermore, its Pottery Barn branch features the PB teen and pottery barn kids lines. Royal Ahold owns 14 retail chains, including Stop and Shop, Giant, and Peapod in the United States and ICA and Albert Heijh in Europe.

Franchising[73]

Franchising is a contractual agreement in which the franchisor (the company) sells the rights to use its business trademark, service mark, or trade name, or another commercial symbol of the company, to the franchisee for a one-time franchise fee and an ongoing royalty fee, typically expressed as a percentage of gross monthly sales. More than 40 percent of all U.S. retail sales are made by franchisees,[74] and this type of retail ownership is growing around the world.[75]

When considering the franchise option, potential franchisees must understand the attractions and drawbacks of buying a franchise versus starting a retail business from scratch. There are many reasons to consider franchise ownership, including the success rate, which results partially from the proven business model that the franchisor offers. Success also results from the unique relationship between the franchisor and the franchisee, in which both parties benefit from the success of the franchisee. To get franchisees off to a good start, most franchisors provide off- and onsite training, location analysis assistance, advertising, and sometimes a protected territory (i.e., no other franchise may open a store within a certain radius of the first store). Some franchisors even provide financing or offer third-party financing opportunities.

There are also several drawbacks to franchise ownership. In addition to having to pay money to the franchisor, the franchisee needs financing for start-up costs, including rent or purchase price of office/retail space; modification of the space according to the guidelines of the franchisor (e.g., paint colors, flooring, lighting, layout); signage; opening inventory; and equipment. In addition to incurring the capital costs, the franchisee must adhere to the franchisor's rules and operating guidelines. In many

McDonald's franchises are growing all over the world.

2.4 RETAILING VIEW Tart Frozen Yogurt—The Sweet Franchise

Frozen yogurt franchise operations Pinkberry and Red Mango both opened in the mid-2000s; they compete with old standby TCBY and some smaller regional chains. The appeal of Pinkberry and Red Mango to customers is not just the low fat of frozen yogurt but also its ability to boost people's immune system and improve calcium absorption. The tart frozen yogurt is dense with active cultures and probiotics. These health benefits, along with the great taste, has changed the way consumers think about frozen yogurt. Consumers are making multiple yogurt purchases each week, instead of buying it as an occasional nonroutine indulgence.

In addition to a limited number of exotic flavors—coconut, lychee and mango, many of which are seasonal—both Pinkberry and Red Mango offer a wide array of high-end toppings. The minimalism in the flavor choices is part of both companies' brand image, as reflected in the stark, bright store layouts. That is, these popular new chains offer consistency across their products and store images, even as it promises that customers can eat healthy, low-fat, hormone-free milk products, and still indulge in unusual yogurt flavors and interesting toppings.

Howard Schultz, the chair of Starbucks, invested $27.5 million in Pinkberry through his venture capital firm and appears to be trying to make it the Starbucks of frozen yogurt chains. Expectations are high, including a growth plan to have one Pinkberry for every 10 Starbucks in the country. Red Mango would like to have 500 units in the United States but is controlling its growth by carefully selecting its franchisees and monitoring their performance. Many franchises become very popular and ultimately fail within five years as a result of growing too large, too fast. An interesting incentive to attract franchisees by reducing their risk is Red Mango's Store Buy Back

New franchises like Red Mango appeal to customers because its frozen yogurt is low-fat, boosts people's immune systems, and improves calcium absorption.

program, in which the corporate franchise will buy back a store in the first six months if the franchisee is not satisfied.

If the frozen yogurt market becomes as competitive as the premium coffee market, then TCBY may become the Dunkin' Donuts of yogurt franchises, while Red Mango and Pinkberry will be the Starbucks.

Sources: Jaime Levy Pessin, "Yogurt Chains Give Power to the People," *The Wall Street Journal*, August 22, 2011; Yolanda Santosa, "The Making of Pinkberry," *Brand Packaging*, November 2, 2011; Blair Chancey, "Red Mango Revolution," *QSR Magazine*, October 1, 2009; and Kelly Bayliss, "Free Fro-Yo Today," *NBC Philadelphia*, September 23, 2009.

cases, the franchisee is required to purchase operating materials from the franchisor, especially in fast-food franchises that rely on standardized products across franchises for the success of the brand. The franchisor also might require the franchisee to purchase the equipment needed to offer a new product, such as fryers at a McDonald's or beds at a Holiday Inn. The hours of operation and days of the year that the business is allowed to close also may be dictated by the franchisor.

Retailing View 2.4 describes the sweet and tart world of frozen-yogurt franchises.

SUMMARY

LO1 List the different characteristics that define retailers.

To collect statistics about retailing, the federal government classifies retailers by the type of merchandise and services they sell. But this classification method may not be useful to determine a retailer's

major competitors. A more useful approach for understanding the retail marketplace is to classify retailers on the basis of the retail mix, merchandise variety and assortment, services, location, pricing, and promotion decisions they make to attract customers.

LO2 Categorize the various types of food retailers.

Food retailing has undergone substantial expansion. Whereas once supermarkets were nearly the only source for food shoppers, today they can choose among traditional supermarkets, hypermarkets or superstores, limited-assortment markets, warehouse clubs, and convenience stores, to name a few.

LO3 Identify the various types of general merchandise retailers.

General merchandise retailers come in various forms, each with its own offerings, benefits, and limitations. These formats include department stores, full-line discount stores, specialty stores, drugstores, category specialists, extreme-value retailers, off-price retailers, and outlet stores.

LO4 Explain the differences between service and merchandise retailers.

The inherent differences between services and merchandise result in services retailers' emphasizing training of employees, whereas merchandise retailers emphasize inventory management issues. Retail institutions have changed in response to a changing marketplace, such that there is significant crossover between these types of retailers.

LO5 Illustrate the types of ownership for retail firms.

Small, independent retailers are usually owned and managed by a single founder. In contrast, corporate retail chains involve vast organizations and operate multiple stores. Another option that allows individual entrepreneurs to enjoy the security of corporate chains is franchising, a growing type of retail organization.

KEY TERMS

assortment, *37*
big-box store, *45*
breadth of merchandise, *37*
category killer, *51*
category specialist, *51*
closeouts, *55*
consignment shop, *53*
convenience store, *46*
conventional supermarket, *42*
department store, *48*
depth of merchandise, *37*
dollar store, *54*
drugstore, *54*
durable goods, *48*
exclusive brand, *49*
extreme-value food retailer, *42*

extreme-value retailer, *54*
factory outlet, *56*
fair trade, *43*
flash sale, *56*
franchising, *61*
full-line discount store, *50*
hard goods, *48*
hypermarket, *45*
irregulars, *55*
limited-assortment
   supermarket, *42*
locavore movement, *43*
North American Industry
   Classification System
   (NAICS), *36*
off-price retailer, *55*

outlet store, *56*
power perimeter, *43*
private-label brand, *49*
retail chain, *61*
services retailer, *56*
soft goods, *48*
specialty store, *52*
stock-keeping unit (SKU), *37*
store brand, *49*
supercenter, *44*
thrift store, *53*
variety, *37*
warehouse club, *45*
wholesale-sponsored voluntary
   cooperative group, *60*

GET OUT AND DO IT!

1. **CONTINUING CASE ASSIGNMENT: GO SHOPPING** The objective of this assignment is to have you take the retailer's, rather than the consumer's, perspective and think about the different strategies that the retailer you selected and another retailer might have, as well as how these strategies result in different retail mixes. The assignment is to conduct a comparison of the retail offerings for a specific merchandise category, such as tablets, men's suits, country/western CDs, women's athletic shoes, or house paint, for two different retailers. The other retailer selected might be a direct competitor using the same format or a retailer selling similar merchandise to a different target market with a different format.

Your comparison should include the following:
- The strategy pursued by the two retailers—each retailer's target market(s) and general approach to satisfying the needs of that target market.
- The retail mixes (store location, merchandise, pricing, advertising and promotion, location of merchandise category in store, store design, customer service) used by each of the retailers.
- With respect to the merchandise category, a detailed comparison of the variety and depth of assortment. In comparing the merchandise offerings, use a table similar to that in Exhibit 2–2.

To prepare this comparison, you need to visit the stores, observe the retail mixes in the stores, and play the role of a customer to observe the service.

2. **GO SHOPPING** Go to an athletic footwear specialty store such as Foot Locker, a department store, and a discount store. Analyze their variety and assortment of athletic footwear by creating a table similar to that in Exhibit 2–2.

3. **GO SHOPPING** Keep a diary for two weeks of where you shop, what you buy, and how much you spend. Get your parents to do the same thing. Tabulate your results by type of retailer. Are your shopping habits significantly different from or are they similar to those of your parents? Do your and your parents' shopping habits coincide with the trends discussed in this chapter? Why or why not?

4. **GO SHOPPING** Describe how the supermarket where you shop is implementing organic, locally grown, ethnic, and private-label merchandise. If any of these categories of merchandise are missing, explain whether you believe it could be a potential opportunity for growth for this supermarket. Then describe any strategies or activities that you believe are providing a better shopping experience than its competition. If you believe that competing stores are providing a better shopping experience than your store, explain what they are doing, and evaluate whether or not these activities would benefit your supermarket.

5. **INTERNET EXERCISE** Data on U.S. retail sales are available from the U.S. Bureau of the Census Internet site at www.census.gov/retail/. Look at the unadjusted monthly sales by NAICS (found in the Monthly Retail Trade Report section). Which categories of retailers have the largest percentage of sales in November and December (the holiday season)? Do your findings make sense to you? Why or why not?

6. **INTERNET EXERCISE** Three large associations of retailers are the National Retail Federation (www.nrf.com), the Food Marketing Institute (www.fmi.org), and the National Association of Convenience and Petroleum Stores (www.nacsonline.com). Visit these sites, and report on the latest retail developments and issues confronting the industry.

7. **INTERNET EXERCISE** Go to Entrepreneur Magazine's Franchise Zone web page at www.entrepreneur.com/franchise500, and view the top 500 franchises for the past year. How many of the retailers in the top 10 have you patronized as a customer? Did you know that they were operated as a franchise? Look at the lists from previous years to see changes in the rankings. Finally, what is the nature of the businesses that seem to lend themselves to franchising?

8. Bed Bath & Beyond is a category specialist with about 1,000 stores throughout the United States and Ontario, Canada. It sells domestics (bed linens, bathroom and kitchen items) and home furnishings (cookware and cutlery, small household appliances, picture frames, and organizing supplies). What are the SIC and NAICS codes used by this retailer? What other retailers compete against Bed Bath & Beyond, and which store format is implemented by each competitor?

DISCUSSION QUESTIONS AND PROBLEMS

1. Distinguish between variety and assortment. Why are these important elements of the retail market structure?

2. What sorts of competitive pressures are confronting traditional grocery stores? What options do these stores have to ease the pressure?

3. What do off-price retailers need to do to compete against other formats in the future?

4. Compare and contrast the retail mixes of convenience stores, traditional supermarkets, supercenters, and warehouse stores. Can all of these food retail institutions be successful over the long run? How? Why?

5. Why is Walmart, the largest retailer in the world, facing slower growth than in the past? What can it do to accelerate its growth?

6. Why are retailers in the limited-assortment supermarket and extreme-value discount store sectors growing so rapidly? From which retailers are they getting these additional sales?

7. The same brand and model of tablet is sold by specialty computer stores, discount stores, category specialists, online retailers, and warehouse stores. Why would a customer choose one retail format over the others?

8. Choose a product category that both you and your parents purchase (e.g., business clothing, casual clothing, music, electronic equipment, shampoo). In which type of store do you typically purchase this merchandise? What about your parents? Explain why there is, or is not, a difference in your store choices.

9. At many optical stores, you can get your eyes checked *and* purchase glasses or contact lenses. How is the shopping experience different for the service as compared to the product? Design a strategy to get customers to purchase both the service and the product. In so doing, delineate specific actions that should be taken to acquire and retain optical customers.

10. There are services and products involved when buying or renting a car, and in both cases, the customer drives away in a car. But buying a car focuses more on the product, whereas renting involves the service. Explain four ways in which marketing for a rental car company differs from marketing for an automobile dealership.

SUGGESTED READINGS

Borghini, Stefania, Nina Diamond, Roberts Kozinets, Mary Ann McGrath, Albert M. Muñiz Jr., and John F. Sherry Jr. "Why Are Themed Brandstores So Powerful? Retail Brand Ideology at *American Girl Place*." *Journal of Retailing* 85, no. 3 (2009).

Cuthbertson, Christine. *Retail Strategy: The View From the Bridge*, Oxford: Elsevier, 2012.

Enrique, Badia. *Zara and Her Sisters: The Story of the World's Largest Clothing Retailer*. New York: Palgrave Macmillan, 2009.

Fishman, Charles. *The Wal-Mart Effect*. New York: Penguin, 2007.

Grewal, Dhruv, Gopalkrishnan Iyer, Rajshekhar G. Javalgi, and Lori Radulovich. "Franchise Partnership and International Expansion: A Conceptual Framework and Research Propositions." *Entrepreneurial Theory & Practice*, May 2011, pp. 533–557.

Hammond, Richard. *Smart Retail: Practical Winning Ideas and Strategies from the Most Successful Retailers in the World*, New Jersey: FT Press, 2012.

Mitchell, Stacy. *Big-Box Swindle: The True Cost of Mega-Retailers and the Fight for America's Independent Businesses*. Boston: Beacon Press, 2006.

Roberts, Bryan, and Natalie Berg. *Walmart: Key Insights and Practical Lessons from the World's Largest Retailer*. Philadelphia: Koran Page, 2012.

Spector, Robert, and Patrick McCarthy. *The Nordstrom Way to Customer Service Excellence: The Handbook For Becoming the "Nordstrom" of Your Industry*. New Jersey: John Wiley & Sons, 2012.

Spector, Robert. *The Mom & Pop Store: True Stories from the Heart of America*. New York: Walker & Company, 2009.

Thain, Greg, and John Bradley. *Store Wards: The Worldwide Battle for Mindspace and Shelfspace, Online and In-Store*. West Sussex, UK: John Wiley & Sons, 2012.

Whitaker, Jan. *Service and Style: How the American Department Store Fashioned the Middle Class*. New York: St. Martin's Press, 2006.

Multichannel Retailing

EXECUTIVE BRIEFING
Luiza Helena Trajano
President, Magazine Luiza

I am from Franca, a small city in the state of São Paulo, Brazil. As a child, I loved to give presents to friends and relatives. When I was 12 years old, my mother told me that I would have to earn money to continue my "hobby" of giving presents. So I started working during vacations at a store owned by my Uncle Pelegrino and Aunt Luiza and have been working there ever since. I went to college in Franca during the evenings, and worked during the day at the store. In 1991, I was selected as the CEO of the company.

The company's early growth came from acquisitions of small town retailers in the state of São Paulo. We catered to the needs of consumers of all social classes. While the lower-income consumers had limited incomes, they sought the same respect shown to upper-income consumers. Our stores offered them respect and credit. With annual sales of about US$ 4 billion in 2012, our company now has more than 800 stores in Brazil selling furniture, appliances, consumer electronics, and home products. Although we are now in the major metro areas of Brazil, we have tried hard to preserve our company culture characterized by respect for our customers and employees and continuous innovation. These elements are in our DNA. Our transparent management system is designed to make associates feel part of the company, and we share the profits of the company with all employees.

In 1992, almost 10 years before e-commerce was introduced in Brazil, we used a multichannel approach. Our sales associates assisted customers placing orders on the stores' computers and having products delivered to their homes.

In 2012, we were invited to present at the National Retail Federation convention, in New York, our creative and very successful "Magazine Voce" (or Your Luiza Store) system. This system allowed our "agents" to create their own virtual Luiza store on Facebook with 20 products and sell these products to their friends. We now have more than 10,000 agents affiliated with our company.

Three years ago, we hired a new CEO, and I no longer am involved in the day-to-day operations. But I maintain our Luiza company culture by holding meetings with the staff of new stores. I also maintain direct supervision of the customer relations

CHAPTER 3

LEARNING OBJECTIVES

LO1 Understand the nonstore channels offered by retailers.

LO2 Compare the benefits offered by the four major retail channels: stores, Internet, mobile, and catalogs.

LO3 Analyze the challenges facing multichannel retailers.

LO4 Consider the multichannel shopping experience in the future.

department. This gives me the opportunity to pass along our values to the new associates, demonstrate the respect we have for them and our customers, and also highlight to all in the company our passion to serve our customers. And I still like to give presents.

A retail channel is the way a retailer sells and delivers merchandise and services to its customers. The most common channel used by retailers is a store. Retailers also use a variety of nonstore channels, including the Internet, mobile, catalogs and direct mail, direct selling, television home shopping, direct-response TV, and automated retailing (vending machines) to make sales to customers. This definition makes a distinction between a channel and a medium such as TV advertising. A *channel* involves the opportunity to complete a transaction—to sell and deliver merchandise—while a *medium* is primarily used to communicate information to consumers. Retailers communicate information through channels as well as complete transactions; however, the primary objective of the channel is to complete transactions.

Multichannel retailing involves using more than one channel to sell and deliver merchandise and services to consumers.[1] Note the term **omniretailing** is frequently used when discussing multichannel retailing; it refers to a coordinated multichannel retail offering that provides a seamless customer experience when using all of the retailer's shopping channels.

The birth of multichannel retailing can be traced back to when Sears opened its first store in 1925, 33 years after it launched its catalog that offered merchandise previously unavailable to the American masses.[2] Now, almost all large retailers

Even small, single-store retailers like Harry's Fishing Supply interact with their customers through multiple channels.

that operate stores are multichannel retailers. Most have added an Internet channel that offers customers an opportunity to buy merchandise or services by accessing their website, as well as patronizing their stores.[3]

Many small, store-based retailers also use multiple channels. For example, in its 8,000-square-foot retail store near Miami's Little River district, Capt. Harry's Fishing Supply's offers more than 20,000 products, including rods and reels, as well as at least 1,000 lures and teasers in every color, designed to tempt fish onto an angler's line. The biggest lure is nearly two feet long and the smallest less than an inch. There are scented lures, mirrored lures, lures with holographic features, and ones designed to move like a frightened fish. In the early 1980s, Harry Vernon, Jr., the company president, noticed that about 40 percent of the foot traffic was from foreign customers. So, he launched a catalog and eventually Internet channels. Now, from a second-floor warehouse, pickers fill orders from nearly every U.S. state and 120 countries.[4]

In this chapter, we take a strategic perspective to examine the four primary channels through which retailers sell merchandise and services to their customers. We first briefly describe all of the nonstore retail channels; retailers typically evolve to multichannel retailers by adding a nonstore channel to their store channel. We then review the unique benefits that each of the four major channels offer to consumers and outline the retailers' benefits from providing a multichannel offering. Next, we describe the challenges multichannel retailers face when using these channels synergistically and how they provide a seamless offering for their customers. At the end of the chapter, we illustrate how integrating these channels and using new technologies will create a compelling shopping experience in the future.

Nonstore Retail Channels

LO1

Understand the nonstore channels offered by retailers.

The estimated percentage of annual retail sales (excluding motor vehicles and food services annual sales) made through each channel is shown in Exhibit 3–1. The vast majority of sales are made through the store channel, but the Internet and catalog channels also account for significant sales, while the mobile channel has the highest growth rate.

Internet Retailing Channels—Electronic and Mobile Retailing

Internet retailing is the fastest growing channel. It involves retailers interacting with consumers via the Internet, whether they use a traditional computer or a laptop, a variety of sizes of tablets or a smartphone. We refer to the channel that

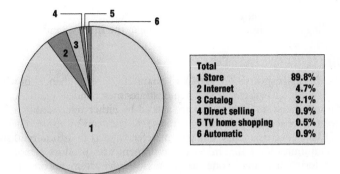

Total	
1 Store	89.8%
2 Internet	4.7%
3 Catalog	3.1%
4 Direct selling	0.9%
5 TV home shopping	0.5%
6 Automatic	0.9%

EXHIBIT 3–1
U.S. Retail Sales by Channel

SOURCES: U.S. Census Bureau, "Estimates of Monthly Retail and Food Services Sales by Kind of Business: 2009," www.census.gov/retail/mrts/www/data/excel/mrtssales92-09.xls; personal communication with the Direct Selling Association, Direct Marketing Association, and National Automatic Merchandising Association.

*Excluding sales of motor vehicles, food services, and travel.

involves accessing the Internet through a traditional computer as the electronic channel. The mobile channel (also called **mobile retailing,** mobile commerce, or m-commerce), involves accessing the Internet using a smartphone. From a retailing perspective, smartphones differ from traditional computers in that they are more portable, have a smaller display, are location-aware, use different touch screen technology to access the Internet, and as a result of these factors produce a different interface experience with the user. Tablets retain some of the advantages and disadvantages of using a traditional computer with some of the mobility benefits and problems associated with shopping with a mobile phone.

Two decades ago, experts thought by now everyone would be doing their shopping over the Internet. These experts predicted that a new breed of high-tech, web-savvy entrepreneurs would dominate the retail industry. Stores would close due to lack of traffic, and paper catalogs would become obsolete. However, these predictions of Internet retailing transforming the retail industry have not occurred. Even though U.S. sales through Internet channels are forecasted to grow at about 10 percent annually, more than three times faster than sales growth through store channels, Internet sales are expected to only account for 11 percent of retail sales (excluding automotive and food services) by 2015, with the mobile channel accounting for 9 percent of Internet retail sales.[6]

The Internet is, therefore, a facilitating, rather than transformational, technology with respect to most sectors of the retail industry. Almost all of the traditional store-based retailers utilize Internet channels to provide a better shopping experience for their customers and now dominate these channels. Almost 75 percent of U.S. consumers use the Internet to search for information about clothes, shoes, toys, and health and beauty aids before they go to a store to buy the items. Eighty-three percent go online before buying electronics, computers, books, music, and movies in stores.[7] Just over half of all adults who own mobile phones use them to get either product reviews or pricing information while in a physical store, a process known as showrooming.[8]

Catalog Channel

The **catalog channel** is a nonstore retail channel in which the retail offering is communicated to customers through a catalog mailed to customers. About half of U.S. consumers shop through catalogs each year. The merchandise categories with the greatest catalog sales are drugs, beauty aids, computers, software, clothing, accessories, furniture, and housewares.[9] The use of catalogs has come under attack from consumer groups that believe that catalogs are an unnecessary waste of natural resources. In the United States, catalogs account for 3 percent of the roughly 80 million tons of paper products used annually. That is more than either magazines or books.[10] Further, catalogs' share of sales is declining relative to the Internet. But

REFACT

The first use of an Internet retail channel was on August 11, 1994, when a CD by Sting was sold by NetMarket over the Internet.[5]

catalogs are not going away. Their role is shifting from primarily generating sales to building a brand image and driving traffic to the Internet and physical stores.[11]

Direct-Response TV Channel

The **direct-response TV (DRTV) channel** is a retail channel in which customers watch a TV advertisement that demonstrates merchandise and then place orders for that merchandise. The orders are placed by either telephoning a phone bank of operators or accessing the Internet to use the company's website. There are two types of DRTV advertisements: a long form, referred to as an **infomercial** and typically 30 to 60 minutes long, that mixes entertainment with product demonstrations, and a short form consisting of one- to two-minute advertisements on television. Approximately $150 million in annual retail sales is made through the DRTV channel.

Unlike most TV advertising, the impact of a DRTV advertisement is precisely measureable. Within 24 hours, retailers using this channel can determine how many customers responded to each exposure to an ad. The results can be analyzed to determine the effects of location, time of week, time of day, and different scripts and creative responses.

Television Home Shopping Channel

Television home shopping is a retail channel in which customers watch a TV network with programs that demonstrate merchandise and then place orders for that merchandise, usually by telephone or via the Internet. Annual U.S. sales through TV shopping networks are approximately $20 billion. The two largest retailers using this channel are HSN and QVC, followed by ShopNBC and Jewelry Television. Although most consumers with cable or satellite television access can patronize a television shopping channel, relatively few watch on a regular basis. Furthermore, most of the purchases are made by a relatively small percentage of viewers. Like catalogs, TV home shopping networks have embraced the Internet for taking customer orders, although it is still possible to place an order by telephone and mail.

The major advantage of TV home shopping is that customers can see the merchandise demonstrated either on their television screens or through streaming videos on the Internet. In response to the increase in cooking, decorating, do-it-yourself, and other lifestyle programming, home shopping retailers have incorporated more demonstrations into their programming in an attempt to educate their potential customers.

TV home shopping retailers are also embracing social media. Today's consumer is interacting with TV home shopping channels on multiple screens. They have a smartphone, laptop computer, or tablet next to them as they view the program. The tweets that these media-savvy customers send to the network appear on live scrolls, adding user comments about various products and guests to the broadcast. At the same time, on HSN's Facebook page, they can ask questions and chat about the program as it happens; the really interesting comments and questions then get read on the air by the customers' favorite hosts.[13]

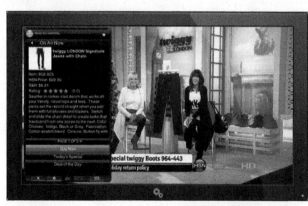

HSN's sales have more than doubled after it started selling more well-known brands.

Direct Selling Channel

Direct selling is a retail channel in which salespeople interact with customers face-to-face in a convenient location, either at the customer's home or at work. Direct salespeople demonstrate merchandise benefits and/or explain a service, take an order, and deliver the merchandise. Direct selling is a highly interactive retail channel in which considerable information is conveyed to customers through face-to-face discussions and demonstrations. However, providing this high level of personalized information, including extensive demonstrations, is costly.

Annual U.S. sales through direct selling are about $30 billion; worldwide, sales are more than $100 billion. More than 60 percent of the products sold through the direct selling channel are home/family care/home durables (cleaning products, cookware, cutlery, etc.), wellness (weight loss products, vitamins, etc.) and personal care (cosmetics, jewelry, skin care, etc.)[15]

Almost all the 15 million salespeople in the United States who work in direct sales are independent agents.[16] They are not employed by the direct sales firm but, rather, act as independent distributors, buying merchandise from the firms and then reselling it to consumers. In most cases, direct salespeople may sell their merchandise to anyone, but some companies, such as Avon, assign territories to salespeople who regularly contact households in their territory. Retailing View 3.1 describes how the direct selling channel is particularly effective in less developed countries.

RETAILING VIEW   Avon's Direct Selling Channel in Brazil   3.1

Baixada Fluminense might be one of the toughest neighborhoods in Rio de Janeiro, but that doesn't mean its residents don't worry about lipstick colors. It might even mean they worry more. Thus, Heloisa Almada Contreira visits her 80 or so customers regularly in their homes, earning weekly sales of about $930 by selling Avon products. Spending 50 reais ($27) on cosmetics might seem like a lot for many low-income consumers, but, according to Almada Contreira, "For them, it's a necessity. Brazilian women can't go without their makeup."

Her impression might be anecdotal, but the statistics back up this claim, in that Brazil constitutes the world's third largest market for beauty care products, behind only the United States and Japan. With its expansive coastline and warm climate, Brazil invites residents to visit beaches all year, though the approach of summer often finds millions of women initiating a diet and beauty regime that will enable them to live *verão sem kanga*—that is, as part of a robe-free summer on the beach. Such hot weather may be great for a beach day, but it also means that people often need at least a couple of showers. Thus, Brazilians use twice the shampoo, conditioner, and soap compared with residents of other countries. And then women need to apply their makeup a second time each day!

The constant demand for cosmetics and beauty products is no problem for Almada Contreira and her 1.1 million sales colleagues. Avon's Brazilian sales force sells door-to-door, whether their customers live in city slums, the Amazonian rainforest, or remote towns. These sorts of direct sales have long been a staple of American life, but companies such as Avon, as well as Herbalife and Amway, increasingly turn to this channel to sell to consumers in less developed countries. In these areas, direct sales can be particularly effective, because the channel does not require a sophisticated or expensive infrastructure. Instead, salespeople handle distribution on their own. These independent agents not only sell and distribute the

Avon's direct selling channel is particularly effective in developing economies such as Brazil.

products to their customers, but they also take responsibility for ordering merchandise to restock their inventory. To reach customers in the Amazon, Avon salespeople might need to hire a small boat or plane, and the product delivery might be delayed for a week or more. But for those waiting for just the right color to apply to their cheeks, a week is not too long to wait.

Sources: Christina Passariello and Emily Glazer, "Coty Knocks on Brazil's Door; Part of Avon's Allure to Fragrance Maker Is Its Sales Network in South America," *The Wall Street Journal (Online)*, April 5, 2012; Jenney Barchfield, "In Beauty-Obsessed Brazil, Clinics Offer Free Plastic Surgery to Poor," *Los Angeles Times*, March 25 2012, A.4; and Jonathan Wheatley, "Beauty Business Turns Heads in Brazil," *Investor's Choice*, January 19, 2010.

DISCUSSION QUESTION

Why is the direct sales channel so much more popular and effective in Brazil than in the United States?

Two special types of direct selling are the party plan and multilevel systems. About one-quarter of all direct sales are made using a **party plan system.** Salespeople encourage customers to act as hosts and invite friends or coworkers to a "party." The host or hostess receives a gift or commission for arranging the party. At the party, the merchandise is demonstrated and attendees place orders.

In a **multilevel system,** independent businesspeople serve as master distributors, recruiting other people to become distributors in their network. The master distributors either buy merchandise from the firm and resell it to their distributors or receive a commission on all merchandise purchased by the distributors in their network. In addition to selling merchandise themselves, the master distributors are involved in recruiting and training other distributors.

Some multilevel direct selling firms are illegal pyramid schemes. A **pyramid scheme** develops when the firm and its program are designed to sell merchandise and services to other distributors, rather than to end-users. The founders and initial distributors in pyramid schemes profit from the inventory bought by later participants, but little merchandise is sold to consumers who use it.

Automated Retailing (Vending Machines) Channel

Automated retailing is a retail channel in which merchandise or services are stored in a machine and dispensed to customers when they deposit cash or use a credit card. Automated retailing machines, also known as **vending machines,** are typically placed at convenient, high-traffic locations. About 80 percent of the automated retailing channel sales are from cold beverages, prepared food service, candy, and snacks. Annual U.S. sales in the channel were $40 billion, but between 2007 and 2010, sales declined by more than 11 percent.[17]

As a result of this decline, vending machines also are disappearing from stores and sidewalks. Unwilling to give up on this channel, some entrepreneurs are reimagining the uses of vending machines. Many of them are going high-tech, with sophisticated service offerings. Machines maintained by Minnesota-based InstyMeds Corp. appear in health clinics and dispense prescription medicines. To prevent fraud, the machines maintain an electronic link to the doctor's computer system, which allows them to confirm each patient's identity and prescription, using a unique code assigned by the doctor to each patient.[19]

Another interesting automated retailing application is taking the DVD rental business by storm. Redbox rents DVDs for $1 a day in more than 22,000 locations, including McDonald's, Walmart, Walgreens, Albertsons, and 7-Eleven Circle-K. The retailer rents more than 7.5 million movies weekly, close to the sales reported by its mail-order rival Netflix. Redbox's success, as well as its challenge, is keeping its inventory of DVDs fresh and available when customers want to rent them. Customers can check the inventory of a particular machine and reserve a copy of any title at Redbox's Internet site.[20]

REFACT

The Greek mathematician Hero invented the first vending machine in 215 B.C., selling holy water to worshippers in Egyptian temples. In the early 1880s, the first coin-operated vending machines allowed customers in London, England, to purchase postcards.[18]

RELATIVE BENEFITS OF RETAIL CHANNELS

LO2

Compare the benefits offered by the four major retail channels: stores, Internet, mobile, and catalogs.

In this section, we discuss the relative benefits and limitations of the four major retail channels: stores, catalogs, electronic, and mobile. Exhibit 3–2 summarizes these unique benefits. In the following section, we discuss how retailers provide a better customer shopping experience by integrating these channels into a true multichannel experience.

Store Channel

Stores offer several benefits to customers that they cannot get when they shop through nonstore channels such as mobile, electronic, or catalogs.

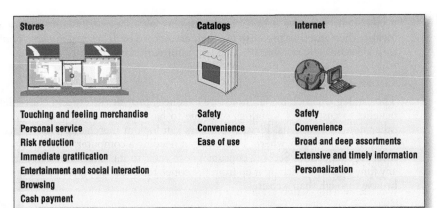

EXHIBIT 3–2
Benefits Provided by
Different Channels

Touching and Feeling Products   Perhaps the greatest benefit offered by stores is the opportunity for customers to use all five senses—touching, smelling, tasting, seeing, and hearing—when examining and evaluating products. Although new technologies such as three-dimensional and 360-degree projections can enhance representations of products on a computer or mobile phone screen, these visual improvements do not provide the same level of information customers get when they actually try on a swimsuit or smell the fragrance of a candle.

Personal Service   Although consumers are often critical of the personal service they get in stores, sales associates still have the unique ability to provide meaningful, personalized information. They can tell customers if a suit looks good on them, suggest a tie to go with a dress shirt, or answer questions customers might have about what is appropriate to wear at a business-casual event.

Risk Reduction   The physical presence of the store reduces perceived risk and increases customers' confidence that any problems with a purchase will be corrected. Customers can easily access people in the store to resolve issues concerning defective or unsuitable merchandise or get additional information on how to use a product.

Immediate Gratification   Customers can use merchandise immediately after they buy it in stores. Thus, when customers have a fever or need a last-minute gift, for example, they do not have to wait a day or two for the delivery of a prescription from Drugstore.com or of a gift from Amazon.com.

Entertainment and Social Experience   In-store shopping can be a stimulating experience for some people, providing a break in their daily routine and enabling them to interact with friends. All nonstore retail formats are limited in the degree to which they can satisfy these entertainment and social needs. Retailing View 3.2 describes how Bass Pro Shops offer an exciting and rewarding shopping experience for their customers.

Browsing   Shoppers often have only a general sense of what they want (e.g., a sweater, something for dinner, a gift) but don't know the specific item they want, so they go to a store to see what is available before they decide what to buy. Although consumers can surf the web or look through catalogs for ideas, most consumers still find it easier to browse in stores.

Cash Payment   Stores are the only channel through which consumers can make cash payments. Some customers prefer to pay with cash because it is quicker, resolves the transaction immediately, and does not result in potential interest payments or excessive debt. Other customers are concerned about security and identity theft and thus prefer to use their credit card or debit card in person rather than electronically sending the payment information via the Internet.

Catalog Channel

The catalog channel, like all nonstore channels, provides safety and convenience benefits to customers. Catalogs continue to have some unique advantages over other nonstore formats. First, consumers can look at merchandise and place an order from almost anywhere, 24/7, without needing a computer, mobile device, or Internet connection. Second, consumers can refer to the information in a catalog any time by simply picking it up from the coffee table. Finally, catalogs are easier to browse through than websites.

3.2 RETAILING VIEW Bass Pro Shops Makes Shopping Fun

How would you like to spend your vacation? Playing in a laser arcade, rock climbing, practicing your aim in a pistol shooting range, or trying out your archery skills? If that sounds great, you're probably among the millions of people who drive for hours just to visit one of Bass Pro Shops' stores. Made to look something like hunting lodges, the stores also feature massive product displays, aided by a professional sales staff who use all the products in their own, outdoorsy lifestyles. Behind the deep product assortment, the stores' decor is enhanced by massive indoor waterfalls, aquariums, and mounted wildlife.

But a cool look isn't all there is to Bass Pro Shops. Shoppers can enjoy free activities, like making their way up the rock climbing wall or challenging their friends to a round of laser tag in the attached arcade. In soundproof rooms, surrounded by shatter-resistant glass, they can pretend to be Dirty Harry—or Katniss Everdeen, if they prefer bows and arrows. For those not quite as practiced, on-hand experts offer advice about how to sight a gun or draw a bow.

It might not be a surprise to learn that customers of Bass Pro Shops tend to be men, who otherwise proclaim just how much they hate shopping. Even a man whose wife claims that in their 35-year marriage, he'd joined her only twice on shopping trips, gets in the spirit at Bass Pro Shops, calling himself, "a kid in a candy store here."

Although these customers might drive hundreds of miles to get to them, the stores reflect their environment. In north-central Alabama, the Leeds store spreads across 120 acres, including a mile-long entryway that moves slowly through the surrounding nature park, including three bridges and a four-acre lake. But one lake isn't enough in this fish-loving area,

More than 100 million people annually visit Bass Pro Shops, compared with 60 million visitors to Disney World in Orlando. The excitement generated in a Bass Pro Shops' store cannot be equaled by other channels.

so an 18,500-gallon aquarium inside the store features fish native to Alabama, and a 3,500-gallon trout pond allows shoppers to test out the fishing equipment available in the store. Fishing too tame for you? Then how about the NASCAR ride simulator that mimics nearby Talladega Speedway? It's waiting outside the store, too.

Sources: www.bassproshop.com; Tom Bailey Jr., "Bass Pro to Open 'Newest Generation' Megastore in Little Rock," *McClatchy–Tribune Business News,* June, 15, 2012; "Outdoors Lovers Find Their 'Disneyland' in Stores Such as Bass Pro Shops," *Sacramento Bee,* September 23, 2009; "Retailer Scores by Luring Men Who Hate to Shop," *The Wall Street Journal,* December 17, 2002.

DISCUSSION QUESTION

What are the pros and cons of Bass Pro Shops' exciting store environment from the perspective of consumers? From the perspective of Bass Pro Shops?

REFACT

Bass Pro Shops' first store in Springfield, Missouri, attracts 4 million visitors a year and is the most visited tourist attraction in Missouri.

IKEA's 2013 catalog illustrates the use of a retailer's website to augment its catalog channel. IKEA dramatically improved the content and user experience with its widely distributed housewares catalog by including augmented reality. In the 2013 catalog, shoppers can place their smartphones over selected pages to get additional content from the retailer's website, such as image galleries and videos. After downloading an app, customers can interact with a series of icons in the catalog to see more information about selected products. The information ranges from how-to videos to "X-ray" photographs of the inside of storage systems. Rooms with and without textiles are shown, allowing users to build up decorative elements and explore color options.[21]

The Internet Channel

In the previous section, we detailed the relative benefits of stores from the consumers' perspective. In this section, we examine how the addition of Internet channels to traditional store-based retailers and catalogers has improved their ability to serve their customers and build a competitive advantage in several ways:

1. The addition of the Internet channels has the potential to offer a greater selection of products.
2. They allow retailers to provide more information.
3. They enable retailers to provide customers with more personalized information about products and services.
4. They offer sellers the unique opportunity to collect information about consumer shopping.
5. Internet channels provide an opportunity for retailers to enter new markets economically.
6. They provide information that they can use to improve the shopping experience across all channels.

While Internet channels offer many benefits to consumers, they also increase consumers' risks, discussed at the end of the section.

Deeper and Broader Selection   One benefit of adding the Internet channels is the vast number of alternatives retailers can make available to consumers without crowding their aisles or increasing their square footage. Stores and catalogs are limited by their size. By shopping on the Internet, consumers can easily "visit" and select merchandise from a broader array of retailers. Individual retailers' websites typically offer deeper assortments of merchandise (more colors, brands, and sizes) than are available in stores or catalogs. This expanded offering enables them to satisfy consumer demand for less popular styles, colors, or sizes. Many retailers also offer a broader assortment (more categories) on their websites. Staples.com, for instance, offers soft drinks and cleaning supplies, which are not available in stores, so that its business customers will view it as a one-stop shop.

More Information for Evaluating Merchandise   An important service offered by retailers is providing information that helps consumers make better buying decisions. Retail channels differ in terms of how much information customers can access. The amount of information available through the store channel is limited by the number and training of sales associates and the space allocated to informative signage. Similarly, the information available through a catalog channel is limited by the number of pages in the catalog. In contrast, the information provided through the Internet channels is unlimited.

The vast amount of information available through these channels enables customers using this channel to solve problems, rather than just get information about specific products. Retailing View 3.3 describes an Internet site that offers products plus information, some of which is generated by customers, that can help couples solve the problems associated with planning their wedding.

Personalization   Due to the Internet's interactive nature, the most significant potential benefit of Internet channels is their ability to economically personalize merchandise offerings and information for each customer. Customers control

3.3 RETAILING VIEW   Helping Couples Get Ready for the Big Day

Not only does the typical engagement and wedding today last seemingly forever (14 months) and cost a lot ($25,000), it also demands that brides, grooms, and their families make often difficult, usually emotionally charged decisions. Who gets invited? What should the invitations look like, and should they be preceded by save-the-date cards? What kind of music should be played at the reception? Wait, where should the reception be held? And just how much can a couple register for before they look greedy?

Although, at one time, the bride and her family were responsible for most of the wedding planning, modern trends—including couples who delay marriage until later, dual-income households, and transient populations who live far from their parents—mean that many of the traditional norms have gone out the window. To help these couples plan, including figuring out how to spend, Internet wedding sites such as The Knot (www.theknot.com) and WeddingChannel (www.weddingchannel.com) provide a budgeting tool. Brides enter the dollar amount they want to spend (e.g., $9,000) and the number of guests (e.g., 30). Using national averages, the website calculates how much they should spend on each feature: $540 for the bride's dress and $68 for her bouquet, in this example. As the plans progress, users enter their spending, and the tool recalculates the amounts available to be expended elsewhere.

Moving beyond the financial questions, visitors to the sites can interact with other couples, as well as etiquette experts, to get advice on how to deal with a meddling mother-in-law or where to seat divorced parents during the reception. Recommendations from other consumers seem less biased and thus more appealing than information provided by a retailer or manufacturer. Thus, shoppers turn to posted reviews of products or services.

Another planning tool sends reminders of key dates, such as the date the band needs to be reconfirmed or when the reception hall deposit is due. The sites also gather registries from various retailers, available for guests to seek out, all in one place. Bands even upload audio clips of their performances, helping bridal couples choose which one will play during their first dance. Once the reception hall and all hotels have been chosen, the website provides maps showing the best routes between

Planning Tools
from the knot

From keeping track of your wedding budget to managing all your to-dos, we've got the best online wedding planning tools -- and they're all free! Keep your RSVPs organized with our wedding guest list tool, spread the word with your own wedding website, and plan on the go with our iPhone wedding apps.

planning checklist
Don't miss a step with our week-by-week to-do list

wedding budgeter
Track your wedding expenses with our easy budget tool

guest list manager
Stay on top of your guest list, RSVPs, and more

save-the-date
Give your guests a heads up with an email save-the-date

wedding websites
Share the details! Choose from 40+ stylish designs

registry central
Get our top registry picks, plus the ultimate registry checklist

my real wedding
Get inspired by other Knotties or upload your own photos

inspiration boards
Show off your wedding style with 1,000s of photos

the knot notebook
See something you like? Save gowns, articles, and more

The Knot offers information and merchandise to help couples plan their wedding.

locations, as well as online booking services for hotel reservations. And then when all is said and done, the married couple can maintain a personal site for recollections and posting wedding pictures.

Sources: www.weddingchannel.com and www.theknot.com.

DISCUSSION QUESTION

Would you use these websites to plan your wedding? Why or why not?

some of this personalization by drilling down through web pages until they have enough information to make a purchase decision. In addition, when using Internet channels, customers can format the information so that it can be effectively used when they are comparing alternatives. For example, Office Depot provides information about alternatives selected by the customer in a side-by-side comparison format. In contrast, customers in stores usually have to inspect each brand, one item at a time, and then remember the different attributes to make a comparison.

The retailer can play a more proactive role in personalizing merchandise and information through the Internet channels. For example, many retailers offer **live chats:** Customers can click a button at any time and have an instant messaging e-mail or voice conversation with a customer service representative. This technology also enables retailers to send a proactive chat invitation automatically to customers on the site. The timing of these invitations can be based on the time the visitor has spent on the site, the specific page the customer is viewing, or a product on which the customer has clicked. For example, Bluefly.com has learned that reviewing several items in a short period implies the visitor has more than a passing interest in its offerings. Therefore, the site displays a pop-up window with a friendly face offering help.[22]

The interactive nature of the Internet also provides an opportunity for retailers to personalize their offerings for each of their customers. For example, Amazon.com serves customers a personalized landing page with information about books and other products of interest based on the customer's past purchases and search behavior on the website. Amazon also sends interested customers customized e-mail messages that notify them that their favorite author or recording artist has published a new book or released a new CD. Amazon further personalizes customers' shopping experience by recommending complementary merchandise.

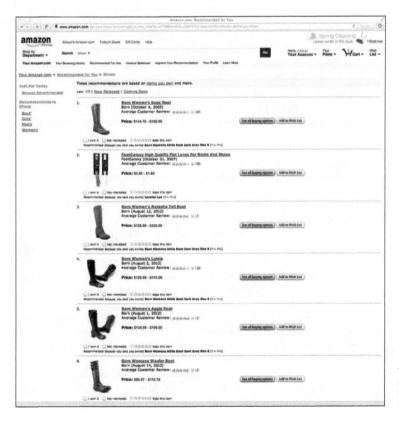

The Internet channels are particularly effective at making personalized recommendations.

Just as a well-trained salesperson would make recommendations to customers before checkout, an interactive web page can make suggestions to shoppers about additional items that they might like to consider.

Some multichannel retailers are able to personalize promotions and Internet homepages on the basis of several attributes tied to the shopper's current or previous web sessions, such as the time of day, time zone as determined by a computer's Internet address, and assumed gender.[23] However, some consumers worry about this ability to collect information about purchase histories, personal information, and search behavior on the Internet. How will this information be used in the future? Will it be sold to other firms, or will the consumer receive unwanted promotional materials online or in the mail?

Expand Market Presence   The market for customers who shop in stores is typically limited to consumers living in proximity those stores. The market for catalogs is limited by the high cost of printing and mailing them and increasing consumer interest in environmentally friendly practices. By adding the Internet channel, retailers can expand their market without having to build new stores or incur the high cost of additional catalogs. Adding an Internet channel is particularly attractive to retailers with strong brand names but limited locations and distribution. For example, retailers such as Neiman Marcus, REI, IKEA, and L.L. Bean are widely known for offering unique, high-quality merchandise. If these retailers only had a store, customers would have to travel vast distances to buy the merchandise they carry.

Provide Information to Improve Shopping Experience Across Channels
It is difficult for most store-based retailers to develop extensive purchase histories of their customers because the retailers are unable to link transactions to customers who pay cash or use third-party credit cards. In contrast, all transactions through the Internet have the customer identification information needed to send the product to the customer as well as their search behavior. This information can be used to provide valuable insights into how and why customers shop and are dissatisfied or satisfied with their experiences.[24]

Collecting data on how customers navigate through a website is quite easy. By placing a cookie (a small computer program that collects information about computer usage) on a customer's hard drive, the retailer can monitor each mouse click. The click-stream data provides insights into what characteristics of products customers considered and what products customers looked at but did not buy.[25] To collect this information from store shoppers would be quite difficult; someone would have to follow them around the store.

This information is useful to retailers in several ways. First, it helps them design stores or websites. By knowing how people shop, a retailer can determine, for instance, whether a store or website should be laid out by brands, size, color, or price point. It can also help the retailer give suggestions about what items a customer might be interested in purchasing. For example, after a customer purchases a book, Amazon recommends additional books that might be of interest to the customer based on purchases made by other customers who have bought that book. Finally, based on what customers clicked on or what they purchased in the past, retailers can provide unique promotions to individual customers.

Perceived Risks in Internet Shopping   Some consumers are concerned about buying products through an Internet channel. Specifically, some believe that the security of credit card transactions is greater than in stores and that there are potential privacy violations.

Although many consumers remain concerned about credit card security, extensive security problems have been rare. Almost all retailers use sophisticated technologies to encrypt communications. Also, all major credit card companies provide some consumer protection for retail transactions. Typically, customers are not liable for more than $50 as long as they report the unauthorized use in a timely manner. The consequences of security breaches can be far worse for the retailer from which the card number was stolen. Security breaches can ruin a retailer's reputation and possibly expose it to legal liability.[26]

Consumers also are concerned about the ability of retailers to collect information about their purchase history, personal information, and search behavior on the Internet without their knowledge.[27] They are worried about how this information will be used in the future. Will it be sold to other retailers, or will the consumer receive unwanted promotional materials online or in the mail? Issues related to privacy are discussed in more detail in Chapters 11 and 15.

Comparison of Electronic and Mobile Phone Internet Channels

Due to the rapid growth of domestic and international broadband access through handheld devices, such as tablets and mobile phones, retailers are very interested in developing this channel's potential. While the mobile Internet channel retains the same benefits over stores as the computer-based electronic Internet channel, it has its own unique benefits and limitations. In particular, customers can easily carry the device in their purses or pockets, and access the retailer's website from any place they are, as long as there is a mobile phone connection available.

Another advantage of a mobile channel is that customer–retailer interactions can be location-sensitive. For example, a retailer can determine where a customer is located and send location-relevant information to the customer, such as promotions, to encourage customers to buy other products nearby the store or go to another area of the store.

The major disadvantage of a mobile channel, compared to a computer-based Internet channel, is the mobile device's smaller screen and slower download speeds. To accommodate the smaller screen size, the software interface for interacting with mobile devices and computers is different. When using mobile channels, customers typically navigate using a touch screen with side scrolling, while a mouse is used with an electronic channel. The smaller screen size and touch screen navigation means that consumers using a mobile channel have to go through many more screens when browsing or trying to locate information.[29]

Apps   To provide their customers with a better shopping experience when using their mobile channels, many retailers have developed mobile shopping apps. **Apps** are software applications designed to improve the consumers' shopping experiences when using smartphones and tablets. Apps developed by retailers are typically used to easily perform some specific functions available on the retailer's website but do not provide access to all of the functions available on the website. The Amazon Mobile app offers product price comparisons with thousands of retailers. Its Snap It feature lets consumers take a photo of a product to search for it, and access to Amazon's one-click purchasing is available. Target's Shop Target makes it easy for consumers to scan barcodes and find daily and weekly deals. Users can also check product availability, search for nearby stores, and set up text alerts for discounts.

The use of tablets may provide the best trade-off between the portability of mobile phones and the navigation ease of websites accessed by computers. Most retailers serve the firm's website, rather a specially designed mobile website when a customer accesses an Internet channel. But now, some retailers are designing websites and apps for tablets. On Anthropologie's app, for example, consumers can not only browse items but also clip pictures of the most appealing options to add to their social networks, as well as check out detailed, thumbnail views of the offerings. The collage option allows them to put together outfits, including accessories

Anthropologie's app improves the usability of mobile devices.

and jewelry, to buy as a set. The percentage of shoppers accessing Anthropologie's website through tablets has tripled, to 6 percent, since the introduction of the app; the retailer expects that number to jump to 20 percent within about a year.[32]

CHALLENGES FACING MULTICHANNEL RETAILERS

LO3

Analyze the challenges facing multichannel retailers.

In the previous section, we outlined the benefits offered by the different retail channels. In this section, we describe how retailers are using multiple channels to improve their offerings to their customers and build a competitive advantage. The typical examples of the evolution toward multichannel retailing are when store-based retailers and catalogers add Internet channels. But retailers that focus on direct selling and TV home shopping network channels have also added Internet channels. Amazon, a retailer using only Internet channels, is even considering establishing a physical presence by having lockers in which customers can access merchandise they purchased online and/or actual stores to overcome some of the limitations of their Internet channel.[33]

Regardless of how they come to find a multichannel retailer, consumers want a seamless experience: Whether they solicit a sales associate for help, seek out an in-store kiosk, call in to the call center, or log on to the website, they also like to be recognized. Once recognized, they also need the retailer to facilitate their ability to find and pick up their purchases, even if they want to buy online and then pick up in the store, or vice versa. In addition, the various channels need to be consistent in the information they provide.

Retailers also benefit by using multiple channels synergistically. Multichannel retailers can use one channel to promote the services offered by other channels. For example, the URL of a store's website can be advertised on in-store signs, shopping bags, credit card billing statements, point-of-sale (POS) receipts, and the print or broadcast advertising used to promote the store. The physical stores and catalogs are also advertisements for a retailer's other channels. The retailer's channels can be used to stimulate store visits by announcing special store events and promotions.

Multichannel retailers can leverage their stores to lower the cost of fulfilling orders and processing returned merchandise. They can use their stores as "warehouses" for gathering merchandise for delivery to customers. Customers also can be offered the opportunity to pick up and return merchandise at the retailer's stores rather than pay shipping charges. Many retailers will waive shipping charges when orders are placed online or through the catalog if the customer physically comes into the store.

Offering customers the opportunity to buy online and pick up merchandise in a store is an example of the seamless interface customers are seeking.

However, as illustrated in Exhibit 3–3, most multichannel retailers have yet to provide these seamless customer-facing processes. This apparent lack of progress should not be interpreted as a lack of interest. The results of a recent survey indicate that cross-channel coordination is extremely important to retailers, even if they have yet to reach their full potential.[34]

In the next section, several challenges and trade-off decisions confronting multichannel retailers are discussed, including multichannel supply chain and information system issues, centralized versus decentralized multichannel retailing, maintaining a consistent brand image across channels, merchandise assortment trade-offs, pricing issues, and the challenge surrounding channel migration and showrooming.

Multichannel Supply Chains and Information Systems

Multichannel retailers still struggle to provide an integrated shopping experience because the various channels demand various skills, as well as unique resources.[35] When retail distribution centers (DCs) support a store channel, they move merchandise, packed in cartons, off the suppliers' trucks, into the DC inventory, and then onto new trucks heading to retail stores. When retailers get efficient enough, merchandise sits in the DC only briefly, often for less than a day. But DCs that supply catalog and Internet channels have other roles to fulfill as well: receive merchandise packed in cartons, then separate out the individual items to be repacked and shipped to individual end-customers. Handling individual items, rather than cartons, and shipping them to individual consumers, instead of retailers, requires unique packaging, different transportation systems, and new intermediaries.

Cross-Channel Fulfillment Activities	High-Performance Retailers	Others
Buy online, return in store	70%	59%
Buy in store, fulfill through online	70	41
Buy online, pick up in store	50	52
Buy via mobile	35	48
Buy via social media source	30	11
Buy online, fulfill through any stop	30	30

EXHIBIT 3–3
Percentage of Multichannel Retailers Offering Cross-Channel Fulfillment

Source: *Omni-Channel 2012: Cross-Channel Comes of Age, 2012 Benchmark*, RSR, June 2012.

Due to these operational differences, many store-based retailers have a separate organization to manage their Internet and catalog operations. But as the multichannel operation matures, retailers tend to integrate all operations under one organization. Both Walmart and JCPenney initially had separate organizations for their Internet channel but subsequently integrated them with stores and catalogs.

Centralized versus Decentralized Multichannel Retailing

Because each of the channels offer a unique set of benefits, the profiles of a retailer's customers who use the different channels are not the same. Thus, a critical decision facing multichannel retailers is the degree to which they should integrate the operations of the channels or have different organizations for each channel. At one extreme of this continuum is complete integration—selling the same products at the same prices through the same distribution system for all channels. At the other extreme is having different organizations manage each channel so that the channels are tailored to different target markets. However, few retailers actually take the extreme route to pursue a strategy at one end of the continuum or the other.

Consistent Brand Image across Channels

Retailers need to provide a consistent brand image of themselves and their private-label merchandise across all channels. For example, Patagonia reinforces its image of selling high-quality, environmentally friendly sports equipment in its stores, catalogs, and website. Each of these channels emphasizes function, not fashion, in the descriptions of Patagonia's products. Patagonia's concerns about the environment are communicated by carefully lighting its stores and using recycled polyester in many of its clothes, as well as only organic, rather than pesticide-intensive, cotton. Its weblog, www.thecleanestline.com, is dedicated to essays and other features on environmental activism, innovative design, and sports. Retailing View 3.4 describes how Build-A-Bear Workshop uses multiple channels to build and reinforce its image.

Merchandise Assortment

Typically, different assortments are often appropriate for each of the channels. For example, multichannel retailers offer a broader and deeper merchandise assortment through their Internet channel than through their store channel. Because the Internet channel can have a much larger assortment, it can satisfy the needs of a larger variety of customer groups. For instance, multichannel apparel retailers can carry fringe sizes on their Internet channel, but it would be too expensive and space constricting to do so in their store channel.

The channels also differ in terms of their effectiveness in generating sales for different types of merchandise. For example, the store channel is better suited for selling products with important "touch-and-feel" attributes such as the fit of a shirt, the taste of an ice cream flavor, or the smell of a perfume. On the other hand, an Internet channel might be just as effective as a store channel for selling products with important "look-and-see" attributes such as price, color, and grams of fat. Evaluating these products does not require senses beyond sight. Because of the problems of providing touch-and-feel information, apparel retailers experience return rates of more than 20 percent on purchases made through Internet channels, but only 5 percent on purchases made in stores.

Pricing

Pricing represents another difficult decision for a multichannel retailer. Many customers expect prices to be the same across channels (excluding shipping charges). However, in some cases, retailers need to adjust their pricing strategy because of the competition they face in different channels. For example, BarnesandNoble.com offers lower prices through its Internet channels than through its stores to compete effectively against Amazon.com.

Retailers with stores in multiple markets often set different prices for the same merchandise to deal with differences in local competition. They can do so because most customers don't know about these price differences because they are exposed only to the prices in their local markets. However, multichannel retailers may have difficulties sustaining regional price differences when customers can easily check prices on the Internet.

Reduction of Channel Migration

An Internet channel helps customers search for information about products and prices. The most common multichannel usage involves an initial search online, followed by a purchase in stores. Whereas approximately 78 percent of U.S. consumers adopt this pattern of consumption, only 8 percent browse through

RETAILING VIEW   The Build-A-Bear Workshop Uses Multiple Channels to Enhance Its Image   3.4

The Build-A-Bear Workshop website reinforces the brand image generated by its stores.

On Bearville.com, stuffed animal fans of all ages and backgounds can enjoy the entertaining content provided by Build-A-Bear Workshop. The content includes online games, access to fun merit "certificates" and thank-you cards, and options for organizing a party. The site thus is closely integrated with the Build-A-Bear Workshop stores, as well as the company's mobile app—and of course, the cuddly products.

Just as youthful customers can name their furry friends, players of the online Bearville game can personalize their characters and purchase virtual outfits for them, then play with other global customers. These visitors spend approximately 25 million hours on the site, playing its free online games. With this Internet channel, Build-A-Bear thus hopes not only to improve its brand image, but also to keep children interested and interacting with the retailer, leading them to beg to make yet another visit to the local store.

Build-A-Bear also promises a safe and useful site. The Find-A-Bear identification program helps users find lost bears. As soon as children register, the company sends an e-mail to their parents, with a link that allows them to determine the level of communications the company will initiate, depending on their children's age, maturity, and comfort level. Furthermore, Build-A-Bear monitors the site to ensure all socialization is appropriate; as the founder of the company notes, "We're conscious of the issues of cyber-bullying, for example."

Sources: www.bearville.com, accessed September 1, 2012; "Build-a-Bear Workshop: The Bear Necessities," *Retail Week,* January 13, 2012; and "Build-A-Bear Workshop Creates Entertainment Destination," *Internet Wire,* February 9, 2011.

DISCUSSION QUESTION

Are these Internet channel activities consistent with its in-store brand?

stores first, then make their purchases via the Internet.[36] As long as the store and the Internet channel represent the same retailer, the firm is happy. But if customers gather information from one of its channels, then buy from a channel hosted by a competitor, the retailer suffers from the frustrating problem of **channel migration**.[37] Modern technologies, including those that allow customers to gather information and buy online or through their mobile devices, also make channel migration really easy. Thus, retaining customers remains a constant challenge for multichannel retailers.

As mentioned earlier in the chapter, a particularly concerning form of channel migration is called showrooming. **Showrooming** occurs when a consumer goes into a store to learn about different brands and products and then searches the Internet for the same product sold at a lower price. Three approaches that multichannel retailers can use to reduce showrooming are (1) providing better customer service, (2) offering uniquely relevant information based on proprietary data the retailer has collected about the customers, and (3) promoting private-label merchandise that can be purchased only from the retailer. These approaches are discussed in more detail in Chapter 5.[38]

MULTICHANNEL SHOPPING IN THE FUTURE

LO4

Consider the multichannel shopping experience in the future.

The following hypothetical scenario illustrates the technologies and seamless interface across channels that customers in the future may experience.

Shopping Experience Scenario

It's Tuesday morning, and Judy Jamison is eating breakfast thinking about buying a new dress for the party she'll be attending this Friday night at the new club downtown. She sends a tweet to her friends about her plans to go shopping after work today and asks for suggestions of retailers she might visit. She gets some suggestions from friends and then decides to do some research on the Internet. She logs on to her tablet, accesses her personal shopper program called FRED, and has the following interactive dialog:

> **FRED:** Do you wish to browse, go to a specific store, or buy a specific item?
>
> **Judy:** Specific item.
>
> **FRED:** What is the item? [Menu appears and Judy selects.]
>
> **Judy:** Dress.
>
> **FRED:** Occasion? [Menu appears and Judy selects.]
>
> **Judy:** Cocktail.
>
> **FRED:** Price range? [Menu appears.]
>
> **Judy:** $175–$200.
> [Now FRED goes out and literally shops the world electronically, visiting the servers for companies selling cocktail dresses in Europe, Asia, Africa, Australia, and North and South America.]
>
> **FRED:** 1,231 items have been identified. How many do you want to review? [Menu appears.]
>
> **Judy:** Just 7
> [FRED selects the seven best alternatives on the basis of information it has about Judy's style preferences. The seven cocktail dresses appear on the screen with the price, brand name, and retailer listed beneath each one. Judy clicks on each dress to get more information about it. With another click, she sees a full-motion video of a woman who looks similar to Judy modeling the dress. She selects several dresses she finds most appealing.]

However, Judy decides not to buy the dress because she is not sure the dress will fit right when it arrives, and she will not have time to return it and get another size. She likes the Robert Rodriguez styles FRED found, so she goes to Brand-Habit.com, types in the designer's name and her zip code, and finds the closest store that carries his designs and has her size in stock. The site directs her to the store's website to look at more dresses. She decides to visit the store after work.

Shortly after Judy walks into the store, a chip in her credit card signals her presence and status as a frequent shopper to a mobile device held by the store sales associate responsible for preferred clients. Information about items in which Judy might be interested, including the items she viewed on the website through FRED, is downloaded from the store server to Judy's and the sales associate's devices.

A sales associate approaches Judy and says, "Hello, Ms. Jamison. My name is Joan Bradford. How can I help you?" Judy tells the associate she needs to buy a dress for a party. She has seen some dresses on the store's website and would like to look at them in the store. The sales associate takes Judy to a virtual dressing room.

In the dressing room, Judy sits in a comfortable chair and views the dresses displayed on her image, which has been drawn from a body scan stored in Judy's customer file. Information about Judy's recent visit to the retailer's website and her past purchases is used to select the dresses displayed.

Using her mobile phone, Judy shares this personalized viewing with her friend, who is still at work in California. They discuss which dress looks best on Judy. Then, using her mobile phone again, Judy drills down to find more information about the dress—the fabric, cleaning instructions, and so forth. Finally, she selects a dress that is of most interest to her and tries it on. When she tries is on, the video cameras in the room enable her to see what she looks like from all angles. She notices that from some angles the dress does not have a flattering fit. The sales associate suggests that this problem can be overcome with a minor alteration and shows Judy how she will look in the altered dress. Using information displayed on her mobile device, the sales associate Joan suggests a handbag and scarf that would complement the dress. These accessories are added to the image of Judy in the dress. Judy decides to buy the scarf but not the handbag. Judy is informed that she will get a message on her mobile when the alterations are completed, and then she can indicate whether she wants the dress delivered to her home or she will pick it up at the store.

As Judy passes through the cosmetics department on her way to her car, she sees an appealing new lipstick shade. She decides to purchase the lipstick and a 3-ounce bottle of her favorite perfume and walks out of the store. The store systems sense her departure, and the merchandise she has selected is automatically charged to her account through signals from radio-frequency identification (RFID) chips.

Supporting the Shopping Experience

This scenario illustrates the advantages of having a customer database shared by all channels and integrated across all systems. The sales associate and the store systems are able to offer superior customer service based on this database, which contains information about Judy's body scan image, her interaction with the retailer's website, and her past purchases and preferences. The technology also supports the retailer's business model, which determines how to offer customers the products and services that will provide the best shopping experience.

Before Judy went into the store, she interacted with a search engine to find where the particular brand and product she was looking for could be found. She then interacted with the retailer's website to review the available merchandise before she went to the store, check the status of her alterations, and decide about having the merchandise delivered to her home. The scenario also includes some new technologies that will exist in the store of the future, such as RFID, self-checkout, and personalized virtual reality displays.

SUMMARY

LO1 Understand the nonstore channels offered by retailers.

A *retail channel* is the way a retailer sells *and* delivers merchandise and services to its customers. The most common channel used by retailers is a store. Retailers also use a variety of nonstore channels including the Internet, mobile, catalogs, direct mail, direct selling, television home shopping, direct response TV, and automated retailing (vending machines) to make sales to customers. *Multichannel retailing* involves using more than one channel to enhance the customer satisfaction experience and exploit the synergies between channels. Some of the challenges facing multichannel retailers are due to the operational and organizational differences inherent in managing multiple information and supply chain systems, channel operations, pricing, branding, and assortments.

LO2 Compare the benefits offered by the four major retail channels: stores, Internet, and catalogs

Stores offer several benefits to customers that they cannot get when they shop through non-store channels such as Internet, or catalogs. These benefits include touching and feeling products, personal service, increased customer service, risk reduction, immediate gratification, cash payments, and entertainment and social experiences.

The catalog channel, like all non-store channels, provides safety and convenience benefits to customers. Using the catalog channel, consumers can look at merchandise and place an order from almost anywhere 24/7 without needing a computer, mobile device, or Internet connection. Second, consumers can refer to the information in a catalog anytime by simply picking it up from the coffee table. Finally, catalogs are easier to browse through than Web sites.

There are five advantages of the Internet channels. First, the addition of the Internet channels has

the potential to offer a greater selection of products. Second, they allow retailers to provide more information. Third, they enable retailers to provide customers with more personalized information about products and services. Fourth, they offer sellers the unique opportunity to collect information about consumer shopping. Fifth, the Internet channels provide an opportunity for retailers to enter new markets economically. Finally, they provide information that they can use to improve the shopping experience across all channels. Some consumers are concerned about buying products through an Internet channel.

LO3 Understand the issues facing multichannel retailers

Multichannel retailers are still struggling to provide an integrated shopping experience across all their channels because unique skills and resources are needed to manage each channel. A critical decision facing multichannel retailers is the degree to which they should integrate the operations of the channels or have different organizations for each channel. Since each of the channels offers a unique set of benefits, the profiles of a retailer's customers who use the different channels are not the same. Retailers need to provide a consistent brand image of themselves and their private-label merchandise across all channels. Pricing represents another difficult decision for a multichannel retailer. Finally, the availability of an Internet channel enables customers to easily search for information about products and their prices during a shopping episode.

LO4 Consider the multichannel shopping experience in the future

This scenario illustrates shopping in the future from an integrated multi-channel retailer.

KEY TERMS

apps, *79*
automated retailing, *72*
catalog channel, *69*
channel migration, *84*
direct-response TV (DRTV) channel, *70*
direct selling, *70*
infomercial, *70*

Internet retailing, *68*
live chat, *77*
m-commerce, *69*
mobile commerce, *69*
mobile retailing, *69*
multichannel retailing, *67*
multilevel system, *72*

omniretailing, *67*
party plan system, *72*
pyramid scheme, *72*
retail channel, *67*
showrooming, *84*
television home shopping, *70*
vending machines, *72*

GET OUT AND DO IT!

1. **CONTINUING CASE ASSIGNMENT: GO SHOPPING** Assume that you are shopping on the Internet for an item in the same merchandise category

you analyzed for the Comparison Shopping exercise in Chapter 2. Go to the retailer's website, and compare the merchandise assortment offered, the prices, and the shopping experience in the store and on the store's website. How easy was it to locate what you were looking for? What were the assortment and pricing like? What was the checkout like? What are the categories and/or sub-categories? How many SKUs were in each category and subcategory? What features of the sites did you like and dislike, such as the look and feel of the site, navigation, and special features?

2. **INTERNET EXERCISE** Go to the websites of J. Crew (www.jcrew.com), JCPenney (www.jcpenney.com), and American Eagle Outfitters (www.ae.com), and shop for a pair of khaki pants. Evaluate your shopping experience at each site. Compare and contrast the sites and your experiences on the basis of characteristics you think are important to consumers.

3. **INTERNET EXERCISE** Assume that you are getting married and planning your wedding. Compare and contrast the usefulness of www.theknot.com and www.weddingchannel.com for planning your wedding. What features of the sites do you like and dislike? Indicate the specific services offered by these sites that you would use.

4. **INTERNET AND SHOPPING EXERCISE** Pick a merchandise category like microwave ovens, power drills, digital cameras, blenders, or coffee makers. Compare a retailer's offering in its local store and on its Internet site. What are the differences in the assortments offered through its store and Internet channel? Are the prices the same or different? What has the retailer done to exploit the synergies between the channels?

5. **INTERNET AND SHOPPING EXERCISE** Access the websites of Home Depot and Macy's using your mobile phone and computer. What are the differences in the ease of navigation when looking at the presentation of merchandise using the two methods of accessing the websites?

DISCUSSION QUESTIONS AND PROBLEMS

1. Why are store-based retailers aggressively pursuing sales through Internet channels?

2. From a customer's perspective, what are the benefits and limitations of stores? Catalogs? Retailer websites?

3. Would you buy clothes on the basis of the way they look on a customized virtual model? Why or why not?

4. Why are the Internet and catalog channels so popular for gift giving?

5. Should a multichannel retailer offer the same assortment of merchandise for sale, at the same price, on its website and in its stores? Why or why not?

6. Which of the following categories of merchandise do you think could be sold most successfully through an Internet channel: jewelry; TV sets; computer software; high-fashion apparel; pharmaceuticals; health care products such as toothpaste, shampoo, and cold remedies? Why?

7. Assume you are interested in investing in a startup Internet retailer that targets people who enjoy active outdoor recreation, such as hiking, rock climbing, and kayaking. What merchandise and information would you offer on the site? What type of entity do you think would be most effective in running the site: a well-known outdoors person, a magazine targeting outdoor activity, or a retailer selling outdoor merchandise, such as Patagonia or REI? Why?

8. What are the advantages to customers of accessing the Internet through a mobile device or a computer when browsing a website? When learning special promotions?

9. When you shop online for merchandise, how much time do you spend browsing versus buying? When you shop in a store for merchandise, how much time do you spend browsing versus buying?

SUGGESTED READINGS

Avery, Jill, Thomas J. Steenburgh, John Deighton, and Mary Caravella, "Adding Bricks to Clicks: Predicting the Patterns of Cross-Channel Elasticities Over Time," *Journal of Marketing* 76(May 2012), 7, pp. 96–111.

Brynjolfsson, Erik, Hu, Yu (Jeffrey), Rahmanand Mohammad S., "Battle of the Retail Channels: How Product Selection and Geography Drive Cross-Channel Competition," *Management Science*, November 2009, Vol. 55 Issue 11, pp. 1755–1765.

Hsiao, Cheng-Chieh; Yen, Ju Rebecca Hsiu, and Eldon Y. Li, "Exploring Consumer Value of Multi-Channel Shopping: A Perspective of Means-End Theory," *Internet Research*, 22: 3, 2012, pp. 318–339.

Lee, Hyun-Hwa and Jihyun Kim (2010), "Investigating Dimensionality of Multichannel Retailer's Cross-Channel Integration Practices and Effectiveness: Shopping Orientation and Loyalty Intention," *Journal of Marketing Channels*, 17:4, 2010, pp. 281–312.

Neslin, S.A. and V. Shankar (2009), "Keys Issues in Multichannel Customer Management: Current Knowledge and Future Directions," *Journal of Interactive Marketing*, 23: 1, pp. 70–81.

Poloian, Lynda Gamans. *Retailing Principles: Global, Multichannel, and Management Viewpoints, 2nd Ed.* Fairchild Publication: New York, 2012.

Schramm-Klein, Hanna, Gerhard Wagner, Sascha Steinmann and Dirk Morschett, "Cross-Channel Integration—Is It Valued By Customers?," *The International Review of Retail, Distribution and Consumer Research*, 21: 5, 2011, pp. 501–511.

Weitz, Barton A. "Electronic Retailing," in Retailing in the 21st Century—Current and Future Trends, 2nd ed., eds. Manfred Kraft and Murali Mantrala. Berlin: Springer, 2010, pp. 309–323.

Zhang, Jie, Paul W. Farris, John W. Irvin, Tarun Kushwaha, Thomas J. Steenburgh, Barton A. Weitz, Crafting Integrated Multichannel Retailing Strategies," *Journal of Interactive Marketing*, Volume 24, Issue 2, May 2010, pp. 168–180.

Customer Buying Behavior

EXECUTIVE BRIEFING

Don Unser, Group President, Retail Business Group, The NPD Group, Inc.

The NPD Group provides information about consumer buying behavior that helps our clients, both retailers and vendors, make better, fact-based decisions. The reports provided by our system are derived from two sources: point-of-sale (POS) data and consumer panel data.

The POS data are supplied by over 900 retail clients around the world, detailing sales in over 150,000 stores. The database provides sales for products and their prices across general merchandise categories offered by a broad cross-section of retailers including department, discount, and specialty stores. Retailers share this sales data in exchange for the knowledge we provide from our analyses.

The online consumer panel consists of over 2 million people who have agreed to participate in surveys and provide information on their purchase behavior. In addition to sales by product and retailer, the database includes demographic and other information about the panel members including customer satisfaction evaluations following specific purchase occasions. This database allows sales tracking across all channels, by demographic segments. Our technology ensures survey samples are representative of the total population or a client's particular target audience.

Our systems are designed to make it easy for retailers to get the data that help them analyze market performance and make fact-based decisions. A variety of reports are available drawing on both databases. For example, an automotive parts retailer reviewed a fair-share report that compared its market share in each merchandise category to its overall market share and discovered some areas in which it was not getting its fair share—it had a market share of 8 percent in the category compared to its overall market share of 11 percent. By drilling down into the data, the buyer for the category adjusted the assortment plan, changing the emphasis placed on specific brands and SKUs. The result was an increase in annual sales of $3 million and a promotion for the buyer.

Due to the breadth and depth of data we collect and analyze, we are able to identify key consumer trends and business opportunities. The choice of food and meals by consumers in their 20s, referred to as Gen Y or millennials, differs from other generations. We find that this segment of consumers has a high degree of confidence in their judgments, heed cravings quickly, and place high value on minimal preparation time. They are more likely than consumers in other age groups to use frozen entrées

CHAPTER 4

LEARNING OBJECTIVES

LO1 Describe the process that consumers go through when making retail patronage and buying decisions.

LO2 Identify the different types of buying processes.

LO3 Summarize how the economy and social factors affect customer purchase decisions.

LO4 Determine why and how retailers group customers into market segments.

and other quick-prep items. These young adults have been among the hardest-hit by the recession and are heavy patrons of low-priced retailers. One-third of millennials shop at Walmart and other mass merchants. For food retailers and restaurants, a major opportunity—and challenge—exists in learning how to communicate effectively with this "connected" generation, as well as offering products and meal/snack solutions that fit their spontaneous, budget-conscious lifestyles.

As discussed in Chapter 1, an effective retail strategy satisfies customer needs better than do competitors' strategies. Successful retailers are customer-centric—their strategic and tactical decisions revolve around their present and potential customers. Thus, understanding customer needs and buying behavior is critical to formulating and implementing an effective retail strategy.

This chapter focuses on how customers process information and make decisions about what stores to patronize, what channels to use, and what products and services to buy.[1] It describes the stages customers go through when making purchase decisions and the factors that influence their buying process. Because typically it is not cost-efficient for retailers to develop unique offerings for individual customers, retailers target their offerings to groups of customers (market segments) with similar needs and buying processes. Thus, this chapter continues with a discussion of how market segments are formed. We use information about the buying process to discuss how retailers can identify the market segments that will be the target of their retail strategy. The appendix to this chapter examines special aspects of consumer behavior that are of concern to retailers selling fashion merchandise.

THE BUYING PROCESS

LO1

Describe the process that consumers go through when making retail patronage and buying decisions.

The following scenario illustrates the steps consumers go through when purchasing merchandise. Eva Mendoza, a student at the University of Washington, is beginning to interview for jobs. Eva planned to wear the blue suit her parents gave her several years ago to the interviews. But looking at her suit, she realizes that it's not very stylish and that the jacket is beginning to show signs of wear. Wanting to make a good first impression during her interviews, she decides to buy a new suit.

Eva surfs the Internet for tips on dressing for interviews and looks through some catalogs to see the styles and prices being offered. Eva surfs fashion blogs such as Nubry and checks what her friends are wearing on Facebook and then checks what they "Like" and what they have "pinned" on Pinterest. She goes to retailers' websites to examine and compare all their suits. She then decides to go to a store so that she can try on a suit and have it altered if necessary. She likes to shop at American Eagle Outfitters and Banana Republic, but neither sells business suits. Before going to the Northgate Mall in Seattle, she issues a status update on her Facebook page, announcing her intentions to go to the mall and inviting friends to join her. Britt responds to her Facebook posting, and they decide to meet at the mall entrance. Betsy also responds, but she has a cold and wants to rest.

Consumers are increasingly turning to fashionista blogs to read reviews and pick up the latest fashion tips.

Eva and Britt first go to Macy's and are approached by a salesperson in the career women's department. After asking Eva what type of suit she wants and her size, the salesperson shows her three suits. Eva talks with Britt about the suits, and they decide to get Betsy's opinion. So Eva takes photos of the suits with her mobile phone and sends them to Betsy at her apartment. Betsy likes all three, so Eva tries them on.

When Eva comes out of the dressing room, she is unsure which suit to select, but after sending Betsy some more photos, she, Britt, and the salesperson decide the second suit is the most attractive and appropriate for interviewing. Eva is happy with the color, fit, fabric, and length of the suit, but she is concerned that it will require dry cleaning. It also costs more than she had planned to spend. Eva decides to buy the suit after another customer in the store, seeing her wearing the suit, tells her she looks very professional.

As Britt and Eva are walking toward the door, they pass the shoe department. Britt tells Eva, "You need to buy shoes that go with your suit." Eva finds a pair of Steve Madden pumps that are perfect. She tries on a few pairs to get

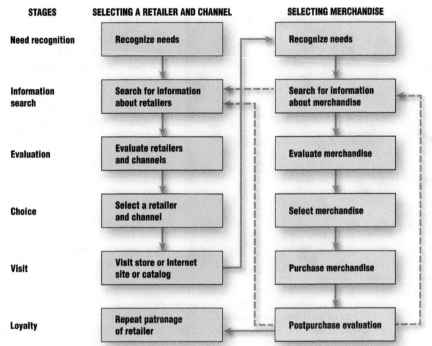

EXHIBIT 4–1
Stages in the Buying
Process

the right size. Then Britt tells her that she thinks the shoes are overpriced. Eva scans the UPC code for the shoes using her mobile phone's shopping app and finds that Zappos is selling the shoes for $20 less and with no sales tax. So she orders the shoes from Zappos for delivery to her apartment the next day.

Consider Eva's shopping trip as we describe the customer buying process. The **buying process**—the steps consumers go through when buying a product or service—begins when customers recognize an unsatisfied need. Then they seek information about how to satisfy the need—what retailers, channels, and products or services might satisfy the need. Customers then evaluate the alternatives and choose a store or Internet site to visit or a catalog to review. Their encounter with a retailer provides more information and may alert customers to additional needs. After evaluating the retailer's offering, customers may make a purchase or go to another retailer to collect more information. Eventually, customers purchase a product, use the product, and then decide whether the retailer, channel, and product satisfy their needs during the postpurchase evaluation stage of the customer buying process.

Exhibit 4–1 outlines the buying process—the stages consumers go through to select a retailer and channel and to buy a specific item. The exhibit suggests that the buying process is linear, as shown by the solid lines. First, the channel and retailer are selected and then the specific items. For each of these decisions, customers go through five stages, beginning with need recognition and ending with loyalty. As we discuss the stages in the buying process, you should recognize that customers might not go through all the stages and/or might not go through the stages in the order shown in Exhibit 4–1. For example, Eva might have decided on the brand of suit she wanted before selecting a store, or she might have collected information about suits sold at Macy's and, on the basis of this information, decided to go to another store or to use another channel, such as the Internet, to buy the suit.

Retailers attempt to influence consumers as they go through the buying process to encourage consumers to buy merchandise and services from them. Each stage in the buying process is examined in the following sections.

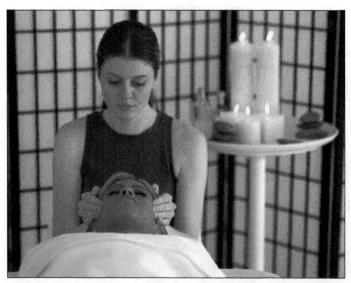

Spas make guests the center of attention and satisfy hedonic needs.

Need Recognition

The buying process is triggered when consumers recognize they have an unsatisfied need. An **unsatisfied need** arises when customers' desired level of satisfaction differs from their present level of satisfaction. For example, Eva recognized that she had a need when she was faced with the prospect of interviewing for jobs in her blue suit. She needed a suit that would make a good impression and realized her worn, outdated blue suit would not satisfy this need. Need recognition can be as straightforward as realizing you need a haircut, feeling the need for an uplifting experience after a final exam, or receiving a message about something a friend bought.

Types of Needs   The needs that motivate customers to go shopping can be classified as utilitarian or hedonic. When consumers go shopping to accomplish a specific task, such as Eva buying a suit for job interviews, they are seeking to satisfy **utilitarian needs.** When consumers go shopping for pleasure, they are seeking to satisfy their **hedonic needs**—their needs for entertaining, emotional, and recreational experiences. Thus, from the consumer's perspective, utilitarian needs are associated with work, whereas hedonic needs are associated with pleasure.[2]

Successful retailers attempt to satisfy both the utilitarian and the hedonic needs of their customers. Consumers motivated by utilitarian needs typically shop in a more deliberate and efficient manner. Thus, retailers need to provide adequate information and an effortless shopping experience for utilitarian shoppers. On the other hand, shoppers with hedonic needs desire excitement, stimulation, status and power, recreation, and adventure.[3] Examples of how retailers satisfy hedonic needs are listed next:

1. *Stimulation*. Retailers and mall managers use background music, visual displays, scents, and demonstrations in stores and malls to create a carnival-like, stimulating experience for their customers. (See Chapter 17.) Such environments encourage consumers to take a break from their everyday lives and visit stores. Retailers also attempt to stimulate customers with exciting graphics and photography in their catalogs and on their websites.

2. *Status and power*. Some people choose retailers based on the attention and respect they receive. For example, Canyon Ranch offers upscale health resorts in Tucson, Arizona, and Lenox, Massachusetts, as well as spa clubs in Las Vegas, Nevada, and on cruises, such as Oceania, Regent Seven Seas, and the Queen Mary 2. All Canyon Ranch resorts and spas make the customer the center of attention, offering spa services, medical and nutritional consultations, workshops, spiritual pursuits, and healthy gourmet cuisine.

3. *Adventure*. Often, consumers go shopping because they enjoy finding bargains, looking for sales, and finding discounts or low prices. They treat shopping as a game to be "won." Off-price retailers like Marshalls and Trader Joe's, warehouse clubs like Costco, and fast-fashion specialty retailers like Zara cater to this need by constantly changing their assortment so that customers never know what kind of treasure they will find.

Saks Fifth Avenue uses its exciting window displays to stimulate need recognition.

Conflicting Needs   Most customers have multiple needs. Moreover, these needs often conflict. For example, Eva Mendoza would like to wear a DKNY suit, which would enhance her self-image and earn her the admiration of her college friends. But satisfying these hedonic needs might conflict with her utilitarian needs—the need to stay within her budget and the need to get a job. Employers might feel that she's not responsible if she wears a suit that is too expensive for an interview for an entry-level position. Later in this chapter, we discuss a model of how customers make trade-offs between conflicting needs.

The needs and decision-making processes may differ depending on the specific situation. For example, a skier may purchase expensive Spyder goggles but wear an inexpensive snowsuit from Target. A grocery shopper might buy an inexpensive store brand of paper towels and a premium national brand of orange juice. This pattern of buying both premium and low-priced merchandise or patronizing both expensive, status-oriented retailers and price-oriented retailers is called **cross-shopping**.[4]

Stimulating Need Recognition   Customers must first recognize unsatisfied needs before they are motivated to visit a store or go online to buy merchandise. Sometimes these needs are stimulated by an event in a person's life, like Eva's impending interviews. But retailers use a variety of approaches to stimulate unmet needs. Advertising, e-mails, direct mail, publicity, and special events communicate the availability of new merchandise or special prices. Visits to SeenOn (www.SeenOn.com) can stimulate need recognition by showing products that celebrities or television characters have worn. In a social media campaign, Melrose Jewelers encouraged visitors to its Facebook page to consider a watch purchase by giving them a personality quiz that claimed to reveal which watch style best suited them.[5] Within a store, visual merchandising and salespeople can stimulate need recognition. For example, the display of shoes stimulated Eva's need for shoes to complement her new suit.

Information Search

Once customers identify a need, they typically seek information about retailers, channels, or products to help them satisfy that need. Eva's search started on the Internet and then narrowed to the three suits shown to her by the salesperson at Macy's and the opinions of her friends.[6] In other situations, Eva might have collected a lot more information by visiting several retailers and/or spending more time on the Internet getting information from fashion blogs like College Fashion, Refinery29, and FabSugar.[7]

Sources of Information   Customers have two sources of information: internal and external. **Internal sources** are information in a customer's memory, such as names, images, and past experiences with different stores. The major source of internal information is the customer's past shopping experience. Even if they remember only a small fraction of the information to which they are exposed, customers have an extensive internal information bank to draw on when deciding where to shop and what to buy.

External sources consist of information provided by a host of sources. People search for products and information using search engines such as Google, visit the websites maintained by manufacturers and retailers, acquire information from traditional media (e.g., advertising), read blogs, watch product demonstrations on YouTube, and ask friends, in person and through social media.

When customers believe that they are not well enough informed or that their internal information is inadequate, they turn to external information sources. For example, Eva asked her friends, Betsy and Britt, to help her make the purchase decision. To find out if the price of the shoes she liked was reasonable, she turned to an online shoe seller. Such external sources of information play a major role in the acceptance of fashions, as discussed in the appendix to this chapter.

Amount of Information Searched   In general, the amount of **information search** undertaken depends on the value customers believe they can gain from searching versus the cost of searching.[9] The value of the search stems from the degree to which the additional information improves the customer's purchase decision. Will the search help the customer find a lower-priced product or one that will give superior performance? The costs of the search include the customer's time and money. Traveling from store to store can cost money for gas and parking, but the major cost incurred is the customer's time.

Technology has dramatically reduced the cost of information search. For example, vast information about merchandise sold across the world is just a smartphone search away. Retailing View 4.1 describes how readily available information on the Web affects the automobile buying process.

The amount of information search is affected by (1) characteristics of the individual customer and (2) aspects of the market and buying situation in which the purchase is made.[10] Some people search more than others. Shoppers seeking hedonic benefits typically spend more time collecting information and shopping because they enjoy the process. Customers who have prior experience purchasing and using the product or service tend to search less.

Two marketplace and situational factors affecting information search are (1) the number of competing brands and retail outlets and (2) the time pressure under which the purchase must be made.[11] When competition is greater and there are more alternatives to consider, the amount of information search increases. However, the amount decreases with greater time pressures.

Reducing Information Search   The retailer's objective for customers in the information search stage is to limit the customer's search to its store or website. One measure of a retailer's performance on this objective is the **conversion rate**—the percentage of customers who enter a store or access a website and then buy a product from that same store or website.

Each element of the retailing mix can be used to increase a retailer's conversion rate. Category specialists such as Best Buy provide a very deep assortment of merchandise, everything a customer might want to consider, so that the customer can collect all the information and make the necessary comparisons between products in their stores or on their websites.

At Old Navy, the remodeled layout features a racetrack format that reduces information search by giving customers a better sense of the vast options available. It also displays more items around the checkout area.[12]

Services provided by retailers can also limit the search once at the retailer's location. By offering credit and having informed salespeople, a retailer can convince consumers that they don't need to collect additional information from other retailers. Lowe's has equipped its floor staff with iPhones to enable them to check

RETAILING VIEW   The Internet Has Changed the Car-Buying Process   4.1

Ten years ago, if consumers wanted to buy a car, they would visit several dealers, look at different models, test drive the cars sold by each dealer, and then negotiate price and financing with a dealer. Many consumers viewed this traditional process of buying a car as about as pleasurable as a visit to the dentist. But now the Internet has changed this experience, as well as the nature of automobile retailing.

The Internet has given consumers more control over the car-buying process. Consumers can visit websites such as www.autobytel.com, www.cars.com, or www.edmunds.com; access a wealth of information, including the dealer's costs for cars and options; compare vehicles in a side-by-side chart that lists their price, features, horsepower, mileage, legroom, and options; read multiple reviews for most models; and even take a 360-degree photo tour of car interiors that gives them an idea of what the view looks like from the driver's seat.

Through the sites' relationships with car dealers, consumers can request prices from dealers in their area. A handy calculator tells customers how much the monthly payment would be if they were to buy a car on credit. The sites also have calculators to help car buyers figure out how much they can afford to spend on a car, whether they should buy a new or used car, and whether they should lease or buy. This information enables consumers to walk into a dealership knowing as much as or more than the dealer's salespeople.

On the TrueCar website, consumers find information about recent purchases in their area. Thus, for a specific car make and model, they see a bell curve that shows them what represents a great price, what is a reasonable price, and what is simply too much to pay. The site also identifies the local dealership that will offer the lowest price, so car buyers know where to start their search.

CarFax (www.carfax.com) enables customers to access a vehicle's history report by typing in its vehicle identification number (VIN). This history describes any accidents the vehicle was in, its past ownership, odometer fraud, and any other events that might be related to the vehicle. Services such as CarFax make it much easier for customers to purchase used cars with confidence.

REFACT

Nearly three-quarters of new-vehicle buyers use the Internet during the shopping process, and 54 percent watch online videos.[13]

The Internet has dramatically reduced the time and effort needed to collect information and increased the quality of information acquired to make a decision when buying an automobile.

Sources: Edward Niedermeyer, "TrueCar Versus Honda: Online Car Buying Challenges Hit Home," *The Truth About Cars*, December 21, 2011; Geoffrey A. Fowler, John D. Stoll, and Scott Morrison, "GM, eBay Will Let Car Buyers Dicker Online," *The Wall Street Journal*, August 11, 2009, p. B1; Thomas Pack, "Kicking the Virtual Tires: Car Research on the Web," *Information Today*, January 2009, pp. 44–45; www.cars.com; and www.carfax.com.

DISCUSSION QUESTIONS

How did you use the Internet to purchase your last car? Was your method of searching for information different than that of your parents?

Lowe's uses iPhones to help customers with their shopping.

inventory levels for customers on the spot. Similarly, Pacific Sunwear gives sales-people iPads that help them create virtual outfits to show customers. Foot Locker is relying on old-fashioned training, such that employees have a better sense of how to engage customers and encourage them to buy in the store.[14]

Walmart utilizes an **everyday low pricing (EDLP) strategy** that stresses conti-nuity of retail prices at a level somewhere between the regular nonsale price and the deep-discount sale price of its competitors. This strategy helps assure customers that they won't find a lower price for these products at a different store the next time they go shopping. In addition, many stores with everyday low prices offer money-back guarantees if a competitor offers the same merchandise at a lower price. These pric-ing policies tend to limit the customer information search to the retailer's offering.

Internet, Mobile, Information Search, and Price Competition   The Internet and smartphones have had a profound impact on consumers' ability to gather external information. In addition to placing their own information on their websites and smartphone apps, retailers encourage their customers to post infor-mation such as product reviews, ratings, and, in some cases, photos and videos. Consumer reviews are emerging as a prime information source for shoppers as they collect information during the buying process.[16] The Internet and new mobile apps that encourage showrooming—a practice in which consumers visit stores to gather information about the product, then buy online—enable consum-ers to find the best prices for any product quickly.

Retailers and manufacturers are concerned that the ease of collecting price infor-mation through the Internet increases price competition. Traditionally, store-based retailers, offering the same merchandise, experienced limited price competition be-cause of their geographic separation. The Internet means that consumers' ability to compare prices no longer is limited by physical distance. In addition, the ease of searching for price information is facilitated by shopping sites such as mysimon. com. Or consumers can use one of the many mobile phone apps to learn about prices and availability of products at stores near where they are located.[18]

The Internet not only helps online consumers collect price information, but also gives them information about the quality and performance of products, all at a low search cost. With more information about product quality, customers might be willing to pay more for high-quality products, which would mitigate the importance of price.[20] Finally, retailers that use an Internet channel can clearly differentiate their offerings by providing better services and information.

Evaluation of Alternatives: The Multiattribute Model

The multiattribute attitude model provides a useful way to summarize how customers use the information they have collected to evaluate and select retailers, channels, and products. We discuss this model in detail because it offers a framework for developing a retailing strategy.[21]

The **multiattribute attitude model** is based on the notion that customers see a retailer, a product, or a channel as a collection of attributes or characteristics. The model is designed to predict a customer's evaluation of a product, retailer, or channel on the basis of (1) its performance on relevant attributes and (2) the importance of those attributes to the customer.

Beliefs about Performance   To illustrate this model, consider the store choice decision confronting a young, single, professional Milwaukee woman who needs groceries. She considers three alternatives: (1) a supercenter store in the next suburb, (2) her local supermarket store, or (3) a grocer that operates only an Internet channel, such as Fresh Direct. Her perception of the offerings provided by these retailers is shown in Exhibit 4–2.

The customer mentally processes the "objective" information about each grocery retailer in part A of Exhibit 4–2 and forms an impression of the benefits each one provides. Part B of Exhibit 4–2 shows her beliefs about these benefits. Notice that some benefits combine several objective characteristics. For example, the convenience benefit combines travel time, checkout time, and ease of finding products. Grocery prices and delivery cost affect her beliefs about the economy of shopping at the various retail outlets.

The degree to which each retailer provides each benefit is represented on a 10-point scale: 10 means the retailer performs very well in providing the benefit; 1 means it performs very poorly. In this example, no retailer has superior performance on all benefits. The supercenter performs well on economy and assortment

A. INFORMATION ABOUT STORES SELLING GROCERIES			
Store Characteristics	Supercenter	Supermarket	Internet Grocer
Grocery prices	20% below average	Average	10% above average
Delivery cost ($)	0	0	10
Total travel time (minutes)	30	15	0
Typical checkout time (minutes)	10	5	2
Number of products, brands, and sizes	40,000	30,000	40,000
Fresh produce	Yes	Yes	Yes
Fresh fish	Yes	Yes	No
Ease of finding products	Difficult	Easy	Easy
Ease of collecting nutritional information about products	Difficult	Difficult	Easy
B. BELIEFS ABOUT STORES' PERFORMANCE BENEFITS*			
Performance Benefits	Supercenter	Supermarket	Internet Grocer
Economy	10	8	6
Convenience	3	5	10
Assortment	9	7	5
Availability of product Information	4	4	8

*10 = excellent, 1 = poor.

EXHIBIT 4–2
Characteristics of Food Retailers

but is low on convenience. The Internet grocer offers the best convenience but is weak on economy and assortment.

Importance Weights   The young woman in the preceding example forms an overall evaluation of each alternative on the basis of the importance she places on each benefit the retailers provide. The importance she places on a benefit can also be represented using a 10-point rating scale, with 10 indicating the benefit is very important to her and 1 indicating it's very unimportant. Using this rating scale, the importance of the retailers' benefits for the young woman and for a parent with four children is shown in Exhibit 4–3, along with the performance beliefs previously discussed. Notice that the single woman values convenience and the availability of product information much more than economy and assortment. But to the parent, economy is very important and assortment is moderately important, whereas convenience and product information aren't very important.

The importance of a retailer's benefits differs for each customer and also may differ for each shopping trip. For example, the parent with four children may stress economy for major shopping trips but place more importance on convenience for a fill-in trip.

In Exhibit 4–3, the single woman and parent have the same beliefs about each retailer's performance, but they differ in the importance they place on the benefits the retailers offer. In general, customers can differ in their beliefs about retailers' performances as well as in their importance weights.

Evaluating Retailers   Research has shown that a customer's overall evaluation of an alternative (in this situation, three retailers) is related to the sum of the performance beliefs multiplied by the importance weights. Thus, we calculate the young, single woman's overall evaluation or score for the supercenter as follows:

$$
\begin{aligned}
4 \times 10 &= 40 \\
10 \times 3 &= 30 \\
5 \times 9 &= 45 \\
9 \times 4 &= \underline{36} \\
&\ 151
\end{aligned}
$$

Exhibit 4–3 shows the overall evaluations of the three retailers using the importance weights of the single woman and the parent. For the single woman, the Internet grocer has the highest score, 221, and thus has the most favorable evaluation. She would probably select this retailer for most of her grocery shopping. On the other hand, the supercenter has the highest score, 192, for the parent, who'd probably buy the family's weekly groceries there.

When customers are about to select a retailer, they don't actually go through the process of listing store characteristics, evaluating retailers' performances on these

EXHIBIT 4–3
Evaluation of Retailers

Characteristic	IMPORTANCE WEIGHTS*		PERFORMANCE BELIEFS		
	Young Single Woman	Parent with Four Children	Supercenter	Supermarket	Internet Grocer
Economy	4	10	10	8	6
Convenience	10	4	3	5	10
Assortment	5	8	9	7	5
Availability of product information	9	2	4	4	8
OVERALL EVALUATION					
Young single woman			151	153	221
Parent with four children			192	164	156

*10 = very important, 1 = very unimportant.

characteristics, determining each characteristic's importance, calculating each store's overall score, and then patronizing the retailer with the highest score. The multiattribute attitude model does not reflect customers' actual decision process, but it does predict their evaluation of alternatives and their choice. In addition, the model provides useful information for designing a retail offering. For example, if the supermarket could increase its performance rating on assortment from 7 to 10 (perhaps by adding a bakery and a wide selection of prepared meals), customers like the parent might shop at the supermarket more often than at the supercenter.

The application of the multiattribute attitude model in Exhibit 4–3 deals with a customer who is evaluating and selecting a retailer. The same model can also be used to describe how a customer evaluates and selects which channel to use (store, Internet, or catalog) or what merchandise to buy from a retailer. For example, the model could be used to describe Eva Mendoza's choice among the three suits she was considering.

Implications for Retailers   In this section, we describe how a retailer can use the multiattribute attitude model to encourage customers to shop at the retailer more frequently. First, the model indicates what information customers use to decide which retailer to patronize or which channel to use. Second, it suggests tactics that retailers can undertake to influence customers' store, channel, and merchandise choices.

To develop a program for attracting customers, retailers need to do market research to collect the following information:

1. Alternative retailers that customers consider.
2. Characteristics or benefits that customers consider when evaluating and choosing a retailer.
3. Customers' ratings of each retailer's performance on the characteristics.
4. The importance weights that customers attach to the characteristics.

Armed with this information, the retailer can use several approaches to influence customers to patronize its store or Internet site.

Getting into the Consideration Set   Retailers need to be included in the customer's **consideration set,** or the set of alternatives the customer evaluates when making a choice of a retailer to patronize. To be included in the consideration set, retailers develop programs to increase the likelihood that customers will remember them when they're about to go shopping. Retailers can increase customer awareness through communication and location decisions. For example, retailers can buy placement at the top of the screen when consumers are using a search engine term for products they sell. They can develop communication programs that link categories they sell with their name. Starbucks locates several stores in the same area so that customers are exposed more frequently to the store name as they drive through the area.

After ensuring that it is in consumers' consideration set, a retailer can use three methods to increase the chances that customers will select it for a visit:

1. Increase beliefs about the store's performance.
2. Change customers' importance weights.
3. Add a new benefit.

Changing Performance Beliefs   The first approach involves altering customers' beliefs about the retailer's performance by increasing the retailer's performance rating on a characteristic. For example, the supermarket in Exhibit 4–3 would want to increase its overall rating by improving its rating on all four benefits. The supermarket could improve its rating on economy by lowering prices and its assortment rating by stocking more gourmet and ethnic foods. Retailing View 4.2 illustrates how Lowe's altered the performance beliefs of women about its stores.

Because it can get costly for a retailer to improve its performance on all benefits, retailers must focus on improving their performance on those benefits that are important to customers in their target market. For example, Best Buy knows that an important benefit for its customers is not to be without their computers for lengthy amounts of time when repairs are needed. So it maintains a 240,000-square-foot "Geek Squad City" warehouse, with more than 1,200 employees, dedicated to reducing the time it takes to repair and return a computer. Geek Squad "agents" fix more than 4,000 laptops per day.[22]

Changing Importance Weights   Altering customers' importance weights is another approach to influencing store choice. A retailer wants to increase the importance customers place on benefits for which its performance is superior and decrease the importance of benefits for which it has inferior performance.

For example, if the supermarket in Exhibit 4–3 tried to attract families who shop at supercenters, it could increase the importance of convenience for them. Typically, changing importance weights is harder than changing performance beliefs because importance weights reflect customers' personal values.

Adding a New Benefit   Finally, retailers might try to add a new benefit to the set of benefits customers consider when selecting a retailer. Senda (www.sendaathletics.com) does not just offer the typical assortment of athletic

4.2   RETAILING VIEW   Do It Herself at Lowe's

You might think that home improvement centers are a retail recreation destination mostly for men. Men visit the stores on the weekends to check out the new tools and buy material for do-it-yourself (DIY) projects. But more than 50 percent of the sales at home improvement centers actually are made to women—who make decisions about what materials to use in home improvement projects and often do much of the work themselves.

Lowe's was early to recognize the importance of female customers—though it is not the only traditionally male-oriented retailer to do so. It redesigned its stores to be brighter, lose the warehouse look, and feature departments more appealing to women. With wider aisles, shoppers can avoid uncomfortable, unintended contact with items on shelves—otherwise known as "butt brush." The shelves also are a bit shorter, to make it easy to reach the easy-to-find products that are well marked by aisle markers and maps.

But these changes need to be restrained, to avoid causing male customers to reject the stores as overly feminine. Moreover, women express negative views of offerings that seem condescending in their "girlie" appeals. To balance its recent findings with its long-standing performance tactics, Lowe's offers workshops to teach women about tools, rather than carrying tools specifically designed for women. One section of its website, www.lowes.com/howto, provides online clinics

REFACT

Women make more than 85 percent of all consumer purchases and purchase 50 percent or more in categories typically considered male—banking and financial services, electronics, automobiles, PCs, and many other big-ticket items. Their purchases represent more than half of the U.S. GDP.[23]

Lowe's changed its store design to change women's beliefs about the pleasantness of its store environment.

and videos to help customers successfully implement their own DIY projects at home.

Sources: Tony Bingham and Pat Galagan, "Training at Lowe's: Let's Learn Something Together," *T + D*, November 2009, pp. 35–41; Amanda Junk, "Women Wield the Tools: Lowe's, Habitat for Humanity Teaches Them How," *McClatchy-Tribune Business News,* July 18, 2009; Cecile B. Corral, "Lowe's Outlines Expansion Plans," *Home Textiles Today*, October 5, 2009, p. 6; and Fara Warner, "Yes, Women Spend (And Saw and Sand)," *The New York Times*, February 29, 2004.

DISCUSSION QUESTION

Does feminizing a Lowe's make it less attractive to men?

gear; it sells unusual items such as customizable soccer balls and training vests. It believes that by providing a wider variety than its competition, its customers will find it more attractive. Other retailers attempt to add new benefits by emphasizing that their merchandise is **fair trade**—made by workers who are paid a fair wage, not just a minimum wage.[24] A fair wage means that workers are able to live relatively comfortably within the context of their local area. Offering fair trade merchandise is a benefit that is important to consumers who are concerned about the welfare of people in less developed countries.

Purchasing the Merchandise or Service

Customers don't always patronize a store or purchase a brand or item of merchandise with the highest overall evaluation. The product or service offering the greatest benefits (having the highest evaluation) may not be available from the retailer, or the customer may feel that its risks outweigh the potential benefits. Other consumers make purchase choices based on a single attribute, regardless of how well the offering performs on other characteristics. For example, Eva visited Macy's because the local store is convenient to her apartment, even though other department stores might have a wider selection of women's suits. One measure of retailers' success at converting positive evaluations to purchases is a reduction in the number of real or virtual abandoned carts in the retailer's store or website.

Retailers use various tactics to increase the chances that customers will convert their positive evaluations into purchases. First, they attempt to make it easy to purchase merchandise. More and more retailers are ensuring that their websites are mobile friendly. In their stores, they can reduce the actual wait time for buying merchandise by having more checkout lanes open and placing them conveniently in the store. In addition to reducing actual waiting time, they can reduce perceived wait times by installing digital displays to entertain customers waiting in line.[25] Many Internet retailers send reminder e-mails to visitors about items in carts they have abandoned.[26]

Second, retailers' ability to turn a positive purchase intention into a sale can also be increased by providing sufficient information that reinforces the customer's positive evaluation. For example, Eva's friend Britt, the salesperson, and another potential customer also provided Eva with positive feedback to support her purchase decision.

Third, retailers can increase the chances of making a sale by reducing the risk of making a purchase mistake. For instance, retailers can offer liberal return policies, money-back guarantees, and refunds if customers find the same merchandise available at lower prices from another retailer.

Finally, retailers often create a sense of urgency or scarcity to encourage customers to make a purchase decision. Zappos.com and Overstock.com alert customers if an item in their shopping carts is about to sell out. Flash-sale sites offer items for a specified time period; Neiman Marcus hosts two-hour online sales. The limited assortments offered by fast-fashion retailers like Zara and off-price retailers like TJX Corporation (TJ Maxx and Marshalls) have conditioned customers to buy it when they see it. Otherwise, it may be gone the next time they visit the store.

REFACT

A recent study found that one in five smartphone shoppers made a purchase via his or her smartphone in April 2012. A third of the purchases were for clothing or accessories.[27]

Postpurchase Evaluation

The buying process doesn't end when a customer purchases a product. After making a purchase, the customer uses the product and then evaluates the experience to determine whether it was satisfactory or unsatisfactory. **Satisfaction** is a postconsumption evaluation of how well a store or product meets or exceeds customer expectations. This **postpurchase evaluation** then becomes part of the customer's internal information and affects store and product evaluations and purchase decisions. Unsatisfactory experiences can motivate customers to complain to the retailer, patronize other stores, and select different brands in the future. Consistently high levels of satisfaction build store and brand loyalty, important sources of competitive advantage for retailers.[28]

To improve postpurchase assessments and satisfaction, retailers can take several steps. First, they must make sure to build realistic customer expectations, so they never let those shoppers down with their performance. Second, they should provide information about proper use and care of the items purchased. Third, as mentioned previously, guarantees and warranties reduce a negative feeling of risk, both before and after the purchase. Fourth, the best retailers make contact periodically with their customers to make sure they are satisfied, correct any problems, and remind customers of their availability. This last effort also can improve the chances that a customer puts the retailer in his or her consideration set for the next purchase occasion.

TYPES OF BUYING DECISIONS

LO2

Identify the different types of buying processes.

In some situations, customers like Eva Mendoza spend considerable time and effort selecting a retailer and evaluating alternative products—going through all the steps in the buying process described in the preceding section. In other situations, buying decisions are made automatically with little thought. This section examines three types of customer decision-making processes: extended problem solving, limited problem solving, and habitual decision making.

Extended Problem Solving

Extended problem solving is a purchase decision process in which customers devote considerable time and effort to analyze their alternatives. Customers typically engage in extended problem solving when the purchase decision involves a lot of risk and uncertainty. **Financial risks** arise when customers purchase an expensive product or service. **Physical risks** are important when customers feel that a product or service may affect their health or safety. **Social risks** arise when customers believe a product will affect how others view them. Lasik eye surgery, for instance, involves all three types of risks: It can be expensive, potentially damage the eyes, and change a person's appearance.

Consumers engage in extended problem solving when they are making a buying decision to satisfy an important need or when they have little knowledge about the product or service, as we described with car buyers in Retailing View 4.1. Due to the high risk in such situations, customers go beyond their internal knowledge to consult with friends, family members, or experts. They might also peruse online blogs; examine online reviews, both retailer-sponsored and independent review sites; and read *Consumer Reports*. They may also visit several retailers before making a purchase decision.

Retailers stimulate sales from customers engaged in extended problem solving by providing the necessary information in a readily available and easily understood manner and by offering money-back guarantees. For example, retailers that sell merchandise involving extended problem solving provide information on their websites describing the merchandise and its specifications, have informational displays in their stores (such as a sofa cut in half to show its construction), and use salespeople to demonstrate features and answer questions.

Limited Problem Solving

Limited problem solving is a purchase decision process involving a moderate amount of effort and time. Customers engage in this type of buying process when they have had some prior experience with the product or service and their risk is moderate. In such situations, customers tend to rely more on personal knowledge than on external information. They usually choose a retailer they have shopped at before and select merchandise they have bought in the past. The majority of customer purchase decisions involve limited problem solving.

Retailers attempt to reinforce this buying pattern and make it habitual when customers are buying merchandise from them. If customers are shopping elsewhere, however, retailers need to break this buying pattern by introducing new information or offering different merchandise or services. A common way to adjust the pattern is through coupons. Companies such as CVS and Walgreens often offer deep coupon discounts on commonly purchased products to get customers into their stores. Retailers are willing to give such steep discounts for two reasons. First, it breaks the established habit a customer may have of shopping elsewhere, and second, they know customers often buy many other, undiscounted items once they are in the store. After customers make these purchases, the retailers analyze their spending patterns and offer targeted coupons to encourage repatronage.[29]

Eva Mendoza's buying process illustrates both limited and extended problem solving. Her store choice decision was based on her knowledge of the merchandise in various stores she had shopped in and her search on Nubry.com. Considering this information, she felt the store choice decision was not very risky; thus, she engaged in limited problem solving when deciding to visit Macy's. But her buying process for the suit was extended. This decision was important to her; thus, she spent time acquiring information from a friend, the salesperson, and another shopper to evaluate and select a suit.

One common type of limited problem solving is **impulse buying,** or **unplanned purchasing,** which is a buying decision made by customers on the spot after seeing the merchandise.[30] Retailers encourage impulse-buying behavior by using prominent point-of-purchase (POP) or point-of-sale (POS) displays to attract customers' attention. Retailers have long recognized that the most valuable real estate in the store is at the point of purchase. An increasing number of non-food retailers (such as Old Navy, as mentioned previously) are looking to increase impulse buys from customers by offering candy, gum, mints, and other fun, hedonic items at their cash registers. Electronic shoppers are also stimulated to purchase impulsively when Internet retailers put special merchandise on their home pages and suggest complementary merchandise just before checkout.

Habitual Decision Making

Habitual decision making is a purchase decision process involving little or no conscious effort. Today's customers have many demands on their time. One way they cope with these time pressures is by simplifying their decision-making process. When a need arises, customers may automatically respond with, "I'll buy the same thing I bought last time from the same store." Typically, this habitual decision-making process occurs when decisions aren't very important to customers and involve familiar merchandise they have bought in the past. When customers are loyal to a brand or a store, they engage in habitual decision making.

Brand loyalty means that customers like and consistently buy a specific brand in a product category. They are reluctant to switch to other brands if their favorite brand isn't available. For example, loyal Coca-Cola drinkers won't buy Pepsi, no matter what. Thus, retailers can satisfy these customers' needs only if they offer the specific brands desired.

Brand loyalty creates both opportunities and problems for retailers.[31] Customers are attracted to stores that carry popular brands, but because retailers must carry these high-loyalty brands, they may not be able to negotiate favorable terms with the suppliers of the popular national brands. If, however, the high-loyalty brands are private-label brands (i.e., brands owned by the retailer), retailer loyalty is heightened.

Retailer loyalty means that customers like and habitually visit the same retailer to purchase a type of merchandise. All retailers would like to increase their customers' loyalty, and they can do so by selecting a convenient location (see Chapters 7 and 8), offering complete assortments of national and private-label brands (Chapter 13), reducing the number of stockouts (Chapter 13), rewarding customers for frequent purchases (Chapter 11), or providing good customer service (Chapter 18).

SOCIAL FACTORS INFLUENCING THE BUYING PROCESS

LO3

Summarize how the economy and social factors affect customer purchase decisions.

Exhibit 4–4 illustrates how customer buying decisions are influenced by four influential social factors: the economy, family, reference groups, and culture.

The Economy

The state of the national and global economy has significant effects on the way people buy. In terms of the most recent global recession, the effects have lingered because consumers continue to feel a sense of uncertainty and risk.[32] At the same time, many shoppers have discovered that shopping for bargains is fun. Even if their incomes have stabilized, they see little reason to switch back to name brands when the private-label offerings they have been buying work just fine.[33]

The outcomes in terms of consumers' buying processes have been both expected and unexpected. Predictably, people have reduced their spending on luxury brands, leading retailers to revamp their offerings. For example, Neiman Marcus broadened its jewelry lines to include more funky, less expensive designs and fewer precious metals.[34] In addition, consumers make fewer shopping trips and appreciate the convenience of one-stop shopping (which also lowers gasoline expenditures) at hypermarkets or supercenters.

More surprising are the trends that suggest some buyers actually are spending a little more on higher-quality products in an effort to gain more value and make purchases last. When they do spend more lavishly, consumers tend to feel guilty. Thus, the Ritz-Carlton began avoiding its "silver tray" image in its advertising and instead encouraged visitors to consider their hotel stay a time to reconnect with family. Consumers want to splurge a little when they can; retailers have to find ways to enable them to do so without guilt.[35]

Family

Many purchase decisions involve products that the entire family will consume or use. The previous discussion of the buying process focused on how one person makes a decision. When families make purchase decisions, they often consider the needs of all family members.[36]

EXHIBIT 4–4
Social Factors
Affecting Buying
Decisions

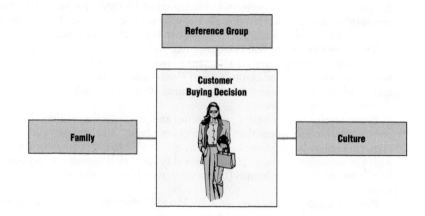

When choosing a vacation site, for example, all family members may participate in the decision making. In other situations, one member of the family may assume the decision-making role. For example, the husband might buy the groceries, which the wife then uses to prepare their child's lunch, which the child consumes in school. In this situation, the store choice decision might be made by the husband, but the brand choice decision might be made by the wife, though it likely is greatly influenced by the child.

Children play an important role in family buying decisions. Resort hotels now realize they must satisfy children's needs as well as those of adults. The Hyatt hotel chain thus cooperates with a mail-order baby supply company, Babies Travel Lite. After parents book a room, they can order all the diapers, formula, and organic baby food they will need for the trip. The items will be ready for them when they check in, which reduces the amount of baggage and increases convenience. For older children, Hyatt offers toys, available to be checked out from the front desk. In addition, working with the famous chef Alice Waters, it has revamped the children's menus in its hotel restaurants to offer nutritious, but also fun meal options.[37]

Retailers also can attract consumers who shop with other family members by satisfying the needs of all those family members. For example, Anthropologie has enlarged its dressing rooms so families (and friends) can provide advice and try on clothes together. Macy's has added comfortable seating and televisions outside dressing rooms to keep other family members entertained.[38]

Reference Groups

A **reference group** includes one or more people whom a person uses as a basis of comparison for beliefs, feelings, and behaviors. A consumer might have a number of different reference groups, such as family, friends, celebrities, and opinion leaders. These reference groups affect buying decisions by (1) offering information, (2) providing rewards for specific purchasing behaviors, and (3) enhancing a consumer's self-image.

Reference groups provide information to consumers directly through conversation, either face-to-face or electronically, or indirectly through observation. For example, Eva received valuable information from her friend about the suits she was considering. On other occasions, Eva might look to women like soccer player Hope Solo and tennis player Caroline Wozniacki to guide her selection of athletic apparel or Demi Lovato and Katy

Shoppers look to celebrities like Katy Perry for fashion tips.

Perry for casual fashion advice. The role of reference groups in creating fashion is discussed in the appendix to this chapter.

By identifying and affiliating with reference groups, consumers create, enhance, and maintain their self-image. Customers who want to be seen as members of an elite social class may shop at prestige retailers, whereas others who want to create the image of an outdoor enthusiast might buy merchandise from the L.L. Bean website.

Retailers are particularly interested in identifying and reaching out to those in a reference group who act as store advocates and actively influence others in the group. **Store advocates** are customers who like a store so much that they actively share their positive experiences with friends and family. Retailing View 4.3 details how social media sites such as Pinterest and Facebook make sharing ideas, reviews, and "likes" even easier. Consumers see so much advertising that they have become suspicious of the claims being made. Thus, they are relying more on their own social networks for information about stores to patronize and merchandise to buy.

Culture

Culture is the meaning, beliefs, morals, and values shared by most members of a society. As the basis of the social factors that influence people's buying decisions, the culture or cultures in which each consumer participates often align with his or her reference groups. For example, Eva's cultural groups include her Latino heritage and the Pacific Northwest culture in which she lives. These cultural influences affect her consumer behavior. Because the culture at Eva's college is rather

---

4.3 RETAILING VIEW   Pinning Consumption Choices on Online Reference Groups

With a simple logo—a thumb pointing up and the word "Like"—Facebook revamped the way people share recommendations and interests. Users can show their approval of other users' posts and pictures. But they also can click the nearly ubiquitous Like button on retailers' sites to show their Facebook friends which retailer, merchandise item, or service they consider worthy of their approval.

The "Like" generation relies heavily on such social media recommendations. A recent study indicated that 62 percent of social media users read their friends' "social sharing" about items to purchase. Of these, 75 percent click on the link. And of the people who click, 53 percent of them actually buy the shared product. Of course, after they buy, they also share their purchase with their social network, starting the virtuous cycle (for retailers) all over again.

But purchasing is not the only promising outcome of social sharing. On Pinterest, a sort of online scrapbook for users' interests, the predominantly female (68 percent) members create pin boards that reflect their interests in their favorite retailers and the merchandise they carry. Then they post pictures to reflect those interests, which others can check to find their own inspiration. Retailers are using pin boards to enhance brand awareness among

consumers who might buy later. American Eagle Outfitters (http://pinterest.com/americaneagle/) has 51 pin boards with 2,020 pins, listing images such as "Fall Shoes from AE" or "Best Gifts to Give." Saks Fifth Avenue has 52 pin boards focusing on topics like decorative fabrics, printed pants, and saturated lip colors.[40]

The increasing popularity of Pinterest seems to reflect the old adage that a picture is worth a thousand words. It also represents a new trend: Everyone is a voyeur. That is, consumers today feel as if they must know what their reference groups are doing, wearing, or buying. Retailers embrace the notion. When a retailer gets Liked or Pinned, the virtuous cycle of social sharing is likely to enhance its sales, profits, and chances of success.

Sources: Andy Kessler, "The Button That Made Facebook Billions," *The Wall Street Journal*, February 2, 2012; Social Labs, "Social Impact Study 2012 Infographic on Social Sharing," March 20, 2012; Tanzina Vega, "Marketers Find a Friend in Pinterest," *The New York Times*, April 17, 2012; and Sarah E. Needleman and Pui-Wing Tam, "Pinterest's Rite of Web Passage—Huge Traffic, No Revenues," *The Wall Street Journal*, February 16, 2012.

DISCUSSION QUESTION

Do you like the "like" button? If yes, why? If no, why not?

fashion conscious, she was immediately aware that her old suit was out of date and considered buying fashionable shoes a reasonable addition.

Many retailers and shopping center managers have recognized the importance of appealing to different cultures and subcultures.[41] For instance, the U.S. Hispanic population is growing faster than any other market segment, and Hispanics' purchasing power is rising faster than that of the general population. Many retailers, particularly supermarkets in areas with large Hispanic populations, have dedicated significant space to products that are indigenous to particular Spanish-speaking countries. The product mix will, however, differ depending on the region of the country. Merchandise should reflect that, for instance, Miami has a large Cuban and Latin American population, whereas Los Angeles and Texas have more people from Mexico. Bilingual employees are a critical success factor for stores catering to the Hispanic population. Some retailers with a long history of serving Hispanic

Many retailers and shopping center managers have adjusted their strategies to appeal to different cultures and subcultures.

customers even found that they needed to start adding more English to their products and marketing materials to better target their customers' children. Thus, Pizza Patrón, a Dallas-based pizza chain, has begun shifting its menu boards from purely Spanish to a combination of Spanish and English, and Curacao, a big box store in California serving Hispanics, has shifted from Spanish-only speaking employees and advertising to a similar mixed format.[42]

MARKET SEGMENTATION

LO4

Determine why and how retailers group customers into market segments.

The preceding discussion focused on (1) how individual customers evaluate and select stores, channels, and merchandise and (2) the factors affecting their decision making. To be cost-effective, retailers identify groups of these customers (market segments) and target their offerings to meet the needs of typical customers in a segment rather than the needs of a specific customer. At one time, Walmart used a "one-size-fits-all" strategy. The merchandise selection was very similar across the United States, without much regard to geographic or demographic variations. This approach worked well when most of its stores were located in rural areas in the Southeast. But as it opened stores in more diverse locations, it realized it had to develop different retail mixes for different market segments. For example, in urban locations, it has begun opening smaller Walmart Express and Market stores, in already-built storefronts, which feature more grocery items and a small selection of lawn furniture.[43]

A **retail market segment** is a group of customers who are attracted to the same retail mix because they have similar needs. For example, young, hip 20-somethings have different needs than executives on business trips. Thus, Marriott offers hotel chains with different retail mixes for each of these segments—AC Hotels by

Marriott for the young and hip and Marriott Hotels and Conference Centers for business executives and conferences.

The Internet enables retailers to target individual customers efficiently and market products to them on a one-to-one basis. This one-to-one marketing concept is discussed in Chapter 11 as it pertains to customer relationship management.

Criteria for Evaluating Market Segments

Customers can be grouped into segments in many different ways. Exhibit 4–5 shows some different methods of segmenting retail markets. There's no simple way to determine which method is best, though four criteria useful for evaluating whether a retail segment is a viable target market are as follows: actionable, identifiable, substantial, and reachable.

Actionable   The fundamental criteria for evaluating a retail market segment are that (1) customers in the segment must have similar needs, seek similar benefits, and be satisfied by a similar retail offering and (2) those customers' needs must differ from the needs of customers in other segments. **Actionable** means that the retailer should know what to do to satisfy needs for the consumers in the

EXHIBIT 4–5
Methods for Segmenting Retail Markets

Segmentation Descriptor	Example of Categories
GEOGRAPHIC	
Region	Pacific, Mountain, Central, South, Mid-Atlantic, Northeast
Population density	Rural, suburban, urban
Climate	Cold, warm
DEMOGRAPHIC	
Age	Under 6, 6–12, 13–19, 20–29, 30–49, 50–65, over 65
Gender	Male, female
Family life cycle	Single, married with no children, married with youngest child under 6, married with youngest child over 6, married with children no longer living at home, widowed
Family income	Under $19,999; $20,000–29,999; $30,000–49,999; $50,000–$74,999; over $75,000
Occupation	Professional, clerical, sales, craftsperson, retired, student, homemaker
Education	Some high school, high school graduate, some college, college graduate, graduate degree
Religion	Catholic, Protestant, Jewish, Muslim
Race	Caucasian, African-American, Hispanic, Asian
Nationality	American, Japanese, British, French, German, Italian, Chinese
PSYCHOSOCIAL	
Social class	Lower, middle, upper
Lifestyle	Striver, driver, devoted, intimate, altruist, fun seeker, creative
Personality	Aggressive, shy, emotional
FEELINGS AND BEHAVIORS	
Attitudes	Positive, neutral, negative
Benefit sought	Convenience, economy, prestige
Stage in decision process	Unaware, aware, informed, interested, intend to buy, bought previously
Perceived risk	High, medium, low
Innovativeness	Innovator, early adopter, early majority, late majority, laggard
Loyalty	None, some, completely
Usage rate	None, light, medium, heavy
Usage situation	Home, work, vacation, leisure
User status	Nonuser, ex-user, potential user, current user

segment. According to this criterion, it makes sense for Banana Republic to segment the apparel market on the basis of the demographic characteristic of physical size. Customers who wear petite sizes have different needs than those who wear regular or large sizes, so they are attracted to a store offering a unique merchandise mix. In the context of the multiattribute attitude model discussed previously, people who wear small sizes place more importance on fit and customer service because it is generally more difficult for them to get the appropriate fit and because they need knowledgeable sales associates who know and can cater to their specific needs.

In contrast, it wouldn't make sense for a supermarket to segment its market on the basis of customer size. Large and small men and women probably have the same needs, seek the same benefits, and go through the same buying process for groceries. This segmentation approach wouldn't be actionable for a supermarket retailer because the retailer couldn't develop unique mixes for large and small customers. However, a segmentation scheme based on geography or demographics such as household income and ethnicity would be actionable.

Identifiable   **Identifiable** means that the retailer is able to determine which customers are in the market segment. When customers are identifiable, the retailer can determine (1) the segment's size and (2) the consumers to whom the retailer needs to target its communications and promotions. For example, supermarket retailers use customer demographics to identify where they should put their stores and the merchandise that they should carry. More prepared and gourmet foods, fancy produce, and expensive cuts of meat would go into stores in neighborhoods with higher average incomes. Snack foods likely predominate in stores located near a college campus. It is equally important to ensure that the segments are distinct from one another because too much overlap between segments means that distinct marketing strategies aren't needed. If, for example, a regional grocery store chain had stores located in neighborhoods containing people with similar demographics, there would be no need to vary its merchandise selection.

Substantial   If a market is too small or its buying power insignificant (i.e., not **substantial**), it cannot generate sufficient profits to support the retailing mix activities. For example, the market for pet pharmaceuticals is probably not large enough in one local area to serve as a target market segment, but a national market could be served through the Internet channel.

Reachable   **Reachable** means that the retailer can target promotions and other elements of the retail mix to consumers in the segment. For example, AutoZone targets men who repair their automobiles themselves. Potential customers in this segment are reachable because they read car magazines, watch NASCAR on TV, and have distinct television viewing habits.

Approaches for Segmenting Markets

Exhibit 4–5 illustrates the wide variety of approaches for segmenting retail markets. No one approach is best for all retailers. Instead, they must explore various factors that affect customer buying behavior and determine which factors are most important for them.

Geographic Segmentation   **Geographic segmentation** groups customers according to where they live. A retail market can be segmented by countries (Japan, Mexico) or by areas within a country, such as states, cities, and neighborhoods.[44] Because customers typically shop at stores convenient to where they live and work, individual retail outlets usually focus on the customer segment reasonably close to the outlet.

4.4 RETAILING VIEW Where Gender Matters—and Where It Doesn't

In the past, the demographic patterns seemed clear: Women bought personal care products, fragrances, women's clothing, and groceries. Men bought stereo equipment, video games, tires, and men's clothing—if they had to. But in modern-day retail environments, virtually all of these easy classifications are being challenged by shoppers who have little time to waste with gender stereotypes. And retailers are quickly catching on.

For example, when Urban Outfitters was redesigning its website, it stumbled on what the web designers thought was a brilliant and simple change. They would personalize the site so that female visitors immediately were directed to dresses and blouses, while male visitors saw work shirts and tough-guy jeans. The response was quick—and negative. Female visitors complained that they were the ones buying most of the clothing for the men in their lives. And on top of that, they found the gender-biased marketing offensive.

At the same time, more and more men are in the market for grooming and personal care products. The suggested reasons are many. Maybe the modern generation simply is more accustomed to shopping for themselves. Or perhaps job seekers in a tight economy need any edge they can get, and feeling confident about their personal grooming as they head to interviews might tip the scales in their favor. But regardless of the reason, the conventional wisdom that personal care and fragrance sellers could market just to women has gone out the window.

Overall, it appears that men and women actually have approximately equal influences on households' spending. In a recent survey, 85 percent of women and 84 percent of men agreed that they shared responsibility for shopping decisions.

Such equality of influence is not to say that women and men shop the same way, though. As men take on more grocery shopping tasks—a role traditionally assigned to women—some grocery retailers are experimenting with ways to appeal to them. For example, men appear to hate to ask for help, so the stores need to be efficient and clearly laid out with good signage, rather than providing an abundance of customer service.

Best Buy similarly recognized that women are a massive market for electronics, smartphones, and mobile devices. But its stores tended to attract very few female shoppers. Therefore, its recent store design revisions aim to appeal to women with household appliance sections that look more like kitchens than like industrial shipyards and hand sanitizer dispensers placed next to the video game test consoles.

Digital Anatomy of the Affluent Male

There are 19 million affluent males on the Internet and they are shopping online and spending more than ever before. Forty percent of them are shopping online 2x a week or more and spending over $30K annually.

Who is the affluent male? How connected is he to his devices?

Source: www.iprospect.com/digital-affluent-male

Sources: Natasha Singer, "E-Tailer Customization: Convenient or Creepy?" *The New York Times*, June 23, 2012; "Who Makes the Call at the Mall, Men or Women?" *The Wall Street Journal*, April 23, 2011; Tom Ryan, "'His' and 'Her' Grocery Aisles," *Retail Wire*, June 6, 2011; Susan Reda, "Guess What? Men Shop, Too!" *Stores*, April 2010; and Miguel Bustillo and Mary Ellen Lloyd, "Best Buy Tests New Appeals to Women," *The Wall Street Journal*, June 16, 2010.

DISCUSSION QUESTION

How are your shopping habits different from someone you are close to of the opposite sex?

REFACT

19 million "affluent males" shop on the Internet. They tend to be over 35 years old and make between $100,000 and $300,000 a year. They generally search for travel, apparel, automotive, and sports. Their favorite brands are Rolex, Louis Vuitton, BMW, Lexus, and Mercedes-Benz.[45]

Segments based on geography can be identifiable, substantial, and reachable. It's easy to determine who lives in a geographic segment, such as the Paris metropolitan area, and then determine how many potential customers are in that area. It is also relatively simple to target communications and locate retail outlets for customers in Paris and then determine if customers are being responsive to those communications. However, when customers in different geographic segments have similar needs, it is inefficient to develop unique retail offerings by geographic markets. For example, a fast-food customer in Detroit probably seeks the same benefits as a fast-food customer in Los Angeles. Thus, it wouldn't be useful to segment the U.S. fast-food market geographically.

Demographic Segmentation   **Demographic segmentation** groups consumers on the basis of easily measured, objective characteristics such as age, gender, income, and education. Demographic variables are the most common means of defining segments, because consumers in these segments can be easily identified, their size can be determined, and the degree to which they can be reached by and are responsive to media can be easily assessed.

However, demographics may not be useful for defining segments for some retailers because the motivations for purchasing transcend simple demographics. For example, demographics are poor predictors of users of activewear, such as jogging suits and running shoes. At one time, retailers assumed that activewear would be purchased exclusively by young athletic people, but the health and fitness trend has led people of all ages to buy this merchandise. Relatively inactive consumers also find activewear to be comfortable. Several other long-held assumptions about who buys what also are being challenged in today's retail environment, as Retailing View 4.4 describes.

Geodemographic Segmentation   **Geodemographic segmentation** uses both geographic and demographic characteristics to classify consumers. This segmentation scheme is based on the principle that "birds of a feather flock together." Consumers in the same neighborhoods tend to buy the same types of cars, appliances, and apparel and shop at the same types of retailers.[46]

One widely used tool for geodemographic market segmentation is the Tapestry Segmentation system developed and marketed by Esri.[47] Tapestry Segmentation classifies all U.S. residential neighborhoods into 65 distinctive segments based on socioeconomic and demographic characteristics.[48] The information in Exhibit 4–6 describes three Tapestry segments. These neighborhoods, with their similar demographics and buying behaviors, can be any place in the United States.

Geodemographic segmentation is particularly appealing for managing the store channel because customers typically patronize stores close to their neighborhoods. Thus, retailers can use geodemographic segmentation to select locations for their stores and tailor the assortment in the stores to the preferences of the local community. In Chapter 8, we illustrate how geodemographic segmentation is used to make store location decisions.

Lifestyle Segmentation   Of the various methods of segmenting, lifestyle is the one that delves the most into how consumers describe themselves. **Lifestyle, or psychographics,** refers to how people live, how they spend their time and money, what activities they pursue, and their attitudes and opinions about the world in which they live. For example, a person may have a strong need for conservation. This need then motivates the person to buy products compatible with that lifestyle. Shoppers at the Austin, Texas–based, environmentally sustainable, zero-waste grocery chain in.gredients bring their own containers and purchase the organic food products they need from bulk bins.[49]

EXHIBIT 4–6
Examples of Tapestry

	Segment 01 - Top Rung	Segment 18 - Cozy and Comfortable	Segment 52 - Inner City Tenants
LifeMode Summary Group	L1 *High Society*	L2 *Upscale Avenues*	L8 *Global Roots*
Urbanization Summary Group	U3 *Metro Cities I*	U8 *Suburban Periphery II*	U4 *Metro Cities II*
Household Type	Married-Couple Families	Married-Couple Families	Mixed
Median Age	44.6	41.7	28.8
Income	High	Upper Middle	Lower Middle
Employment	Prof/Mgmt	Prof/Mgmt	Srvc/Prof/Mgmt/Skilled
Education	Bach/Grad Degree	Some College	No HS Diploma; HS; Some Coll
Residential	Single Family	Single Family	Multiunit Rentals
Race/Ethnicity	White	White	White; Black; Hispanic
Activity	Participate in public/civic activities	Dine out often at family restaurants	Play football, basketball
Financial	Own stock worth $75,000+	Have personal line of credit	Have personal education loan
Activity	Vacation overseas	Shop at Kohl's	Go dancing
Media	Listen to classical, all-news radio	Listen to sporting events on radio	Read music, baby, fashion magazines
Vehicle	Own/Lease luxury car	Own/Lease minivan	Own/Lease Honda

SOURCE: Esri, "Tapestry Segmentation: The Fabric of America's Neighborhoods."

Lifestyle segments can be identified through consumer surveys that ask respondents to indicate whether they agree or disagree with statements such as, "My idea of fun in a national park would be to stay in an expensive lodge and dress up for dinner," "I often crave excitement," or "I could not stand to skin a dead animal." Retailers today are placing more emphasis on lifestyles than on demographics to define a target segment.

One of the most widely used tools for **lifestyle segmentation** is **VALS**, by Strategic Business Insights. On the basis of responses to the VALS survey (www.strategicbusinessinsights.com/vals/presurvey.shtml), consumers are classified into the eight segments shown in Exhibit 4–7. On the horizontal dimension, the segments reflect people's primary motivation for buying, which stem from their self-image. There are three primary motivations of U.S. consumers: ideals, achievement, and self-expression. People who are primarily motivated by ideals are guided by knowledge and principles. Those who are motivated by achievement look for products and services that demonstrate success to their peers. Consumers who are primarily motivated by self-expression desire social or physical activity, variety, and risk. On the vertical dimension, the descriptions refer instead to consumers' resources, including their income, education, health, and energy level, as well as their degree of innovativeness. The segments on top have more resources and are more innovative; those on the bottom have fewer resources and are less innovative. The demographics of each group are provided in the figure.

EXHIBIT 4–7
VALS American
Lifestyle

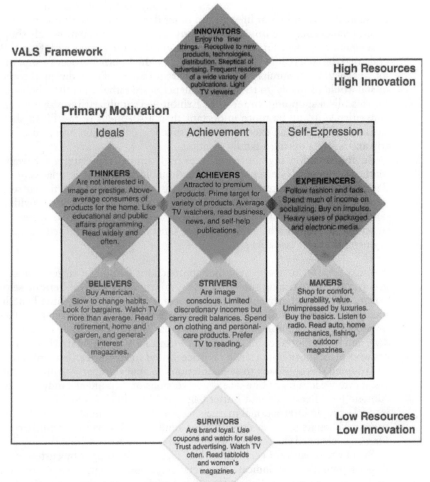

SOURCE: Strategic Business Insights (SBI) (www.strategicbusinessinsights.com/).

Firms are finding that lifestyles are often more useful for predicting consumer behavior than are demographics. In particular, VALS enables firms to identify target segments and their underlying motivations. It also reveals correlations between psychology and lifestyle choices. People who share demographics actually tend to have varying psychological traits. Two shoppers with similar demographic appearances still might have different levels of risk-taking propensity, social consciousness, or preferred benefits. College students and day laborers might earn similar incomes, but they spend that income quite differently because of their very different values and lifestyles.

There are limitations to using lifestyle segmentation, however. Lifestyles are not as objective as demographics, and it is harder to identify potential customers. With demographics, a firm like Nike can easily identify its customers as men or women and direct its marketing strategies to each group differently. For these reasons, lifestyle segmentation is often used in conjunction with other segmentation methods. In addition, psychographics are more expensive as a means to identify potential customers. To identify VALS segments, companies use the VALS questionnaire in surveys or focus groups. Then VALS provides segment description linkages with consumer product and media data, communication styles, and zip code location.

Buying Situation Segmentation The buying behavior of customers with the same demographics or lifestyle can differ depending on their buying situation. Thus, retailers may use **buying situations,** such as fill-in versus weekly shopping, to segment a market. For example, in Exhibit 4–3, the parent with four children evaluated the supercenter more positively than the Internet grocer or supermarket for weekly grocery purchases. But if the parent ran out of milk during the week, he or she would probably go to the convenience store rather than the wholesale club for this fill-in shopping. In terms of Exhibit 4–3's multiattribute attitude model, convenience would be more important than assortment in the fill-in shopping situation. Similarly, an executive might stay at a convention hotel on a business trip and a resort during a family vacation.

Buying situation segmentation rates high among the criteria for evaluating market segments. The segments are actionable because it is relatively easy to determine what a marketer should do to satisfy the needs of a particular segment. They are identifiable and accessible because retailers or service providers can determine who the customers are on the basis of who has purchased the product or service and under what circumstances. Once they have identified the customer segment, they can assess its size.

Benefit Segmentation Another approach for defining a target segment is to group customers seeking similar benefits; this method is called **benefit segmentation.** In the multiattribute attitude model, customers in the same benefit segment would have a similar set of importance weights for the attributes of a store or product. For example, customers who place high importance on fashion and style and low importance on price might form a fashion segment, whereas customers who place more importance on price would form a price segment. Hershey's has adopted this approach to segmentation: To appeal to hand-to-mouth munchers, it offers packages of bite-size candy versions of its popular candy bars, such as Almond Joys, Reese's Peanut Butter Cups, and Hershey's Chocolate. It also tailors its packaging in international markets to offer the key benefits demanded by consumers. When its research showed that Chinese consumers prefer gold over silver, Hershey's changed the foil that wraps its Kisses candies in China.[50]

Benefit segments are very actionable. The benefits sought by customers in the target segment clearly indicate how retailers should design their offerings to appeal to those customers. But customers in benefit segments aren't easily identified or accessed; it's hard to look at a person and determine what benefits he or she is seeking. Typically, the audience for the media used by retailers is described by demographics rather than by the benefits they seek.

Composite Segmentation Approaches

No segmentation approach meets all the criteria. For example, segmenting by demographics and geography is ideal for identifying and accessing customers, but these characteristics often are unrelated to customers' needs. Thus, these approaches may not indicate the actions necessary to attract customers in these segments. In contrast, knowing what benefits customers are seeking is useful for designing an effective retail offering; the problem is identifying which customers are seeking these benefits. For these reasons, **composite segmentation** uses multiple variables to identify customers in the target segment according to their benefits sought, lifestyles, and demographics.

CVS uses what it calls the "CVS personalities" to target three composite segments. Each of these segments, referred to by a first name, is used to develop a retail strategy for the market segment.[51] **"Caroline,"** is a segment composed of 18- to 24-year-old single or new moms who have a lower income but have the highest number of items purchased per trip. **"Vanessa"** targets a segment of 35- to 54-year-old women with children, at the peak of their income and generating the highest spending, frequency of purchases, and overall basket size. Finally, "Sophie" is a 55-plus empty nester woman with a median income and a health focus. These segments are useful in developing positioning messages that can be used in their ads, flyers, and displays. This information is also useful for manufacturers who sell their products through CVS. For example, for "Caroline," Dove could be positioned as a convenient reenergizer. For "Vanessa," it could be positioned as an escape. Finally, for "Sophie," it could be touted as beneficial to health.

SUMMARY

LO1 **Describe the process that consumers go through when making retail patronage and buying decisions.**

Consumers go through several stages when making a purchase decision: need recognition, information search, evaluation of alternatives, choice of alternatives, purchase, and postpurchase evaluation. It is important for retailers to understand how they can nudge their customers closer to a buying decision at each step of their buying process

LO2 **Identify the different types of buying processes.**

The importance of the stages depends on the nature of the customer's decision. When decisions are important and risky, the buying process is longer because customers spend more time and effort on the information search and evaluation of alternatives. When buying decisions are less important to customers, they spend little time in the buying process, and their buying behavior may become habitual.

LO3 **Summarize how the economy and social factors affect customer purchase decisions.**

The buying process of consumers is influenced by their personal beliefs, attitudes, and values, as well as by their social environment. The primary social influences are provided by the economy, consumers' families, their reference groups, and culture.

LO4 **Determine why and how retailers group customers into market segments.**

To develop cost-effective retail programs, retailers group customers into segments. Some approaches for segmenting markets are based on geography, demographics, geodemographics, lifestyle, usage situations, and benefits sought. Because each approach has its advantages and disadvantages, retailers typically define their target segment by several characteristics.

KEY TERMS

actionable, 108
benefit segmentation, 114
brand loyalty, 103
buying process, 91
buying situation, 114
compatibility, 119
complexity, 119
composite segmentation, 114
consideration set, 99
conversion rate, 94
cross-shopping, 93
culture, 106
demographic segmentation, 111
everyday low pricing (EDLP) strategy, 96
extended problem solving, 102
external sources, 94
fair trade, 101
fashion, 117

fashion leader, 118
financial risks, 102
geodemographic segmentation, 111
geographic segmentation, 109
habitual decision making, 103
hedonic needs, 92
identifiable, 109
impulse buying, 103
information search, 94
innovator, 118
internal sources, 94
knockoff, 118
lifestyle, 111
lifestyle segmentation, 112
limited problem solving, 102
mass-market theory, 119
multiattribute attitude model, 97
observability, 119
physical risks, 102

postpurchase evaluation, 101
psychographics, 111
reachable, 109
reference group, 105
retailer loyalty, 103
retail market segment, 107
satisfaction, 101
social risks, 102
store advocate, 106
subculture theory, 119
substantial, 109
trend setter, 118
trialability, 119
trickle-down theory, 118
unplanned purchasing, 103
unsatisfied need, 92
utilitarian needs, 92
VALS, 112

116   SECTION I   The World of Retailing

GET OUT AND DO IT!

1. **CONTINUING CASE ASSIGNMENT: GO SHOPPING** Visit the retail store operated by the target firm for your continuing assignment. Determine all the things that the store does to try to stimulate customers to buy merchandise at each stage of the buying process. In which types of buying decisions are most customers involved? Based on your observations and what you know about the target firm, what type(s) of market segmentation strategies are they involved in? Do you believe these are the best strategies for this firm?

2. **GO SHOPPING** Go to a supermarket, and watch people selecting products to put in their shopping carts. How much time do they spend selecting products? Do some people spend more time than others? Why is this the case? Does consumer behavior vary in the store perimeter versus in the aisles? Explain your observations.

3. **OLC EXERCISE** Go to the student side of the book's website to develop a multiattribute attitude model describing your evaluation of and decision about some relatively expensive product you bought recently, such as a car or a consumer electronics product. Open the multiattribute model exercise. List the attributes you considered in the left-hand column. List the alternatives you considered in the top row. Fill in the importance weights for each attribute in the second column (10 = very important, 1 = very unimportant); then fill in your evaluation of each product on each attribute (10 = excellent performance, 1 = poor performance). Based on your importance weights and performance beliefs, the evaluation of each product appears in the bottom row. Did you buy the product with the highest evaluation?

4. **INTERNET EXERCISE** To better understand the segmentation classification of consumers, Strategic Business Insights has developed the VALS tool, which uses psychology to segment people according to their distinct personality traits. Go to the firm's home page at www.strategicbusinessinsights.com/vals/presurvey. shtml, and take the survey to identify your VALS profile according to your values, attitudes, and lifestyle. According to the results, what is your VALS profile type? Do you agree with your consumer profile? Why or why not? How can retailers effectively use the results of this survey when planning and implementing their business strategies?

5. **INTERNET EXERCISE** Retailers want to segment the market on the basis of the geographic classification of customers to select the best sites for their businesses. Go to the Esri Business Information Solutions home page at www.esri.com/data/esri_data/ tapestry, type in the zip code for your hometown or your campus, and read the results. How would a retailer, such as a local restaurant, use the information in this report when making a decision about whether to open a location in this zip code?

6. **INTERNET EXERCISE** Go to the following Internet sites offering information about the latest fashions: *New York Magazine's* The Cut at http://nymag. com/thecut/, *New York Times'* Fashion & Style at www.nytimes.com/pages/fashion/index.html, and the U.K. *Telegraph* at fashion.telegraph.co.uk, Write a brief report describing the latest apparel fashions that are being shown by designers. Which of these fashion trends do you think will be popular with college students? Why?

DISCUSSION QUESTIONS AND PROBLEMS

1. Does the customer buying process end when a customer buys some merchandise? Explain your answer.

2. Describe how service retailers, such as hotels, provide information to potential customers to answer questions about rates, services offered, and other amenities.

3. Considering the steps in the consumer buying process (Exhibit 4–1), describe how you (and your family) used this process to select your college or university. How many schools did you consider? How much time did you invest in this purchase decision? When you were deciding on which college to attend, what objective and subjective criteria did you use in the alternative evaluation portion of the consumer buying process?

4. In Exhibit 4–6, The Inner City Tenant is described. How should banks, restaurants, drugstores, and car dealers alter their retail mixes to meet the needs of this segment compared to the Top Rung segment?

5. Any retailer's goal is to get customers in its store so that they can find the merchandise that they are looking for and make a purchase at this location. How could a sporting goods retailer ensure that the customer buys athletic equipment at its outlet?

6. A family-owned used-book store across the street from a major university campus wants to identify the various segments in its market. What approaches might the store owner use to segment this market? List two potential target market segments based on this segmentation approach. Then contrast the retail mix that would be most appropriate for the two potential target segments.

7. How does the buying decision process differ when consumers are shopping on the Internet or mobile device compared with shopping in a store in terms of locations or sites visited, time spent, and brands examined?

8. Using the multiattribute attitude model, identify the probable choice of a local car dealer for a young, single woman and for a retired couple with limited income (see the accompanying table). What can the national retail chain do to increase the chances of the retired couple patronizing its dealership? You can use the multiattribute model template on the student side of the book's website to analyze this information.

	IMPORTANCE WEIGHTS		PERFORMANCE BELIEFS		
Performance Attributes	Young, Single Woman	Retired Couple	Local Gas Station	National Service Chain	Local Car Dealer
Price	2	10	9	10	3
Time to complete repair	8	5	5	9	7
Reliability	2	9	2	7	10
Convenience	8	3	3	6	5

9. Think of a recent purchase that you made, and describe how economic and social environmental factors (e.g., reference group, family, and culture) influenced your buying decision. How are retailers using social media to affect your buying decisions?

10. Think about the merchandise sold at Office Depot, Staples, and Office Max, and list three to four types of merchandise that fall into extended problem solving, limited problem solving, and habitual decision making for college students. Explain how the categories of merchandise would change for each type of buying decision if the customer was the owner of a medium-size business.

SUGGESTED READINGS

Arnold, Mark J., and Kristy E. Reynolds. "Approach and Avoidance Motivation: Investigating Hedonic Consumption in a Retail Setting." *Journal of Retailing* 88, no. 3 (September 2012), pp. 399–411.

Dahl, Darren W., Jennifer J. Argo, and Andrea C. Morales. "Social Information in the Retail Environment: The Importance of Consumption Alignment, Referent Identity, and Self-Esteem." *Journal of Consumer Research*, February 2012, pp. 860–71.

Gauri, Kulkarni, Brian Ratchford, and P. K. Kannan. "The Impact of Online and Offline Information Sources on Automobile Choice Behavior." *Journal of Interactive Marketing* 26, no. 3 (2012), pp. 167–75.

Hawkins, Delbert, David L. Mothersbaugh, and Roger J. Best. *Consumer Behavior: Building Marketing Strategy*, 12th ed. New York: McGraw-Hill/Irwin, 2012.

Iverson, Annemarie. *In Fashion: From Retail to the Runway, Everything You Need to Know to Break into the Fashion Industry*. New York: Clarkson Potter, 2010.

Ma, Yu, Kusum L Ailawadi, Dinesh K Gauri, and Dhruv Grewal, "An Empirical Investigation of the Impact of Gasoline Prices on Grocery Shopping Behavior." *Journal of Marketing* 75, no. 2 (2011), pp. 18–35.

Solomon, Michael. *Consumer Behavior: Buying, Having, and Being*, 10th ed. Englewood Cliffs, NJ: Prentice Hall, 2012.

Sorensen, Herb. *Inside the Mind of the Shopper*. Philadelphia: Wharton School, 2009.

Underhill, Paco. *Why We Buy: The Science of Shopping*, updated and revised. New York: Simon & Schuster, 2008.

APPENDIX 4A   Customer Buying Behavior and Fashion

Many retailers sell fashionable merchandise. To sell this type of merchandise profitably, retailers need to (1) understand how fashions develop and diffuse throughout the marketplace and (2) use operating systems that enable them to match supply and demand for this seasonal merchandise. This appendix reviews the consumer behavior aspects of fashion; the operating systems for matching supply of and demand for fashion merchandise are discussed in Chapter 12.

Fashion is a type of product or a way of behaving that is temporarily adopted by a large number of consumers because the product, service, or behavior is considered socially appropriate for the time and place.[52] For example, in some social groups, it is or has been fashionable to have brightly colored hair or tattoos, wear a coat made from animal fur, or have a beard. Even though a wide range of activities and products go in and out of fashion, in many retail environments the term *fashion* is associated with apparel and accessories.

CUSTOMER NEEDS SATISFIED BY FASHION

Fashion gives people an opportunity to satisfy many emotional and practical needs. Through fashions, people develop their own identity. They also can use fashions to manage their appearance, express their self-image and feelings, enhance their egos, and make an impression on others. Through the years, fashions have become associated with specific lifestyles or the roles people play. You wear different clothing styles when you are attending class, going out on a date, or interviewing for a job.

People use fashions to both develop their own identity and gain acceptance from others. These two benefits of fashion can be opposing forces. If you choose to wear something radically different, you will achieve recognition for your individuality but might not be accepted by your peers. To satisfy these conflicting needs, manufacturers and retailers offer customers designs that are fashionable but that still enable consumers to express their individuality.

Consumers also adopt fashions to overcome boredom. People get tired of wearing the same clothing and seeing the same furniture in their living rooms. They seek changes in their lifestyles by buying new clothes or redecorating their houses to meet their changing tastes, preferences, and income.

HOW DO FASHIONS DEVELOP AND SPREAD?

Fashions are not universal. A fashion might be accepted in one geographic region, country, or age group and not in another. Consider how your idea of "fashionable" differs from that of your parents. Many of you might have a hard time imagining them dressed in distressed, hip-hugging jeans and a tight T-shirt. Well, they might have just as much trouble picturing you in a double-breasted business suit. One interesting sports fashion trend has been the uniforms for college and NBA basketball players. Forty years ago, they sported long hair and wore tight, short shorts and Converse shoes. Now they have short hair and wear baggy shorts and Nike shoes (see www.nba.com/photostore/).

The stages in the fashion life cycle are shown in Exhibit 4–8. The cycle begins with the creation of a new design or style. Then some consumers recognized as fashion leaders or innovators adopt the fashion and start a trend in their social group. The fashion spreads from the leaders to others and is accepted widely as a fashion. Eventually, the fashion is accepted by most people in the social group and can become overused. Saturation and overuse

set the stage for that fashion's decline in popularity and the creation of new fashions. The time span of a fashion life cycle varies depending on the type of product and the market. The cycle for apparel fashions for young teenagers is measured in months or even weeks, whereas the fashion cycle for home furnishings may last several years.

Creation

New fashions arise from a number of sources. Fashion designers are one source of creative inspirations, but fashions are also developed by creative consumers, celebrities, and even retailers. When high-profile actors, performers, and athletes wear the latest styles in television shows and movies, on stage, or on the red carpet, consumers interested in fashion often adopt and follow these trends.

Adoption by Fashion Leaders

The fashion life cycle really starts when the fashion is adopted by leading consumers. These initial adopters of a new fashion are called **fashion leaders, innovators,** or **trendsetters,** and they are the first people to display the new fashion in their social group or write about them in social media, like fashion blogs. If the fashion is too innovative or very different from currently accepted fashion, it might not be accepted by the social group, thereby prematurely ending its life cycle.

Three theories have been proposed to explain how fashion spreads within a society. The **trickle-down theory** suggests that fashion leaders are consumers with the highest social status—wealthy, well-educated consumers. After they adopt a fashion, the fashion trickles down to consumers in lower social classes. When the fashion is accepted in the lowest social class, it is no longer acceptable to the fashion leaders in the highest social class.

Manufacturers and retailers stimulate this trickle-down process by copying the latest styles displayed at designer fashion shows and sold in exclusive specialty stores. These copies, referred to as **knockoffs,** are sold at lower prices through retailers targeting a broader market. For example, designers at retailers like Forever 21 view fashion shows and interpret the designs for their market.[53] If the designers in Paris and Milan are showing turtlenecks, the

REFACT

The bikini was designed by a former civil engineer, Louis Reard, in 1947.[54]

EXHIBIT 4–8
Stages in the Fashion Life Cycle

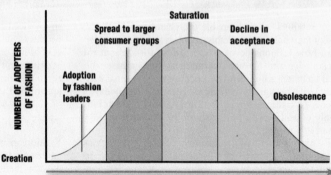

Forever 21 designers determine what aspects of that fashion will appeal to their broader market and then have their designs manufactured in Asia. It is likely that the knockoff turtlenecks will be on the shelves at Forever 21 well before the higher-priced originals get to the high-end specialty and department stores.

The second theory, the **mass-market theory,** suggests that fashions spread across different peer groups. Each group has its own fashion leaders who play key roles in their own social networks. Fashion information trickles across groups rather than down from the upper classes to the lower classes. Spain-based fast-fashion retailer Zara solicits new fashion advice from its store management all over the world. These managers funnel information to the corporate offices in Spain about fashion requests from its customers, what they are wearing, and how they are interpreting and changing off-the-rack apparel to adapt to their unique fashion senses. Zara's fashion designers synthesize the information and reinterpret this information into their own new fashions.

The third theory, the **subculture theory,** is based on the development of recent fashions. Subcultures of mostly young and less affluent consumers, such as urban youth, started fashions for such things as colorful fabrics, T-shirts, sneakers, jeans, black leather jackets, and surplus military clothing. Many times, fashions are started unintentionally by people in lower-income consumer groups and trickle up to mainstream consumer classes. For example, workers wear blue jeans that have holes in them and are distressed from manual labor, their T-shirts are faded from working in the sun, and people who paint houses are covered in splashes of paint. These looks have been adapted by manufacturers and sold to many different consumer groups. The more distress, the more people are willing to pay.

These theories of fashion development indicate that fashion leaders can come from many different places and social groups. In our diverse society, many types of consumers have the opportunity to be the leaders in setting fashion trends.

Spread to Large Consumer Groups

During this stage, the fashion is accepted by a wider group of consumers referred to as early adopters. The fashion becomes increasingly visible, receives greater publicity and media attention, and is readily available in retail stores. The relative advantage, compatibility, complexity, trialability, and observability of a fashion affect the time it takes for that fashion to spread through a social group. New fashions that provide more benefits have a higher relative advantage compared with existing fashions, and these new fashions spread faster. Fashions are often adopted by consumers because they make people feel special. Thus, more exclusive fashions like expensive clothing are adopted more quickly in an affluent target market. On a more utilitarian level, clothing that is easy to maintain, such as wrinkle-free pants, will diffuse quickly in the general population.

Compatibility is the degree to which the fashion is consistent with existing norms, values, and behaviors. When new fashions aren't consistent with existing norms, the number of adopters and the speed of adoption are lower. Head-to-toe leather apparel is only compatible with a relatively small percentage of the public. Although this look may be moderately successful for a season or two, it will never achieve widespread acceptance.

Complexity refers to how easy it is to understand and use the new fashion. Consumers have to learn how to incorporate a new fashion into their lifestyles. For example, a platform, 6-inch, stiletto-heeled pump is difficult to walk in unless you are only taking a quick strut down the runway.

Trialability refers to the costs and commitment required to adopt the fashion initially. For example, consumers buying fashions through Internet channels or catalogs cannot examine the garments or try them on before making a purchase commitment—the trialability is low compared to shopping in stores. New size-matching machines are being used in several shopping centers around the United States. The machines take consumers' measurements and match them with specifications provided by clothing manufacturers, thus providing a proper fit and increasing trialability by reducing the risk associated with buying apparel that has not been tried on.[55]

Observability is the degree to which the new fashion is visible and easily communicated to others in the social group. Clothing fashions are very observable compared with fashions for the home, such as sheets and towels. It is, therefore, likely that a fashion in clothing will spread more quickly than a new color scheme or style for the bedroom.

Fashion retailers engage in many activities to increase the adoption and spread of a new fashion throughout their target market. Compatibility is increased and complexity is decreased by showing consumers how to coordinate a new article of fashion clothing with other items the consumer already owns. Trialability is increased by providing actual or virtual dressing rooms so that customers can try on clothing and see how it looks on them. Providing opportunities for customers to return merchandise also increases trialability because it reduces purchase risk. Retailers increase observability by displaying fashion merchandise in their stores, advertising it in the media, and facilitating coverage through social media like YouTube and fashion blogs.

Saturation

In this stage, the fashion achieves its highest level of social acceptance. Almost all consumers in the target market are aware of the fashion and have decided to either accept or reject it. At this point, the fashion has become old and boring to many people.

Decline in Acceptance and Obsolescence

When fashions reach saturation, they have become less appealing to consumers. Because most people have already adopted the fashion, it no longer provides an opportunity for people to express their individuality. Fashion creators and leaders thus are beginning to experiment with new fashions. The introduction of a new fashion speeds the decline of the preceding fashion.

Retail Market Strategy

EXECUTIVE BRIEFING
David Berg, President and CEO of Outback
Steakhouse International LLC

My career path in retailing is somewhat unusual. After graduating from Emory University with a degree in economics, I went to law school at the University of Florida. During law school, I was attracted to corporate law, which was a good fit with my undergraduate training in economics. I took a position in the corporate counsel's office at Nordic-Track. At the time, NordicTrack was best known for its cross-country ski simulator, which dominated the home fitness market in the late 1980s.

As the U.S. market for the NordicTrack's simulator matured, the company became interested in expanding internationally. I volunteered to set up a network of international distributors. While I did not have a lot of retail experience, in law school, I had learned how to be an effective negotiator and how to logically analyze situations—skills that were very valuable in developing a worldwide distribution network.

After NordicTrack, I went to work for Best Buy and eventually was promoted to COO of Best Buy International, responsible for the operations of all of Best Buy's brands and businesses outside of the United States. I was deeply involved in the sale of Best Buy's Musicland subsidiary; its acquisition of a majority interest in Jiangsu Five Star Appliance in China; its

expansion into Mexico and Turkey; and the creation of its joint venture with The Carphone Warehouse, which provided an opportunity to introduce the Best Buy brand in Europe.

My present position is challenging and exciting. Our corporation owns and operates more than 400 restaurants under the brands names of Outback Steakhouse, Carrabba's Italian Grill, Bonefish Grill, Roy's, and Fleming's Prime Steakhouse & Wine Bar. While we have more than 200 Outback Steakhouses in 19 countries, our potential for international expansion is tremendous.

The dining experience for our international customers is similar to our domestic experience. Our international restaurants tend to follow U.S. design guidelines with some modifications to account for local needs and customs. Most restaurants are in shopping centers or office buildings; very few are free standing. In Asian cities, where space is at a particular premium, many restaurants are located above the ground floor and sometimes split in two separate floors.

The international menu is also similar to the U.S. menu, with some changes made to meet local taste preferences. For example, we feature local beef cuts

CHAPTER 5

 such as Picanha in Brazil or Neobiani in Korea, in addition to the traditional Outback Special sirloin. Product and ingredient availability in a region also drive specific menu offerings. For example, our iconic Bloomin' Onion is replaced by the Typhoon Bloom in Southeast Asia because the exact onion needed for the Bloomin' Onion is not readily available there.

Going global with retail services, particularly restaurants, is more challenging than the international expansion of product-focused retailing. Tastes in food vary significantly from country to country and even within countries, but preferences for products is pretty homogenous across the globe—shopping for flat-panel TVs is pretty universal. While we need a great deal of local input as we expand internationally, we have found that direct foreign investment is more than three times more profitable than franchising.

Retailers need to focus on long-term strategic planning to cope effectively with the growing intensity of retail competition as well as the emergence of new channels, technologies, and globalization. The retail strategy indicates how a retailer will deal effectively with its environment, customers, and competitors.[1] As the retail management decision-making process (discussed in Chapter 1) indicates, the retail strategy (Section II) is the bridge between understanding the world of retailing (Section I) and the more tactical merchandise management and store operations activities (Sections III and IV) undertaken to implement the retail strategy.

The first part of this chapter defines the term *retail strategy* and discusses three important elements of retail strategy: (1) the target market segment, (2) the retail format, and (3) the retailer's bases of sustainable competitive advantage. Then we outline approaches retailers use to build a sustainable competitive advantage. After reviewing the various growth opportunities, specifically international expansion, that retailers can pursue, the chapter concludes with a discussion of the strategic retail planning process.

WHAT IS A RETAIL STRATEGY?

LO1

Define the retail strategy.

REFACT

The word *strategy* comes from the Greek word meaning the "art of the general."[2]

The term *strategy* is frequently used in retailing. For example, retailers talk about their merchandise strategy, promotion strategy, location strategy, channel strategy, or branding strategy. The term is used so commonly that it might appear that all retailing decisions are strategic decisions, but retail strategy isn't just another expression for retail management.

Definition of Retail Market Strategy

A **retail strategy** is a statement identifying (1) the retailer's target market, (2) the format and resources the retailer plans to use to satisfy the target market's needs, and (3) the bases on which the retailer plans to build a sustainable competitive advantage.[3] The **target market** is the market segment(s) toward which the retailer plans to focus its resources and retail mix. A **retail format** describes the nature of the retailer's operations—its retail mix (type of merchandise and services offered, pricing policy, advertising and promotion programs, store design and visual merchandising, typical locations, and customer services)—that it will use to satisfy the needs of its target market. A **sustainable competitive advantage** is an advantage the retailer has over its competition that is not easily copied by competitors and thus can be maintained over a long period of time. The following are Founder's name is Ells. a few examples of retail strategies:

REFACT

Chipotle is by far the largest purchaser of natural meat in the United States.[5]

- *Chipotle Mexican Grill.* Steve Ells, founder and co-chair of Chipotle Mexican Grill, is changing the way America eats, one burrito at a time. The first store of this fast, casual restaurant chain was opened in Denver in 1993 and has grown to 1,200 locations with annual sales of more than $2 billion. Its menu consists of only four items: burritos, burrito bowls, tacos, and salads. When asked about expanding the menu, Steve Ells said, "[I]t's important to keep the menu focused, because if you just do a few things, you can ensure that you do them better than anybody else." Its mission statement, Food With Integrity, highlights its efforts to increase the use of naturally raised meat, organic produce, and dairy without added hormones. This philosophy goes beyond using fresh ingredients to understanding how the animals are raised. The majority of food is prepared in each restaurant. None of the restaurants have freezers, microwave ovens, or can openers.[4]

Lululemon's retail strategy is selling merchandise that appeals to consumers seeking spiritual enrichment through yoga.

- *Lululemon Athletica.* Lululemon is a Canadian specialty store chain selling apparel and accessories that support the practice of yoga. The products it sells include headbands, bamboo blocks, and yoga mats printed with encouraging healthy-living slogans like "Drink fresh water." The signature Lulu item is the Groove Pant, cut with special gussets and flat seams to create a feeling of a drop of water free from gravity. Lululemon's apparel is made with special materials, Silverescent and Luon, enabling customers to engage in vigorous yoga exercises and still look attractive. Lululemon stores are a community hub where people can learn about and discuss the physical aspects of healthy living, from yoga and diet to running and cycling, as well as the spiritual aspects of life. To create this community, the company recruits local ambassadors before opening a store. These ambassadors, usually popular yoga teachers, are featured on Lululemon's website and on bulletin boards in the store.[6]

- *Chico's.* Chico's is a specialty apparel chain serving the lifestyle needs of fashion-savvy women over 30 years old with a household income of $50,000 to $100,000. Its apparel uses easy-to-care-for fabrics; distinctive, fashionable designs; and a comfortable, relaxed fit. Accessories, such as handbags, belts, scarves, earrings, necklaces, and bracelets, are designed to coordinate with the assortment of clothing, allowing customers to easily personalize their wardrobes. All of the merchandise offered is private label, so Chico's designers and buyers specify the patterns, prints, construction, designs, fabrics, finishes, and colors. The distinctive nature of Chico's clothing is carried through to its sizing. Chico's uses sizes of 0, 1, 2, 3, rather than the more commonly used sizes of 1 to 16 so women are less sensitive to large sizes. The relaxed styles of the clothing allow Chico's to utilize a reduced number of sizes and still offer a wide selection of clothing without having to invest in a large number of different sizes within a single style.[7]

- *Save-A-Lot.* From a single store in 1977, Save-A-Lot, a wholly owned subsidiary of SuperValu, has grown to more than 1,300 stores, making it the nation's 13th-largest U.S. supermarket chain. Save-A-Lot stores offer a limited assortment of 1,250 SKUs compared to 20,000 to 30,000 SKUs in a conventional supermarket. By offering only the most popular items in each category, most of which are private-label merchandise, Save-A-Lot reduces its costs and is able to price its merchandise 40 percent lower than prices at conventional supermarkets. Due to its buying power, Save-A-Lot is able to develop customized product specifications that provide high-quality, private-label merchandise at low prices. Because the stores generally do not feature grocery store–style shelving, items instead are available in specially printed, cut-out shipping containers. Finally, most customers bring their own bags; the stores charge those customers who forget their own and need to obtain bags from the retailer.[8]

CENTRAL CONCEPTS IN A RETAIL MARKET STRATEGY

Each of these retail strategies described in the preceding section involves (1) the selection of target market segment(s), (2) the selection of a retail format (the elements in the retailer's retail mix), and (3) the development of a sustainable competitive advantage that enables the retailer to reduce the level of competition it faces. Now let's examine these central concepts of a retail strategy.

LO2

Illustrate how retailers build a sustainable competitive advantage.

Target Market and Retail Format

A **retail market** is a group of consumers with similar needs and a group of retailers that satisfy those needs using a similar retail channels and format.[9] Exhibit 5–1 illustrates a set of retail market segments for women's clothing. It lists various retail formats in the left-hand column. Each format offers a different retail mix to its customers. Market segments are listed in the exhibit's top row. As mentioned in Chapter 4, these segments could be defined in terms of the customers' geographic location, demographics, lifestyle, buying situation, or benefits sought. In this exhibit, we divide the market into three fashion-related

EXHIBIT 5–1   Retail Market Segments for Apparel

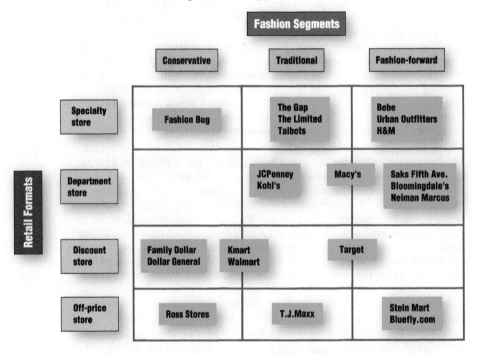

segments: (1) conservative—consumers who place little importance on fashion; (2) traditional—those who want classic styles; and (3) fashion-forward—those who want the latest fashions.

Each square of the matrix in Exhibit 5–1 describes a potential retail market in which retailers compete for consumers with similar needs. For example, Walmart and Kmart stores in the same geographic area compete with each other using a full-line discount store format to target conservative customers. Bloomingdale's and Neiman Marcus compete against each other using a department store format targeting the fashion-forward segment.

Exhibit 5–1's matrix describes the battlefields on which women's apparel retailers compete. The position in each battlefield (cell in the matrix) indicates the first two elements of a retailer's strategy: the fashion segment (the *x*-axis) and the retail format (the *y*-axis).

Consider the situation confronting Target as it refines its retail strategy for the women's clothing market. Should Target compete in all 15 retail markets shown in Exhibit 5–1, or should it focus on a limited set of markets? If Target decides to focus on a limited set of markets, which should it pursue? Target's answers to these questions define its retail strategy and indicate how it will focus its resources.

The women's clothing market in Exhibit 5–1 is just one of several representations that we could have used. Retail formats might be expanded to include off-price stores and category specialists. Although Exhibit 5–1 isn't the only way to describe the women's retail apparel market segments, it does illustrate how retail market segments can be defined in terms of retail format and customer market segments.

Building a Sustainable Competitive Advantage

After selecting a target market and a retail mix, the final element in a retail strategy is the retailer's approach to building a sustainable competitive advantage.[10] Establishing a competitive advantage means that the retailer, in effect, builds a wall around its position in a retail market, that is, around its present and potential

Sources of Advantage	SUSTAINABILITY OF ADVANTAGE	
	Less Sustainable	More Sustainable
Customer loyalty (Chapters 11 and 16)	Habitual repeat purchasing because of limited competition in the local area	Building a brand image with an emotional connection with customers; using databases to develop and utilize a deeper understanding of customers
Location (Chapters 7 and 8)		Convenient locations
Human resource management (Chapter 9)	More employees	Committed, knowledgeable employees
Distribution and information systems (Chapter 10)	Bigger warehouses; automated warehouses	Shared systems with vendors
Unique merchandise (Chapters 12 and 13)	More merchandise; greater assortment; lower price; higher advertising budgets; more sales promotions	Exclusive merchandise
Vendor relations (Chapter 13)	Repeat purchases from vendor due to limited alternatives	Coordination of procurement efforts; ability to get scarce merchandise
Customer service (Chapter 18)	Hours of operation	Knowledgeable and helpful salespeople

EXHIBIT 5–2
Approaches for Developing a Sustainable Competitive Advantage

customers and its competitors. When the wall is high, it will be hard for competitors outside the wall (i.e., retailers operating in other markets or entrepreneurs) to enter the market and compete for the retailer's target customers.

Any business activity that a retailer engages in can be the basis for a competitive advantage. But some advantages are sustainable over a long period of time, while others can be duplicated by competitors almost immediately. For example, it would be hard for Peets Coffee & Tea to establish a long-term advantage over Starbucks by simply offering the same coffee specialties at lower prices. If Peets' lower prices were successful in attracting a significant number of customers, Starbucks would soon realize that Peets had lowered its prices and would quickly match the price reduction. This might lead to a price war that Starbucks is likely to win because it has lower costs due to its larger size. Similarly, it's hard for retailers to develop a long-term advantage by offering broader or deeper assortments of national brands. If the broader and deeper assortment attracts a lot of customers, competitors will simply go out and buy the same branded merchandise. Exhibit 5–2 indicates which aspects of these potential sources of advantage are more and less sustainable.

Over time, all advantages erode due to competitive forces, but by building high walls, retailers can sustain their advantage for a longer time. Thus, establishing a sustainable competitive advantage is the key to long-term financial performance.

Three approaches for developing a sustainable competitive advantage are (1) building strong relationships with customers, (2) building strong relationships with suppliers, and (3) achieving efficient internal operations. Each of these approaches involves developing an asset—loyal customers, strong vendor relationships, committed effective human resources, efficient systems, and attractive locations—that is not easily duplicated by competitors. Let's look at each of these approaches.

Relationships with Customers—Customer Loyalty

Customer loyalty means that customers are committed to buying merchandise and services from a particular retailer. Loyalty is more than simply liking one retailer over another. Loyalty means that customers will be reluctant to switch and patronize a competitive retailer. For example, loyal customers will continue to have their car serviced at Jiffy Lube, even if a competitor opens a store nearby and charges

REFACT

Approximately half of food and beverage shoppers and nearly 60 percent of consumers of health/beauty and household goods would purchase their preferred brands, even if a less expensive alternative were to become available.[11]

McDonald's has developed a competitive advantage by projecting an image of fast service, consistent quality, and clean restrooms.

REFACT

Brooks Brothers, a men's specialty store chain, sold the rights to the Polo brand name to Ralph Lauren.[12]

REFACT

Because brands build loyalty, they are very valuable. The five most valuable U.S. retail brands are Walmart (worth $142 billion), Target ($32 billion), Home Depot ($20 billion), Best Buy ($19 billion), and CVS ($17 billion).[13]

slightly lower prices. Approaches for developing loyalty discussed in this section are building a strong brand image, creating a unique positioning in the target market, offering unique merchandise, providing excellent customer service, implementing a customer relationship management program, and building a retail community.

Brand Image   Retailers build customer loyalty by developing a well-known, attractive image of their brands and of the name over their doors. For example, when most consumers think about fast food or hamburgers or French fries, they immediately think of McDonald's. Their image of McDonald's includes many favorable beliefs such as fast service, consistent quality, and clean restrooms.

Strong brand images facilitate customer loyalty because they reduce the customers' risks associated with purchases. They assure customers that they will receive a consistent level of quality and satisfaction from the retailer. The retailer's image can also create an emotional tie with a customer that leads the customer to trust the retailer. The steps retailers take to develop a strong brand image are discussed in Chapter 15.

Positioning   A retailer's brand image reflects its positioning strategy. **Positioning** is the design and implementation of a retail mix to create an image of the retailer in the customer's mind relative to its competitors. A **perceptual map** is frequently used to represent the customer's image and preferences for retailers.

Exhibit 5–3 offers a hypothetical perceptual map of retailers selling women's clothing. The two dimensions in this map, fashion and service, represent two important characteristics that consumers in this example use in forming their images of retailers.

Perceptual maps are developed in a way so that the distance between two retailers' positions on the map indicates how similar the stores appear to consumers. For example, Neiman Marcus and Saks Fifth Avenue are very close to each other on the map because consumers in this illustration see them as offering similar services and fashion. In contrast, Nordstrom and Marshalls are far apart, indicating consumers think they're quite different. Note that stores close to each other compete vigorously because consumers feel they provide similar benefits and have similar images.

Hypothetical Perceptual Map of Women's Apparel Market   **EXHIBIT 5–3**

In this example, Macy's has an image of offering moderately priced, fashionable women's clothing with good service. TJ Maxx offers slightly less fashionable clothing with considerably less service. Sears is viewed as a retailer offering women's clothing that is not very fashionable with moderate customer service.

The ideal points (marked by red dots on the map) indicate the characteristics of an ideal retailer for consumers in different market segments. For example, consumers in segment 3 prefer a retailer that offers high-fashion merchandise with low service, while consumers in segment 1 want more traditional apparel and aren't concerned about service. The ideal points are located so that the distance between the needs of customers in the segment (marked with a blue "x"), and the perception of the retailer's offering (marked with a red dot) indicates the consumer's probability the consumers in the segment with patronize the retailer.

Retailers that are closer to an ideal point are evaluated more favorably by the consumers in the segment than are retailers located farther away. Thus, consumers in segment 6 prefer Forever 21 and Bebe to Neiman Marcus because these retailers are more fashion-forward and their target customers do not require such high service levels. Retailers strive to develop an image desired by customers in their target segment and thus develop loyalty with those customers.

Unique Merchandise   It is difficult for a retailer to develop customer loyalty through its merchandise offerings because most competitors can purchase and sell the same popular national brands. But many retailers build customer loyalty by developing **private-label brands** (also called **store brands** or **own brands**)—products developed and marketed by a retailer and available only from that retailer.[14] For example, Costco's highly regarded private-label brand, Kirkland Signature, engenders strong brand loyalty and consequently generates considerable loyalty toward Costco. The quality image of its private-label products makes a significant contribution to the image of Costco. Retailing View 5.1 describes how IKEA builds customer loyalty through its unique merchandise. Issues pertaining to the development of store-brand merchandise are discussed in Chapter 13.

Customer Service   Retailers also can develop customer loyalty by offering excellent customer service.[15] Consistently offering good service is difficult because customer service is provided by retail employees who are less consistent than machines. Machines can be programmed to make every box of Cheerios identical, but employees do not provide a consistent level of service because they vary in their training, motivation, and mood.

REFACT

The Ritz-Carlton is the only hotel chain and the first service company to win the annual Malcolm Baldrige National Quality Award. It has won the award twice.[16]

5.1   RETAILING VIEW   The IKEA Way

IKEA, a global retailer headquartered in Sweden, offers a wide range of well-designed, functional home furnishing products at low prices. It's easy to make high-quality products and sell them at a high price or make low-quality products to sell at a low price. But IKEA has to be cost-effective and innovative to sell quality products at low prices.

Creating IKEA's unique merchandise starts on the factory floor. IKEA product developers and designers work closely with suppliers to efficiently use production equipment and raw materials and keep waste to a minimum. For example, an IKEA product developer learned about board-on-frame construction touring a door factory. This technique is cost-effective and environmentally friendly because sheets of wood are layered over a honeycomb core to provide a strong, lightweight structure with a minimal wood content. This type of construction is used in many IKEA products, such as its LACK tables.

Many items IKEA sells are shipped and sold disassembled in flat packs to reduce transportation costs and make it easier for customers to take them home. However, some products like lamps take up a lot of space even when disassembled. The LAMPAN illustrates the IKEA way of offering extremely low price with beautiful design and high quality. This was achieved by developing a new packing method in which the lamp shade could be used as a bucket for the lamp base.

IKEA reduces labor costs in its stores by providing signage with extensive information about its products and their quality, presenting its products in room settings, and prominently displaying price tags. These features enable customers to serve themselves and reduce IKEA's labor costs.

REFACT

Annually 600 million customers visit IKEA's stores, eat two billion of those meatballs, and carry off 168 million catalogues.[17]

The LACK table and LAMPAN are classic IKEA designs only available at IKEA's stores and website.

Sources: www.IKEA.com; Deniz Caglar, Marco Kesteloo, and Artt Kleiner, "How Ikea Reassembled Its Growth Strategy," *Strategy+Business*, May 2012; "The Man Who Named the Furniture," *Financial Times*, January 16, 2010, p. 30; and Yongquan Hu and Huifang Jiang, "Innovation Strategy of Retailers: From the View of Global Value Chains," *6th International Conference on Service Systems and Service Management*, 2009, pp. 340–345.

DISCUSSION QUESTION

Why does IKEA's private-label furniture create a sustainable competitive advantage?

It takes considerable time and effort to build a tradition and reputation for customer service. But once a retailer has earned a service reputation, it can sustain this advantage for a long time because it's hard for a competitor to develop a comparable reputation. For example, Ritz-Carlton hotels are world-renowned for providing outstanding customer service. Employees gather daily for a 15-minute staff meeting, during which they share accounts of how they or their peers have gone above and beyond the call for conventional customer service, also known as "WOW stories." A great example involved a chef in a Balinese

Ritz-Carlton who learned that a guest had extensive food allergies and responded by having special eggs and milk flown in from a small grocery store, located in another country. Such WOW stories help maintain employees' focus on customer service and gives them recognitions for the efforts they make.[18] Chapter 18 discusses how retailers develop a customer service advantage.

Ritz Carlton's outstanding service builds customer loyalty.

Customer Relationship Management Programs   **Customer relationship management (CRM) programs,** also called **loyalty** or **frequent shopper programs,** are activities that focus on identifying and building loyalty with a retailer's most valued customers.[19] These programs typically involve offering customers rewards based on the amount of services or merchandise they purchase. For example, airlines offer free tickets to travelers who have flown a prescribed number of miles, and Subway gives customers a free sandwich for each 10 they purchase.

The discounts offered by these programs may not create loyalty. Customers may join loyalty programs of competing retailers and continue to patronize multiple retailers. However, the data collected about customer shopping behavior by these programs can provide insights that enable retailers to build and maintain loyalty. For instance, CVS Caremark's CRM program enables the retailer to collect extensive information about each of its customers and use this information to increase sales. For example, if customers shop relatively infrequently, e.g., once a month for prescriptions, CVS Caremark may provide incentives that expire in a week to encourage more frequent visits. Alternatively, if customers buy frequently, but buy less than $20 per visit, CVS Caremark offers incentives to increase each visit's purchases to, say, $25. It may provide incentives to get customers who are purchasing only national brands to purchase more private-label merchandise. CVS also uses the loyalty data to determine if a household is purchasing less of a category than it should based on usage in similar households, and therefore provide it with a "buy one, get one free" coupon. Thus, the data developed through the loyalty program enable a retailer to develop a personal relationship with customers that builds loyalty. CRM programs are discussed in detail in Chapter 11.

Building a Retail Community Using Social Media   Retailers are beginning to use their websites and social media to develop retail communities. A **retail community** is a group of consumers who have a shared involvement with a retailer. The members of the community share information with respect to the retailer's activities. The involvement in the community can range from simply becoming a fan of a retailer's Facebook page to meeting face-to-face with community members to share experiences. Increased involvement in the community by its members leads to a greater emotional feeling and loyalty toward the retailer.[20]

REFACT

Starbucks, with 29 million fans, ranks second after Coca-Cola on Facebook and ranks third after Facebook and Whole-Foods on Twitter.[21]

Starbucks builds customer loyalty by developing a community of customers who offer suggestions for improving Starbucks' offering.

Starbucks started building a community in 2008 when it launched My Starbucks Ideas (http://mystarbucksidea.force.com). The website was initially a hub for Starbucks customers to share their ideas, suggestions, and even frustrations on this mini social network. As Starbucks customers started enjoying their time interacting with other customers, the website evolved into a community. Now, the online community gives customers the ability to see what others are suggesting, vote on ideas, and check out the results. Starbucks actually implements the most popular ideas, resulting in customers feeling that they have a say on what their favorite coffee does.[22] Starbucks has extended its online efforts into the social media space. Its Facebook page (www.facebook.com/Starbucks) has more than 32 million likes.

Relationships with Suppliers

A second approach for developing a competitive advantage is to develop strong relationships with companies that provide merchandise and services to the retailer, such as real estate developers, advertising agencies, and transportation companies. Of these relationships with suppliers, the most important are relationships with vendors. For example, the relationship between Walmart and Procter & Gamble initially focused on improving supply chain efficiencies. Today, the partners in this relationship share sensitive information with each other so that Walmart is better able to plan for the introduction of new P&G products and even develop some unique packaging for P&G's national brands exclusively available at Walmart. Walmart shares its sales data with P&G so that P&G can better plan its production and use a just-in-time inventory management system to reduce the level of inventory in the system. By strengthening relationships with each other, both retailers and vendors can develop mutually beneficial assets and programs that give the retailer–vendor pair an advantage over competing pairs.[23]

Relationships with vendors, like relationships with customers, are developed over a long time and may not be easily offset by a competitor.[25] Chapter 13

examines how retailers work with their vendors to build mutually beneficial, long-term relationships.

Efficiency of Internal Operations

In addition to strong relationships with external parties, customers, and suppliers, retailers can develop competitive advantages by having more efficient internal operations. Efficient internal operations enable retailers to have a cost advantage over competitors or offer customers more benefits than competitors at the same cost.

Larger companies typically have greater internal operations efficiency. Larger retailers can invest in developing sophisticated systems and spread the fixed cost of these systems over more sales. In addition to size, other approaches for improving internal operating efficiencies are human resource management and information and supply chain management systems.

Human Resource Management   Retailing is a labor-intensive business, in which employees play a major role providing services to customers and building customer loyalty.[26] Some retailers view employees as an expense that needs to be reduced over the long run. But research has found that highly successful retail chains such as Costco invest heavily in store employees, but still have low prices, solid financial performance, and better customer service than their competitors. They recognize that under-investing in their employees makes their operations more inefficient and, therefore, much less profitable. Knowledgeable and skilled employees committed to the retailer's objectives are critical assets that support the success of these retailers. The retail landscape is increasingly dominated by retailers such as Wegman's and Costco that have adapted to this new reality.[27]

Chapter 9 examines how retailers build their human resource assets by developing programs to motivate and coordinate employee efforts, provide appropriate incentives, foster a strong and positive organizational culture and environment, and manage diversity. In Chapter 16, additional information is presented on increasing employee productivity and retention through recruiting, training, and leadership.

Distribution and Information Systems   The use of sophisticated distribution and information systems offers an opportunity for retailers to reduce operating costs—the costs associated with running the business—and make sure that the right merchandise is available at the right time and place.[28] Information flows seamlessly from Walmart to its vendors to facilitate quick and efficient merchandise replenishment and reduce stockouts. Walmart's distribution and information systems have enabled it to have a cost advantage that its competitors cannot overcome. This component of competitive advantage is discussed in Chapter 10.

In addition to using information systems to improve supply chain efficiency, the customers' purchase data collected by information systems provide an opportunity for retailers to tailor store merchandise assortments to the market served by each of its stores and to tailor promotion to the specific needs of individual customers. These data about its customers' buying behavior are a valuable asset offering an advantage that is not easily duplicated by competitors. These applications of information systems are discussed in more detail in Chapter 11.

Location

While committed relationships with customers and vendors and efficient internal operations are important sources of advantage, location is a pervasive source of advantage in retailing. The classic response to the question, "What are the three most important things in retailing?" is "Location, location, location." Location is a critical opportunity for developing competitive advantage for two reasons: (1) Location is the most important factor determining which store a consumer patronizes. For example, most people shop at the supermarket closest to where they live. (2) Location is a sustainable competitive advantage because it is not easily duplicated. Once Walgreens has put a store at the best location at an

REFACT

Seventy-four percent of U.S. consumers said that shopping locations should be located no more than a 15-minute travel time from their homes.[29]

Starbucks creates a competitive advantage by saturating an area with stores, which makes it difficult for competitors to find good locations.

intersection, CVS is relegated to the second-best location.

Starbucks has developed a strong competitive advantage with its locations. As it expanded across the United States, it saturated each market before entering a new market. For example, there were more than 100 Starbucks outlets in the Seattle area before the company expanded to a new region. Starbucks frequently opens several stores close to one another. It has two stores on two corners of the intersection of Robson and Thurlow in Vancouver. By having such a high density of stores, Starbucks makes it very difficult for a competitor to enter a market and find good locations. Approaches for evaluating and selecting locations are discussed in Chapters 7 and 8.

Multiple Sources of Advantage

To build an advantage that is sustainable for a long period of time, retailers typically cannot rely on a single approach, such as good locations or excellent customer service. Instead, they use multiple approaches to build as high a wall around their position as possible.[30] For example, McDonald's long-term success is based on providing customers with a good value that meets their expectations, having efficient customer service, possessing a strong brand name, and offering convenient locations. By building strategic assets in all of these areas, McDonald's has developed a strong competitive position in the quick-service restaurant market.[31]

In addition to its unique products and associated customer loyalty, IKEA has a large group of loyal customers due to its strong brand image and the stimulating shopping experience it provides its customers. Walmart complements its size advantage with strong vendor relationships and the clear positioning of a retailer that offers superior value. Starbucks combines its location advantage with unique products, committed employees, a strong brand name, and strong relationships with coffee growers to build an overall advantage that is very difficult for competitors to erode. Retailing View 5.2 describes The Container Store, a retailer that has also built multiple bases of sustainable competitive advantages through unique merchandise, excellent customer service, and strong customer and vendor relationships.

GROWTH STRATEGIES

LO3

Classify the different strategic growth opportunities retailers pursue.

In the preceding sections, we have focused on a retailer's strategy, its target market and retail format, and the approaches that retailers take to build a sustainable competitive advantage and defend their position from competitive attacks. When retailers develop these competitive advantages, they have valuable assets. In this section, we discuss how retailers leverage these assets to expand their businesses.

Growth Opportunities

Four types of growth opportunities that retailers may pursue—market penetration, market expansion, retail format development, and diversification—are shown in Exhibit 5–4.[32] The vertical axis indicates the synergies between the retailer's present markets and the growth opportunity—whether the opportunity involves markets the retailer is presently pursuing or new markets. The horizontal axis indicates the synergies between the retailer's present retail mix and the retail mix of the growth opportunity—whether the opportunity exploits the retailer's skills and knowledge in operating its present format or requires new capabilities to operate a new format.

Market Penetration   A **market penetration growth opportunity** is a growth opportunity directed toward existing customers using the retailer's present retailing format. Such opportunities involve either attracting new consumers from the retailer's current target market who don't patronize the retailer currently or devising approaches that get current customers to visit the retailer more often and/or buy more merchandise on each visit.

Market penetration approaches include opening more stores in the target market and/or keeping existing stores open for longer hours. Other approaches involve displaying merchandise to increase impulse purchases and training salespeople to

RETAILING VIEW   The Container Store—Building a Competitive Advantage by Selling Products That Make Life Simpler   5.2

The Container Store sells products to help customers solve problems, or challenges, as the company likes to call them, in organizing their lives. It offers more than 10,000 innovative products, including multipurpose shelving and garment bags to organize closets; portable file cabinets and magazine holders to create order in home offices; backpacks, modular shelving, and DVD holders to make dorm rooms less cluttered; and recipe holders, bottles, jars, and recycling bins to bring harmony to kitchens. More than 1,500 new products are added to its assortment every year.

Over the years, the company has developed strong vendor relationships. Most of its vendors' primary focus was to manufacture products for industrial use. Yet, over time, the company has worked closely with its vendors to develop products that are appropriate for the home.

The Container Store's sales associates provide outstanding customer service. The company actively recruits customers who are intrigued with helping people organize. It spends considerable time educating sales associates about the merchandise (240 hours versus the typical 12 hours for new retail employees) and then empowering them to use their own intuition and creativity to solve customer challenges.

Employees are very committed to the company; as a result, its turnover rate is among the lowest in the retail industry. The Container Store also has appeared on *Fortune*'s list of the "100 Best Companies to Work For" in each of the last 11 years.

The Container Store has multiple sources of competitive advantage, including unique merchandise, excellent customer service, strong vendor relationships, and committed employees.

and Angela Ellis, "Inside the Container Store: Secrets of America's Favorite Stores," *ABC News*, March 30, 2010; and "Three Good Hires? He'll Pay More for One Who's Great," *The New York Times*, March 14, 2010.

DISCUSSION QUESTION

How does the Container Store maintain its competitive advantage?

Sources: Steven R. Thompson, "Container Store Uses Personal Approach in New Strategy," *Dallas Business Journal*, April 27, 2012; Bianna Golodryga

EXHIBIT 5–4
Growth Opportunities

TARGET MARKETS

	Existing	New
RETAIL FORMAT Existing	Market Penetration	Market Expansion
New	Format Development	Diversification (unrelated/related)

cross-sell. **Cross-selling** means that sales associates in one department attempt to sell complementary merchandise from other departments to their customers. For example, a sales associate who has just sold a Blu-Ray player to a customer will take the customer to the accessories department to sell special cables to improve the performance of the player.

Market Expansion   A **market expansion growth opportunity** involves using the retailer's existing retail format in new market segments. For example, Dunkin' Donuts has been opening new stores outside its traditional target market in the northeastern United States.[33] When Chico's acquired White House Black Market, it engaged in a market expansion growth opportunity. Chico's and White House Black Market have similar retail formats. They are both mall-based specialty apparel stores. But Chico's targets women over 30 years old, while White House Black Market targets a younger age segment. In contrast, Chico's acquisition of Soma, a mall-based specialty store chain offering lingerie for women between 35 and 55, was a market penetration opportunity—same market and similar operations; however, Chico's and Soma offer different products.

Retail Format Development   A **retail format development growth opportunity** is an opportunity in which a retailer develops a new retail format—a format with a different retail mix—for the same target market. The U.K.-based retailer Tesco has employed a retail format development growth strategy by operating several different food store formats that all cater to essentially the same target market. The smallest is Tesco Express, up to 3,000 square feet. These stores are located close to where customers live and work. Tesco Metro stores are 7,000 to 15,000 square feet, bring convenience to city center locations, and specialize in offering a wide range of ready-to-eat meals. Tesco Superstores, up to 50,000 square feet, are the oldest format. In recent years, the company has added nonfood products, such as Blu-Rays and books, to improve customer satisfaction. Finally, Tesco Extra stores, more than 60,000 square feet, are designed to be a one-stop destination, with the widest range of food and nonfood products, from housewares and clothing to garden furniture.[34]

Diversification   A **diversification growth opportunity** is one in which a retailer introduces a new retail format directed toward a market segment that's not currently served by the retailer. Diversification opportunities are either related or unrelated.

Related versus Unrelated Diversification

In a **related diversification growth opportunity,** the retailer's present target market and retail format shares something in common with the new opportunity. This commonality might entail purchasing from the same vendors, operating in similar locations, using the same distribution or management information system, or advertising in the same newspapers to similar target markets. In contrast, an **unrelated diversification growth opportunity** has little commonality between the retailer's present business and the new growth opportunity.

Through acquisition, Home Depot built a wholesale building supply business, called HD Supply, which had generated more than $3 billion in annual sales. Management felt that this growth opportunity would be synergistic with the firm's retail business, because its stores were already selling similar merchandise to contractors. Thus, Home Depot viewed this growth opportunity as a related diversification, because the targeted customers (i.e., contractors) would be similar, and the new large contractor market could be served using a retail mix similar to Home Depot's present retail mix. In addition, Home Depot would realize cost savings by placing larger orders with vendors because it would be selling to both retail and wholesale large and small customers.

In hindsight, though, the HD Supply actually was an unrelated diversification. The large contractor market served by HD Supply sold primarily pipes, lumber, and concrete—products with limited sales in Home Depot's retail stores. Selling these supplies to large contractors involved competitive bidding and transporting large, bulky orders to job sites—skills that Home Depot lacked. So Home Depot sold this unrelated diversification to concentrate on its core retail, small-contractor business.[35]

Vertical Integration

Vertical integration describes diversification by retailers into wholesaling or manufacturing. For example, some retailers go beyond designing their private-label merchandise to owning factories that manufacture the merchandise. When retailers integrate backward and manufacture products, they are making risky investments because the requisite skills to make products are different from those associated with retailing them. In addition, retailers and manufacturers have different customers. The immediate customers for a manufacturer's products are retailers, while a retailer's customers are consumers. Thus, a manufacturer's marketing activities are very different from those of a retailer. Note that designing private-label merchandise is a related diversification because it builds on the retailer's knowledge of its customers, whereas actually making the merchandise is an unrelated diversification.

Growth Opportunities and Competitive Advantage

Typically, retailers have the greatest competitive advantage and most success when they engage in opportunities that are similar to their present retail operations and markets. Thus, market penetration growth opportunities have the greatest chances of succeeding because they build on the retailer's present bases of advantage and don't involve entering new, unfamiliar markets or operating new, unfamiliar retail formats.

When retailers pursue market expansion opportunities, they build on their advantages in operating a retail format and apply this competitive advantage in a new market. A retail format development opportunity builds on the retailer's relationships and loyalty of present customers. Even if a retailer doesn't have experience and skills in operating the new format, it hopes to attract its loyal customers to it. Retailers have the least opportunity to exploit a competitive advantage when they pursue diversification opportunities.

GLOBAL GROWTH OPPORTUNITIES

LO4

Identify issues that arise as domestic retailers become global retailers.

In this section, we provide a more detailed discussion of one type of growth opportunity—expanding operations to international markets. This growth opportunity is becoming particularly attractive to large retailers as they begin to saturate their domestic market. Of the 20 largest retailers in the world, only 3 operate in one country.[36] By expanding internationally, retailers can increase their sales, leverage their knowledge and systems across a greater sales base, and gain more bargaining power with vendors. But international expansion is risky because retailers must deal with different government regulations, cultural traditions, consumer preferences, supply chains, and languages. Retailing View 5.3 describes the substantial differences in grocery shopping in Shanghai.

We first discuss the attractiveness of different opportunities for global expansion and then the keys to success for expanding globally. Finally, we review the approaches that retailers can take to enter international markets.

Attractiveness of International Markets

Three factors that are often used to determine the attractiveness of international opportunities are (1) the potential size of the retail market in the country, (2) the degree to which the country does and can support the entry of foreign retailers engaged in modern retail practices, and (3) the risks or uncertainties in sales and profits.[37] Some indicators of these factors are shown in Exhibit 5–5. The (+) or (−) indicates whether the indicator is positively or negatively related to the factor.

Note that the importance of some country characteristics depends on the type of retailer evaluating the country for entry. For example, a retailer of video games, such as Gamestop, would find a country with a large percentage of people under 19 to be more attractive than a country with a large percentage of people over 65. High-fashion retailers that sell expensive merchandise, such as Neiman Marcus and Cartier, would find a country that has a significant percentage of the population with high incomes to be more attractive than a country that has a large percentage of people in poverty.

Most retailers considering entry into foreign markets are successful multinational retailers that use sophisticated management practices. Thus, they would find countries that have modern retailing, more advanced infrastructures, and significant urban populations to be more supportive. In addition, countries lacking strong domestic retailers but having a stable economy and political environment would be more supportive.

The factors outlined in Exhibit 5–5 are weighted to develop an index scoring each country on the attractiveness dimensions. One index ranking the 20 most

EXHIBIT 5–5   Indicators of the Potential, Support, and Risk in International Markets

Country Potential	Country Support	Country Risk
Population (+)	Market share of modern retailing (+)	Political stability (+)
Population growth rate (+)	Quality of infrastructure (roads, trains, etc.) (+)	Business-friendly laws and regulations (+)
GDP (+)	Urban population (+)	Access to bank financing (+)
GDP growth rate (+)	Market share of domestic retailers (+)	National debt (−)
GDP per capita (+)	Market share of international retailers (+)	Crime (−)
Retail sales (+)	Market share of largest retailers (+)	Violence (−)
Retail sales growth rate (+)		Corruption (−)
Retail sales per capita (+)		
Population (+)		
Income distribution (+ or −)		
Age (+ or −)		

attractive international retail markets on market potential (country potential and support) and risk is shown in Exhibit 5–6. Of the top 20 counties in this ranking, 10 are emerging economies. The emerging international markets that receive the most attention from global retailers are India, China, Russia, and Brazil, collectively referred to as "the BRIC" (Brazil, Russia, India, China) countries. However, in this analysis, Russia is not in the top 20 because of its high risk.

RETAILING VIEW   Wet Markets in Shanghai

5.3

Shanghai, with more than 23 million inhabitants, is the largest city by population in the world. It is a sophisticated international city, like New York, London, and Tokyo, with substantial influence in global commerce, culture, finance, media, fashion, technology, and transportation. It is a major financial center and the busiest container port in the world. The major international food retailers (Walmart, Carrefour, Metro, and Tesco) have now opened more than 200 Western-style hypermarkets in Shanghai. In addition, there are more than 2,000 modern supermarkets operated mostly by Chinese firms. But the majority of perishable goods (fish, meat, chicken, pork, vegetables, and fruit) sales still are made in traditional wet markets.

Wet markets are buildings divided into small stalls lined along narrow corridors with small, independent retailers selling perishables in the stalls. The retailers lease the stalls from market operators. They buy the perishables from various sources, including wholesale markets, rural merchants, and farmers' cooperatives, and then sort, clean, and package the perishables for sale to their customers. These markets are called "wet markets" because the concrete floor is constantly wet from the spraying of perishables and cleaning of live meat and fish. There are more than 900 wet markets in Shanghai.

The Chinese government would like to close all wet markets because they do not reflect the modern China and because they pose health risks due to poor hygiene. But Chinese urban consumers cross-format shop for groceries: They buy manufactured goods in supermarkets and hypermarkets but perishables in wet markets. Two factors contribute to this preference for wet markets.

First, Chinese consumers place great importance on freshness. Perishables sold at supermarkets and hypermarkets usually get to the store around eight o'clock the night before and have been shelved for at least half a day before reaching consumers. At wet markets, vendors buy their perishables around four o'clock in the morning and constantly trim, spray, clean, and sort the perishables to keep them fresh. Also, wet-market vendors do not have or use refrigerators for storage; thus, they have to replenish their inventory with fresh supplies every day. The modern-format retailers simply cannot win the freshness contest.

Even though there are many modern supermarkets and hypermarkets in Shanghai, the majority of perishable groceries are still bought at traditional wet markets.

Second, for logistical reasons, most Chinese consumers shop for groceries every day and buy just enough to prepare for that day's meals. In their small homes, the average kitchen size is about 60 square feet, leaving little room to store any items for extended periods, especially perishable foods that require refrigeration. Furthermore, though the automotive market is growing in China, many families still travel by other means. In Shanghai for example, bicycles (20 percent), buses (30 percent), and walking (40 percent) are more common means of transport for shopping trips. In these locations, the small wet markets provide far more convenient locations than larger super- or hypermarkets.

Sources: "Buying the Store," *China Economic Review*, June 14, 2012; Louise Herring, Daniel Hui, Paul Morgan, and Caroline Tufft, *Inside China's Hypermarkets: Past and Prospects* (Hong Kong: McKinsey By McKinsey, 2012); and Qian Forrest Zhang and Zi Pan, *The Transformation of Urban Vegetable Retail in China: Wet Markets, Supermarkets, and Informal Markets in Shanghai*, Research Collection School of Social Sciences, 2012.

DISCUSSION QUESTION

Given the Chinese government's disdain for wet markets, do you think they will endure?

Retailing

140   SECTION II   Retailing Strategy

EXHIBIT 5–6   Country Attractiveness

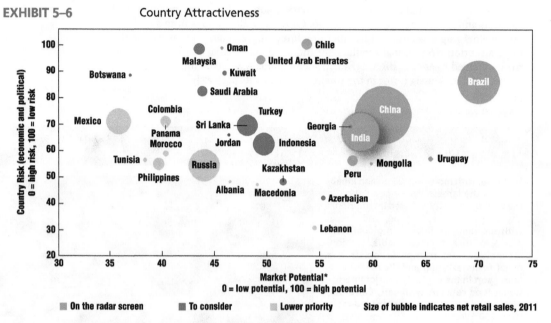

On the radar screen   ■ To consider   ■ Lower priority   Size of bubble indicates net retail sales, 2011

*Based on weighted score of market attractiveness, market saturation, and time pressure of top 30 countries

SOURCE: Hana Ben-Shabat, Helen Rhim, Mike Moriarity, and Fabiola Salman, *Global Retail Expansion Keeps Moving—2012* (New York: ATKearney, 2012).

India and China are by far the largest and most attractive retail markets. However, these two countries offer different opportunities and challenges for retailers contemplating entry.[38]

India   In India and most emerging economies, the retail industry is divided into organized and unorganized sectors. The **unorganized retailing** includes the small independent retailers—the local *kirana* shops, owner-operated general stores, *paan/beedi* shops, convenience stores, and handcart and street vendors. Most Indians shop in open markets and millions of independent grocery shops called *kirana*. However, India's growing, well-educated, aspirational middle class wants a more sophisticated retail environment and global brands.

REFACT

Less than 5 percent of India's retail sales are through organized retail channels.[39]

While the demand for modern (organized) retailing exists in India, entering the Indian market is challenging. As the world's largest pluralistic democracy, with myriad cultures and 22 official languages, India actually is a conglomeration of discrete markets. In addition, government regulations impede foreign investment in retailing. Retailers must comply with a myriad of regulations before opening stores and shipping merchandise. For example, there are taxes for moving goods to different states and even within states. Initially, Walmart's entry into India is a partnership with Bharti Enterprises to open wholesale outlets called Best Price Modern Wholesale. The outlets initially were allowed to

In India, most consumers shop at small, independent retail outlets.

sell only to firms that register by showing tax documents that prove they own retail outlets. The development of organized retailing is being undertaken by industrial conglomerates that have limited expertise in running retail chains.[40]

China   Government regulations of retailing are much less onerous in China than in India, and direct foreign investment is encouraged. Since the lifting of most operational restrictions on international retailers, six global food retailers (Auchan, Carrefour, Ito-Yokado, Metro, Tesco, and Walmart) have entered China, although much of this retail development has been in the large eastern coastal cities of Shanghai, Beijing, Guangzhou, and Shenzhen.[41]

China is rapidly developing the infrastructure to support modern retailing. Highway density in China is already approaching similar levels as the United States. China has a number of high-quality airports and a rapidly developing sophisticated railroad network.

However, doing business in China is still challenging. Operating costs are increasing, managerial talent is becoming more difficult to find and retain, and an underdeveloped and inefficient supply chain predominates.

Brazil   Brazil has the largest population and strongest economy in Latin America. It is a country of many poor people and a few very wealthy families. Brazilian retailers have developed some very innovative practices for retailing to low-income families, including offering credit and installment purchases. The very wealthy Brazilians provide a significant market for luxury goods and retailers. Even though they are approximately 1 percent of the population, this equates to approximately 19 million people, a market just a little smaller than all of Australia.

Russia   In Russia, the impediments to market entry are less visible but more problematic. Corruption is rampant, with various administrative authorities capable of impeding operations if payments are not made. Retailers encounter severe logistical challenges in supporting operations in Russia. There are long delays at borders and ports and a scarcity of containers. More than 70 percent of international container shipments come through the St. Petersburg port, which is very congested. Retailers often cannot rely on domestic products because the quality of products made in Russia is poor. Most major retailers offer their own credit card facility, with "signing up" booths at the entrances to their stores. Many low-income customers go from week to week paying their credit card commitments. Finally, much of the purchasing power is concentrated in Moscow, where salaries are about double those in other regions. But Moscow is already saturated with shopping centers.

> **REFACT**
> The anticorruption group Transparency International ranks Russia 143th out of 183 countries on its most recent index of the most corrupt countries.[42]

Keys to Success in Global Retailing

Four characteristics of retailers that have successfully exploited international growth opportunities are (1) a globally sustainable competitive advantage, (2) adaptability, (3) a global culture, and (4) financial resources.

Globally Sustainable Competitive Advantage   Entry into nondomestic markets is most successful when the expansion opportunity builds on the retailer's core bases of competitive advantage. For example, Walmart and ALDI have a significant cost advantage that facilitates success in international markets in which price plays an important role in consumer decision making and a distribution infrastructure is available to enable these firms to exploit their logistical capabilities. In contrast, H&M and Zara are more successful in international markets that value lower-priced, fashionable merchandise.

Some U.S. retailers have a competitive advantage in global markets because American culture is emulated in many countries, particularly by young people. Due to rising prosperity, the rapidly increasing access to broadband Internet, social media like Facebook and networks such as MTV that feature American programming, fashion trends in the United States have spread to young people in emerging countries. The global MTV generation prefers Coke to tea, Nikes to sandals, Chicken McNuggets to rice, and credit cards to cash. China's major cities have American stores and restaurants, including KFC, Pizza Hut, and McDonald's. Shanghai and Beijing have more than 100 Starbucks stores even though coffee had never been the drink of choice before Starbucks came to town. But Chinese urban dwellers go to Starbucks to impress a friend or because it's a symbol of a new kind of lifestyle. Although Western products and stores have gained a reputation for high quality and good service in China, in some ways it is the American culture that many Chinese consumers want.

Adaptability Although successful global retailers build on their core competencies, they also recognize cultural differences and adapt their core strategy to the needs of local markets. Retailing View 5.4 illustrates how 7-Eleven changed its retail offering to be more appealing in Indonesia.

Carrefour is an expert at understanding and integrating itself into local regions. For example, it realized early on that the merchandising of fish differs for each local market. In San Francisco, fish is sold dead and filleted; in France, fish is sold

---

5.4 RETAILING VIEW 7-Eleven Is Trendy Hangout in Indonesia

In a local hangout in Jakarta, hipsters gather to drink iced coffee, gossip, eat nachos, listen to a live band, and text their friends. This sort of hanging out is so popular and common among young Indonesians that their language includes a word to describe sitting around, chatting, and generally doing nothing productive: *nongkrong*. For years, the most popular gathering spots were food stalls, located along the sides of roads, known as *warung*. But the *warung* are giving way to another popular *nongkrong* location: local 7-Eleven stores.

This shift is exactly the response that 7-Eleven hoped to achieve when it instituted a new strategy in Indonesia: adding seating to its existing small supermarkets and offering inexpensive, ready-to-eat meals, such as fried rice and pillow bread (i.e., small cheese- or chocolate-filled sandwiches). Jakarta is notably lacking in outdoor recreation space, so the little hangouts effectively attract social customers. And Indonesia has plenty of those, as evidenced by its massive social networking rates. In Indonesia alone, 7-Eleven has attracted nearly 60,000 Twitter followers and almost as many Facebook fans.

The strategy also means that the franchise mainly targets young customers, who constitute 65 percent of its market. These Millennials make use of the 24/7 access that 7-Eleven offers, surfing the Internet at all hours, before or after gathering with their friends. In Indonesia, one of the most electronically connected nations in the world, customers constantly update their social networks to alert them about when a band is about to start playing at the local 7-Eleven, for example. Among this generational cohort, the store appeals to a wide range of economic classes, such that the parking lots fill with Mercedes-Benzes interspersed with rusted-out motor bikes.

Despite these unique offerings, 7-Elevens are still 7-Elevens: They sell Big Gulps, flavored Slurpees, doughnuts,

7-Eleven is a trendy place for young Indonesians to hang out with their friends.

and hot coffee. But in locations in the world's most populous Muslim country, 7-Eleven only sells alcohol after conducting neighborhood surveys to obtain community approval.

Sources: Sara Schonhardt, "7-Eleven Finds a Niche by Adapting to Indonesian Ways," *The New York Times*, May 28, 2012; and Anthony Deutsch, "7-Eleven Becomes Indonesia's Trendy Hangout," *Financial Times*, September 13, 2011.

DISCUSSION QUESTION

Could 7-Eleven adapt what it has learned in Indonesia to the United States to attract young urban customers? Would it want to?

dead but whole on ice with the head still intact; and in China, fish is sold live. However, consumers in the middle and western parts of China have more confidence in frozen fish, because they are so far from the ocean.[43] Carrefour and Tesco make sure that more than 90 percent of the merchandise they sell is produced in the country in which it is sold.[44]

Peak selling seasons also vary across countries. In the United States, many stores experience a sales increase in August, when families stock up on back-to-school supplies and apparel. However, this month is one of the slowest sales periods in Europe because most people are on vacation. Back-to-school season in Japan occurs in April.

Store designs and layouts often need to be adjusted in different parts of the world. In the United States, for instance, supercenters are usually quite large and on one level, except in a few urban areas. In other parts of the world, such as Europe and parts of Asia, where space is at a premium, stores must be designed to fit smaller footprints and are often housed in multiple levels. In some cultures, social norms dictate that men's and women's clothing cannot be displayed next to each other.

Government regulations and cultural values can also affect store operations. Some differences, such as holidays, hours of operation, and regulations governing part-time employees and terminations, are easy to identify. Other factors require a deeper understanding. For example, Latin American culture is very family oriented, so traditional U.S. work schedules would need to be adjusted so that Latin American employees could have more time with their families during family meals. Boots, a U.K. drugstore chain owned by Walgreens, has the checkout clerks in its Japanese stores stand up because it discovered that Japanese shoppers found it offensive to pay money to a seated clerk, but retailers have to provide seating for checkout clerks in Germany. Retailers in Germany also must recycle packaging materials sold in their stores. Also in Germany, seasonal sales can be held only during specific weeks and apply only to specific product categories, and the amount of the discounts are limited. Spanish and French retailers work under government-controlled operating hours and must mind policies prohibiting midseason sales.

Global Culture   To be global, retailers must think globally. It is not sufficient to transplant a home-country culture and infrastructure to another country. In this regard, Carrefour is truly global. In the early years of its international expansion, it started in each country slowly, an approach that reduced the company's ethnocentrism. Further enriching its global perspective, Carrefour has always encouraged the rapid development of local management and retains few expatriates in its overseas operations. Carrefour's management ranks are truly international. One is just as likely to run across a Portuguese regional manager in Hong Kong as a French or Chinese one. Finally, Carrefour discourages the classic overseas "tour of duty" mentality often found in U.S. firms. International assignments are important in themselves, not just as stepping stones to ultimate career advancement back in France. The globalization of Carrefour's culture is perhaps most evident in the speed with which ideas flow throughout the organization. A global management structure of regional committees, which meet regularly, advances the awareness and implementation of global best practices. The proof of Carrefour's global commitment lies in the numbers: It has had more than 30 years of international experience in 30 countries, both developed and developing.[45]

Financial Resources   Expansion into international markets requires a long-term commitment and considerable up-front planning. Retailers find it very difficult to generate short-term profits when they make the transition to global retailing. Although firms such as Walmart, Carrefour, Office Depot, and Costco often initially have difficulty achieving success in new global markets, these large firms generally are in a strong financial position and therefore have the ability to keep investing in projects long enough to become successful.

144   SECTION II   Retailing Strategy

Entry Strategies

Four approaches that retailers can take when entering nondomestic markets are direct investment, joint venture, strategic alliance, and franchising.[46]

Direct Investment   **Direct investment** occurs when a retail firm invests in and owns a retail operation in a foreign country. This entry strategy requires the highest level of investment and exposes the retailer to the greatest risks, but it also has the highest potential returns. A key advantage of direct investment is that the retailer has complete control of the operations. For example, McDonald's chose this entry strategy for the U.K. market, building a plant to produce buns when local suppliers could not meet its specifications.

Joint Venture   A **joint venture** is formed when the entering retailer pools its resources with a local retailer to form a new company in which ownership, control, and profits are shared. A joint-venture entry strategy reduces the entrant's risks. In addition to sharing the financial burden, the local partner provides an understanding of the market and has access to local resources, such as vendors and real estate. Many foreign countries require that foreign entrants partner with domestic firms. Problems with this entry approach can arise if the partners disagree or the government places restrictions on the repatriation of profits.

Strategic Alliance   A **strategic alliance** is a collaborative relationship between independent firms. For example, a retailer might enter an international market through direct investment but use independent firms to facilitate its local logistical and warehousing activities.

Franchising   **Franchising** offers the lowest risk and requires the least investment, but also has the lowest potential return on investment. The retailer has limited control over the retail operations in the foreign country, its potential profit is reduced, and the risk of assisting in the creation of a local domestic competitor increases. The U.K.-based Marks & Spencer, for example, has franchised stores in 30 countries.[47]

THE STRATEGIC RETAIL PLANNING PROCESS

LO5

Know the steps retailers go through to develop a strategic plan.

In the previous sections, we reviewed the elements in a strategy statement, the approaches for building a sustainable competitive advantage, the growth opportunities that retailers consider, and the factors they consider when evaluating and pursuing a global growth opportunity. In this section, we outline the process retailers use to review their present situation and decide on a strategy to pursue.

The **strategic retail planning process** is the set of steps a retailer goes through to develop a strategy and plan[48] (see Exhibit 5–7). It describes how retailers select target market segments, determine the appropriate retail format, and build sustainable competitive advantages. As indicated in Exhibit 5–7, it is not always necessary to go through the entire process each time a strategy and plan are developed (step 7). For instance, a retailer could evaluate its performance and go directly to step 2 to conduct a SWOT analysis.

The planning process can be used to formulate strategic plans at different levels within a retail corporation. For example, the corporate strategic plan of Tesco indicates how to allocate resources across the corporation's various divisions, such as Tesco, Tesco Extra, Tesco Express, Tesco Metro, Tesco Homeplus, and One Stop. Each division, in turn, develops its own strategic plan.

As we discuss the steps in the retail planning process, we will apply each step to the planning process for a hypothetical retailer owned by Kelly Bradford. Kelly owns Gifts To Go, a small, two-store chain in the Chicago area. One of her 1,000-square-foot stores is located in the downtown area; the other is in an upscale suburban mall. The target market for Gifts To Go is upper-income men and women looking for gifts in the $50 to $500 price range. The stores have an eclectic

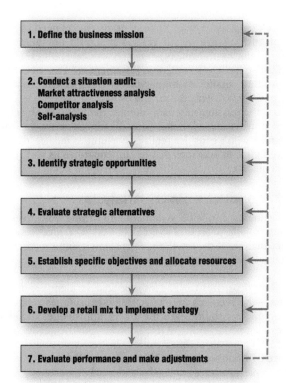

EXHIBIT 5–7
Stages in the Strategic
Planning Process

selection of merchandise, including handmade jewelry and crafts, fine china and glassware, perfume, watches, writing instruments, and a variety of one-of-a-kind items. Gifts To Go also has developed a number of loyal customers who are contacted by sales associates when family anniversaries and birthdays come up. In many cases, customers have a close relationship with a sales associate and enough confidence in the associate's judgment that they tell the associate to pick out an appropriate gift. The turnover of Gifts To Go sales associates is low for the industry because Kelly treats associates as part of the family. The company pays for health insurance for all associates, and the associates share in the profits of the firm.

Step 1: Define the Business Mission

The first step in the strategic retail planning process is to define the business mission. The **mission statement** is a broad description of a retailer's objectives and the scope of activities it plans to undertake.[49] While the principle objective of a publicly held firm is to maximize its stockholders' wealth, firms also are concerned about their impact on society.

For example, Maxine Clark, founder and chief executive bear at Build-A-Bear Workshop, in discussing her goals for the company, says, "We also believe strongly that we need to give back to the communities in which we have stores. For example, as part of our on-going commitment to children's health and wellness, we introduced a series of Nicki Bears to honor Nicki Giampolo, a young girl who lost her life to cancer. A portion of the sales of each Nicki is donated to support programs that help children maintain normal lives while they struggle with difficult health issues."[50] Owners of small, privately held firms frequently have other objectives, such as achieving a specific level of income and avoiding uncertainty rather than maximizing income.

The mission statement defines the general nature of the target segments and retail formats on which the firm will focus. For example, the mission statement "Serve the customer, build value for shareholders, and create opportunities for associates," is too broad. It fails to provide a sense of strategic direction.

In developing the mission statement, managers need to answer five questions: (1) What business are we in? (2) What should our business be in the future? (3) Who are our customers? (4) What are our capabilities? (5) What do we want to accomplish? Gifts To Go's mission statement is "The mission of Gifts To Go is to be the leading retailer of higher-priced gifts in Chicago and provide a stable income of $100,000 per year for the owner."

Because the mission statement defines the retailer's objectives and the scope of activities it plans to undertake, Gifts To Go's mission statement clarifies that its management won't consider retail opportunities outside the Chicago area, selling low-priced gifts, or activities that might jeopardize its ability to generate $100,000 in annual income.

Step 2: Conduct a SWOT Analysis

After developing a mission statement and setting objectives, the next step in the strategic planning process is to conduct a **SWOT analysis.** A SWOT analysis involves an analysis of the retailer's internal environment (strengths and weaknesses) and external environment (opportunities and threats).

Internal Environment   The internal analysis identifies the retailer's *strengths and weaknesses*—the retailer's unique strategic capabilities relative to its competition. These unique capabilities are the assets, knowledge, and skills that the retailer possesses such as the loyalty of its customers and the quality of its relationships with its vendor. These capabilities reflect the retailer's ability to develop a strategic advantage as an opportunity it is considering. Exhibit 5–8 outlines some issues to consider in performing a **strengths and weaknesses analysis.**

Here is Kelly Bradford's analysis of Gifts To Go's strengths and weaknesses:

Capabilities	Gifts To Go Strength and Weaknesses
Financial resources	Good—Gifts To Go had no debt and a good relationship with a bank. Kelly has saved $255,000 that she has in liquid securities.
Customer loyalty	Good—While Gifts To Go did not achieve the sales volume in gifts done in department stores, the company has a loyal base of customers.
Locations	Excellent—Both of Gifts To Go's locations are excellent. The downtown location is convenient for office workers. The suburban mall location is at a heavily trafficked juncture.
HUMAN RESOURCES	
Merchandise management	Limited—Kelly has a flair for selecting unique gifts but has no systems to support her.
Store management	Excellent—The store managers and sales associates are excellent. They are very attentive to customers and loyal to the firm. Employee and customer theft is kept to a minimum.
Other staff and systems	Limited—An accounting firm keeps the financial records for the business.
Vendor relationships	Kelly has excellent relationships with vendors providing one-of-a-kind merchandise.
Supply chain management and information systems	Poor—While Kelly feels Gifts To Go has relatively low overhead, the company does not have a computer-based inventory control system or management and customer information systems. Her competitors (local department stores, catalog, and Internet retailers) certainly have superior systems. No skills in developing and utilizing customer databases.

EXHIBIT 5–8
Elements in a
Strengths and
Weaknesses Analysis

Financial resources	Human resources
Customer loyalty	Top managers
Strength of brand image	Store manager
Development of unique merchandise	Merchandise managers
Quality of customer service	Operation managers
Information about customers	Vendor relationships
Size and involvement of community	Supply chain management systems
Locations	Information systems

Market Factors	Competitive Factors	Environmental Dynamics
Market size	Barriers to entry	New technology
Market growth	Bargaining power of vendors	Economic conditions
Cyclicality of sales	Competitive rivalry	Changes in governmental regulations
Seasonality		Social changes

EXHIBIT 5–9
Opportunities and Threats

External Environment   The external analysis identifies the retailer's opportunities and threats—the aspect of the environment that might positively or negatively affect the retailer's performance. These factors associated with the market, competition, and environment dynamics are typically beyond the retailer's control. Exhibit 5–9 outlines some issues to consider when doing an **opportunities and threats analysis.**

Market Factors   The attractiveness of a target market in which a retailer is involved or considering is affected by the size of the market, market growth, cyclicality of sales, and seasonality. Market size is important because it indicates a retailer's opportunity to generate revenues to cover its investment.

Growing markets are typically more attractive than mature or declining markets. For example, retail markets for limited-assortment, extreme-value retailers are growing faster than are those for department stores. Typically, the return on investment may be higher in growing markets because competition is less intense than in mature markets. Because new customers are just beginning to patronize stores in growing markets, they may not have developed strong store loyalties and thus might be easier to attract to new retail offerings.

Firms are often interested in minimizing the business cycle's impact on their sales. Thus, retail markets for merchandise that is affected by economic conditions (such as cars and major appliances) are less attractive than retail markets that are less affected by economic conditions (such as food). In general, markets with highly seasonal sales are unattractive because a lot of resources are needed to accommodate the peak season and then the resources go underutilized the rest of the year. Retailers can take steps to reduce seasonality; for instance, ski resorts can promote summer vacations.

To conduct an analysis of the market factors for Gifts To Go, Kelly Bradford went on the Internet to get information about the size, growth, and cyclical and seasonal nature of the gift market in general and, more specifically, in Chicago. On the basis of her analysis, she concluded that the market factors were attractive. The market for more expensive gifts was large, growing, and not vulnerable to business cycles. The only negative aspect was the high seasonality of gifts, with peaks at Valentine's Day, June (due to weddings), Christmas, and other holidays.

Competitive Factors   The nature of the competition in retail markets is affected by barriers to entry, the bargaining power of vendors, and competitive rivalry.[51] Retail markets are more attractive when competitive entry is costly. **Barriers to entry** are conditions in a retail market that make it difficult for other firms to enter the market. Some of these conditions are (1) scale economies, (2) customer loyalty, and (3) the availability of great locations.

Scale economies are cost advantages due to a retailer's size. Markets dominated by large competitors with scale economies are typically unattractive because the dominant firms have sustainable cost advantages. For example, an entrepreneur would view the drugstore market as unattractive because it is dominated by three large firms: Walgreens, CVS, and Rite Aid. These firms have considerable cost advantages over an entrepreneur because they have significant bargaining power over suppliers and can buy merchandise at lower prices. They have the resources to invest in the latest technology and can spread the fixed costs of such investments across more outlets.

Retail markets dominated by a well-established retailer that has developed a loyal group of customers also are unattractive. For example, Home Depot's high customer loyalty in Atlanta, where it has its corporate offices, makes it hard for a competing home improvement center like Lowe's to compete effectively in the Atlanta market.

The availability of locations may impede competitive entry. Staples, for instance, attributes part of its success over its rivals in the northeastern United States to its first-mover advantage. The Northeast has a preponderance of mature but stable retail markets, so finding new locations is more difficult there than it is in most of the rest of the United States. Because Staples started in the Northeast, it was able to open stores in the best available locations.

Entry barriers are a double-edged sword. A retail market with high entry barriers is very attractive for retailers presently competing in that market, because those barriers limit competition. However, markets with high entry barriers are unattractive for retailers not already in the market.

Another competitive factor is the **bargaining power of vendors.** Markets are less attractive when only a few vendors control the merchandise sold in the market. In such situations, vendors have the opportunity to dictate prices and other terms (like delivery dates), reducing the retailer's profits. For example, the market for retailing fashionable cosmetics is less attractive because two suppliers, Estée Lauder (Estée Lauder, Clinique, Prescriptives, Aveda, Jo Malone, Bumble and Bumble, Tommy Hilfiger, MAC, and Origins) and L'Oréal (Maybelline, Giorgio Armani, Redken, Lancôme, Garnier, and Ralph Lauren) provide most of the desirable premium brands. Because department stores need these brands to support a fashion image, the vendors have the power to sell their products to retailers at high prices.

The final competitive factor is the level of competitive rivalry in the retail market. **Competitive rivalry** is the frequency and intensity of reactions to actions undertaken by competitors. When rivalry is high, price wars erupt, retailers attempt to "steal" employees from one another, advertising and promotion expenses increase, and profit potential falls. Conditions that may lead to intense rivalry include (1) a large number of competitors that are all about the same size, (2) slow growth, (3) high fixed costs, and (4) a lack of perceived differences between competing retailers. For example, Home Depot and Lowe's have an intense rivalry in many markets.

When Kelly Bradford started to analyze the competitive factors for Gifts To Go, she realized that identifying her competitors wasn't easy. Although there were no gift stores carrying similar merchandise at the same price points in the Chicago area, there were various other retailers from which a customer could buy gifts. She identified her primary competitors as department stores, craft galleries, catalogs, and Internet retailers. Kelly felt there were some scale economies in developing customer databases to support gift retailing. The lack of large suppliers meant that vendors' bargaining power wasn't a problem, and competitive rivalry was minimal because the gift business was not a critical part of a department store's overall business. In addition, merchandise carried by the various retailers offered considerable differentiation opportunities.

Environmental Dynamics   Environmental dynamics that can affect market attractiveness include technological, economic, regulatory, and social changes. When a retail market is going through significant changes in technology, existing competitors are vulnerable to new entrants that are skilled at using the new technology. Many traditional store-based retailers were slow to develop their multichannel strategies fully. For instance, even today, many multichannel retailers do not offer customers the ability to purchase over the Internet and return merchandise to a store. Retailing View 5.5 illustrates how changes in the competitive environment forced Hot Topic to reevaluate its entire retail format.

Government regulations can reduce the attractiveness of a retail market. For example, until recently, government regulations made it difficult for retailers to open big-box stores in France and Germany.[52] Also, many local governments within the United States have tried to stop Walmart from entering their markets in an attempt to protect locally owned retailers.

Retailers need to answer three questions about each environmental factor:

1. What new developments or changes might occur, such as new technologies and regulations or different social factors and economic conditions?

2. What is the likelihood that these environmental changes will occur? What key factors affect whether these changes will occur?

3. How will these changes affect each retail market, the firm, and its competitors?

Kelly Bradford's primary concern when she did an environmental analysis was the potential growth of Internet gift retailers such as RedEnvelope. Gifts seem ideal for an electronic channel, because customers can order the item over the Internet and have it shipped directly to the gift recipient. Kelly also recognized that the electronic channel could effectively collect information about customers and then target promotions and suggestions to them when future gift-giving occasions arose.

RETAILING VIEW   Hot Topic Emphasizes Its Strength in Indie Music   5.5

Hot Topic, which started in the late 1980s, differentiated itself from other mall-based retailers targeting the Generation Y segment by offering an edgier alternative. It offered goth merchandise in its stores, which were frequented by customers and sales associates with tattoos, multiple piercings, spiked hair, and all-black clothing. Over time, Hot Topic looked like an also-ran in the crowded teen-retailer market. The tastes of fickle teens had changed. Its sales were stagnant. Mall foot traffic was down.

Hot Topic analyzed its situation and discovered that its basis of advantage among teens wasn't its goth image but its connection to the indie music scene—the small avant-garde bands it promoted with its private-label T-shirts. So it repositioned itself, reducing its emphasis on goth-look apparel and placing more emphasis on merchandise linked to cutting-edge music and entertainment.

Today, its stores feel more like campus student centers with loud music, dark walls, and bulletin boards crammed with concert flyers and staff music picks. Hot Topic began hosting free acoustic shows, called Local Static, featuring bands chosen by salespeople in its local stores. The company stresses its connection with music through its music download site, ShockHound.

It also licensed exclusively *Twilight's* four-book-and-film franchise about teen vampire love. The movie's stars did a national tour of Hot Topic stores, and the retailer supplied hot chocolate and pizza to thousands of fans.

When Hot Topic's market declined, it altered its strategic positioning to target young consumers that prefer local bands.

Sources: Schuyler Velasco, "How 'The Hunger Games' Scored a Marketing Win," *Christain Science Monitor*, March, 2012, p. 10; Nivedita Bhattacharjee, "And Hot Topic Gets Hunger Games Lift but May Not Last," *March*, March 2012: and http://community.hottopic.com/content/about-hot-topics, accessed September 6, 2012.

DISCUSSION QUESTION

Describe Hot Topic's target market. How has this changed over time?

Step 3: Identify Strategic Opportunities

After completing the SWOT analysis, the next step is to identify opportunities for increasing retail sales. Kelly Bradford presently competes in gift retailing using a specialty store format. The strategic alternatives she is considering are defined in terms of the growth opportunities in Exhibit 5–4. Note that some of these growth strategies involve a redefinition of her mission.

Step 4: Evaluate Strategic Opportunities

The fourth step in the strategic planning process is to evaluate opportunities that have been identified in the SWOT analysis. The evaluation determines the retailer's potential to establish a sustainable competitive advantage and reap long-term profits from the opportunities being evaluated. Thus, a retailer must focus on opportunities that utilize its strengths and its competitive advantage.

Both the market attractiveness and the strengths and weaknesses of the retailer need to be considered in evaluating strategic opportunities. The greatest investments should be made in market opportunities for which the retailer has a strong competitive position. Here's Kelly's informal analysis:

Growth Opportunity	Market Attractiveness	Competitive Position
Increase size of present stores and amount of merchandise in stores	Low	High
Open additional gift stores in Chicago area	Medium	Medium
Open gift stores outside the Chicago area (new geographic segment)	Medium	Low
Sell lower-priced gifts in present stores or open new stores selling low-priced gifts (new benefit segment)	Medium	Low
Sell apparel and other nongift merchandise to same customers in same or new stores	High	Medium
Sell similar gift merchandise to same market segment using the Internet	High	Low
Open apparel stores targeted at teenagers	High	Low
Open a category specialist selling low-priced gifts	High	Low

Step 5: Establish Specific Objectives and Allocate Resources

After evaluating the strategic investment opportunities, the next step in the strategic planning process is to establish a specific objective for each opportunity. The retailer's overall objective is included in the mission statement; the specific objectives are goals against which progress toward the overall objective can be measured. Thus, these specific objectives have three components: (1) the performance sought, including a numerical index against which progress may be measured; (2) a time frame within which the goal is to be achieved; and (3) the level of investment needed to achieve the objective. Typically, the performance levels are financial criteria such as return on investment, sales, or profits. Kelly's objective is to increase profits by 20 percent in each of the next five years. She expects she will need to invest an additional $25,000 in her apparel and other nongift merchandise inventory.

Step 6: Develop a Retail Mix to Implement the Strategy

The sixth step in the planning process is to develop a retail mix for each opportunity in which an investment will be made and control and evaluate performance. Decisions related to the elements in the retail mix are discussed in Sections III and IV.

Step 7: Evaluate Performance and Make Adjustments

The final step in the planning process is to evaluate the results of the strategy and implementation program. If the retailer is meeting or exceeding its objectives, changes aren't needed. But if the retailer fails to meet its objectives, reanalysis is required. Typically, this reanalysis starts with reviewing the implementation programs, but it may indicate that the strategy (or even the mission statement) needs to be reconsidered. This conclusion would result in starting a new planning process, including a new SWOT analysis.

Strategic Planning in the Real World

The planning process in Exhibit 5–7 suggests that strategic decisions are made in a sequential manner. After the business mission is defined, the SWOT analysis is performed, strategic opportunities are identified, alternatives are evaluated, objectives are set, resources are allocated, the implementation plan is developed, and, finally, performance is evaluated and adjustments are made. But actual planning processes have interactions among the steps. For example, the SWOT analysis may uncover a logical alternative for the firm to consider, even though this alternative isn't included in the mission statement. Thus, the mission statement may need to be reformulated. The development of the implementation plan might reveal that the resources allocated to a particular opportunity are insufficient to achieve the objective. In that case, the objective would need to be changed, the resources would need to be increased, or the retailer might consider not investing in the opportunity at all.

SUMMARY

LO1 **Define the retail strategy.**

A retail strategy is a statement that identifies (1) the retailer's target market, (2) the format and resources the retailer plans to use to satisfy the target market's needs, and (3) the bases on which the retailer plans to build a sustainable competitive advantage. The target market is the market segment(s) toward which the retailer plans to focus its resources and retail mix. A retail format describes the nature of the retailer's operations—its retail mix. A sustainable competitive advantage is an advantage the retailer has over its competition that is not easily copied by competitors and thus can be maintained over a long period of time.

LO2 **Illustrate how retailers build a sustainable competitive advantage.**

Three approaches for developing a sustainable competitive advantage are (1) building strong relationships with customers, (2) building strong relationships with suppliers, and (3) achieving efficient internal operations. Each of these approaches involves developing an asset—loyal customers, strong vendor relationships, committed effective human resources, efficient systems, and attractive locations—that is not easily duplicated by competitors. Three approaches for developing a sustainable competitive advantage are (1) building strong relationships with customers, (2) building strong relationships with suppliers, and (3) achieving efficient internal operations. To build an advantage that is sustainable for a long period of time, retailers typically cannot rely on a single approach, such as good locations or excellent customer service. Instead, they use multiple approaches to build as high a wall around their position as possible.

LO3 **Classify the different strategic growth opportunities retailers pursue.**

Four types of growth opportunities that retailers may pursue are market penetration, market expansion, retail format development, and diversification. The success in pursuing these growth opportunities is the synergies between the retailer's present markets and the growth opportunity—whether the opportunity involves markets the retailer is presently pursuing or new markets—and the synergies between the retailer's present retail mix and the retail mix of the growth opportunity—whether the opportunity exploits the retailer's skills and knowledge in operating its present format or requires new capabilities to operate a new format.

LO4 **Identify issues that arise as domestic retailers become global retailers.**

By expanding internationally, retailers can increase their sales, leverage their knowledge and systems across a greater sales base, and gain more bargaining power with vendors. But international expansion is risky because retailers must deal with different government regulations, cultural traditions, consumer preferences, supply chains, and languages. The attractiveness of international opportunities is assessed by (1) the potential size of the retail market in the country, (2) the degree to which the country does and can support the entry of foreign retailers engaged in modern retail practices, and (3) the risks or uncertainties in sales and profits. The most attractive international markets are India, China, and Brazil.

152   SECTION II   Retailing Strategy

LO5 **Know the steps retailers go through to develop a strategic plan.**

Strategic planning is an ongoing process. Every day, retailers audit their situations, examine consumer trends, study new technologies, and monitor competitive activities. But the retail strategy statement does not change every year or every six months; the strategy statement is reviewed and altered only when major changes in the retailer's environment or capabilities occur.

When a retailer undertakes a major reexamination of its strategy, the process for developing a new strategy statement may take a year or two.

Potential strategic directions are generated by people at all levels of the organization and then evaluated by senior executives and operating personnel to ensure that the eventual strategic direction is profitable in the long run and can be implemented.

The strategic planning process consists of a sequence of steps: (1) define the business mission, (2) conduct a SWOT analysis, (3) identify strategic opportunities, (4) evaluate the alternatives, (5) establish specific objectives and allocate resources, (6) develop a retail mix to implement the strategy, and (7) evaluate performance and make adjustments.

KEY TERMS

bargaining power of vendors, *148*
barriers to entry, *147*
competitive rivalry, *148*
cross-selling, *136*
customer loyalty, *127*
customer relationship management (CRM) program, *131*
direct investment, *144*
diversification growth opportunity, *136*
franchising, *144*
frequent shopper program, *131*
joint venture, *144*
loyalty program, *131*
market expansion growth opportunity, *136*

market penetration growth opportunity, *135*
mission statement, *145*
opportunities and threats analysis, *147*
own brand, *130*
perceptual map, *128*
positioning, *128*
private-label brand, *130*
related diversification growth opportunity, *137*
retail community, *131*
retail format, *124*
retail format development growth opportunity, *136*
retail market, *125*

retail strategy, *124*
scale economies, *147*
SWOT analysis, *146*
store brand, *130*
strategic alliance, *144*
strategic retail planning process, *144*
strengths and weaknesses analysis, *146*
sustainable competitive advantage, *124*
target market, *124*
unorganized retailing, *140*
unrelated diversification growth opportunity, *137*
vertical integration, *137*

GET OUT AND DO IT!

1. **CONTINUING CASE ASSIGNMENT** Prepare an analysis of the company you selected for the continuing assignment. Identify its direct competitors, its target market and positioning, its strategy with respect to its competitors, its retail format (the elements in its retail mix—merchandise variety and assortment, pricing, locations), and its bases for developing a competitive advantage relative to its competitors. Outline the retailer's strengths, weaknesses, opportunities, and threats relative to its competitors. Pick a specific country in which the firm does not operate, and make a recommendation about whether the retailer should enter the country and, if so, how it should do so.

2. **INTERNET EXERCISE** Visit the websites for IKEA (www.ikea.com) and Starbucks (www.starbucks.com). Are the look and feel of these Internet sites consistent with the in-store experience of these retailers?

3. **INTERNET EXERCISE** Go to the websites for Walmart (www.walmartstores.com), Carrefour (www.carrefour.fr), Royal Ahold (www.ahold.com), and Metro AG (www.metro.de). Which chain has the most global strategy? Justify your answer.

4. **GO SHOPPING** Visit two stores that sell similar merchandise categories and cater to the same target segment(s). How are their retail formats (the elements in their retail mixes) similar? Dissimilar? On what bases do they have a sustainable competitive advantage? Explain which you believe has a stronger position.

5. **WEB OLC EXERCISE** Go to the student side of the book's website, and click on "Market Position Matrix."
Exercise 1: This spreadsheet describes an analysis of international growth opportunities. What numbers in the matrices would have to change to make China and France more attractive opportunities? To make Brazil and Mexico less attractive opportunities? Change the numbers in the matrices, and see what effect this has on the overall position of the opportunity in the grid.

Exercise 2: The market attractiveness/competitive position matrix can also be used by a department store to evaluate its merchandise categories and determine how much it should invest in each category. Fill in the importance weights (10 = very important, 1 = not very important) and the evaluations of the merchandise categories (10 = excellent, 1 = poor), and then see what is recommended by the plot on the opportunity matrix.

Exercise 3: Think of another investment decision that a retailer might make, and analyze it using the strategic analysis matrix. List the alternatives and the characteristics of the alternatives, and then put in the importance weights for the characteristics (10 = very important, 1 = not very important) and the evaluation of each alternative on each characteristic (10 = excellent, 1 = poor).

DISCUSSION QUESTIONS AND PROBLEMS

1. For each of the four retailers discussed at the beginning of the chapter (Chipotle Mexican Grill, Lululemon, Chico's, and Save-A-Lot), describe its strategy and the basis of its competitive advantage.

2. Choose a retailer, and describe how it has developed a competitive strategic advantage.

3. Give an example of a market penetration, a retail format development, a market expansion, and a diversification growth strategy that Best Buy might use.

4. Choose your favorite retailer. Draw and explain a positioning map, like that shown in Exhibit 5–3, that includes your retailer, retailers that sell the same types of merchandise, and the target customer segments (ideal points).

5. Do a SWOT analysis for McDonald's. What is its mission? What are its strengths and weaknesses? What opportunities and environmental threats might it face over the next 10 years? How could it prepare for these threats?

6. What are Neiman Marcus's and PetSmart's bases for sustainable competitive advantage? Are they really sustainable, or are they easily copied?

7. Assume you are interested in opening a restaurant in your town. Go through the steps in the strategic planning process shown in Exhibit 5–7. Focus on conducting a SWOT analysis of the local restaurant market, identifying and evaluating alternatives, and selecting a target market and a retail mix for the restaurant.

8. The Gap owns several chains, including Old Navy, Banana Republic, Piperlime, and Athleta. What type of growth opportunity was The Gap pursuing when it opened each of these retail concepts? Which is most synergistic with the original Gap chain?

9. Identify a store or service provider that you believe has an effective loyalty program. Explain why it is effective.

10. Choose a retailer that you believe could be, but is not yet, successful in other countries. Explain why you think it could be successful.

11. Amazon.com started as an Internet retailer selling books. Then it pursued a variety of growth opportunities, including expanding to groceries, DVDs, apparel, software, and travel services; introducing e-readers (Kindle); operating the Internet channel for other retailers; and hosting virtual stores for small, independent retailers. Evaluate these growth opportunities in terms of the probability that they will be profitable businesses for Amazon.com. What competitive advantages does Amazon.com bring to each of these businesses?

SUGGESTED READINGS

Aaker, David. *Strategic Market Management*, 6th ed. New York: Wiley, 2009.

Cao, Lanlan, and Marc Dupuis. "Strategy and Sustainable Competitive Advantage of International Retailers in China." *Journal of Asia-Pacific Business* 11, no. 1 (2010), pp. 6–27.

Cuthbertson, Christine, and Jonathan Reynolds. *Retail Strategy*. London: Routledge, 2012.

Etgar, M., and D. Rachman-Moore. "The Relationship between National Cultural Dimensions and Retail Format Strategies." *Journal of Retailing and Consumer Services* 18, no. 5 (2011), pp. 397–404.

Fox, Edward J., and Raj Sethuraman. "Retail Competition." In *Retailing in the 21st Century—Current and Future Trends*, 2nd ed., eds. Manfred Kraft and Murali Mantrala. Berlin: Springer, 2010, pp. 239–256.

Gamble, John E., Arthur A Thompson Jr., and Margaret Peteraf. *Essentials of Strategic Management: The Quest for Competitive Advantage*, 3rd ed. New York: McGraw-Hill, 2013.

Grewal, Dhruv, Ram Krishnan, Michael Levy, and Jeanne Mungar. "Retail Success and Key Drivers." In *Retailing in the 21st Century—Current and Future Trends*, 2nd ed., eds. Manfred Kraft and Murali Mantrala. Berlin: Springer, 2010, pp. 15–30.

Lehmann, Donald, and Russell Winer. *Analysis for Marketing Planning*, 8th ed. Burr Ridge, IL: McGraw-Hill/Irwin, 2010.

Ortinau, D. J., B. J. Babin and J. C. Chebat, "Retailing Evolution Research: Introduction to the Special Section on Retailing Research," *Journal of Business Research* 64, no. 6 (2011), pp. 541–542.

Rothaermel, Frank T. *Strategic Management: Concepts*. New York: McGraw-Hill, 2013.

Zentes, Joachim, Dirk Morschett, and Hanna Schramm-Klein. *Strategic Retail Management: Text And International Cases*, 2nd ed. Weisbaden: Springer, 2011.

Retail Locations

EXECUTIVE BRIEFING

Michael Kercheval, President and CEO
International Council of Shopping Centers

While I was going to college, I became very concerned about the poor quality of life in much of the world and volunteered to work on several economic development projects in Latin America sponsored by the Peace Corps and the Pan American Health Organization. From these experiences, I decided to go to medical school, become a doctor, and then return to Latin America. But pre-med chemistry did not agree with me. I discovered economics and majored in developmental economics.

After graduate school, I went to work for Equitable Life Insurance and eventually became involved in managing real estate investment activities in Latin America. I observed keenly how retail developments are a catalyst for economic development. They create a virtuous cycle: retail developments → more goods, more choices, lower prices, and greater income → more retail development. The shopping centers provided goods to people with higher quality at lower prices and greater convenience. By saving people money on necessities, they can have a higher standard of living and greater disposable income. In addition, the retail developments provided jobs that increased the incomes. Then the increased incomes spurred more retail developments.

I am president of the International Council for Shopping Centers (ICSC), which offers me a chance to serve an industry that is very involved in economic development around the world, as well as in U.S. urban and rural communities.

The retail development industry is at an interesting crossroads now. Demand for retail space across the globe is far greater than supply, and there is considerable capital available to invest in new retail developments. The primary restraint to growth is from government policymakers who are tempering new development out of concern for small retail businesses, the environment, and what they see as suburban sprawl. ICSC and its members are working on ways to meet the retail needs of consumers, stimulate economic growth, and address the concerns of policymakers.

CHAPTER 7

LEARNING OBJECTIVES

LO1 Describe the types of retail locations available to retailers.

LO2 Review the types of unplanned locations.

LO3 Analyze the characteristics of the different types of shopping centers.

LO4 Discuss nontraditional retail locations.

LO5 Match the locations to the retailer's strategy.

LO6 Review the societal and legal considerations in selecting locations.

The oft-referenced response to the question "What are the three most important things in retailing?" is "Location, location, location." Why is store location such an important decision for a retailer? First, location is typically one of the most influential considerations in a customer's store-choice decision. For instance, when choosing where you're going to have your car washed, you usually pick the location closest to your home or work. Most consumers similarly shop at the supermarket closest to them.

Second, location decisions have strategic importance because they can be used to develop a sustainable competitive advantage. If a retailer has the best location, that is, the location that is most attractive to its customers, competitors can't copy this advantage. Competitors are relegated to occupying the second-best location.

Third, location decisions are risky. Typically, when retailers select a location, they either must make a substantial investment to buy and develop the real estate or must commit to a long-term lease with developers. Retailers often commit to leases for 5 to 15 years.

In the first part of this chapter, we discuss the types and relative advantages of three types of locations available to retailers—unplanned, planned, and nontraditional. We then examine how the location decision fits into the retailer's strategy. For example, the best locations for a 7-Eleven convenience store are not the best locations for a category specialist such as a Best Buy. We end this chapter by discussing the societal and legal considerations affecting a retailer's location decisions. In the next chapter, we discuss the issues involved in selecting areas of the country in which to locate stores and how to evaluate specific locations and negotiate leases.

184   SECTION II   Retailing Strategy

TYPES OF RETAIL LOCATIONS

LO1

Describe the types of retail locations available to retailers.

Many types of locations are available for retail stores, each type with its benefits and limitations. The two basic types of location are unplanned (freestanding and urban sites) and planned (shopping centers). **Unplanned locations** do not have centralized management that determines what stores will be in a development, where the specific stores will be located, and how they will be operated. In **planned locations,** the shopping center developer and/or manager makes and enforces policies that govern store operations, such as the hours that a store must be opened. The shopping center management also maintains the common facilities such as the parking area—an arrangement referred to as **common area maintenance (CAM)**—and is responsible for providing security, parking lot lighting, outdoor signage for the center, advertising, special events to attract consumers, and so on.

In the United States, about 47 percent of the gross leasable square feet of retail space is in planned locations and the remaining in unplanned locations.[1] **Gross leasable area (GLA)** is the real estate industry's term for the total floor area designed for the retailer's occupancy and exclusive use, including any basements, mezzanines, or upper floors.

When choosing a particular location type, retailers evaluate a series of trade-offs involving the size of the trade area, the occupancy cost of the location (rent, maintenance, energy cost, etc.), the pedestrian and vehicle customer traffic associated with the location, the restrictions placed on store operations by the shopping center management, and the convenience of the location for customers. The **trade area** is the geographic area that encompasses most of the customers who would patronize a specific retail site. The following sections describe the characteristics of each type of location, as summarized in Exhibit 7–1.

EXHIBIT 7–1   Characteristics of Different Retail Locations

	Size (000 sq. ft.)	Trading Area (Miles)	Annual Occupancy Cost ($ per sq. ft.)	Shopping Convenience	Pedestrian Traffic	Vehicular Traffic	Restrictions on Operations	Typical Tenants
UNPLANNED AREAS								
Freestanding	Varies	3–7	15–30	High	Low	High	Limited	Convenience, drug stores, category specialists
Urban locations/ central business district	Varies	Varies	8–20	Low	High	Low	Limited to medium	Specialty stores
SHOPPING CENTERS								
Neighborhood and community shopping centers	30–350	3–6	8–20	High	Low	High	Medium	Supermarkets, discount stores
Power centers	250–600	5–10	10–20	Medium	Medium	Medium	Limited	Category specialists
Regional and super-regional enclosed malls	400–1,000	5–25	10–70	Low	High	Low	High	Department and specialty apparel stores
Lifestyle centers	150–800	5–15	15–35	Medium	Medium	Medium	Medium to high	Specialty apparel and home stores, restaurants
Outlet centers	50–400	25–75	8–15	Low	High	High	Limited	Off-price retailers and factory outlets
Theme/festival centers	80–250	N/A	20–70	Low	High	Low	Highest	Specialty stores and restaurants

Sources: Personal communications with industry executives; "North American Retail Highlights 2009," http://www.colliers.com/Content/Repositories/Base/Corporate/English/Market_Report_Corporate/PDFs/RetailNaHighlightsSpring2009.pdf; http://www.icsc.org/srch/lib/2009_S-C_CLASSIFICATION_May09.pdf.

UNPLANNED LOCATIONS

The three types of unplanned retail locations are freestanding sites, urban locations, and mainstreet locations.

Freestanding Sites

Freestanding sites are retail locations for an individual, isolated store unconnected to other stores; however, they might be near other freestanding stores or near a shopping center. The advantages of freestanding locations are their convenience for customers (easy access and parking); high vehicular traffic and visibility to attract customers driving by; modest occupancy costs; and fewer restrictions on signs, hours, or merchandise that might be imposed by management of planned locations.

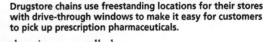

There are several disadvantages to freestanding sites. First, is their limited trade area. Typically, there are no other nearby retailers to attract customers interested in conveniently shopping for multiple categories of merchandise on one trip. In addition, freestanding locations typically have higher occupancy costs than shopping centers because they do not have other retailers to share

Drugstore chains use freestanding locations for their stores with drive-through windows to make it easy for customers to pick up prescription pharmaceuticals.

the common area maintenance costs. Finally, freestanding locations generally have little pedestrian traffic, limiting the number of customers who might drop in because they are walking by.

Some retailers are shifting from planned locations to freestanding locations to offer their customers a better shopping experience. The three major drugstore chains (CVS, Walgreens, and Rite Aid) have shifted their emphasis from strip malls to freestanding locations because they want accessible drive-through windows for pharmacies, more floor space, and better access for receiving merchandise.

Outparcels are freestanding stores that are not connected to other stores in a shopping center, but are located on the premises of a shopping center, typically in a parking area. Some advantages of outparcels compared to other freestanding locations are that they can offer customers the convenience of a drive-through window, extensive parking, and clear visibility from the street. These locations are popular for fast-food restaurants and banks.

Urban Locations

Urban areas in large cities offer three types of locations: the central business district, inner city, and gentrified residential sites.

Central Business District   The **central business district (CBD)** is the traditional downtown financial and business area in a city or town. Due to its daily activity, it draws many people and employees into the area during business hours. There is a high level of pedestrian traffic, but shopping flow in the evening and on weekends is slow in many CBDs. Vehicular traffic is limited due to congestion in urban areas, and parking problems reduce consumer convenience. Many CBDs have a large number of residents living in nearby areas.

Risk-taking entrepreneurial developers working with forward-thinking urban planners and city leaders are slowly attracting more people to the CBD at night and during weekends. For example, coal and steel are no longer the backbone of Cleveland's economy. City leaders and local developers reinvented the CBD using an entertainment-focused strategy to redevelop East Fourth Street. Retail stores occupy about one-third of the 600,000-square-foot, $110 million, historic redevelopment project. The rest is housing. The area is spectacularly designed

Cleveland's East Fourth Street development attracts consumers to the CBD.

with art, flowers, decorative paving, planters, outdoor seating, and special overhead lighting. To increase the foot traffic, two new stadiums for the city's football and baseball teams, a new arena for its basketball team, and the Rock and Roll Hall of Fame were built. Today, city residents and suburbanites flock to East Fourth Street before and after sports and entertainment events, as well as for an interesting afternoon or evening "on the town."[2]

Inner City   During the 1970s and 1980s, many U.S. and some European cities experienced urban decay. **Urban decay** is the process of a previously functioning city, or part of a city, falling into disrepair. The **inner city** is a low-income residential area within a large city. Empty lots, buildings, and condemned houses attract criminals and street gangs that make living in the inner city dangerous. One of the major causes of urban decay is when businesses relocate from the inner city to suburbs.

Some U.S. retailers avoid opening stores in the inner city because they think these stores are riskier and produce lower returns than other areas. Although income levels are lower in inner cities than in other neighborhoods, inner-city retailers often achieve a higher sales volume and higher margins, resulting in higher profits.

Inner-city residents and public policy advocates are concerned about the offerings at inner-city grocery stores. Instead of offering fresh meat and produce, they tend to feature lower-priced packaged foods that have longer shelf lives. As a result, inner-city consumers often have to travel to the suburbs using buses to shop for healthy food items. Government programs, in partnership with nonprofit organizations, are working to change the inner-city supermarket landscape. For instance, in an inner-city Philadelphia neighborhood, a new supermarket, stocked with fresh produce, a pharmacy, and various ethnic products, has opened within walking distance of most of the neighborhood. Nonprofit organizations such as Philadelphia's Food Trust lobby for loans and government subsidies to support supermarkets in lower-income areas.[3] Retailing View 7.1 describes how Magic Johnson has brought retailing to the inner city.

Retailing can play an important role in inner-city redevelopment activities by providing needed services and jobs for inner-city residents, as well as property taxes to support the redevelopment. Because of the potential of this untapped market and incentives from local governments, developers are increasing their focus on opportunities in the inner city. However, inner-city redevelopments can be controversial. Often local governments will use the right of eminent domain to buy buildings and land and then sell it to developers at an attractive price. For instance, people are concerned about the residents displaced by the development, increased traffic, and parking.

Gentrified Residential Areas   Many inner-city areas are going through a process of **gentrification**—the renewal and rebuilding of offices, housing, and retailers in deteriorating areas—coupled with an influx of more affluent people that displaces the former, lower-income residents. Young professionals and retired empty-nesters are moving into these areas to enjoy the convenience of shopping, restaurants, and entertainment near where they live.

Some retailers are finding urban locations attractive, particularly in cities that are redeveloping their urban areas. Big-box retailers like Target, Walmart, Office Depot, Home Depot, and Costco, which usually locate in the suburbs, are now opening outlets in cities, typically with smaller stores.[4]

While some U.S. cities are still struggling to rekindle their business, social, cultural, and retail vitality, others like New York, Chicago, and many Canadian and European cities have not experienced significant urban decay. These cities offer very attractive markets for retailers. For example, the world's five most famous locations for high-fashion retailers are in these locations—Oxford and Regent Street in London, Fifth Avenue between 49th and 58th Streets in New York City, Rue du Faubourg Saint-Honoré in Paris, Rodeo Drive in Los Angeles, and Passeig de Gràcia in Barcelona.[5]

Retailers need to tailor their offerings to the unique characteristics of urban gentrified consumers and the restrictions associated with these locations. When selecting a store to patronize, these urban consumers, compared with suburban consumers, typically place more importance on reducing their shopping time rather than the

RETAILING VIEW   Magic Johnson Brings Retailing to the Inner City   7.1

They called him "Magic" because of the way he knew where to pass the ball without looking and his ability to make jump shots that seemingly had no hope of going in. But since retiring from the NBA and becoming one of the first public figures to announce his HIV-positive status, Earvin Johnson also has turned his magic touch to urban redevelopment and growth, creating a whole new meaning for his famous nickname.

In the mid-1990s, Magic Johnson announced a partnership with Loews Cineplex, which would seek to open more movie theaters in underserved inner-city markets. Research showed that approximately one-third of movie tickets were being purchased by lower-income, minority audiences. Yet most of these consumers had to travel long distances, often taking up to an hour, to get to a theater, because few theaters were located in urban locations. For Johnson, the natural response was to build more urban movie theaters.

Once the Magic Johnson Theaters group had built a few facilities, Johnson and his partners recognized that their success depended on attracting customers by offering complementary entertainment as well. People love to have dinner before or dessert after catching a movie, but many casual dining franchises avoided urban locations. Instead, their conventional strategies involved targeting middle-class, suburban markets, with little consideration of diverse demographics. Again weaving his magic, Johnson ultimately convinced Starbucks to enter into an exclusive joint partnership with the theater group, after which T.G.I. Fridays came on board as well.

Today, the Johnson Development Corporation (JDC) consists of four separate enterprises. In addition to Magic Johnson Theatres, it includes Urban Coffee Opportunities, Magic Johnson's T.G.I. Friday's, and the Canyon Johnson Urban Fund. Through these entitites, the JDC seeks to establish entertainment complexes, featuring theaters, coffee shops, restaurants, and retailing, in underserved U.S. markets. The 50–50 partnerships thus give JDC connections to some of the most successful names in each

Doris Jackson, 8, left, sits at a computer as Earvin "Magic" Johnson looks over her shoulder at the Mattie Koonce Learning Center in the Overtown section in Miami, Florida. Through his foundation, Johnson has helped donate $200,000 in computer equipment to the learning center.

market, such as Loews Cineplex Entertainment, Starbucks, and T.G.I. Friday's—and they give urban consumers a fun way to spend their Saturday nights.

Sources: Roger Vincent, "Magic Johnson Built Business Empire after Court Glories Ended," *Los Angeles Times*, March 28, 2012; "Meet Magic Johnson, the Media Mogul," *CNN Money*, March 15, 2012; and Danielle Kwateng, "Decoding the Business of Earvin "Magic" Johnson," *Black Enterprise*, March 30, 2012.

DISCUSSION QUESTION

Among all of the potential retailers that could be interested in an inner-city location, why have Loews Cineplex Entertainment, Starbucks, and T.G.I. Friday's been particularly interested in working with Magic Johnson?

Rodeo Drive is an CBD location that is one the most highly regarded locations by retailers of high-fashion merchandise.

breadth and depth of the retailer's assortment. For example, Office Depot's urban stores are 5,000 square feet, about a fifth of a suburban store. The shelves are about 6 feet high, much shorter than in a suburban store, so visitors can navigate quickly. The signs above the aisles are simplified so customers do not waste time interpreting them. A suburban Office Depot store has 9,000 SKUs for sale, while its urban stores have half that number. The merchandise offered focuses on immediate-replacement items (a pen) versus stock-up items (a 25-pack of pens).

Retailers with urban locations also need to recognize the differences in consumer needs within these markets. For example, the Walgreens store in New York City's Union Square attracts commuters and tourists using the subway; the store a few blocks north draws mostly local residents. So the Union Square site carries lots of products such as umbrellas for the unprepared tourists, along with cosmetics and snacks; the other store is more heavily stocked with household-cleaning items and toothpaste.[6]

Finally, to deal with the traffic and parking problems in these gentrified residential areas, many residents use public transportation or walk when they go shopping. As a result, they are reluctant to buy bulky items like a 24-pack of toilet paper and are active users of Internet retail channels.

Main Street

Main Street refers to the traditional downtown shopping area in smaller towns and secondary shopping areas in large cities and their suburbs. Over the past 30 years, many downtowns in small U.S. towns have experienced decay similar to that of inner cities. When Walmart and other big-box retailers opened standalone stores on the outskirts of these towns, local retailers could not compete effectively with these big boxes and went out of business. In response, smaller towns are undertaking redevelopment programs to draw residents back to their downtown areas, and retailers play a major role in these efforts.

To attract consumers and retailers, these Main Street redevelopment efforts focus on providing a better shopping experience than big-box retailers do. Instead of streets, they develop pedestrian walkways. Next to major crosswalks, pedestrian shelters equipped with benches provide shady resting spots for mobile shoppers, helping them extend their visits and prolong their shopping excursions. Property owners can also receive grants if they agree to maintain and enhance their shops' appearance with necessary repairs, new signage, attractive entrances, attention-grabbing windows, and nice awnings. Furthermore, the town administrations work to improve downtown aesthetics with landscaping, which surrounds repaved sidewalks and updated (and functioning) street lights.[7]

Main Street locations share most of the characteristics of locations in gentrified urban areas, but their occupancy costs are generally lower. Main Street locations do not draw as many people as the CBD because fewer people work in the area, and the fewer stores generally mean a smaller overall draw to the area. In addition, Main Streets typically don't offer the range of entertainment and recreational activities available in the more successful primary CBDs. Finally, the planning organization for the town or redevelopment often imposes some restrictions on Main Street store operations.

SHOPPING CENTERS AND PLANNED
RETAIL LOCATIONS

In this section, we discuss the different types of shopping centers—planned locations. A **shopping center** is a group of retail and other commercial establishments that are planned, developed, owned, and managed as a single property. After discussing the role of shopping center developers and management, each type of center is discussed.

By combining many stores at one location, developments attract more consumers to the shopping center than would be the case if the stores were at separate locations. The developer and shopping center management carefully select a set of retailers that are complementary to provide consumers with a comprehensive shopping experience at one, convenient location.

Lease agreements typically require that retailers in the center pay a portion of the common area maintenance (CAM) costs for the center according to the size of their store's space and/or sales volume and a retail fee based on sales. As mentioned earlier, the shopping center management group can place restrictions on the operating hours, signage, and even the type of merchandise sold in the stores.

Most shopping centers have at least one or two major retailers, referred to as **anchors,** such as Macy's, Walmart, or Kroger. These retailers are courted by the center's developer because they attract a significant number of consumers and consequently make the center more appealing for other retailers. To get these anchor retailers to locate in a center, developers frequently give them special deals, such as reduced lease costs.

These shopping centers are generally managed by a **shopping center property management firm,** which is a company that specializes in developing, owning, and/or managing shopping centers. Management of these shopping malls entails selecting and negotiating leases with retail tenants, maintaining the common areas, marketing the centers to attract consumers, and providing security. Retailing View 7.2 describes the evolution of Simon Properties—the largest retail management company in the world.

In Exhibit 7–2, the characteristics of the different types of shopping centers are outlined followed by a discussion of each type. As you can see, strip centers account for the vast majority of retail GLA. The growth rate in terms of the number of shopping centers is limited; however, the greatest growth has been lifestyle centers followed by power centers. Regional and super-regional enclosed malls have the highest sales per square foot.

LO3

Analyze the characteristics of the different types of shopping centers.

REFACT

There are 23.1 square feet of retail GLA per person in the United States.[8]

REFACT

Highland Park Shopping Village in Dallas, Texas, developed by Hugh Prather in 1931, was the first planned shopping center. Its stores were built with a unified image and managed under the control of a single owner.[9]

REFACT

There are more than 107,000 shopping centers in the United States and fewer than 7,000 in the European Union.[10]

Number, Sales per Square Foot, and Growth Rate of Shopping Centers   **EXHIBIT 7–2**

	Number	Total GLA (millions of square feet)	Percentage of Overall Shopping Center GLA	Growth in Number of Centers 2008–2011	Anchor GLA Percentage of Total Center GLA	Sales per Square Foot ($)	Growth Rate in Sales per Square Foot 2009–2011
Community, neighborhood, and convenience	101,630	4,981	67.8%	1.3%	30–60%	12.68	5.7%
Regional and super-regional enclosed malls	1,505	1,321	18.0	1.1%	40–70	21.20	1.7
Power centers	2,023	822	11.2	2.8%	N/A	10.85	4.1
Lifestyle center	396	126	1.7	6.9%	0–50	N/A	N/A
Outlet centers	334	71	1.0	1.9%	N/A	N/A	N/A
Theme/festival centers	201	27	0.4	1.2%	N/A	N/A	N/A

Source: eData, International Council of Shopping Centers.

190   SECTION II   Retailing Strategy

Convenience, Neighborhood, and Community Shopping Centers

Convenience, neighborhood, and **community shopping centers** (also called **strip shopping centers**) are attached rows of open-air stores, with onsite parking usually located in front of the stores. The most common layouts are linear, L-shaped, and inverted U-shaped. Historically, the term *strip center* has applied to the linear configuration.

Smaller centers (convenience and neighborhood centers) are 10,000 to 60,000 square feet and are typically anchored by a supermarket. They are designed for convenience shopping. These centers typically have 10 to 15 smaller retailers such as a bakery, dollar store, dry cleaner, florist, laundry center, barber shop, and mail service. The larger centers (community centers) are typically 25,000 to

7.2   RETAILING VIEW   Simon Properties: The Largest Shopping Center Management Company in the World

Simon Properties owns, develops, and manages 326 retail real estate properties in the United States, including 151 regional malls, 58 premium outlet malls, and 66 lifestyle centers. This empire got its start in 1960, when Melvin Simon and Associates (MSA; the associates were Melvin's brothers Fred and Herbert) opened a shopping plaza in Bloomington, Indiana, followed quickly thereafter by four similar Indianapolis-area plazas. Melvin had previously established himself as a leasing agent in a local real estate firm, and MSA soon gained a reputation for managing its plazas well. Large tenants flocked to the retail centers; with big-name contracts with retailers such as Sears, Roebuck, MSA had easy access to bank financing for still more construction projects.

One of those projects was MSA's first enclosed mall, opened in the early 1960s. This format dominated its developments for years; then in the 1990s, MSA reinvented the retail real estate development market yet again by combining its malls with entertainment options. These multi-use centers attracted vast numbers of visitors, most of whom remained in the centers for hours. For example, The Forum Shops at Caesars Palace in Las Vegas sit between Caesars Palace and The Mirage, evoking an ancient Roman street. Visitors interact with animatronic statues, stop to rest at bubbling fountains, and enjoy simulated views of the awesome Mediterranean sky. In addition, MSA is responsible for perhaps the best known mall in America, that is, the Mall of America in Minnesota.

Today, the U.S. market allows for fewer new shopping centers, so Simon Properties—now led by Melvin's son David—aggressively pursues international growth and earns approximately 5.4 percent of its new operating income from international operations. In addition to investments in outlet centers in Japan, South Korea,

The Forum Shops at Caesars Palace in Las Vegas, developed and managed by Simon Properties, meld entertainment with shopping.

Malaysia, and Mexico, Simon Properties and its Paris-based Klépierre SA own nearly 300 shopping centers in 13 European countries. The global financial crisis has made Europe less attractive as a market for shopping center development; instead, Asia—particularly Shanghai, Mumbai, Dubai, and Tokyo—represent the most attractive regions with the greatest growth in rental rates.

Sources: "Buy Simon Property Group: Growth to Come from International Expansion," September 18, 2012; www.seekingalpha.com; "David Simon: Most Respected CEOs," and www.simon.com.

DISCUSSION QUESTION

What are the challenges facing Simon Properties as it pursues international growth opportunities?

50,000 square feet and are anchored by at least one big-box store such as a discount department store, an off-price retailer, or a category specialist.

The primary advantages of these centers are that they offer customers convenient locations and easy parking, and they have relatively low occupancy costs. The primary disadvantage is that smaller centers have a limited trade area due to their size, and they lack entertainment and restaurants to keep customers in the center for a longer time. In addition, there is no protection from the weather. As a result, neighborhood and community centers do not attract as many customers as do larger, enclosed malls.

National chains such as The Children's Place, Kohl's, Radio Shack, and Marshalls compete effectively against their rival mall-based retailers by offering the convenience of a neighborhood or community center. In these locations, they can offer lower prices, partly because of the lower occupancy cost, and their customers can drive right up to the door.[12]

Power Centers

Power centers are shopping centers that consist primarily of collections of big-box retail stores, such as full-line discount stores (Target), off-price stores (Marshalls), warehouse clubs (Costco), and category specialists (Lowe's, Staples, Michaels, Barnes & Noble, Best Buy, Sports Authority, and Toys "R" Us). Although these centers are open air, unlike traditional strip centers, power centers often consist of a collection of freestanding (unconnected) "anchor" stores and only a minimum number of smaller specialty store tenants. Many power centers are located near an enclosed shopping mall.

Power centers offer low occupancy costs and modest levels of consumer convenience and vehicular and pedestrian traffic. The growth in power centers reflects the growth of category specialists. Many power centers are now larger than regional malls and have trade areas as large as regional malls.

Enclosed Shopping Malls

Shopping malls are enclosed, climate-controlled, lighted shopping centers with retail stores on one or both sides of an enclosed walkway. Parking is usually provided around the perimeter of the mall. Shopping malls are classified as either **regional malls** (less than 800,000 square feet) or **super-regional malls** (more than 800,000 square feet). Super-regional centers are similar to regional centers, but because of their larger size, they have more anchors, specialty stores, and recreational opportunities and draw from a larger geographic area. They often are considered tourist attractions.

Enclosed shopping malls have several advantages over alternative locations. First, shopping malls attract many shoppers and have a large trade area because of the number of stores and the opportunity to combine shopping with an inexpensive form of entertainment. Older citizens get their exercise by walking the malls, and teenagers hang out and meet their friends, though some malls are restricting their admittance in the evenings. Thus, malls generate significant pedestrian traffic inside the mall and have sales per square foot almost twice that of power centers and strip centers. Second, customers don't have to worry about the weather, and thus malls are appealing places to shop during cold winters and hot summers. Third, mall management ensures a level of consistency that benefits all the tenants. For instance, most major malls enforce uniform hours of operation.

However, malls also have disadvantages. First, mall occupancy costs are higher than those of strip centers, freestanding sites, and most central business districts. For example, the occupancy cost (rent, common area maintenance, and taxes) for an enclosed mall is almost 140 percent greater than that for an open-air shopping center ($35.42 compared to $14.55 per square foot).[15] Second, some retailers may not like mall management's control of their operations,

REFACT

The first power center was the 280 Metro Center in Colma, California, which opened in 1993.[13]

REFACT

The first enclosed mall, called Southdale, opened in Edina, Minnesota (near Minneapolis), in 1956.[14]

such as strict rules governing window displays and signage. Third, competition within shopping centers can be intense. Several specialty and department stores might sell very similar merchandise and be located in close proximity. Fourth, freestanding locations, strip centers, lifestyle centers, and power centers are more convenient because customers can park in front of a store, go in and buy what they want, and go about their other errands. Fifth, some malls were built more than 40 years ago and have not been subject to any significant remodeling, so they appear run-down and unappealing to shoppers. Furthermore, these older malls are often located in areas with unfavorable demographics because the population has shifted from the near suburbs to outer suburbs. Sixth, the consolidation in the department store sector has decreased the number of potential anchor tenants and diminished the drawing power of enclosed malls. Finally, the growing sales through the Internet channel is cannibalizing sales through the store channel.

For these reasons, mall traffic and sales are declining. The last new mall was opened in 2006, and it is estimated that 10 percent of the 1,500 enclosed malls will close in the next three years (see www.deadmalls.com).[17] Most malls that close are razed; however, mall managers and developers are trying to redevelop failing malls. Some redevelopment projects become mixed-used spaces, incorporating unconventional tenants like government offices, churches, medical clinics, and satellite university campuses. Others seek to turn malls into one-stop sources for various services, not just fashionable apparel. A busy working mother visiting The Westside Pavilion mall in Los Angeles can thus drop off her kids for piano lessons at Music Stars & Masters on the second floor. During their lesson, she also can send an overnight package, get a haircut, have her purse repaired, and check out some books for the kids from the public library. If the kids do well with their lessons, mom might treat them to ice cream, too.[18]

Another approach for dealing with aging malls and the changing demographics in their trade areas is to tailor the offerings to the markets that do exist today. Older shopping centers such as Northridge Mall in northern California (built in 1972) can be repositioned to appeal to immigrant populations. In recent decades, the demographics of Monterey County have changed, producing a rich Latino culture in which approximately 75 percent of the population in the mall's trade area is of Latino heritage. Thus, the courtyard at the entryway to the mall hosts mariachi bands on weekend afternoons, while clowns and dancers provide family-friendly entertainment underneath colorful piñatas that have been suspended from the ceiling. To appeal to the large Roman Catholic population, the mall also offers services with religious themes, such as celebrations on Día de los Santos Reyes and shrines to the Virgen de Guadalupe Las Posadas. The idea is that the mall can be so welcoming that the local community views it more like a weekend home than a retail destination.[19]

While the percentage of mall retail sales has declined over the past 10 years, recently malls have experienced a slight increase in market share. This increase is due to the redevelopment efforts previously described plus an influx of exciting new tenants such as Aeropostale, Forever 21, Sephora, and H&M and the improved performance of anchors such as Macy's and Nordstrom.[20]

An increasing number of malls are using exciting stores like Forever 21 to attract younger customers.

Lifestyle Centers

Lifestyle centers are shopping centers that have an open-air configuration of specialty stores, entertainment, and restaurants, with design ambience and amenities such as fountains and street furniture. Lifestyle centers resemble the main streets in small towns, where people stroll from store to store, have lunch, and sit for a while on a park bench talking to friends. Thus, they cater to the "lifestyles" of consumers in their trade areas. Lifestyle centers are particularly attractive to specialty retailers.

People are attracted to lifestyle centers not only because of their shops and restaurants but also because of their outdoor attractions such as a pop-up fountain, ice cream carts, stilt walkers, balloon artists, magicians, face painters, concerts, and other events. Because lifestyle centers have some limited auto access, customers can be dropped off right in front of a store.

Because lifestyle centers are open air, bad weather can be an impediment to traffic. But some centers, like the Easton Town Center in Columbus, Ohio, thrive despite the climate.[21] When the weather is bad, tough Ohioans simply bundle up and take a stroll.

Due to the ease of parking, lifestyle centers are very convenient for shoppers, and the occupancy costs, like those of all open-air developments, are considerably lower than those for enclosed malls. But they typically have less retail space than enclosed malls and thus may attract fewer customers than enclosed malls. Many lifestyle centers are located near higher-income areas, so the higher purchases per visit compensate for the fewer number of shoppers. Finally, many lifestyle centers are part of larger, mixed-use developments, which are described in the next section.

Mixed-Use Developments

Mixed-use developments (MXDs) combine several different uses into one complex including retail, office, residential, hotel, recreation, or other functions. They are pedestrian-oriented and therefore facilitate a live-work-play environment.[22] They appeal to people who have had enough of long commutes to work and the social fragmentation of their neighborhoods and are looking for a lifestyle that gives them more time for the things they enjoy and an opportunity to live in a genuine community. In addition, MXDs are popular with retailers because they bring additional shoppers to their stores. They are also popular with governments, urban planners, developers, and environmentalists because they provide a pleasant, pedestrian environment and are an efficient use of space. For instance, land costs the

Mizner Park in Boca Raton, Florida, combines retail, residential, and entertainment offerings in one location with unique boutiques, eateries, music, movies, and art galleries conveniently located close to ocean-front apartments and condos.

same whether a developer builds a shopping mall by itself or an office tower on top of the mall or parking structure.

The Boca Mall, a 430,000-square-foot regional shopping mall in Boca Raton, Florida, opened in 1974. Decades later, the mall was plagued by two trends: population growth occurring elsewhere and competing malls that were attracting most of its patrons. The original anchors and many of the specialty stores departed. The Boca Mall was demolished and replaced with a mixed-use development called Mizner Park. Mizner Park has commercial office space located above the ground-floor retail space on one side of the street, and residential units sit above the retail space on the opposite side of the street.[23]

Outlet Centers

Outlet centers are shopping centers that contain mostly manufacturers' and retailers' outlet stores.[24] Some outlet centers have a strong entertainment component, including movie theaters and restaurants to keep customers on the premises longer. For example, the Outlets at Orange, in Orange, California, has a multiplex theater, with an IMAX movie theater; a children's play area; and Thrill It Fun Center.[25]

In the past, outlet stores sold damaged merchandise or excess production overruns. However, retailers have improved their demand forecasting, reducing the availability of production overruns. In addition, the availability of damaged goods has been reduced because these goods are weeded out before being shipped to the United States. Thus, 82 percent of products at outlet centers are made specifically for the outlets. The quality of these made-for-outlet products is not always the same quality as the branded merchandise sold in department or specialty stores.[26]

Typically, outlet centers are in remote locations. These remote locations offer lower costs and reduce the competition between the outlet stores and department and specialty stores offering the branded merchandise at full price.

Tourism represents 50 percent of the traffic generated for many outlet centers. Thus, many are located with convenient interstate access and close to popular tourist attractions. Some center developers actually organize bus tours to bring people hundreds of miles to their malls. As a result, the primary trade area for some outlet centers is 50 miles or more.

Outlet centers are also very popular in Europe, Japan, and China. Retailing View 7.3 describes an upscale outlet center with a unique theme in China.

Theme/Festival Centers

In **theme/festival centers,** a unifying theme generally is reflected in each individual store, both in their architecture and the merchandise they sell. This seemingly simple idea was introduced relatively late in the progression of retail ideas. In the late 1970s, a private developer took Boston's historic Faneuil Hall and reconceived it as a "festival marketplace." The goal was to attract multitudes of tourists and local visitors by being more fun and interesting than a basic suburban mall. The Faneuil Hall Marketplace resonates with a colonial history theme. Subsequent applications of the idea have included Baltimore's Inner Harbor and the Grand Canal Shops at the Venetian Hotel in Las Vegas.

When they first opened, some of these festival locations were successful at drawing visitors and reinvigorating urban centers suffering from crime and an exodus of population. But now, with invented themes, generic stores, and vigorous competition from other nearby retailers, such centers are viewed by many as tourist traps and are avoided by many locals. In 1985, the themed shopping center that opened on Pier 17 in Lower Manhattan promised to reinvigorate the South Street

Seaport, but today, its owners are seeking to tear down the three-story building to replace it with a different, upscale shopping center.[27]

Larger, Multiformat Developments—Omnicenters

New shopping center developments are combining enclosed malls, lifestyle centers, and power centers. Although centers of this type do not have an official name, they may be referred to as **omnicenters.**

Omnicenters represent a response to several trends in retailing, including the desire of tenants to lower CAM charges by spreading the costs among more tenants and to function inside larger developments that generate more pedestrian traffic and longer shopping trips. In addition, they reflect the growing tendency of consumers to **cross-shop,** which is a pattern of buying both premium and low-priced merchandise or patronizing expensive, status-oriented retailers and price-oriented retailers, as occurs when a customer shops at both Walmart and Nordstrom's. Time-scarce customers are also attracted to omnicenters because they can get everything they need in one place. For example, the 1.3 million-square-foot St. John's Town Center in Jacksonville, Florida, is divided into three components: a lifestyle center with a Dillard's department store anchor, a mini-power center anchored by Dick's Sporting Goods and a Barnes & Noble bookstore, and a Main Street with Cheesecake Factory and P.F. Chang's restaurants as anchors.[28]

 RETAILING VIEW   For China's High-End Fashion Consumers, "Italy" Is Now Just a Bullet Train Away   **7.3**

 Between Beijing and Tijanjin, you can find an Italian village—or at least a themed outlet mall that seeks to recreate one. With its luxury brand offerings, Florentia Village draws approximately 25,000 visitors daily, most of whom come to check out a sixteenth-century Italian village, with its narrow streets and piazzas. Once they have experienced a trip back in history, they can indulge in the purchase of Italian luxury brands, including Zegna, Armani, Ferragamo, Prada, Fendi, Bulgari, and Moncler. Near the "Colosseum," Tod's, Frette, Piquadro, and Brooks Brothers maintain their storefronts, whereas customers move through the "Grand Canal Promenade" to find Fendi, Gucci, and Prada.

China is both the largest source of counterfeits in the world and one of the biggest markets for luxury goods. The visitors who arrive at Florentia Village in the morning come by train. Wearing Western clothes, they are mostly young, evidently wealthy, and obviously Chinese. Later in the day, wealthy women wearing designer clothing drive their SUVs into the parking lots; they actively avoid the crowds of visitors on the weekends.

Although Chinese-owned outlet malls have existed for more than a decade, their success has been limited by their failure to attract top brands. These top brands worried about the effect of outlet sales on their brand images. The lesson learned is that an outlet mall's quality image is crucial; it must look like a location that sells luxury. Although "re-creating the Italian style has not been easy, with these kinds of projects, details make the difference. Asking Chinese workers to re-create Italian

The Florentia Village outlet center in China draws young and evidently wealthy customers from around the country.

style pink rock, pilasters, frames, and copper eaves was hard. But we did it."

Sources: Christopher Carothers, "A New Outlet for China's Consumerism," *The Wall Street Journal*, March 8, 2012; and Peter Foster, "China Builds Replica of Italian Town Called Florentia Village," *The Telegraph*, June 27, 2011.

DISCUSSION QUESTION

Why is the Florentia Village outlet center successful while Chinese-owned outlet centers have not been?

NONTRADITONAL LOCATIONS

LO4

Discuss nontraditional retail locations.

Pop-up stores, stores within a store, kiosks, and airports are other location alternatives for many retailers. Retailing View 7.4 describes some of Subway's nontraditional locations and the accommodations it needed to make to secure those locations.

Pop-Up Stores and Other Temporary Locations

Pop-up stores are stores in temporary locations that focus on new products or a limited group of products. These "stores" have been around for centuries as individuals sold merchandise on city streets and at festivals or concerts, such as the Newport Jazz Festival, weekend crafts fairs, or farmers' markets. For instance, in New York's Columbus Circle, 100 vendors sell a variety of gifts from yogawear to handmade glass jewelry. Cities around the United States generally welcome these temporary retailers because they bring people and money to areas, creating excitement. Local retailers, who pay high rents, aren't necessarily so enthusiastic because some of the temporary retailers sell competing merchandise.

7.4   RETAILING VIEW   Subway Goes to Church

In 2011, Subway Restaurants passed McDonald's to become the largest restaurant chain in the world, in terms of number of locations. Subway has achieved this rapid growth partly by opening stores in nontraditional locations: an appliance store in Brazil, a California automobile showroom, a Goodwill store in South Carolina, a riverboat in Germany. One of the more remarkable locations is its One World Trade Center construction site in New York City, where the restaurant gets hoisted up to the next level as each floor of the 105-story building is completed. As the chain's chief development officer puts it, "We're continually looking at just about any opportunity for someone to buy a sandwich, wherever that might be. The closer we can get to the customer, the better." Noting the nearly 8,000 Subways in unusual locations, he adds, "The non-traditional is becoming traditional."

With its menu of sandwiches, Subway has an easier time opening in unusual venues because it has a simpler kitchen than traditional fast-food restaurants, which require frying and grilling equipment. Hospitals and religious facilities have a favorable attitude toward Subway because it promotes its sandwiches as a fresher, healthier alternative to traditional fast food.

Subway often has to make special accommodations when opening stores in nontraditional locations, though. For example, the first of many kosher Subway stores opened in the Jewish Community Center of Cleveland in 2006, and Subway is now the largest kosher chain in the United States. The kosher stores still have steak and cheese subs, except the cheese is a soy-based product. In observance of the Jewish Sabbath, these restaurants are closed on Friday afternoon and all day Saturday.

When a Subway opened in the True Bethel Baptist Church of Buffalo, New York, in a low-income area of town, the franchisee worked closely with church leaders. To support the congregation and create jobs, church leaders had approached several fast-food franchisers about

To maintain growth, Subway has opened outlets in nontraditional locations like this one at a Baptist church in Buffalo, New York.

opening a franchise in a corner of the church. Subway was the only chain that was flexible enough toward the space available and the operating hours to accommodate the church. The chain agreed to waive its requirement of a Subway sign on the outside of the building and created a parking pattern to keep restaurant traffic from displacing churchgoers during services.

Sources: Julie Jargon, "Unusual Store Locations Fuel Subway's Growth," *The Wall Street Journal*, March 10, 2011; and Alan J. Liddle, "10 Non-Traditional Subway Restaurants," *Nation's Restaurants*, July 26, 2011.

DISCUSSION QUESTION

What are the advantages and disadvantages to Subway's nontraditional location strategy?

Due to the recession and retail industry consolidation, shopping center vacancies have increased and occupancy costs have decreased. Retailers and manufacturers are opening pop-up stores in these vacant locations. Pop-up stores are particularly attractive to retailers with highly seasonal sales such as Toys "R" Us. Toys "R" Us has been experimenting with pop-ups for several years. In 2009, Toys "R" Us had 90 "Express" pop-up stores, and in 2010 it increased the number dramatically to 600. Opening, managing, and closing that large number of stores strained the management capabilities of the company. So, the company only opened 160 pop-ups in 2011. In 2012, it complemented its own pop-ups with pop-ups inside Macy's stores. The temporary Toys "R" Us units inside 24 Macy's stores were leased from October 15 through January 15. Each pop-up is roughly 1,500 square feet and includes items such as dolls, action figures, and puzzles.[29]

This Kate Spade pop-up store is an attractive temporary location for the high-fashion retailer/designer.

Cities have adopted the pop-up store concept to revitalizing their urban neighborhoods. In Oakland, California, the Pop-Up Hood concept grants six months' worth of rent-free space to independent retailers if they agree to test their innovative retail concepts in designated parts of the city.[30]

Store-within-a-Store

Store-within-a-store locations involve an agreement in which a retailer rents a part of the retail space in a store operated by another independent retailer. The host retailer basically "sublets" the space to the store-within retailer.[31] The store-within retailer manages the assortment, inventory, personnel, and systems and delivers a percentage of the sales or profits to the host. Grocery stores have been experimenting with the store-within-a-store concept for years with service providers such as coffee bars, banks, film processors, and medical clinics. Starbucks operates cafés in many retail stores.

Department stores in the United States have traditionally leased some space to other retailers, such as retailers of beauty salons, fine jewelry, and furs. However, most department stores in Europe, Japan, and China are a collection of store-

within-a-store retailers. For example, Modern Plaza, a luxury department store in Beijing, "rents" all of the space in its store to a set of luxury brands, and the brands operate a store within Modern Plaza. Thus, Modern Plaza and European department stores perform the role of mall managers rather than retail stores.

In contrast, JCPenney's relationship with Sephora is more of a partnership. Sephora designs and develops the merchandise, and JCPenney is responsible for managing the sales associates and inventory sold in the Sephora boutique within a JCPenney store. The sales are made through JCPenney's POS system, and customers can use their JCPenney card when shopping in the Sephora boutique. The Sephora stores do not have a separate entrance, so there is some sense of creating a cohesive JCPenney experience.[32]

JCPenney has a partnership with Sephora using a store-within-a-store strategy.

Stores-within-a-store can be mutually beneficial to the store within and the host retailer. The store within gets an excellent location with high pedestrian traffic of customers in its target market. The host retailer generates increased revenue from the space and enhances its brand image. For example, JCPenney's relationship with Sephora enables it to offer a fashionable brand that it would not be able to offer normally through its channels. Similarly, Banfield Veterinarian services within PetSmart stores offers pet owners a true one-stop shop.[33] However, there are risks associated with this arrangement. Over time, the host or store within could have conflicting, rather than synergistic, target markets and/or brand images.

Merchandise Kiosks

Merchandise kiosks are small selling spaces, typically located in the walkways of enclosed malls, airports, college campuses, or office building lobbies. Some are staffed and resemble a miniature store or cart that could be easily moved. Others are twenty-first-century versions of vending machines, such as the Apple kiosks that sell iPods and other high-volume Apple products.

For mall operators, kiosks are an opportunity to generate rental income in otherwise vacant space and offer a broad assortment of merchandise for visitors. They also can generate excitement from retailers like national cell phone provider Sprint to smaller niche products like Israeli Dead Sea cosmetics, leading to additional sales for the entire mall. Moreover, mall kiosks can be changed quickly to match seasonal demand.

When planning the location of kiosks in a mall, operators are sensitive to their regular mall tenants' needs. They are careful to avoid kiosks that block any storefronts, create an incompatible image, or actually compete directly with permanent tenants by selling similar merchandise.

Airports

A high-pedestrian area that has become popular with national retail chains is airports.[34] Passengers arrive earlier for their flights than they did in the past, leaving them more time to shop. In addition, a cutback in airline food service has more people seeking sustenance in the airport. As a result, sales per square foot at airport malls are often much higher than at regular mall stores. However, rents are higher too. Also, costs can be higher—hours are longer, and because the location is often inconvenient for workers, the businesses have to pay higher wages. The best airport locations tend to be ones where there are many connecting flights (Atlanta and Frankfurt) and international flights (New York's Kennedy and London's Heathrow) because customers have downtime to browse through stores. The best-selling products are those that make good gifts, necessities, and easy-to-pack items. However, airport sales of consumer electronics accessories are increasing. The largest retailer of electronics at airports is InMotion Entertainment that rents DVD players and sells a wide variety of electronics and accessories in its 68 stores at 33 airports in the United States.

REFACT

Passengers spend an average of 136 minutes at Kennedy International Airport in New York from arrival to boarding.[35]

LOCATION AND RETAIL STRATEGY

LO5

Match the locations to the retailer's strategy.

The selection of a location type reinforces the retailer's strategy. Thus, the location-type decision is consistent with the shopping behavior and size of the target market and the retailer's positioning in its target market. Each of these factors is discussed next.

Shopping Behavior of Consumers in Retailer's Target Market

A critical factor affecting the type of location that consumers select to visit is the shopping situation in which they are involved. Three types of shopping situations are convenience shopping, comparison shopping, and specialty shopping.

Convenience Shopping   When consumers are engaged in **convenience shopping** situations, they are primarily concerned with minimizing their effort to get the product or service they want. They are relatively insensitive to price and indifferent about which brands to buy. Thus, they don't spend much time evaluating different brands or retailers; they simply want to make the purchase as quickly and easily as possible. Examples of convenience shopping situations are getting a cup of coffee during a work break, buying gas for a car, or buying milk for breakfast in the morning.

Retailers targeting customers involved in convenience shopping, such as quick service restaurants, convenience stores, and gas stations, usually locate their stores close to where their customers are and make it easy for them to access the location, park, and find what they want. Thus, convenience stores, drugstores, fast-food restaurants, supermarkets, and full-line discount stores are generally located in neighborhood strip centers and freestanding locations.

Comparison Shopping   Consumers involved in **comparison shopping** situations are more involved in the purchase decision. They have a general idea about the type of product or service they want, but they do not have a well-developed preference for a brand or model. Because the purchase decisions are more important to them, they seek information and are willing to expend effort to compare alternatives. Consumers typically engage in this type of shopping behavior when buying furniture, appliances, apparel, consumer electronics, and hand tools.

Furniture retailers, for instance, often locate next to one another to create a "furniture row." In New York City, a number of retailers selling houseplants and flowers are all located in Chelsea between 27th and 30th Streets on 6th Avenue, and diamond dealers are located on West 47th Street between 5th and 6th Avenues. These competing retailers locate near one another because doing so facilitates comparison shopping and thus attracts many customers to the locations.

Enclosed malls offer the same benefits to consumers interested in comparison shopping for fashionable apparel. Thus, department stores and specialty apparel retailers locate in enclosed malls for the same reason that houseplant retailers locate together on 6th Avenue in New York City. By co-locating in the same mall, they attract more potential customers interested in comparison shopping for fashionable apparel. Even though the enclosed mall might be inconvenient compared with a freestanding location, comparison shopping is easier after the customers have arrived.

Category specialists offer the same benefit of comparison shopping as a collection of co-located specialty stores like those described previously. Rather than going to a set of small hardware stores when comparison shopping for an electric drill, consumers know they can get almost anything they need to fix or build a house in either Home Depot or Lowe's. Thus, category specialists are **destination stores,** places where consumers will go even if it is inconvenient, just like enclosed malls are destination locations for fashionable-apparel comparison shopping. Category specialists locate in power centers, primarily to reduce their costs and create awareness of their location and secondarily to benefit from multiple retailers that attract more consumers and the resulting potential for cross-shopping. Basically, power centers are a collection of destination stores.

200   SECTION II   Retailing Strategy

Specialty Shopping   When consumers go **specialty shopping,** they know what they want and will not accept a substitute. They are brand and/or retailer loyal and will pay a premium or expend extra effort, if necessary, to get exactly what they want. Examples of these shopping occasions include buying organic vegetables, a luxury automobile, or a high-end road or mountain bike. The retailers they patronize when specialty shopping also are destination stores. Thus, consumers engaged in specialty shopping are willing to travel to an inconvenient location. Having a convenient location is not as important for retailers selling unique merchandise or services.

Density of Target Market

A second, but closely related, factor that affects the retailer's choice of location type is the density of the retailer's target market in relation to the location. A good location has many people in the target market who are drawn to it. Thus, a convenience store located in a CBD can be sustained by customers living or working in fairly close proximity to the store. Similarly, a comparison shopping store located next to a Walmart is a potentially good location because Walmart draws lots of customers from a very large area. It is not as important to have high customer density near a store that sells specialty merchandise because people are willing to search out this type of merchandise. A Porsche dealer, for instance, need not be near other car dealers or in close proximity to its target market, because those seeking this luxury car will drive to wherever the dealer may be.

Uniqueness of Retail Offering

Finally, the convenience of their locations is less important for retailers with unique, differentiated offerings than for retailers with an offering similar to other retailers. For example, Bass Pro Shops provides a unique merchandise assortment and store atmosphere. Customers will travel to wherever the store is located, and its location will become a destination.

SOCIETAL AND LEGAL CONSIDERATIONS

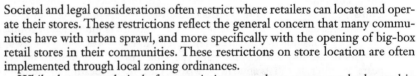

LO6

Review the societal and legal considerations in selecting locations.

Societal and legal considerations often restrict where retailers can locate and operate their stores. These restrictions reflect the general concern that many communities have with urban sprawl, and more specifically with the opening of big-box retail stores in their communities. These restrictions on store location are often implemented through local zoning ordinances.

While there are relatively few restrictions on where stores can be located in the United States, location decisions are more restricted in other areas of the world. For example, western Europe and Asia have higher population densities and more people living and shopping in urban environments. Thus, less space is available for retailing, and the space that is available is costly. In addition, many western European countries restrict retailing to specific areas and then restrict the sizes of the stores that can be built.

In this section, we discuss the nature of the restrictions, reasons communities impose these restrictions, and the impact of these restrictions on society.

Urban Sprawl

Urban sprawl is the increased expansion of residential and shopping center development in suburban and rural areas outside of their respective urban centers. Before World War II, the downtown urban area was a community's commercial hub. Consumers shopped at local businesses downtown. The presence of offices, banks, and libraries guaranteed traffic in the downtown center. Downtown also

was an important part of an area's social life. On weekends, people met to
window shop, eat at restaurants, and
go to the movies.

The interstate highway system and
growth of the suburbs changed the
way Americans live and work. With
improved transportation, people could
travel longer distances to work or
shop. As a result, many downtown retailers went out of business. As customers and sales dwindled, property
values and tax revenues dropped.
Historic buildings were neglected and
storefronts boarded up, reinforcing
the decline of downtown areas.

In addition to the decline of the
downtown, some other negative consequences of urban sprawl are congestion
and air pollution due to increased auto-

Main Street locations in the U.K. and in U.S. towns face intense competition from hypermarkets located on the outskirts of the towns.

mobile travel, loss of farmland, concentrated poverty, and racial and economic seg-
regation. On the other hand, some desirable outcomes of this migration to the
suburbs are better housing opportunities, public schools, and less crime.[36]

The European Union is very concerned about urban sprawl and the effects of
big-box retailers locating outside the city limits. The EU is trying to restrain the
growth of big-box retailers, limiting their size and subsidizing the redevelopment
of inner city (called the High Street in the United Kingdom) to help local retailers
compete. Europe has greater population density and less space than the United
States, and stricter planning and greenbelt laws provide a sharp division between
town and country. Suburbs are few, thus minimizing urban sprawl. But preserving
the environment comes at a cost for Europe. The limits on out-of-town, big-box
retailing reduce competition and retailing efficiency, causing higher prices.[37]

Opposition to Big-Box Retailers

Retailers that operate big-box stores like Walmart, Target, Costco, and Home
Depot often meet with a great deal of resistance when they plan to build a store in
a community. Many people vehemently oppose big-box stores entering their
community. The opponents of the store openings argue that these retailers sell
merchandise at lower prices that drive local retailers out of business; do not provide a living wage for employees; hire part-time workers to avoid providing health
insurance benefits; and achieve their low prices by manufacturing merchandise
outside the United States, thus contributing to the decline of U.S. jobs.

Discussions between big-box stores and local communities continue to occur
throughout the United States and other countries. Some communities have allowed for the building of such stores when the retailers agree to pay employees a
set wage or fund low-cost housing for employees. Zoning, discussed in the following section, is one method used by local communities to restrict big-box retailers.

Zoning

Local governments in the United States use **zoning** to regulate land uses in specific
areas to prevent any interference with existing uses by residents or businesses, as
well as encourage the preservation of a community's sense of identity. Thus, zoning
ordinances might keep McDonald's from opening a franchise in a residential
neighborhood. In other nations, such as France and Germany, zoning regulations
and planning are enforced at national or state levels instead of locally.

EXHIBIT 7–3   Zoning Map for a Small Town

In urban areas, zoning ordinances often specify five categories of activities that are acceptable in a certain region or on a particular site: residential, commercial, mixed residential and commercial, industrial, or special. In addition, most zoning regulations include detailed density limitations, such as those indicating whether an area may host high-density high rises or instead is limited to low-density, single-family housing. Noting that exceptions can exist, most ordinances denote the conditions—usually hardship-related—that must be met for variances to be granted.

Exhibit 7–3 describes the zoning restrictions in Superior, Wisconsin. These zoning maps are typically developed by a planning commission and approved by the city council. Note that the areas dedicated for retailing shown in red are adjacent to the two major highways. Some areas (shown in green) are dedicated open spaces and residential areas are shown in yellow.

Building Codes

Building codes are legal restrictions that specify the type of building, signs, size and type of parking lot, and so forth, that can be used at a particular location. Some building codes require a certain-size parking lot or a particular architectural design. In Santa Fe, New Mexico, for instance, building codes require that buildings keep a traditional mud stucco (adobe) style.

Signs   Restrictions on the use of signs can affect a particular site's desirability. Sign sizes and styles may be restricted by building codes, zoning ordinances, or even the shopping center management group. At the Bal Harbour Shops in North Miami Beach, for example, all signs (even sale signs) must be approved by the shopping center management group before implementation by each individual retailer.

Licensing Requirements   Licensing requirements may vary in different parts of a region. For instance, some Dallas neighborhoods are dry, meaning no alcoholic beverages can be sold; in other areas, only wine and beer can be sold. Such restrictions can affect retailers other than restaurants and bars. For instance, a theme/festival shopping center that restricts the use of alcoholic beverages may find its clientele limited at night.

Legal issues such as those mentioned here can discourage a retailer from pursuing a particular site. These restrictions aren't always permanent, however. Although difficult, time consuming, and possibly expensive, lobbying efforts and court battles can change these legal restrictions.

SUMMARY

LO1 **Describe the types of retail locations available to retailers.**

Store location decisions are important decisions for a retailer because location is typically one of the most influential considerations in a customer's store-choice decision. Location decisions also have strategic implications because they can be used to develop a sustainable competitive advantage and location decisions are risky.

LO2 **Review the types of unplanned locations.**

Two basic types of location are unplanned (free-standing and urban sites) and planned (shopping centers). Unplanned locations do not have centralized management that determines what stores will be in a development, where the specific stores will be located, and how they will be operated. The three types of unplanned retail locations are freestanding sites, urban and Main Street locations. Freestanding locations are convenient for customers and have high vehicular traffic and visibility, modest occupancy costs, and few restrictions. But freestanding sites are higher in cost and have smaller trade areas. In general, urban locations have lower occupancy costs than enclosed malls; vehicular traffic is limited, and parking problems reduce consumer convenience.

LO3 **Analyze the characteristics of the different types of shopping centers.**

By combining many stores at one location, shopping centers attract more consumers to the center than would be the case if the stores were at separate locations. The developer and shopping center management carefully select a set of retailers that are complementary to provide consumers with a comprehensive shopping experience at one, convenient location. Each of the types of shopping centers has its advantages and disadvantages. Many central business

districts, inner-city, and Main Street locations have become more viable options than they were in the past because of gentrification of the areas, tax incentives, and lack of competition. There also are a wide variety of shopping center types for retailers. They can locate in a strip or power center; an enclosed mall; or a lifestyle, theme/festival, or outlet center.

LO4 **Discuss nontraditional retail locations.**

Pop-up stores, stores-within-a-store, kiosks, and airports are other location alternatives for many retailers. Pop-up stores are particularly attractive to retailers with highly seasonal sales. Store-within-a-store locations involve an agreement in which a retailer rents a part of the retail space in a store operated by another independent retailer. These locations are mutually beneficial to the host and store within.

LO5 **Match the locations to the retailer's strategy.**

The selection of a location type reinforces the retailer's strategy. Thus, the location-type decision is consistent with the shopping behavior and size of the target market and the retailer's positioning in its target market. Different shopping locations are more appropriate for consumers engaged in three types of customer shopping situations: convenience shopping, comparison shopping, and specialty shopping.

LO6 **Review the societal and legal considerations in selecting locations.**

Societal and legal considerations often restrict the locations and operations of standalone stores and shopping centers. These restrictions reflect the general concern that many communities have with urban sprawl and, more specifically, with the opening of big-box retail stores in their communities. Shopping center developers and retailers often need to deal with zoning ordinances before they open stores in a community.

KEY TERMS

204   SECTION II   Retailing Strategy

GET OUT AND DO IT!

1. **CONTINUING CASE ASSIGNMENT** Interview the manager of the shopping center that contains the retailer you selected for the Continuing Assignment. Write a report summarizing which retailers the shopping center manager thinks are his or her best tenants and why they are valued. How does the manager rate the retailer you have selected? What criteria does he or she use?

2. **INTERNET EXERCISE** Go to the web page for Faneuil Hall Marketplace at www.faneuilhallmarketplace.com and the online site for CocoWalk at www.cocowalk.net. What kinds of centers are these? List their similarities and differences. Who is the target market for each of these retail locations?

3. **GO SHOPPING** Go to your favorite shopping center, and analyze the tenant mix. Do the tenants appear to complement one another? What changes would you make in the tenant mix to increase the overall performance of the center?

4. **GO SHOPPING** Visit a lifestyle center. What tenants are found in this location? Describe the population characteristics around this center. How far would people drive to shop at this lifestyle center? What other types of retail locations does this lifestyle center compete with?

5. **INTERNET EXERCISE** Go to the home page for Simon Property Group, www.simon.com/about_simon/our_business/default.aspx, and read about the businesses that Simon is in. What is the difference between their businesses?

6. **INTERNET EXERCISE** Go to the home page of your favorite enclosed mall, and describe the mall in terms of the following characteristics: number of anchor stores, number and categories of specialty stores, number of sit-down and quick-service restaurants, and types of entertainment offered. What are the strengths and weaknesses of this assortment of retailers? What are the unique features of this particular mall?

7. **GO SHOPPING** Visit a power center that contains a Target, Staples, Sports Authority, Home Depot, or other category specialists. What other retailers are in the same location? How is this mix of stores beneficial to both shoppers and retailers?

8. **INTERNET EXERCISE** Go to www.pbs.org/itvs/storewars/. This site contains information about the Ashland town council's decision to allow Walmart to open a store in Ashland, Virginia. Summarize the pros and cons of allowing Walmart to open a store in town. Were you surprised by the town council's decision? Why or why not?

DISCUSSION QUESTIONS AND PROBLEMS

1. Why is store location such an important decision for retailers?

2. Pick your favorite store. Describe the advantages and disadvantages of its current location, given its store type and target market.

3. Home Depot typically locates in either a power center or a freestanding site. What are the strengths of each location for this home improvement retailer?

4. As a consultant to 7-Eleven convenience stores, American Eagle Outfitters, and Porsche of America, what would you say is the single most important factor in choosing a site for these three very different types of stores?

5. Retailers are locating in shopping centers and freestanding locations in central business districts that have suffered decay. As a result, these areas are rejuvenating, a process known as gentrification. Some people have questioned the ethical and social ramifications of this process. Discuss the benefits and detriments of gentrification.

6. Staples, Office Max, and Office Depot all have strong multichannel strategies. How do competition and the Internet affect their strategies for locating stores?

7. In many malls, quick-service food retailers are located together in an area known as a food court. What are the advantages and disadvantages of this location for the food retailers? What is the new trend for food retailers in the shopping environment?

8. Why would a Payless ShoeSource store locate in a neighborhood shopping center instead of a regional shopping mall?

9. How does the mall near your home or university combine the shopping and entertainment experiences?

10. Consider a big city that has invested in an urban renaissance. What components of the gentrification project attract both local residents and visiting tourists to spend time shopping, eating, and sightseeing in this location?

SUGGESTED READINGS

Brooks, Charles, Patrick J. Kaufmann, and Donald R. Lichtenstein. "Trip Chaining Behavior in Multi-Destination Shopping Trips: A Field Experiment and Laboratory Replication." *Journal of Retailing* 84, no. 1 (2008), pp. 29–38.

Curtiss, Donald L. *Operation Shopping Centers; Guidebook to Effective Management & Promotion.* Ulan Press, 2011.

Gibbs, Robert J. *Principles of Urban Retail Planning and Development.* New York: Wiley, 2012.

International Council of Shopping Centers. *Winning Shopping Center Designs,* 35th ed. New York: ICSC, 2012.

Kim, Jung-Hwan, and Rodney Runyan. "Where Did All the Benches Go? The Effects of Mall Kiosks on Perceived Retail Crowding." *International Journal of Retail & Distribution Management* 39, no. 2 (2011), pp. 130–143.

Roslin, Rosmimah, and Mohd Herwina Rosnan. "Location as a Strategic Retail Decision: The Case of the Retail Cooperative." *International Journal of Commerce and Management* 22, no. 2 (2012), pp. 152–158.

Ruoh-Nan, Yan, and Molly Eckman. "Are Lifestyle Centres Unique? Consumers' Perceptions across Locations." *International Journal of Retail & Distribution Management* 37, no. 1 (2009), pp. 24–42.

Schewel, Laura B., and Lee J. Schipper. "Shop 'Till We Drop: A Historical and Policy Analysis of Retail Goods Movement in The United States." *Environmental Science and Technology* 46, no. 18 (2012), pp. 9813–9821.

Yiu, C. Y., and Sys Xu. "A Tenant-Mix Model for Shopping Malls," *European Journal of Marketing,* 46, no. 3 (2012), pp. 234–256.

Retail Site Location

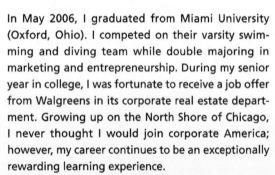

EXECUTIVE BRIEFING
Brenden O'Brien, Senior Real Estate Manager
Walgreen Co.

In May 2006, I graduated from Miami University (Oxford, Ohio). I competed on their varsity swimming and diving team while double majoring in marketing and entrepreneurship. During my senior year in college, I was fortunate to receive a job offer from Walgreens in its corporate real estate department. Growing up on the North Shore of Chicago, I never thought I would join corporate America; however, my career continues to be an exceptionally rewarding learning experience.

Our locations are critical strategic assets, and we take a long-term perspective in developing each and every store. A team comprised of market planning and research, a market VP from operations, and a real estate manager evaluate new opportunities. Accessing a vast amount of collected data in a geographic information system, the team identifies ideal target locations for our stores. Walgreens strives to lock down the best real estate deal in each neighborhood, which generally equates to the intersection with the most amount of traffic. Because we target the best locations for future stores, the real estate is not easy to put under contract nor are all locations commercially feasible. Sometimes the real estate prices are so high that the economics become cost prohibitive. To finalize each and every opportunity,

real estate managers must present them for approval to the Walgreens real estate committee. This committee is comprised of a panel of executives at corporate headquarters. Many of the highest-level executives in Walgreens are involved in the final decision, which includes the location, the economics, and a specific plan for each store. I am amazed that after only six years from college graduation, I am interacting with corporate-level executives in one of the 10 largest retail companies in the world.

Walgreens gives me the opportunity to be creative, develop new ideas, and also learn from others in the company. For example, one of my most exciting projects was developing a location directly across from SeaWorld on International Drive in Orlando, Florida. International Drive attracts a massive number of tourists who flock to the area to spend money at stores, restaurants, and attractions. Walgreens already had five successful stores on International Drive; however, I negotiated a deal to include a nontraditional store at an underserved fabulous location. We designed the exterior of the store to include unique architectural elements and designed the interior of the store to include special features

CHAPTER 8

LEARNING OBJECTIVES

LO1 Summarize the factors considered in locating a number of stores.

LO2 Review the characteristics of a particular site.

LO3 Understand how retailers analyze the trade area for a site.

LO4 Determine the forecasted sales for a new store location.

LO5 Illustrate the site selection process.

LO6 Explain the different types and terms of leases.

such as a curved ceiling, in order to enhance the customer experience. The merchandise is uniquely designed for tourists with an emphasis on souvenirs, an expanded food offering, and an assortment of health and beauty aids.

To be successful in any endeavor, you need to stay ahead of the curve by continuing to learn.

Walgreens provides an atmosphere that supports my interest in developing my knowledge in real estate (my job), finance, and business in general. The company was very supportive of my efforts to complete the course work and examinations required to become a certified commercial investment member, or CCIM.

Chapter 5 emphasized the strategic importance of location decisions. Although location decisions can create strategic advantage, like all strategic decisions, they are also risky because they involve a significant commitment of resources. Opening a store at a site often involves committing to a lease of five years or more or purchasing land and building a store. If the store's performance is below expectations, the retailer may not be able to recover its investment easily by having another party move in and assume the lease or buy the building.

Chapter 7 reviewed the different types of locations available to retailers and why certain types of retailers gravitate toward particular locations. This chapter takes a closer look at how retailers choose specific sites to locate their stores.

Selecting retail locations involves the analysis of a large amount of data and the use of sophisticated statistical models. Because most retailers make these decisions infrequently, it is not economical for them to employ full-time real estate analysts with state-of-the-art skills. Thus, small retailers often use firms that provide the geographic and demographic data and consulting services needed to evaluate specific sites. However, there continues to be an element of art in making these location decisions.

This chapter reviews the steps retailers go through in selecting their store locations and negotiating leases. The first part of the chapter examines the factors retailers consider when selecting a general area for locating stores and determining the number of stores to operate in each area. Then this chapter reviews different approaches used to evaluate specific sites and estimate the expected sales if and when a store is located at that site. Finally, the chapter looks at the various terms that are negotiated when a retailer commits to leasing space for its store.

EVALUATING AREAS FOR LOCATIONS AND DETERMINING THE NUMBER OF STORES IN AN AREA

LO1

Summarize the factors considered in locating a number of stores.

The first part of this section discusses the areas retailers typically analyze when making location decisions, and the second section reviews factors retailers consider when evaluating these areas for locating stores and determining the number of stores to put in an area.

Metropolitan Statistical Area

Areas that retailers consider for locating stores might be countries, areas within a country such as a province in France or a state in the United States, particular cities, or areas within cities. In the United States, retailers often focus their analysis on a **metropolitan statistical area (MSA)** because consumers tend to shop within an MSA, and media coverage and demographic data for analyzing location opportunities often are organized by MSA.

An MSA is a core urban area containing a population of more than 50,000 inhabitants, together with adjacent communities that have a high degree of economic and social integration with the core community. For example, many people in an MSA commute to work in the central business district but live in the surrounding areas. An MSA can consist of one or several counties and usually is named after the major urban area in the MSA. For example, the Cincinnati-Middleton MSA consists of 15 counties (3 in Indiana, 7 in Kentucky, and 5 in Ohio) with a population of 2,172,191; the Missoula, Montana, MSA consists of one county with a population of 110,138.

In contrast, a **micropolitan statistical area (μSA)** is somewhat removed from larger U.S. cities, often by up to 100 miles. Although they lack big cities' pull and economic significance, these notable population centers often are responsible for substantial production capabilities and provide reasonable housing accommodations for many residents. The designation refers to the core population of a central town, so regardless of their name, a micropolitan area could be larger than a metropolitan area. The largest μSA is Seaford, Delaware, with a population of 200,330.[3]

REFACT

California has the most shopping centers (6,379) and Wyoming has the fewest (55).[1]

REFACT

There are 366 MSAs and 576 μSAs in the United States.[2]

Considerations in Evaluating Store Locations

The best areas for locating stores are those that generate the highest long-term profits for a retailer. Some factors affecting the long-term profit generated by stores that should be considered when evaluating an area include: (1) the economic conditions, (2) competition, (3) the strategic fit of the area's population with the retailer's target market, and (4) the costs of operating stores (see Exhibit 8–1). Note that these factors are similar to those that retailers consider when evaluating an investment in a new business growth opportunity or entry into a foreign market, as discussed in Chapter 5.

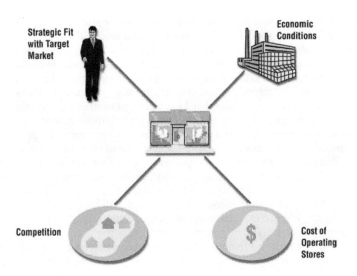

Economic Conditions   Because locations involve a commitment of resources over a long time horizon, it is important to examine an area's level and growth of population and employment. A large, fully employed population means high purchasing power and high levels of retail sales.

But population and employment growth alone aren't enough to ensure a strong retail environment in the future. Retail location analysts need to determine how long such growth will continue and how it will affect demand for merchandise sold in the stores. For instance, if growth is not diversified in various industries, the area may be unattractive because of extreme cyclical trends. The economies of some Rust Belt cities like Flint, Michigan, experience greater peaks and valleys because of their dependence on specific industries such as automobiles.

Also, it is useful to determine which areas are growing quickly and why. For instance, the east side of Seattle, Washington, has become a desirable retail location because of its proximity to Microsoft's corporate headquarters. But the performance of these retail locations is linked to the financial performance of Microsoft.

In most cases, areas where the population is large and growing are preferable to those with declining populations. However, some retailers, such as Subway, often go into new strip shopping centers with few nearby households with the anticipation that the surrounding suburban area will eventually be built up enough to support the stores.

Competition   The level of competition in an area affects the demand for a retailer's merchandise. Walmart's early success was based on a location strategy of opening stores in small towns with little competition. It offered consumers in small towns quality merchandise at low prices. Previously, rural consumers either shopped in small stores with limited assortments or drove to larger towns.

Although they once were viewed as undesirable areas, inner-city neighborhoods today host many full-service restaurant chains, including Chili's, Denny's, IHOP, and so forth. For such casual restaurants, underserved urban locations offer some strong attractions, including minimal competition levels; a large, readily accessible labor force; and, in some neighborhoods, a surrounding market of customers with high disposable incomes.

Retailing View 8.1 describes the success realized by Stage Stores targeting small towns with limited competition for fashionable apparel.

210   SECTION II   Retailing Strategy

Strategic Fit   Economic conditions and competition alone don't tell the whole story. The area needs to have consumers who are in the retailer's target market—who are attracted to the retailer's offerings and interested in patronizing its stores. Thus, the area must have the right demographic and lifestyle profile. The size and composition of households in an area can be an important determinant of success. For instance, electronics, appliance, and home goods store, La Curacao, focuses on Hispanic consumers. Thus it has 11 locations in southern California and Arizona—all locations are areas with at least 250,000 Hispanics.[4] Ethnic composition of the trade area, however, is not a particularly critical issue for Toys "R" Us, which is interested in locations with heavy concentrations of families with young children.

Party City, the world's largest party supply retailer, sells celebratory merchandise for happy occasions—birthdays, holiday parties, anniversaries—through more than 600 company-owned franchised stores. Party City chooses locations that have a high density of middle-income shoppers with children.[5]

Finally, lifestyle characteristics of the population may be relevant, depending on the target market(s) that a particular retailer is pursuing. For example, areas with consumers interested in outdoor activities are attractive for REI and Bass Pro Shops.

Operating Costs   The cost of operating stores can vary across areas. For example, store rental and advertising costs in the Missoula, Montana, MSA are significantly lower than those in the Cincinnati-Middletown MSA. But, of course,

---

8.1   RETAILING VIEW   Big Payoff from Small Towns

Even though Stage Stores is a billion-dollar retail chain operating in more than 800 locations, it is relatively unknown because most of its stores are located in small towns. Being outside the big city has advantages, though. "The beauty of our business model is that we have no natural competitor," said Andy Hall, former president and CEO of Stage Stores: "Most small towns are not big enough for two stores like ours. The first one in wins." Typically, the nearest thing to competition for Stage Stores' small-town locations are regional malls 40 miles away and online sites.

Among the 801 stores, 521 are in small markets (small MSAs and larger μSAs), mostly in strip centers in towns with less than 50,000 people within a 10-mile radius. Stage Stores operates under the names Palais Royal, Bealls, Goody's, Peebles, and Stage. Of the 521 small-town Stage Store locations, 510 are near a Walmart. Customers buy their groceries and hard goods at Walmart and their apparel at Stage stores. Name brands, such as Lee, Levi's, Calvin Klein Jeans, Izod, Nike, Nautica, Dockers, Nine West, Clinique, and Estee Lauder, are 80 percent of sales.

A downside of being small-town-focused is being overlooked by many investors, according to Hall. "Most city dwellers don't understand the vibrancy of small markets. It's an amazing culture in small markets," Hall said.

Bealls, a subsidiary of Stage Stores focus on small towns where it faces little competition for its assortment of designer fashion apparel and accessories.

Sales associates and customers there are more likely to know each other, and their relationships in the stores are often warm.

Sources: David Kaplan, "Stage Stores' Strategy Pays Off Big in Small Towns," *Houston Chronicle*, August 1, 2011; www.stagestores.com.

DISCUSSION QUESTION

What are the opportunities and threats Stage Stores faces?

the potential sales and profits from stores located in the Cincinnati-Middletown MSA are substantially greater due to its larger and denser population.

Operating costs are also affected by the proximity of the area being considered to other areas in which the retailer operates stores. For example, if a store is located near other stores and the retailer's distribution centers, the cost of shipping merchandise to the store is lower, as is the cost and travel time spent by the district manager supervising the stores' operations.

The local and state legal and regulatory environment can have a significant effect on operating costs. Some retailers are reluctant to locate stores in California because they feel that the state and local governments, the political process of voter-initiated referendums, and a legal environment that fosters class-action lawsuits result in higher operating costs.[6]

Number of Stores in an Area

Having selected an area in which to locate its stores, a retailer's next decision is how many stores to operate in the area. At first glance, you might think that a retailer should choose the one best location in each MSA, but clearly, larger MSAs can support more stores than smaller MSAs. It may, therefore, be more advantageous to locate several stores in one MSA and none in others. But there is a limit to how many stores can be operated in even the largest MSAs. When making the decision about how many stores to open in an area, retailers must consider the trade-offs between lower operating costs and potential sales cannibalization from having multiple stores in an area.

Economies of Scale from Multiple Stores   Most retail chains open multiple stores in an area to lower promotion and distribution by realizing economies of scale. A retailer's total promotional costs are the same for newspaper advertising that promotes 20 stores in a MSA or only 1 store. Multiple stores in an MSA can be serviced by the same distribution center. Thus, chains like Walmart expand into areas only where they have a distribution center in place to support the stores.[7] When Kohl's entered the Florida market, it opened 14 stores in Jacksonville and Orlando on the same day. Finally, when stores are located close each other, district store managers visit each of their stores more frequently.

Cannibalization   Although retailers gain scale economies from opening multiple locations in an MSA, they also suffer diminishing returns associated with locating too many additional stores in an area. For example, suppose the first four stores opened in an MSA by a specialty store retailer generate sales of $2 million each. Because they are located far apart from one another, customers consider patronizing only the store nearest to them, and there is no cannibalization. When the retailer opens a fifth store close to one of the existing stores, it hopes for a net sales increase for the area of $2 million; the new store should generate the same sales level as the four existing stores. Instead, the increase in incremental sales might be only $1.5 million because the sales in the nearest existing store's sales drop to $1.7 million and sales from the new store are only $1.8 million because its location is only the fifth best in the area. Thus, because the new store cannibalizes sales from the closest store, it only contributes sales of $1.5 million.

Because a primary retailing objective is to maximize profits for the entire chain, retailers should continue to open stores only as long as profits continue to increase or, in economic terms, as long as the marginal revenues achieved by opening a new store are greater than the marginal costs. Exhibit 8–2 shows the location of customers that are 3 (yellow), 6 (pink), and 9 (blue) minutes from a retailer's four stores in an area. Note how there is very little overlap, thus little cannibalization except for the City East and the South East stores.

For franchise retail operations, the objectives of the franchisor and franchisee differ, and thus, disputes can arise over the number of locations in an area. The

EXHIBIT 8–2
Location of Customers
Patronizing a Retailer's
Store

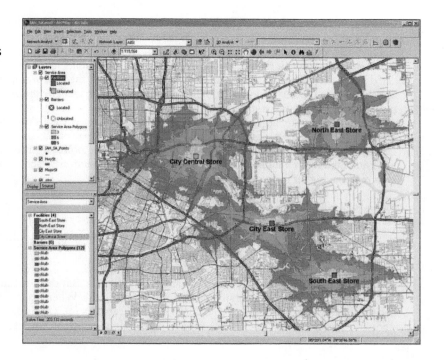

franchisor is interested in maximizing the sales of all stores because it earns a royalty based on total store sales. The franchisee is interested in just the sales and profits from its store(s). Thus, the franchisor is not as concerned about cannibalization as the franchisee is. To reduce the level of conflict, most franchise agreements grant franchisees an exclusive territory to protect them from another franchisee cannibalizing their sales.[8]

CONSIDERATIONS IN EVALUATING STORE LOCATIONS

LO2

Review the characteristics
of a particular site.

Having decided to locate stores in an area, the retailer's next step is to evaluate and select a specific site. In making this decision, retailers consider three factors: (1) the characteristics of the site, (2) the characteristics of the trading area for a store at the site, and (3) the estimated potential sales that can be generated by a store at the site. The first two sets of factors are typically considered in an initial screening of potential sites. The methods used to forecast store sales, the third factor, can involve a more complex analytical approach. Each of these factors is discussed in the following sections.

Site Characteristics

Some characteristics of a site that affect store sales and thus are considered in selecting a site are (1) the traffic flow past the site and accessibility to the site, (2) parking, (3) visibility, (4) adjacent tenants, and (5) restrictions and costs.

Traffic Flow and Accessibility   One of the most important factors affecting store sales is the **traffic flow**—the number of vehicles and pedestrians that pass by the site. When the traffic is greater, more consumers are likely to stop in and shop at the store. Thus, retailers often use traffic count measures to assess a site's attractiveness. Traffic counts are particularly important for retailers offering merchandise and services bought on impulse or on frequent trips such as grocery stores, convenience, and car washes. In contrast, traffic flow is not as important for destination retailers such as The Container Store.

More traffic flow is not always better. Traffic volume counts for surrounding roadways are often used to assess the attractiveness of a retail site. But these measures can be misleading. While these measures can give a reasonable estimate of the level of activity in an area, they do not provide any indication of how much of that volume actually stops and shops at a particular retail location. Most shopping centers are located along heavily traveled roads and highways. As such, these roads are heavily traveled by drivers commuting to and from work or carrying out a number of other daily activities that don't include shopping. As such, daily traffic counts are skewed during rush hours, which creates congestion that impedes access to the stores. Also, traffic volume counts are collected over a 24-hour period, and average rates are reported, whereas retail properties are typically only open for 8 to 12 hours each day.

The **accessibility** of the site, which can be as important as traffic flow, is the ease with which customers can get into and out of the site. Accessibility is greater for sites located near major highways, on uncongested highways, and at streets with traffic lights and lanes that enable turns into the site. Retailing View 8.2 describes the importance of accessibility to a retailer's business.

Natural barriers, such as rivers or mountains, and **artificial barriers,** such as railroad tracks, divided or limited-access highways, or parks, may also affect accessibility. These barriers' impact on a particular site primarily depends on whether the merchandise or services will appeal to customers so strongly that they cross the barrier. For example, a supermarket on one side of a divided highway with no convenient crossover point will appeal only to consumers going in one direction.

A more accurate measure of traffic, which can be obtained from several specialized companies, is the number of consumers entering the shopping center, collected at store entrances within the shopping center. This measure provides a more accurate picture of the number of consumers actually patronizing the shopping center. Additionally, the measure is available for every day of the year individually, rather than the annual averages provided by firms specializing in traffic counts. This allows for more detailed and targeted analyses based on seasonal or week-to-week comparisons.

In the United States, most consumers drive to shopping centers, and thus vehicular traffic is an important consideration when evaluating a site. However, pedestrian traffic flow and access by public transportation are more important for analyzing sites in countries such as China where consumers do not drive to shop or for evaluating urban sites and sites within an enclosed mall.

Parking The amount and quality of parking facilities are critical for evaluating a shopping center. On the one hand, if there aren't enough spaces or the spaces are too far from the store, customers will be discouraged from patronizing the site and the store. On the other hand, if there are too many open spaces, the shopping center may be perceived as having unpopular stores. A standard rule of thumb is 5.5:1,000 (five and one-half spaces per thousand square feet of retail store space) for a shopping center and 10 to 15 spaces per 1,000 square feet for a supermarket.

The parking around this Best Buy store contributes to the quality of this location.

214   SECTION II   Retailing Strategy

8.2   RETAILING VIEW   It Pays to Locate on the Right Side of the Road

For U.S. drivers, businesses and stores located on the right side of the road, rather than on the left, are the ones they see most readily on their commutes home from work or school. That is, if we were to measure the volume of traffic on a road, we would find that the right-hand side of the yellow lines takes up far more afternoon volume. Accordingly, for many businesses, a location on that right-hand side can be highly desirable because it is easy for customers to make a quick right turn into their properties, then an easier right turn out of the retail parking area, without having to cross many lanes of traffic.

In the morning, a right-side location might be ideal for a coffee shop or newspaper stand. But most commuters have little time to spare in the mornings, so they reserve their stops to fill up on gas, grab a gallon of milk, or perhaps sneak in an afternoon candy bar for their rides home.

For Hess gas stations and convenience stores, locating on the right-hand side for afternoon commuters is a priority. As a vertically integrated energy company, Hess is involved in oil exploration and refining, but its most familiar presence is its approximately 1,400 green-logoed retail stores, running up and down the East Coast of the United States. For its 1.3 million daily customers, "The location of our stores is critical to providing value . . . and is paramount to our success," according to Rick Lawlor, vice president of retail marketing for Hess. To generate its $6 billion in annual sales, Hess maintains

Rick Lawlor at Hess positions Hess's convenience stores on the right side of the road.

a staff that evaluates the location of stores we are considering to build or acquire. When evaluating locations, we look at all the numbers—the size and characteristics of the store's trading area, the demographics and geodemographics of the customers that drive by the location and live in the area. However, the most important factors for us are visibility and access—that is, can customers see the signage for our stores and easily make a right turn into the location on their way home? While the data on a location are useful, we never open a location without looking at it in person to assess its visibility and access.

Right turns into and out of Hess locations are particularly important for its customers, who demand a maximum of convenience from their convenience stores. For many drivers, being required to cross multiple lanes of traffic (and hold up frustrated drivers behind them) to make a left turn simply isn't worth the hassle. If they also need to make a left turn out of the parking lot to continue their commute, their quick pit stop could turn into an extended chore as they wait for gaps in the heavy rush hour traffic to enter the flow of cars.

Locations on the left-hand side of the road, from commuters' perspective, also have grown increasingly problematic with the expansion of "access control" policies by local, county, and state transportation agencies. Such controls include the installation of medians and curbing that limit left turns, as well as prohibitions on U-turns at traffic signals.

As a result of these consumer preferences and governmental policies, being on the "wrong" side of the road can result in a 5 to 20 percent decrease in customer transactions, depending on the road's specific traffic volume patterns.

The bottom line is thus that it is no longer just "location, location, location" that matters for retail sales. Location questions must be evaluated in the context of "access, access, access," especially for customers seeking convenience. Any retailer evaluating locations for stores therefore should think carefully about the traffic patterns whizzing by. Are you on the right side, or the wrong side, of the road?

Sources: "It Pays to Be on the Right Side of the Road," *TSImaster,* 2011; Rick Lawlor, personal communication.

DISCUSSION QUESTIONS

For what types of retailers is being on the right side more important during afternoon commutes? For which types of retailers is it more important during the morning commute? Are there any types of retailers for which a right-hand side location is not particularly important?

Retailers need to observe the shopping center at various times of the day, week, and season. They also must consider the availability of employee parking, the proportion of shoppers using cars, parking by non-shoppers, and the typical length of a shopping trip.

An issue closely related to the amount of available parking facilities but extended into the shopping center itself is the relative congestion of the area. **Congestion** is an excess level of traffic that results in customer delays. There is an optimal level of congestion for customers. Too much congestion can make shopping slow, irritate customers, and generally discourage sales. However, a relatively high level of activity in a shopping center creates excitement and can stimulate sales.

The location of this store is poor because the store and its signage are not visible.

Visibility   **Visibility** refers to customers' ability to see the store from the street. Good visibility is less important for stores with a well-established and loyal customer base, but most retailers still want a direct, unimpeded view of their store. In an area with a highly transient population, such as a tourist center or large city, good visibility from the road is particularly important.

Adjacent Tenants   Locations with complementary, as well as competing, adjacent retailers have the potential to build traffic. Complementary retailers target the same market segment but have a different, noncompeting merchandise offering. For example, Save-A-Lot, a limited-assortment supermarket targeting price-sensitive consumers, prefers to be co-located with other retailers targeting price-sensitive consumers, such as Big Lots, Family Dollar, or even Walmart.

Have you ever noticed that competing fast-food restaurants, automobile dealerships, antique dealers, or even shoe and apparel stores in a mall are located next to one another? Consumers looking for these types of merchandise are involved in convenience or comparison shopping situations, as we described in Chapter 7. They want to be able to make their choice easily in the case of convenience shopping, or they want to have a good assortment so that they can "shop around," in the case of shopping goods. This grouped location approach is based on the principle of **cumulative attraction,** which states that a cluster of similar and complementary retailing activities will generally have greater drawing power than isolated stores that engage in the same retailing activities.[9]

Restrictions and Costs   As we learn later in this chapter, retailers may place restrictions

Save-A-Lot prefers locations next to Big Lots or Family Dollar because the presence of the two retailers will attract additional consumers.

on the type of tenants that are allowed in a shopping center in their lease agreement. Some of these restrictions can make the shopping center more attractive for a retailer. For example, a specialty men's apparel retailer may prefer a lease agreement that precludes other men's specialty apparel retailers from locating in the same center. A florist in a strip center may specify that if the grocery anchor tenant vacates the center, it can be released from its lease. Retailers would look unfavorably on a shopping center with a sign size restriction that prevented easy visibility of the store's name from the street. At the end of the chapter, we discuss some other restrictions and cost issues involved in negotiating a lease.

Locations within a Shopping Center

While the previous discussion focused on factors affecting the attractiveness of a shopping center location, the location within a shopping center has a significant effect on both sales and occupancy costs. The better locations have higher occupancy costs. In a strip shopping center, the locations closest to the supermarket are more expensive because they attract greater foot traffic. So a flower shop or sandwich shop that may attract impulse buyers should be close to the supermarket. But a shoe repair store, which does not cater to customers shopping on impulse, could be in a lower-traffic location farther away from the supermarket because customers in need of this service will seek out the store. In other words, it is a destination store.

The same issues apply to evaluating locations within a multilevel, enclosed shopping mall. Stores that cater to consumers engaging in comparison shopping, such as shoppers buying fashionable apparel, benefit from being in more expensive locations near the department store anchors, which are destinations for comparison apparel shoppers. As apparel shoppers enter and leave the department store, they walk by and may be attracted to neighboring specialty store retailers. In contrast, a retailer such as Foot Locker, another destination store, need not be in the most expensive location, because many of its customers know they're in the market for its type of product before they even go shopping.

Another consideration is how to locate stores that appeal to similar target markets. In essence, customers want to shop where they'll find a good assortment of merchandise. The principle of cumulative attraction applies to both stores that sell complementary merchandise and those that compete directly with one another. Consider the location of retailers in The Mall in Columbia, the centerpiece of the planned community of Columbia, Maryland. The mall's trade area includes about three-quarters of a million people, located in wealthy Howard County, which is positioned halfway between Baltimore, Maryland, and Washington, DC. Many of the tenants are positioned within the mall into category zones to better match their target markets.[10] For example, at the Mall in Columbia, retailers selling jewelry are located near each other. On the lower level are Zales Jewelers, Shaw's Jewelers, Pandora, Littman Jewelers, Monica Jewelers, and Fire and Ice. A short escalator ride to the upper level are Eastern Coral, Edward Arthur, Helzberg Diamond, Michael Kors, Reed's Jewelers, and Icing Ice.

TRADE AREA CHARACTERISTICS

LO3

Understand how retailers analyze the trade area for a site.

After identifying several sites that have acceptable traffic flow, accessibility, and other location characteristics, the next step is to collect information about the trade area that can be used to forecast sales for a store located at the site. The retailer first needs to define the trade area for the site. Once the trade area is defined, the retailer can use several different information sources to develop a detailed understanding of the nature of consumers in the site's trade area.

EXHIBIT 8–3
Zones in a Trade Area

Trade Area Definition

A **trade area** is a contiguous geographic area that accounts for the majority of a store's sales and customers. Trade areas can be divided into three zones, as shown in Exhibit 8–3. The exhibit shows the trade area zones for a shopping center located at the red square: the 5-minute drive-time zone (light brown), the 10-minute zone (blue), and the 15-minute zone (green).

The trade area zones shown in Exhibit 8–3 are not concentric circles based on distance from the store but, rather, are irregular polygons based on the location of roads, highways, and natural barriers, like rivers and valleys, that affect the driving time to the store. The location of competitive stores can also affect the actual trade area configuration.

The **primary trading area** is the geographic area from which the shopping center or store site derives 50 to 70 percent of its customers. The **secondary trading area** is the geographic area of secondary importance in terms of customer sales, generating about 20 to 30 percent of the site's customers. The **tertiary trading area** or **fringe** (the outermost area) includes the remaining customers who shop at the site but come from widely dispersed areas. These customers might travel an unusually long distance because they do not have comparable retail facilities closer to home, or they may drive near the store or center on their way to or from work.

The best way to define the three zones is based on driving time rather than distance. Thus, the primary trading area might be defined as customers within 5 minutes' driving time of the site; the secondary trading area, as customers with a 10-minute drive; and the tertiary zone, as customers more than 15 minutes away from the site by car. In bigger cities where driving times are lengthy, such as Los Angeles, the primary trading area may be 15 minutes; the secondary trading area, 40 minutes; and the tertiary trading area, more than 1 hour. However, it is much easier to collect information about the number of people and their characteristics in the different zones by geographic distance than by driving time. Thus, retailers often define the zones by distance—such as 3, 5, and 10 miles from the site—rather than driving time.

Factors Affecting the Size of the Trade Area

The actual boundaries of a trade area are determined by the store's accessibility, natural and physical barriers, level of competition, nature of the merchandise sold, the assortment offered, and the location of alternative sources for the merchandise.

A Starbucks in a central business district, for example, may have a trade area of only two or three blocks; a category specialist like Michaels may draw customers from 10 miles away; and The Container Store, which is the only store of its kind in a city, might draw customers from 30 miles away. Category specialists offer a large choice of brands and products for which customers are engaged in comparison shopping. Thus, customers generally drive some distance to shop at these stores. In general, destination stores have a large trade area—people are willing to drive farther to shop there.

Measuring the Trade Area for a Retail Site

Retailers can determine the trade area for their existing stores by customer spotting. **Customer spotting** is the process of locating the residences of customers for a store on a map and displaying their positions relative to the store location. The addresses for locating the customers' residences usually are obtained by asking the customers, recording the information from a check or Internet channel purchase, or collecting the information from customer loyalty programs. The data collected from customer spotting can be processed in two ways: manually plotting the location of each customer on a map or using a geographic information system like those described later in this chapter.

Multichannel retailers use their catalog and Internet sales data to spot customers and use that information to identify potential store locations. The number of catalog and Internet channel customers in an area can be used predict the sales of a store placed in the area.

Sources of Information about the Trade Area

To analyze the attractiveness of a potential store site, retailers use information about both the consumers and the competitors in the site's trade area. Two widely used sources of information about the nature of consumers in a trade area are (1) data published by the U.S. Census Bureau, based on the Decennial Census of the United States, and (2) data from geographic information systems, provided by several commercial firms.

Demographic Data from U.S. Census Bureau   Every 10 years, **census** takers gather demographic information (sex, age, ethnicity, education, marital status, etc.) from every household in the United States. The decennial census is more than just a head count; it provides a snapshot of the country's demographic, social, and economic characteristics. The U.S. Census Bureau prepares periodic reports summarizing the data. There are 8 million **census blocks** in the United States, each containing the residences of about 40 people. The smallest unit of analysis is the **block group**, a collection of adjacent blocks that contain between 300 and 4,000 people.[12]

Although the data from the U.S. Census Bureau can be used to develop a better understanding of the nature of consumers in a region or trade area, these data have several limitations. First, because they are based on information collected every 10 years, they are not very current, although the projections are reasonably accurate. Second, the data are not particularly user-friendly. It is difficult to utilize census data to examine the trade areas for various locations for specific products or services. Thus, most retailers rely on the geographic information system data offered by a number of companies to examine trade areas for potential stores.

Geographic Information System Suppliers   A **geographic information system (GIS)** is a system of hardware and software used to store, retrieve, map, and analyze geographic data; a GIS also includes the operating personnel and the data that go into the system. The key feature of GIS data is that they are identified with a coordinate system (latitude and longitude) that references a particular place on Earth. The data in the systems include spatial features such as rivers and roads,

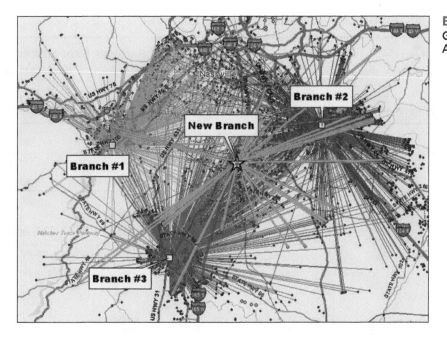

EXHIBIT 8–4
GIS Map for the Trade
Area of a Bank

as well as descriptive information associated with the spatial features, such as the street address and the characteristics of the household at the address.

Firms such as ESRI (www.esri.com), Nielsen, which purchased Claritas (www.claritas.com/sitereports/Default.jsp), and Pitney Bowes, which purchased MapInfo (www.pbinsight.com/welcome/mapinfo/) offer services that combine updated demographic census data with data from other sources that describe consumer spending patterns and lifestyles in a geographic area. In addition, they provide a user-friendly interface so that the data can be accessed and analyzed easily. Frequently, the outputs from the system are maps that enable retailers to visualize the implications of the data quickly. For example, the map in Exhibit 8–4 shows the trade areas for three branch banks that a retailer has in an MSA and a fourth branch it is considering, as well as the residences of its customers relative to the branch at which they bank. This map suggests that people bank near their work and, thus, that the new location might cannibalize from the other branches.

Retailers interested in developing a deeper understanding of their trade areas for several sites can provide one of these firms with the street addresses for the sites under consideration. The system then provides the projected data shown in the following table for current year estimates and five-year projections pertaining to people living within a 3-, 5-, and 10-mile radius of the sites. In addition, these GIS firms can provides data on the lifestyles of consumers, consumer spending potential, and the locations of competitive retailers. An example of a report on the retail goods and services purchased by residents in a trade area is shown in Exhibit 8–5.

Gender	Occupation
Income	Travel time to work
Disposable income	Transportation mode to work
Net worth	Household composition
Education	Household expenditures by NAICS categories
Age	Geodemographic market segment
Race/ethnicity	Market potential index
Employment status	Spending potential index

EXHIBIT 8–5   GIS Data for Retail Expenditures in a Trade Area

esri

Retail Goods and Services Expenditures

Sample Report

Proposed Location
100 S Wacker Dr, Chicago, IL 60606-4006
Ring: 1 mile radius

Latitude: 41.8805
Longitude: -87.63715

Top Tapestry Segments:		Demographic Summary	2010	2015
Metro Renters	68.4%	Population	45,534	50,151
Laptops and Lattes	23.4%	Households	24,338	26,808
City Strivers	2.7%	Families	7,223	7,843
Main Street, USA	1.8%	Median Age	35.7	35.8
Metropolitans	1.6%	Median Household Income	$81,441	$100,632

	Spending Potential Index	Average Amount Spent	Total
Apparel and Services	120	$2,873.94	$69,945,928
Men's	112	$512.65	$12,476,953
Women's	104	$861.55	$20,968,522
Children's	121	$485.96	$11,827,277
Footwear	84	$349.13	$8,497,153
Watches & Jewelry	173	$335.43	$8,163,589
Apparel Products and Services[1]	352	$329.21	$8,012,434
Computer			
Computers and Hardware for Home Use	169	$324.62	$7,900,647
Software and Accessories for Home Use	169	$48.15	$1,171,788
Entertainment & Recreation	155	$4,996.06	$121,594,105
Fees and Admissions	155	$960.54	$23,377,534
Membership Fees for Clubs[2]	155	$253.65	$6,173,216
Fees for Participant Sports, excl. Trips	145	$154.42	$3,758,358
Admission to Movie/Theatre/Opera/Ballet	172	$260.56	$6,341,578
Admission to Sporting Events, excl. Trips	149	$88.77	$2,160,410
Fees for Recreational Lessons	147	$201.16	$4,895,736
Dating Services	257	$1.98	$48,236
TV/Video/Audio	161	$2,003.60	$48,763,617
Community Antenna or Cable TV	157	$1,130.81	$27,521,629

Tapestry Segmentation   ERSI and other GIS suppliers have developed schemes for classifying geographic areas in the United States by combining census and survey data about people's lifestyles and purchasing behavior with the mapping capabilities of GIS. The analysis is based on the premise that "birds of a feather flock together." Specifically, people who live in the same neighborhoods tend to have similar lifestyles and consumer behavior patterns.

The ESRI Tapestry Segmentation system classifies all U.S. residential neighborhoods into 65 distinctive segments, based on demographic and socioeconomic characteristics. Exhibit 8–5 is a hypothetical report for the area within a 1.5-mile radius of 100 S. Wacker Drive in Chicago. Each segment provides a description of the typical person in that segment. The largest segment in the trade area report in Exhibit 8–5 is Metro Renters.[14] According to ESRI, residents of Metro Renters neighborhoods are young (approximately 30 percent are in their 20s), well-educated singles beginning their professional careers in some of the largest U.S. cities such as New York City, Los Angeles, and Chicago. The median age is 33.6 years; the median household income is $56,311. Most rent apartments in high-rise buildings, living alone or with a roommate. They travel, read two or more daily newspapers, listen to classical music and public radio, and go online. To stay fit, they work out regularly at clubs, play tennis and volleyball, practice yoga, ski, and jog. They go dancing and to the movies, attend rock concerts, visit museums, and

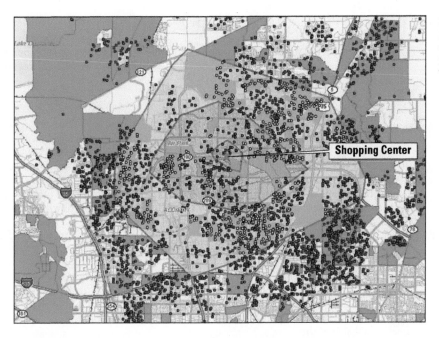

EXHIBIT 8–6
Location of Target
Customers in a
Shopping Center
Trade Area

throw frisbees. Painting and drawing are favorite hobbies. They are politically liberal. Several similar, competing segmentation systems are currently commercially available, including PRIZM (Potential Rating Index for Zip Markets), which was developed by Nielsen Claritas.

Exhibit 8–6 shows the location of customers who have the desired geodemographic profile on a trade area map for a shopping center. Note that most of the retailer's desirable customers are not even in the tertiary trade area; thus, this shopping center would not be a desirable location. (The shopping center is designated by the red star. The primary trade area is green; the secondary trade area is lavender; and the tertiary trade area is turquoise.)

Spending Potential Index   Data in ESRI's consumer spending database is reported by product or service; variables include total expenditures, average amount spent per household, and a **Spending Potential Index (SPI).** The SPI compares the local average expenditure by product to the national average amount spent. An index of 100 is average. For example, an SPI of 120 shows that average spending by local consumers is 20 percent above the national average; an SPI of 80 means that average local spending is 20 percent below the national average. (See Exhibit 8–5.)

Competition in the Trade Area

In addition to needing information about the residents in a trade area, retailers need to know about the amount and type of competition in the trade area. Although GIS vendors provide data on the location of competitive retailers, there are also other sources for this information. For example, most retailer websites list not only all current store locations, but future sites as well. A more traditional method of accessing competitive information is to look through the Yellow Pages of the telephone book. Other sources of competitive information include directories published by trade associations, chambers of commerce, Chain Store Guide (published by CSG Information Services, www.csgis.com), and municipal and county governments.

ESTIMATING POTENTIAL SALES FOR A STORE SITE

LO4

Determine the forecasted sales for a new store location.

Three approaches for using information about the trade area to estimate the potential sales for a store at the location are (1) the Huff gravity model, (2) regression analysis, and (3) the analog method.

Huff Gravity Model

The **Huff gravity model** is used to predict the probability that a consumer will patronize a store.[15] The model specifies two factors that assess the probability: (1) the attractiveness of the store's location (larger stores and shopping centers are more attractive) and (2) the time it takes a consumer to travel to the store (stores that take more time to get to are less attractive). The mathematical formula for predicting the probability of a customer's going to a specific store location is

$$P_{ij} = \frac{S_j/T_{ij}^{\lambda}}{\Sigma S_j/T_{ij}^{\lambda}}$$

where

P_{ij} = probability that customer i shops at location j

S_j = size of the store at location j

T_{ij} = travel time for customer i to get to location j

The formula indicates that the larger the size (S_j) of the store compared with competing stores' sizes, the greater the probability that a customer will shop at the location. A larger size is generally more attractive in consumers' eyes because it means more merchandise assortment and variety. Travel time or distance (T_{ij}) has the opposite effect on the probability that a consumer will shop at a location. The greater the travel time or distance from the consumer, compared with that of competing locations, the lower the probability that the consumer will shop at the location. Generally, customers would rather shop at a close store than a distant one.

The exponent λ reflects the relative effect of travel time versus store size. When λ is equal to 1, store size and travel time have an equal but opposite effect on the probability of a consumer's shopping at a store location. When λ is greater than 1, travel time has a greater effect, and when λ is less than 1, store size has a greater effect. The value of λ is affected by the nature of the shopping trips consumers generally take when visiting the specific type of store. For instance, travel time or distance is generally more important for convenience goods than for shopping goods because people are less willing to travel a great distance for a quart of milk than they are for a new pair of shoes. Thus, a larger value for λ is assigned if the store being studied specializes in convenience shopping trips rather than comparison shopping trips. The value of λ is usually estimated statistically using data that describe shopping patterns at existing stores.

To illustrate the use of the Huff model, consider the situations shown in Exhibit 8–7. A small town has two communities, Rock Creek and Oak Hammock. The town currently has one 5,000-square-foot drugstore with annual sales of $8 million, $3 million of which come from Oak Hammock residents and $5 million from Rock Creek residents. A competitive chain is considering opening a 10,000-square-foot store. As the exhibit illustrates, the driving time for the average Rock Creek resident to the existing store is 10 minutes, but it would be only 5 minutes to the new store. In contrast, the driving time for the typical Oak Hammock resident to the existing drugstore is 5 minutes and would be 15 minutes

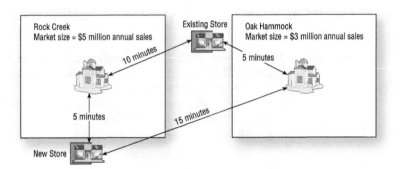

EXHIBIT 8–7
Application of the
Huff Gravity Model for
Estimating Store Sales

to the new store. Based on its past experience, the drugstore chain has found that λ equals 2 for its store locations. Using the Huff formula, the probability of a Rock Creek resident's shopping at the new location, P_{RC}, is

$$P_{RC} = \frac{10,000/5^2}{10,000/5^2 + 5,000/10^2} = .889$$

The probability of Oak Hammock residents shopping at the new location, P_{OH}, is

$$P_{OH} = \frac{10,000/15^2}{10,000/15^2 + 5,000/5^2} = .182$$

This simple application assumes that the market size for drugstores in the community will remain the same at $8 million with the addition of the new store. We also could have considered that two drugstores would increase the total size of the market. In addition, rather than doing the calculations for the average customer located in the middle of each community, we could have calculated the probabilities that each customer in the two communities would go to the new location.

Even though the Huff gravity model considers only two factors affecting store sales—travel time and store size—its predictions are quite accurate because these two factors typically have the greatest effect on store choice.[16] The regression approach discussed in the next section provides a way to incorporate additional factors into the sales forecast for a store under consideration.

Regression Analysis

The **regression analysis** approach is based on the assumption that factors that affect the sales of existing stores in a chain will have the same impact on stores located at new sites being considered. When using this approach, the retailer employs a technique called multiple regression to estimate a statistical model that predicts sales at existing store locations. The technique can consider the effects of the wide range of factors discussed in this chapter, including site characteristics, such as visibility and access, and characteristics of the trade area, such as demographics and lifestyle segments represented.

Consider the following example: A chain of sporting goods stores has analyzed the factors affecting sales in its existing stores and found that the following model is the best predictor of store sales (the weights for the factors, such as 275 for the number of households, are estimated using multiple regression):

$$
\begin{aligned}
\text{Stores sales} = {} & 275 \times \text{Number of households in trade area (15-minute drive time)} \\
& + 1{,}800{,}000 \times \text{Percentage of households in trade area with} \\
& \quad \text{children under 15 years of age} \\
& + 2{,}000{,}000 \times \text{Percentage of households in trade area in} \\
& \quad \text{Tapestry segment "aspiring young"} \\
& + 8 \times \text{Shopping center square feet} \\
& + 250{,}000, \text{if visible from street} \\
& + 300{,}000, \text{if Walmart in center}
\end{aligned}
$$

The sporting goods retailer is considering the following two locations:

Variable	Estimated Weight	Location A	Location B
Households within a 15-minute drive time of the location	275	11,000	15,000
Percentage of households with children under 15	1,800,000	70%	20%
Percentage of households in the Aspiring Young Tapestry geodemographic segment	2,000,000	60%	10%
Gross leasable square feet of shopping center	8	200,000	250,000
Visibility of store (1 = yes, 0 = no)	250,000	yes	no
Walmart store in shopping center (1 = yes, 0 = no)	300,000	yes	no

Using the regression model, the forecasted sales for location A are:

$$
\begin{aligned}
\text{Stores sales at location A} = \$7{,}635{,}000 = {} & 275 \times 11{,}000 \\
& + 1{,}800{,}000 \times 0.7 \\
& + 200{,}000 \times 0.6 \\
& + 8 \times 200{,}000 \\
& + 250{,}000 \times 1 \\
& + 300{,}000 \times 1
\end{aligned}
$$

and forecasted sales for location B are:

$$
\begin{aligned}
\text{Store sales at location B} = \$6{,}685{,}000 = {} & 275 \times 15{,}000 \\
& + 1{,}800{,}000 \times 0.2 \\
& + 2{,}000{,}000 \times 0.1 \\
& + 8 \times 250{,}000 \\
& + 250{,}000 \times 0 \\
& + 300{,}000 \times 0
\end{aligned}
$$

Note that location A has greater forecasted sales, even though it has fewer consumers in its trading area and shopping center size, because the profile of its target market fits the retailer's target market (families with children under 15 and in the Aspiring Young Tapestry segment) better.

Analog Approach

To estimate a regression model to predict sales from a site, a retailer needs data about the trade area and site characteristics from a large number of stores. Because small chains cannot use the regression approach, they use the similar but more subjective analog approach. When using the **analog approach,** the retailer simply describes the site and trade area characteristics for its most successful stores and attempts to find a site with similar characteristics. The use of this approach is described in the following illustration.

ILLUSTRATION OF SITE SELECTION: EDWARD BEINER PURVEYOR OF FINE EYEWEAR

Edward Beiner Purveyor of Fine Eyewear is an 11-store Florida retailer specializing in upper-end, high-fashion eyewear. Its store in South Miami lacks the entertainment and recreation found in shopping centers. Other problems with the location are a lack of protection against the heavy rains that characterize the area's subtropical climate, security, and parking. However, some positive features of the location are the low rent, high pedestrian traffic, few restrictions, and no other high-quality and fashion optical stores in the area, although there are other optical stores in the general area.

Edward Beiner Purveyor of Fine Eyewear wants to open a new location. Because the South Miami site is its best store, it would like to find a location whose trade area has similar characteristics. It has identified several potential locations that it is evaluating.

Using the analog approach, Edward Beiner undertakes the following steps:

1. Conduct a competitive analysis.

2. Define present trade area.

3. Analyze trade area characteristics.

4. Match characteristics of present trade area with potential sites.

L05

Illustrate the site selection process.

Edward Beiner Purveyor of Fine Eyewear specializes in high-fashion eyewear and targets affluent customers.

EXHIBIT 8–8   Competitive Analysis of Potential Locations

(1) Trade Area	(2) Eyeglasses/ Year/ Person	(3) Trade Area Population	(4) Total Eyeglasses Potential	(5) Estimated Eyeglasses Sold	(6) Trade Area Potential Units	(7) Trade Area Potential Percentage	(8) Relative Level of Competition
South Miami	0.2	85,979	17,196	7,550	9,646	56.09%	Low
Site A	0.2	91,683	18,337	15,800	2,537	13.83	Medium
Site B	0.2	101,972	20,394	12,580	7,814	38.32	Low
Site C	0.2	60,200	12,040	11,300	740	6.15	High
Site D	0.2	81,390	16,278	13,300	2,978	18.29	Medium

Step 1: Conduct Competitive Analysis

The competitive analysis of the four potential sites being considered by Edward Beiner is shown in Exhibit 8–8. To perform the analysis, Edward Beiner first estimated the number of eyeglasses sold per year per person (column 2), obtained from industry sources. Then the area population was taken from U.S. Census data (column 3). Column 4 is an estimate of the trade area potential reached by multiplying column 2 by column 3.

The estimates of the number of eyeglasses sold in the trade areas, column 5, are based on visits to competitive stores. Column 6 represents the unit sales potential for eyeglasses in the trade areas, or column 4 minus column 5. Then the trade area potential penetration is calculated by dividing column 6 by column 4. For instance, because the total eyeglass potential for the South Miami store trade area is 17,196 pairs and an additional 9,646 pairs could be sold in that trade area, 56.1 percent of the eyeglass market in this area remains untapped. The bigger the number, the lower the competition.

Column 8, the relative level of competition, is subjectively estimated on the basis of column 7. Unlike other optical stores in the trade area, Edward Beiner carries a very exclusive merchandise selection. In general, however, the higher the trade area potential, the lower the relative competition will be.

On the basis of the information in Exhibit 8–8, Edward Beiner should locate its new store at site B. The trade area potential is high, and competition is relatively low. Of course, relative competition is only one issue to consider. Later in this section, we'll consider competition along with other issues to determine which is the best new location for Edward Beiner.

Step 2: Define Present Trade Area

On the basis of customer spotting data gathered from Beiner's data warehouse of current customers, the trade area map in Exhibit 8–9 was generated using ESRI's GIS software. The zones are based on drive times: 5 minutes for the primary trade area (red), 10 minutes for the secondary trade area (purple), and 20 minutes for the tertiary trade area (green). Note that the trade area boundaries are oblong because the major highways, especially U.S. 1, run north and south. Not only do the north–south highways bring traffic to the area, but heavy traffic often makes them difficult to cross. Biscayne Bay also limits the trade area on the east.

Edward Beiner trade area is smaller than it would be if the store were located in a regional shopping mall. However, Edward Beiner is one of several optical shops in this business district. Having similar shopping goods stores in the same vicinity expands its trade area boundaries; more people are drawn to the area to shop because of its expanded selection. In addition, Edward Beiner's trade area is limited

Trade Area for Edward Beiner Purveyor of Fine Eyewear   **EXHIBIT 8–9**

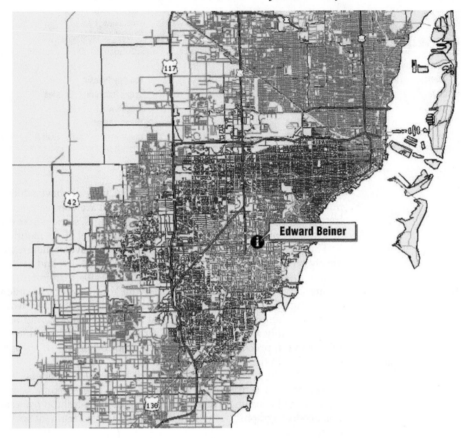

on the south by a large regional shopping center that has several stores carrying similar merchandise.

Step 3: Identify Trade Area Characteristics

Having defined its trade area, Edward Beiner reviewed a number of reports describing the characteristics of its trade area. Some of interesting findings from these reports were:

- The average household income is $92,653. In addition, 27.6 percent of the households have incomes between $75,000 and $149,000, and 13.7 percent have incomes greater than $150,000. The 3-mile ring surrounding Edward Beiner is very affluent.

- The area surrounding Edward Beiner has a population that is more than 50 percent Hispanic.

Step 4: Match Characteristics of Present Trade Area with Potential Sites

Edward Beiner believes that the profile of its current trade area is high income, predominantly white-collar occupations, a relatively large percentage of older residents, upscale geodemographic segments, and relatively low competition for expensive, high-fashion eyewear. Exhibit 8–10 compares Edward Beiner's current location with four potential locations on these five factors.

EXHIBIT 8–10   Four Potential Locations for a New Store

Store Location	Average Household Income	White-Collar Occupations	Percentage Residents Age 45 and Over	Predominant Geodemographic Segments	Level of Competition
Edward Beiner					
Optical	$100,000	High	37%	Top One Percent	Low
Site A	60,000	High	25	Young Immigrant Families	Medium
Site B	70,000	Low	80	Gray Power	Low
Site C	100,000	High	30	Young Literati	High
Site D	120,000	High	50	Upper-Income Empty-Nesters	Medium

Although the potential customers of site A typically have white-collar occupations, they also have relatively low incomes and are comparatively young. Young Immigrant Families also tend to have young families, so expensive eyewear may not be a priority purchase. Finally, there's a medium level of competition in the area.

The Gray Power residents surrounding site B have moderate incomes and are mostly retired. Even though competition would be low and most residents need glasses, these customers are more interested in value than in fashion.

Site C has strong potential because the Young Literati residents in the area are young and have a strong interest in fashion. Although working, they are busy furnishing their first homes and apartments and paying off college loans. They probably would appreciate Edward Beiner's fashionable assortment, but they won't appreciate the high prices. Also, other high-end optical stores are entrenched in the area.

Site D is the best location for Edward Beiner. The residents are older professionals or early retirees with high incomes. Upper-Income Empty-Nesters are sophisticated consumers of adult luxuries like high-fashion eyewear. Importantly, this geodemographic segment is similar to a large segment in Edward Beiner's current location.

Unfortunately, finding analogous situations isn't always as easy as in this example. The weaker the analogy, the more difficult the location decision will be. When a retailer has a relatively small number of outlets (say, 20 or fewer), the analog approach is often best. As the number of stores increases, it becomes more difficult for the analyst to organize the data in a meaningful way. More analytical approaches, such as regression analysis, then are necessary.

NEGOTIATING A LEASE

LO6

Explain the different types and terms of leases.

Once a particular site is chosen, retailers still face a multitude of decisions, including the types and terms of the lease.

Types of Leases

There are two basic types of leases: percentage and fixed rate.

Percentage Leases   Although there are many combinations within each type of lease, the most common form is a **percentage lease,** in which the rent is based on a percentage of sales. In addition to the percentage of sales, retailers typically pay a common area maintenance (CAM) fee based on a percentage of their gross leasable square footage. Most malls use some form of percentage lease. Because retail leases typically run for 5 to 10 years, they appear equitable to both parties if rents go up (or down) with sales and inflation.

A **percentage lease with a specified maximum** is a lease that pays the shopping center manager a percentage of sales up to a maximum amount. This type of lease rewards good retailer performance by allowing the retailer to hold rent constant above a certain level of sales. A similar variation, the **percentage lease with a specified minimum,** specifies that the retailer must pay a minimum rent, no matter how low sales are.

Another type of percentage lease is a **sliding scale lease,** in which the percentage of sales paid as rent decreases as the sales go up. For instance, a retailer may pay 4 percent on the first $200,000 in sales and then 3 percent on sales greater than $200,000. Similar to the percentage lease with a specified maximum, the sliding scale rewards high-performing retailers.

Fixed-Rate Leases   The second basic type of lease is a **fixed-rate lease,** most commonly used by community and neighborhood centers. A retailer pays a fixed amount per month over the life of the lease. With a fixed-rate lease, the retailer and shopping center management know exactly how much will be paid in rent, but this type of lease is not as popular as the various forms of percentage leases.

A variation of the fixed-rate lease is the **graduated lease,** in which rent increases by a fixed amount over a specified period of time. For instance, rent may be $1,000 per month for the first three years and $1,250 for the next five years.

Terms of the Lease

Although leases are formal contracts, they can be changed to reflect the relative power of the retailer and shopping center management and specific needs of the retailer. In addition to the rent, some other negotiable aspects of the lease are cotenancy, prohibited-use, and exclusive-use clauses.

Cotenancy Clause   Some retail leases contain **cotenancy clauses.** These clauses may require that a certain percentage of a shopping center be leased or that specified stores be in the center. For example, if The Gap goes into a mall, it doesn't want to be by itself. In all likelihood it has a group of retailers that it views as complements. These may include Abercrombie and Fitch, Banana Republic (also owned by The Gap), Aeropostale, American Eagle Outfitters, Ann Taylor, Anthropologie, and bebe, among others. It would not be uncommon to see a lease requirement where The Gap will only sign if at least four of the seven retailers just listed are also in the development.

If these terms are violated, the retailers with the cotenancy clauses may demand rent reductions or leave altogether. Cotenancy clauses have become particularly important in the past few years because many retailers, including several large chains like Circuit City, Borders, and Linens 'N Things, have created vacancies as a result of their bankruptcies.[17]

Prohibited-Use Clause   A **prohibited-use clause** limits the shopping center management from leasing to certain kinds of tenants. Many retailers don't want the shopping center space to be leased to establishments that take up parking spaces but do not bring in shoppers, such as a bowling alley, skating rink, meeting hall, dentist, or real estate office. Retailers may also wish to restrict the use of space from those establishments that could harm the shopping center's image. Prohibited-use clauses often specify that bars, pool halls, game parlors, off-track betting establishments, massage parlors, and pornography retailers are unacceptable.

Suppose, for instance, that Tiffany & Co., the famous jeweler, has a store in a high-end shopping center that is about to sign a lease with H&M. It could envoke its lease's prohibited-use clause in a lawsuit against the shopping center management company. Specifically, the lease forbids retailers "whose merchandise and/or price points are not considered to be luxury, upscale or better by conventional retail industry standards" to use or lease certain spaces within, fronting, or adjacent to the Tiffany store.

Exclusive-Use Clause   An **exclusive-use clause** prohibits the shopping center management from leasing to retailers that sell competing products. For example, a discount store's lease may specify that the landlord cannot lease to other discount stores, variety stores, or limited-assortment value retailers.

Some retailers also are particular about how the storefront appears. For instance, a women's specialty store may specify that the storefront must have floor-to-ceiling glass to maximize window displays and improve customers' ability to see into the store. Other retailers believe it is important that nothing blocks the view of the store from the street, so they specify that the landlord cannot place any outparcels in the parking lot. An **outparcel** is a building (such as a bank or McDonald's) or kiosk (such as an automatic teller machine) that sits in the parking lot of a shopping center but is not physically attached to the center.

Common Area Maintenance Costs   In retail leases, **common area maintenance (CAM) clauses** often require the most extensive negotiations. These clauses traditionally assign responsibilities for taking care of common areas, including sidewalks or parking lots. Modern versions have extended these responsibilities such that tenants might need to agree to contribute to capital improvement projects, pay for new roofing, or participate in the purchase of adjoining land parcels. As a result of this expansion of the meaning of CAM clauses, many leases today call them simply operating costs; in some cases, these costs outpace even rents. This status helps explain why they require such extensive negotiations. Retail tenants seek to limit their responsibilities, and they ask for the right to monitor any common area costs, to confirm their portion is charged legitimately.[18]

SUMMARY

LO1 Summarize the factors considered in locating a number of stores.

Four factors that retailers consider when evaluating an area for store locations are economic conditions, competition, strategic fit, and operating costs. Areas where the population is large and growing, have limited competition, and have a profile that matches the retailer's target market are more attractive. Finally, the cost of servicing an area needs to be considered. When determining the number of stores to locate in an area, retailers need to determine the incremental sales and profits from exploiting scale economies and increasing cannibalization by adding more stores.

LO2 Review the characteristics of a particular site.

Some characteristics of a site that affect store sales and thus are considered in selecting a site are (1) the traffic flow past the site and accessibility

to the site, (2) parking, (3) visibility, (4) adjacent tenants, and (5) restrictions and costs.

LO3 Understand how retailers analyze the trade area for a site.

Trade areas are typically divided into primary, secondary, and tertiary zones. The boundaries of a trade area are determined by how accessible it is to customers, the natural and physical barriers that exist in the area, the type of shopping area in which the store is located, the type of store, and the level of competition. Two sources of information to assess the trade areas are census data and GIS.

LO4 Determine the forecasted sales for a new store location.

Once retailers have the data that describe their trade areas, they use several analytical techniques to estimate demand. The Huff gravity model predicts the probability that a customer will choose a particular store in a trade area. The model is based on the premise that customers are more likely to shop at a given store or shopping center if it is conveniently located and offers a large selection. Regression analysis is a statistically based model that estimates the effects of a variety of factors on existing store sales and uses that information to predict sales for a new site. The analog approach—one of the easiest to use—can be particularly useful for smaller retailers. Using the same logic as regression analysis, the retailer can make predictions about sales by a new store on the basis of sales in stores in similar areas.

LO5 **Illustrate the site selection process.**

Edward Beiner Purveyor of Fine Eyewear is used to illustrate the analysis involved in opening a new location using the analog technique. This example illustrates how to (1) conduct a competitive analysis, (2) define the present trade area, (3) analyze the trade area's characteristics, and (4) match characteristics of the present trade area with potential sites.

LO6 **Explain the different types and terms of leases.**

Retailers need to negotiate the terms of a lease. Although leases are formal contracts, they can be changed to reflect the relative power of the retailer and shopping center management and specific needs of the retailer. These lease terms affect the cost of the location and may restrict retailing activities. There are two basic types of leases: percentage and fixed rate. In addition to the rent, some other negotiable aspects of the lease are cotenancy, prohibited-use, and exclusive-use and common area maintenance clauses.

KEY TERMS

accessibility, *213*

analog approach, *225*

artificial barrier, *213*

block group, *218*

census, *218*

census block, *218*

common area maintenance (CAM) clause, *230*

congestion, *215*

cotenancy clause, *229*

cumulative attraction, *215*

customer spotting, *218*

exclusive-use clause, *230*

fixed-rate lease, *229*

fringe, *217*

geographic information system (GIS), *218*

graduated lease, *229*

Huff gravity model, *222*

metropolitan statistical area (MSA), *208*

micropolitan statistical area (μSA), *208*

natural barrier, *213*

outparcel, *230*

percentage lease, *228*

percentage lease with a specified maximum, *229*

percentage lease with a specified minimum, *229*

primary trading area, *217*

prohibited-use clause, *229*

regression analysis, *223*

secondary trading area, *217*

sliding scale lease, *229*

Spending Potential Index (SPI), *221*

tertiary trading area, *217*

trade area, *217*

traffic flow, *212*

visibility, *215*

GET OUT AND DO IT!

1. **CONTINUING CASE ASSIGNMENT** Evaluate the location of a store operated by the retailer you have selected for the Continuing Case. What is the size and shape of the retailer's trade area? Describe the positive and negative aspects of its location. Compare the store's location with the locations of its competitors.

2. **INTERNET EXERCISE** Go to www.esri.com/library/fliers/pdfs/tapestry_segmentation.pdf, and

identify five segments that you would expect to find in your zip code. Then go to http://www.arcwebservices.com/services/servlet/EBIS_Reports?serviceName=FreeZip&errorURL=http%3A%2F%2Fbao.esri.com%2Fesribis%3Fcommand%3Dzipcodelookup&zipcode=02453&x=0&y=0, and type in your zip code. Compare the segments that are found in your zip code with your initial prediction. Are they similar or different?

3. **INTERNET EXERCISE** Go to http://www.esri.com/what-is-gis, the home page for ESRI Geographical Information Systems, and read about GIS. Afterwards, explain how retailers can make better decisions with GIS.

4. **INTERNET EXERCISE** The U.S. Census Bureau tracks key population characteristics, such as age, gender, disability, employment, income, language, poverty, and race. Go to the U.S. Census Bureau home page at http://factfinder2.census.gov/faces/nav/jsf/pages/index.xhtml, and, using the Population Finder, look up key demographic data for your state. Explain which factors would be most important for retailers considering this location to evaluate.

5. **GO SHOPPING** Go to a shopping mall. Get or draw a map of the stores. Analyze whether the stores are clustered in some logical manner. For instance, are all the high-end stores together? Is there a good mix of retailers catering to comparison shoppers near one another?

6. **GO SHOPPING** Visit a jewelry store in an enclosed mall and one in a neighborhood strip shopping center. List the pros and cons for each location. Which location is the most desirable? Why is this the case?

7. **WEB OLC EXERCISE** Go to the student side of the book's website, and click on "Location." You will see an Excel spreadsheet that contains the sales for 45 retail locations of a sporting goods retail chain, plus the characteristics of each location: number of households in trading area, percentage of households with children under 15 years old, percentage of households in appropriate Tapestry segments that the retailer is targeting, distance from a Walmart store, and distance from a Sports Authority store. Estimate a multiple regression model that predicts sales as a function of the site characteristics, and use the estimate weights to evaluate the two sites at the bottom of the spreadsheet.

DISCUSSION QUESTIONS AND PROBLEMS

1. Which factors do retailers consider when evaluating an area of the country to locate stores? How do retailers determine the trade area for a store?

2. True Value Hardware plans to open a new store. Two sites are available, both in middle-income neighborhood centers. One neighborhood is 20 years old and has been well maintained. The other was recently built in a newly planned community. Which site is preferable for True Value? Why?

3. Trade areas are often described as concentric circles emanating from the store or shopping center. Why is this practice used? Suggest an alternative method. Which would you use if you owned a store in need of a trade area analysis?

4. Under what circumstances might a retailer use the analog approach for estimating demand for a new store? What about regression analysis?

5. Retailers have a choice of locating on a mall's main floor or second or third level. Typically, the main floor offers the best, but most expensive, locations. Why would specialty stores such as Radio Shack and Foot Locker choose the second or third floor?

6. What retail locations are best for department stores, consumer electronics category killers, specialty apparel stores, and warehouse stores? Discuss your rationale.

7. If you were considering the ownership of a Taco Bell franchise, what would you want to know about the location in terms of traffic, population, income, employment, and competition? What else would you need to research about a potential location?

8. A drugstore is considering opening a new location at shopping center A, with hopes of capturing sales from a new neighborhood under construction. Two nearby shopping centers, B and C, will provide competition. Using the following information and the Huff gravity model, determine the probability that residents of the new neighborhood will shop at shopping center A:

Shopping center	Size (000's sq. ft.)	Distance from new neighborhood (miles)
A	3,500	4
B	1,500	5
C	300	3

Assume that $\lambda = 2$.

SUGGESTED READINGS

Baumgartner, H., and J. B. E. M. Steenkamp. "Retail Site Selection." In L.A.M. Moutinho and G.D. Hutcheson (Eds), *The SAGE Dictionary of Quantitative Management Research*. Thousands Oak, CA: Sage, 2011.

Can, Cui, Jiechen Wang, Yingxia Pu, Jinsong Ma, and Gang Chen, "GIS Based Method of Delimitating Trade Area for Retail Chains," *International Journal of Geographical Information Science* 26, 19 (2012), pp. 1863–1879.

Cox, Emmett. *Retail Analytics: The Secret Weapon*. Hoboken, NJ: Wiley, 2011.

Duggal, Nini. *Use of GIS in Retail Location Analysis*. Saarbrücken, Germany: VDM Verlag, 2008.

Gibbs, Robert. *Principles of Urban Retail Planning and Development*. Hoboken, NJ: Wiley, 2012.

Joseph, Lawrence, and Michael Kuby. "Gravity Modeling and Its Impacts on Location Analysis." In H. A. Eiselt (Ed), *Foundations of Location Analysis*. New York: Springer, 2011.

Ki, Yingru Li, and Lin Liu. "Assessing the Impact of Retail Location on Store Performance: A Comparison of Wal-Mart and Kmart Stores in Cincinnati." *Applied Geography* 32, no. 2 (March 2012), pp. 591–600.

Suárez-Vega, Rafael, Dolores R. Santos-Peñate, and Pablo Dorta-González. "Location Models and GIS Tools for Retail Site Location." *Applied Geography* 35, no. 1–2 (November 2012), pp. 2, 35.

Teller, Christoph, and Thomas Reutterer. "The Evolving Concept of Retail Attractiveness: What Makes Retail Agglomerations Attractive When Customers Shop at Them?" *Journal of Retailing and Consumer Services* 15, no. 3 (2008), pp. 127–143.

Tyman, Jeff, and Lewis Poi. "Retail Site Selection and Geographic Information Systems." *Journal of Applied Business Research* 11, no. 2 (2011), pp. 46–54.

Wood, Steve, and Sue Browne. "Convenience Store Location Planning and Forecasting—a Practical Research." *International Journal of Retail and Distribution Management* 35, no. 4 (2007), pp. 233–255.

Information Systems and Supply Chain Management

EXECUTIVE BRIEFING

Don Ralph, Senior Vice President,
Supply Chain & Logistics, Staples, Inc.

Prior to joining Staples, I worked 27 years in the department store business, for both Federated Department Stores and The May Department Stores Company where I held positions that included vice president of logistics and senior vice president of operations. Then I moved to Staples, the world's largest office products company, as senior vice president of supply chain and logistics. I have been at Staples for the last 14 years. Staples conducts retail and B2B operations in 27 countries in North and South America, Europe, Asia, and Australia.

I am responsible for the development of Staples' supply chain and logistics strategy and the execution of supply chain operations including its fulfillment, delivery, transportation, inventory management, wholesaler, and merchandising operations areas, as well as its planning and engineering, logistics strategy, and project management office. It is a big job! We have over 15,000 associates who work in our supply chain globally and operate over 300 facilities worldwide.

One of my most important responsibilities is to make sure we get our processes right before we make investments in technology. For instance, since inventory is one of the largest components of our balance sheet, a lot of time and effort is devoted to inventory management.

The new technologies we are developing are particularly fascinating to me personally, and important to Staples. For instance, Staples has developed a portal called StaplesPartners.com through which our partners can see the inventory available in each store and fulfillment center and what is sold every day—in real time! It has been a very effective tool to help us with our collaborative efforts with our partners.

We supply like products for like prices in many cases. I believe that the value chain is a strategic competitive differentiator and it adds shareholder value. The supply chain sits in the middle of the company and integrates the majority of the functions. It is a fun place to be. I view my job being like an orchestra conductor—synchronizing the various functional experts (my direct reports—all very smart folks in their own areas). The fun and challenging

CHAPTER 10

LEARNING OBJECTIVES

LO1 Understand the strategic advantage generated by a supply chain.

LO2 Describe the information and merchandise flows in a supply chain.

LO3 Consider the activities that are undertaken in a distribution center.

LO4 Review the considerations in the design of supply chains.

LO5 Explain how retailers and vendors collaborate to make sure the right merchandise is available when customers are ready to buy it.

LO6 Discuss RFID and its implications for retailers.

part of the job is optimizing all the moving parts (thousands of SKUs and hundreds of distribution and fulfillment centers). Having inquisitive DNA is a real plus in my job.

Supply chain management is a great place to start a career. Supply chain managers have to coordinate with marketing, finance, inventory management, and merchandising, among others. As such, they learn from the ground up how the company really works. As a result, I think that in the future a lot of corporate-level executives will have some tenure in supply chain management.

Joe Jackson wakes up in the morning, takes a shower, dresses, and goes to his kitchen to make a cup of coffee and toast a bagel. He slices the bagel and puts it in his toaster oven, but, to his dismay, the toaster oven is not working. He reviews his e-mails as he is eating his untoasted bagel with his coffee and notices an electronic coupon from Target for home appliances. He reviews the toaster ovens sold by Target on its website, decides he likes a Michael Graves toaster oven best, and sees it available at a store near his apartment. So, on his way home from work, he stops at a Target store. He finds the Michael Graves model his likes on the shelf and buys it.

Joe expected to find the Michael Graves toaster oven, as well as other models, available at Target, but he probably didn't realize that a lot of behind-the-scenes activities were going on to get those toaster ovens to the store. Target uses sophisticated information and supply chain management systems to make sure that the Michael Graves toaster ovens and other brands are available in its stores whenever Joe and other customers want them. When Joe bought the toaster oven, the information about his transaction was automatically forwarded by the information systems to Target's regional distribution center (DC), the home appliance planner at Target's corporate headquarters in Minneapolis, and the toaster oven manufacturer in China. A computer information system monitors all toaster oven sales and inventory levels in every Target store and indicates when to have toaster ovens shipped from the manufacturer in China to the regional distribution centers and then from the centers to the stores. Shipments to the DCs and stores are monitored using a satellite tracking system that locates the ships and trucks transporting the toaster ovens.

Of course, Target could ensure the availability of toaster ovens and other merchandise by simply keeping a large number of units in the stores at all times. But stocking a large number of each model would require much more space to store the items and a significant investment in additional inventory. So the challenge for Target is to limit its inventory and space investment but still make sure products are always available when customers want them.

This chapter begins by outlining how retailers can gain a strategic advantage through supply chain management and information systems. Then the chapter describes information and product flows in the supply chain and the activities undertaken in DCs. Next, it examines a set of decisions that retailers make to determine the structure of the supply chain, such as whether to use DCs or direct store deliveries and whether to outsource some supply chain functions. The chapter continues with a discussion of how vendors and retailers work together to efficiently manage the movement of merchandise from the vendor through the retailer's DCs to its stores and customers. The chapter concludes with a discussion of how radio frequency identification (RFID) is being used to improve supply chain efficiency.

CREATING STRATEGIC ADVANTAGE THROUGH SUPPLY MANAGEMENT AND INFORMATION SYSTEMS

LO1

Understand the strategic advantage generated by a supply chain.

As discussed in Chapter 1, retailers are the connection between customers and manufacturers. It is the retailer's responsibility to gauge customers' wants and needs and work with the other members of the supply chain—distributors, vendors, and transportation companies—to make sure the merchandise that customers want is available when they want it. A simplified supply chain is illustrated in Exhibit 10–1. Vendors ship merchandise either to a **distribution center** (DC) (as is the case for vendors V_1 and V_3) or directly to stores (as is the case for vendor V_2). The factors considered in deciding to ship directly to stores versus to DCs are discussed later in this chapter.

Supply chain management is a set of activities and techniques firms employ to efficiently and effectively manage the flow of merchandise from the vendors to the retailer's customers. These activities ensure that the customers are able to purchase merchandise in the desired quantities at a preferred location and appropriate time.[1]

Retailers are increasingly taking a leadership role in managing their supply chains. When retailers were predominantly small businesses, larger manufacturers and distributors dictated when, where, and how merchandise was delivered. But with the consolidation and emergence of large, international retail chains, retailers often play a dominant role in coordinating supply chain management activities. As we will discuss later in the chapter, retailers are sharing their data on shopping behaviors with suppliers to plan production, promotions, deliveries, assortments, and inventory levels. Efficient supply chain management is important to retailers because it can provide a strategic advantage from increases in product availability and inventory turnover and produces a higher return on assets.

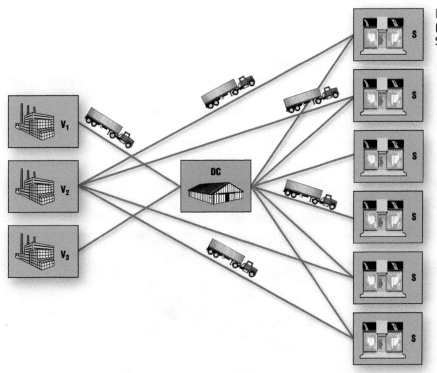

EXHIBIT 10–1
Illustration of a
Supply Chain

Improving supply chain efficiency has significant implications with respect to environmental sustainability. Retailing View 10.1 outlines Walmart's efforts toward making its supply chain greener.

Strategic Advantage

As we discussed in Chapter 5, strategic advantages are unique, and sustainable advantages enable retailers to realize a higher-than-average return on their assets. Of course, all retailers strive to develop a competitive advantage, but not all retailers can develop a competitive advantage from their information and supply chain systems.[3] However, if they do develop such an advantage, the advantage is sustainable because it is difficult for competitors to duplicate.

For example, a critical factor in Walmart's success is its information and supply chain management systems. Even though competitors recognize this advantage, they have difficulty achieving the same level of performance as Walmart's systems for four reasons. First, Walmart has made substantial initial and continuing investments in developing its systems over a long time period. Second, it has the size and scale economies to justify these investments. Third, its supply chain activities take place within the firm and are not easily known and copied by competitors. Its systems are not simply software packages that any firm can buy from a software supplier. Through its continuous learning process, Walmart is always refining its systems to improve its performance. Fourth, the coordinated effort of employees and functional areas throughout the company is supported by Walmart's top management and organization culture.

Consider the various activities that retailers undertake to keep merchandise in stock:

- Accurately forecast sales and needed inventory levels for each category and SKU.
- Monitor sales to detect deviations from the forecast.
- Transport the right amount of merchandise from the DCs to each store.

268   SECTION II   Retailing Strategy

- Make sure that accurate information is available that indicates where the merchandise is—in the vendor's warehouse, the DC, the store, sold to customer, or in transit.
- Place accurate, timely orders with vendors.
- Replenish merchandise from DCs with the right quantities when the stores need it.
- Ensure that buyers and marketing managers coordinate merchandise delivery with special sales and promotional materials.
- Collect and process returned merchandise.

10.1   RETAILING VIEW   Walmart Builds a Greener Supply Chain

Walmart has made significant strides in recent years to become a green company. Some of Walmart's green logistical activities involve improving the efficiency of its truck fleet and reducing transportation miles and packaging material. To improve the efficiency of its U.S. truck fleet, Walmart has sought to include more pallets on each truck, both in initial deliveries and in their return trips to eliminate empty "backhauls," and it closely monitors the routes that its trucks travel. **Backhauls** are trucks returning to the DCs after delivering merchandise to the stores. Typically, these trucks only have some packaging material and returns when making a backhaul. Rather than having these half-empty trucks returning to the DCs, Walmart has them picking up loads from vendors that need to ship their merchandise to Walmart's DCs.

Walmart is greening its supply chain by making its trucks more efficient.

Walmart is also making significant investments in developing and testing a number of advanced technologies to improve truck efficiencies. For example, Walmart is testing various configurations of hybrid trucks and studying improvements that make its trucks more aerodynamic. These and other technologies are helping Walmart achieve its objective of doubling the efficiency of its truck fleet, such that even as it reduced its driving distances by 28 million miles, Walmart achieved the delivery of 65 million more cases. These efficiency gains also led to another benefit: a 41,000-metric-ton reduction in CO_2 emissions.

In addition, Walmart works with its vendors to eliminate a variety of single-use packaging, such as wire ties from most toys, and reduce the weight and materials associated with a number of grocery items. Although plastic is an essential element to packaging, the 5.85 billion pounds of plastic sent annually to U.S. landfills produces 3.8 million tons of greenhouse gas (GHG). One example of Walmart's activities in this area involves thermoform, the plastic clamshell packaging used for berries, mixed salads, toys, and even some electronics. Walmart helped its vendors to identify the types of plastics that were reusable and encourages them to use more of these plastics in the packaging of their products.

Finally, Walmart is encouraging its vendors to propose green supply chain projects. For example, one of Walmart's tier 1 vendors suggested a project to increase the temperature of the vendors' cold supply chain and reduce temperature spikes. The work Walmart is doing with the vendor on this project has the potential to reduce energy consumption, product waste, and associated GHG emissions.

Sources: *2012 Global Responsibility Report*, Walmart, Bentonville, Arkansas; Andrew Winston, "How Walmart's Green Performance Reviews Could Change Retail for Good," *HBR Blog*, October 2, 2012; and Stephanie Rosenbloom, "Wal-Mart Unveils Plan to Make Supply Chain Greener," *The New York Times*, February 25, 2010.

DISCUSSION QUESTION

What are the benefits and costs of Walmart's efforts to make its supply chain greener?

REFACT

More than 80 percent of Walmart's physical waste in the United States is recycled. In the United Kingdom, its ASDA stores send no waste to landfills.[2]

Improved Product Availability

Efficient supply chain management provides two benefits to retailers and their customers: (1) fewer stockouts and (2) tailored assortments. These benefits translate into greater sales, lower costs, higher inventory turnover, and lower prices (markdowns) for retailers.

Fewer Stockouts   A **stockout** occurs when an SKU that a customer wants is not available. What would happen if Joe went to the Target store and the store did not have the Michael Graves toaster oven he wants because the DC did not ship enough to the store? The store would give Joe a **rain check** so that he could come back and still pay the sale price when the store receives a new shipment. But Joe would not be pleased because he would have made a wasted trip to the store. As a result of the stockout, Joe might decide to buy another model, or he might go to a nearby Walmart to buy a toaster oven. While at Walmart, he could buy other items in addition to the toaster oven. He also might be reluctant to shop at Target in the future and might tell his friends about the negative experience he had or post a negative review on Yelp or Twitter. This bad experience could have been avoided if Target had done a better job of managing its supply chain.

In general, stockouts have significant negative short- and long-term effects on sales and profits. Data from apparel shoppers show that when experiencing a stockout, 17 percent of consumers will switch to another brand, 39 percent will go to another store to buy the product, and the remaining 44 percent will just stop shopping. In addition, when experiencing multiple stockouts, customers typically switch to another retailer.[4]

Tailored Assortments   Another benefit provided by information systems that support supply chain systems is making sure that the right merchandise is available at the right store. Most national retail chains adjust assortments in their stores on the basis of climate—stocking more wool sweaters in northern stores and cotton sweaters in southern stores during the winter. Some retailers are now using sophisticated statistical methods to analyze sales transaction data and adjust store assortments for a wide range of merchandise on the basis of the characteristics of customers in each store's local market. (See Chapter 12 for more information on assortment planning.)

Higher Return on Assets

From the retailer's perspective, an efficient supply chain and information system can improve its return on assets (ROA) because the system increases sales and net profit margins, without increasing inventory. Net sales increase because customers are offered more attractive, tailored assortments that are in stock. Consider Joe Jackson's toaster oven purchase. Target, with its information systems, could accurately estimate how many Michael Graves toaster ovens each store would sell during the special promotion. Using its supply chain management system, it would make sure sufficient stock was available at Joe's store so that all the customers who wanted to buy one could.

Net profit margin is improved by increasing the gross margin and lowering expenses. An information system that coordinates buyers and vendors allows retailers to take advantage of special buying opportunities and obtain the merchandise at a lower cost, thus improving their gross margins. Retailers also can lower their operating expenses by coordinating deliveries, thus reducing transportation expenses. With more efficient DCs, merchandise can be received, prepared for sale, and shipped to stores with minimum handling, further reducing expenses.

By efficiently managing their supply chains, retailers can carry less backup inventory, yet still avoid stockouts. Thus, inventory levels are lower, and with a lower inventory investment, total assets are also lower, so the asset and inventory turnovers are both higher. Retailing View 10.2 describes how supply chain management is changing the way fashion comes to market.

10.2   RETAILING VIEW   Zara Delivers Fast Fashion

Fast fashion is a strategy used by fashion apparel retailers that offers customers inexpensive fashionable merchandise early in the fashion life cycle. The approach is particularly effective for specialty apparel retailers that target fashion-conscious consumers who simply must have the latest looks but are also on a very limited budget. These retailers motivate shoppers to buy new fashionable apparel every few weeks instead of purchasing a few higher-priced items every few months. The strategy was pioneered by Zara, a global specialty apparel chain located in La Coruña, Spain, and has been adopted by other retailers, including H&M (headquartered in Sweden), TopShop (United Kingdom), World (Japan), and Forever 21 (United States).

To achieve a short time between design concept and availability in stores, the fast-fashion process starts with the receipt of timely information from store managers. Headquarters staff, using the company's information system, knows what is currently selling. But the store managers interacting directly with customers find out what customers want that is not available in the stores. At Zara, store managers always have their reporting devices literally in hand. These handheld devices, which are linked directly to the company's corporate office in Spain, enable daily reports on what customers are asking for but not finding.

For example, customers might want a purple version of a pink shirt that they see in the store. Managers immediately pass the information on to the designers in Spain. If the firm believes there will be sufficient demand for the purple shirt, the designers communicate electronically with the factory that produces fabric for shirts. Assembler firms have highly automated equipment to dye the fabric purple and sew the shirts. Finally, to ensure timely delivery, the shirts get shipped by truck to stores in Europe and by air express to stores in the rest of the world.

Zara's main advantage over its more traditional competitors is its highly responsive and tightly organized supply chain. Unlike its competitors, Zara uses factories located in close geographic proximity to the company's headquarters in Spain. Although this approach increases labor costs compared with outsourced production in lower-cost countries in Asia, it also improves communication, reduces shipping costs and time, and reduces the time to get new fashions in stores.

Due to its efficient supply chain, Zara can get new fashionable apparel from design to stores in six weeks, compared to the six months that department stores typically take.

Instead of shipping new products every three months like other fashion apparel retailers, Zara's stores have new merchandise delivered several times during a month. The purple shirts would be in stores in six weeks, compared with the several months it would take for most department stores and other specialty apparel stores. Because its fast-fashion system ensures a relatively short time to get merchandise to stores, it is less likely that any Zara store will be out of stock before the next shipment arrives. Limiting the stock in stores can create a sense of scarcity among its customers. If they don't buy now, the item might not be available the next time they visit the store.

Sources: Seth Stevenson, "Polka Dots Are In? Polka Dots It Is! How Zara Gets Fresh Styles to Stores Insanely Fast—Within Weeks," *Slate*, June 21, 2012; Suzy Hansen, "How Zara Grew into the World's Largest Fashion Retailer," *The New York Times*, November 9, 2012; and Greg Petro, "The Future of Fashion Retailing—The Zara Approach," *Forbes.com*, October 25, 2012.

DISCUSSION QUESTION

What are some of the ways that Zara's supply chain management system has helped create value for its customers? Provide specific examples.

THE FLOW OF INFORMATION AND MERCHANDISE IN A SUPPLY CHAIN

LO2

Describe the information and merchandise flows in a supply chain.

The complexities of the merchandise and information flows in a typical multistore chain are illustrated in Exhibit 10–2. Although information and merchandise flows are intertwined, in the following sections we describe first how information about customer demand is captured at the store, which triggers a series of responses from buyers and planners, DCs, and vendors. This information is used to make sure that merchandise is available at the store when the customer wants it. Then we discuss the physical movement of merchandise from vendors through DCs to the stores.

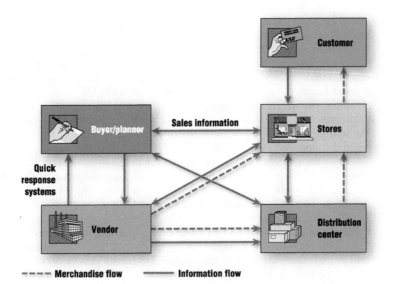

EXHIBIT 10–2
Information and
Merchandise Flows

Information Flows

When Joe Jackson bought his toaster oven at Target, he initiated the information flows illustrated in Exhibit 10–3 (the numbers in parentheses refer to the path in the exhibit).

The Target cashier scans the **universal product code (UPC)** tag on the toaster oven box (1), and a sales receipt is generated for Joe. The UPC tag is a black-and-white UPC bar code containing a 13-digit code that indicates the manufacturer of the item, a description of the item, information about special packaging, and special promotions. The codes for all products are issued by GS1 US (gs1us.org), formerly the Uniform Code Council. In the future, RFID tags, discussed later in this chapter, may replace UPC tags.

The information about the transaction is captured at the **point-of-sale (POS) terminal** and sent to Target's information system, where it can be accessed by the merchandise planner for the toaster oven product category (2). The planner uses

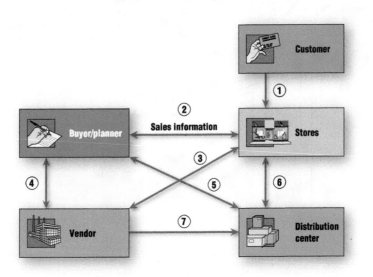

EXHIBIT 10–3
Information Flows

this information to monitor and analyze sales and decide when to reorder more toaster ovens or reduce their prices if sales are below expectations.

The sales transaction data also are sent to Target's DC (6). When the store inventory drops to a specified level, more toaster ovens are shipped to the store, and the shipment information is sent to the Target computer system (5) so that the planner knows the inventory level that remains in the DC.

When the inventory drops to a specified level in the DC (4), the planner negotiates terms and shipping dates and places an order with the manufacturer of the toaster ovens. The planner then informs the DC about the new order and when the store can expect delivery (5).

When the manufacturer ships the toaster ovens to the Target DC, it sends an advanced shipping notice to the DC (7). An **advance shipping notice (ASN)** is a document that tells the DC what specifically is being shipped and when it will be delivered. The DC then makes appointments for trucks to make the delivery at a specific time, date, and loading dock. When the shipment is received at the DC and checked, the planner is notified (5) and then authorizes payment to the vendor.

In some situations, discussed later in this chapter, the sales transaction data are sent directly from the store to the vendor (3), and the vendor decides when to ship more merchandise to the DC and stores. The fulfillment of sales from nonstore channels may involve the vendor shipping merchandise directly to the customer. In other situations, especially when merchandise is reordered frequently, the ordering process is done automatically, bypassing the planners.

Data Warehouse   Purchase data collected at the point of sale goes into a database known as a *data warehouse*. The information stored in the data warehouse is accessible on various dimensions and levels, as depicted in the data cube in Exhibit 10–4.

As shown on the horizontal axis, data can be accessed according to the level of merchandise aggregation—SKU (item), vendor, category (toaster ovens), or all merchandise. Along the vertical axis, data can be accessed by level of the

EXHIBIT 10–4   Retail Data Warehouse

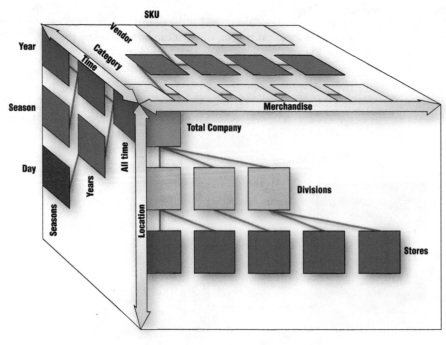

company—store, division, or total company. Finally, along the third dimension, data can be aggregated to day, season, or year.

The CEO might be interested in how the corporation is generally doing and could look at the data aggregated by quarter for a merchandise division, a region of the country, or the total corporation. A buyer may be more interested in a particular vendor in a specific store on a particular day. Analysts from various levels of the retail operation extract information from the data warehouse to make a plethora of retailing decisions about developing and replenishing merchandise assortments.

Data warehouses also contain detailed information about customers, which is used to target promotions and group products together in stores. These applications are discussed in Chapter 11. To economically collect this information, most of the communication between vendors and retailers and within the retailer is done via electronic data interchange (EDI).

Electronic Data Interchange   In the past, retailer–vendor information flows were accomplished by sending handwritten or typed documents through the mail or by fax. Now most communications between vendors and retailers occur via electronic data interchange. **Electronic data interchange (EDI)** is the computer-to-computer exchange of business documents using a standardized format. To facilitate the adoption of EDI, the retail industry agreed to use specific symbols to delineate the purchase order number, the vendor's name, the address the merchandise is being shipped to, and so forth.[7]

Retailers also have developed standards for exchanging information about purchase order changes, order status, transportation routings, advance shipping notices, on-hand inventory status, and vendor promotions, as well as information that enables vendors to put price tags on merchandise. The development and use of these standards is critical to the use of EDI because they enable all retailers to use the same format when transmitting data to their vendors.

EDI transmissions between retailers and vendors occur over the Internet. Because the Internet is a publicly accessible network, its use to communicate internally and externally with vendors and customers raises security issues. Some potential implications of security failures are the loss of business data essential to conducting business, disputes with vendors and customers, loss of public confidence and its effect on brand image, bad publicity, and loss of revenue from customers using an electronic channel.

To help secure information, retailers have incorporated security policies. A **security policy** is the set of rules that apply to activities involving computer and communication resources that belong to an organization. Retailers also train employees and add the necessary software and hardware to enforce the rules. The objectives of a security policy are:

- *Authentication.* The system ensures or verifies that the person or computer at the other end of the communication really is who or what it claims to be.
- *Authorization.* The system ensures that the person or computer at the other end of the communication has permission to carry out the request.
- *Integrity.* The system ensures that the arriving information is the same as that sent, which means that the data have been protected from unauthorized changes or tampering through a data encryption process.

The Physical Flow of Merchandise—Logistics
Exhibit 10–5 illustrates the physical flow of merchandise within the supply chain.

1. Merchandise flows from vendor to DC.
2. Merchandise goes from DC to stores.
3. Alternatively, merchandise can go from vendor directly to stores or even the customer.

EXHIBIT 10–5   Merchandise Flow

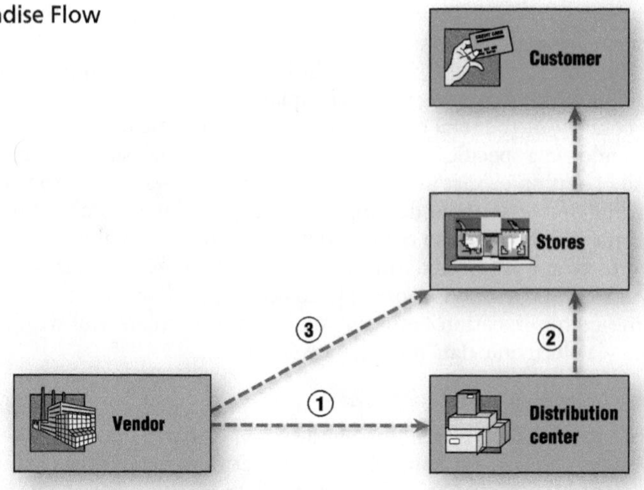

REFACT

Located strategically across the United States, Walmart's disaster DCs are well stocked with supplies that communities affected by a natural disaster are likely to need so that the company can ensure a rapid response.[9]

Logistics is the aspect of supply chain management that refers to "the planning, implementation, and control of the efficient flow and storage of goods, services, and related information from the point of origin to the point of consumption to meet customers' needs."[8] In addition to managing inbound and outbound transportation, logistics involves the activities undertaken in the retailer's DC. For example, sometimes merchandise is temporarily stored at the DC; other times it just passes directly through the center from an inbound to an outbound truck. Merchandise shipments also might be prepared for stores in the center. For example, the center might break down received shipping cartons into smaller quantities that can be more readily utilized by the individual stores and/or apply price tags and the retailer's labels. The next section describes activities undertaken in a DC.

THE DISTRIBUTION CENTER

LO3

Consider the activities that are undertaken in a distribution center.

DCs perform the following activities: coordinating inbound transportation; receiving, checking, storing, and cross-docking merchandise; getting merchandise "floor-ready"; and coordinating outbound transportation. To illustrate these activities, we will follow a shipment of Nintendo's WiiU consoles that arrive at a Best Buy DC.

Management of Inbound Transportation

REFACT

On Cyber Monday, Amazon shipped more than 17 million items, 200 items per second, from its 40 DCs.[10]

Traditionally, buyers focused their efforts, when working with vendors, on developing merchandise assortments, negotiating prices, and arranging joint promotions. Now, buyers and planners are much more involved in coordinating the physical flow of merchandise to the stores. The Best Buy video game buyer has arranged for a truckload of WiiU consoles to be delivered to its Houston, Texas, DC on Monday between 1 and 3 p.m. The buyer has also specified the number of units per carton and the particular way that the merchandise should be placed on pallets for easy unloading.

The truck must arrive within the specified time because the DC has all of its 100 receiving docks allocated throughout the day, and much of the merchandise on this particular inbound truck is going to be cross-docked and loaded into an outbound truck going to a store that evening. Unfortunately, the truck was delayed due to an engine problem. The **dispatcher**—the person who coordinates deliveries to the DC—reassigns the truck delivering the WiiU consoles to a Wednesday morning delivery slot, notifies the planner, and charges the vendor several hundred dollars for missing its delivery time. Although many manufacturers pay transportation expenses, some retailers negotiate with their vendors to absorb this expense.

Receiving and Checking

Receiving is the process of recording the receipt of merchandise as it arrives at a DC. **Checking** is the process of going through and verifying the merchandise listed on the ASN is the same as the merchandise received.

Checking merchandise is a very labor-intensive and time-consuming task. When retailers have developed good relationships with vendors, they often do not check the number of items received on each carton compared to the number sent as indicated on the vendor's ASN. They might randomly check a sample of shipments to monitor the accuracy of the vendor's ASNs. In the future, as discussed later in this chapter, retailers may be able to automatically check the contents of each carton by detecting signals sent from RFID chips placed on each item of merchandise in a carton.

Storing and Cross-Docking

After the WiiU consoles are received and checked, they are either stored or cross-docked. When the WiiU consoles are stored, the cartons are transported by a conveyor system and forklift trucks to racks that go from the DC's floor to its ceiling. Then, when the consoles are needed in the stores, a forklift driver goes to the rack, picks up the carton, and places it on a conveyor system that routes the carton to the loading dock of a truck going to the stores.

Cross-Docking   The cartons with WiiU consoles that are cross-docked are prepackaged by Nintendo for a specific store. The UPC label attached to the carton indicates the store to which it is to be sent. Nintendo may also affix a price tag to each item in the carton. The WiiU cartons are unloaded from the inbound truck and placed on a conveyor system that routes them across the loading dock to the truck going to the specific store—thus, the term **cross-docked**. The cartons are routed on the conveyor system automatically by sensors that read the UPC labels on the cartons. These cross-docked cartons are only in the DC for a few hours before they are shipped to the stores.

REFACT

Cartons on the conveyor belt at Amazon's DC travel at 20 miles per hour.[11]

Not all of the cartons received can be cross-docked. For example, it would be inefficient to cross-dock toothbrush cartons if a received carton contained 600 units but a store only sold 50 units a day. In this situation, the received toothbrush carton would be opened and a smaller number of units along with other merchandise would be put in a carton going to a store. This is done in a **break pack area** in the DC. Finally, when cross-docking cartons, retailers assume that the number and type of merchandise in each carton and the store designations are correctly encoded in the vendor's UPC labels. Thus, retailers are reluctant to cross-dock merchandise from unreliable vendors. These errors are ultimately uncovered when the cross-docked cartons are opened at the store. At this point, it is very costly to send the incorrect merchandise back to the DC or vendor through the retailers' reverse logistics system, as discussed later in the chapter.

No hands are needed to cross-dock merchandise. The automated conveyor systems move merchandise from the unloading area for a vendor's inbound truck to the loading area for a retailer's outbound truck going to its store.

Ticketing and marking are often done in the DC so that the merchandise is floor-ready—that is, ready to put on the sales floor when the carton is opened at the store.

Getting Merchandise Floor-Ready

For some merchandise, additional tasks are undertaken in the DC to make the merchandise floor-ready. **Floor-ready merchandise** is merchandise that is ready to be placed on the selling floor in a store. Getting merchandise floor-ready entails ticketing, marking, and, in the case of some apparel, placing garments on hangers.

Ticketing and marking refer to affixing price and identification labels to the merchandise. It is more efficient for a retailer to perform these activities at a DC than in its stores. In a DC, an area can be set aside and a process implemented to efficiently add labels and put apparel on hangers. Conversely, getting merchandise floor-ready in stores can block aisles and divert sales associates' attention from their customers. An even better approach from the retailer's perspective is to get vendors to ship floor-ready merchandise, thus totally eliminating the expensive, time-consuming, ticketing and marking process.

Preparing to Ship Merchandise to a Store

At the beginning of the day, the computer system in the DC generates a list of items to be shipped to each store on that day. For each item, a pick ticket and shipping label are generated. The **pick ticket** is a document or display on a screen in a forklift truck that indicates how many cartons to get from specific storage areas. The forklift driver goes to the storage area, picks up the number of cartons indicated on the pick ticket, places UPC shipping labels on the cartons that indicate the stores to which the cartons are to be shipped, and puts the cartons on the conveyor system, where they are automatically routed to the loading dock for the truck going to the stores.

Pick tickets and labels are also generated for the break pack area. In the break pack area, open cartons shipped by the vendors are placed on shelves. Employees with pick tickets, or robots, pick the number of items designated for a store and put the items into a new carton designated for the store. When the new carton for the store is full, a label with the UPC code is affixed, and the carton is put on the conveyor system, directing it to the loading dock for the truck going to the store.

When it is not economical to send a carton of a single item to a store, the multiple items are picked from the shelves and put into a carton for shipment to the store.

Thus, the conveyor system feeds cartons from three sources to the loading dock for a truck going to a specific store: (1) cross-docked cartons directly from the vendor's delivery trucks, (2) cartons stored in the DC, and (3) cartons from the break pack area. The cartons are then loaded onto the trucks by employees.

Management of Outbound Transportation

The management of outbound transportation from DC to stores is quite complex. Most DCs run 50 to 100 outbound truck routes each day. To handle this complex transportation problem, the centers use sophisticated routing and scheduling software that considers the locations of the stores, road conditions, and transportation operating constraints for developing the most efficient routes possible. As a result, stores are provided with an accurate estimated time of arrival, and vehicle utilization is maximized.

Retailers also need to determine the mode of transportation—planes, ships, or trucks. Some retailers mix modes of transportation to reduce overall costs and time delays. For example, many Chinese vendors send Europe-bound cargo by ship to the U.S. West Coast. From there, the cargo is flown to its final destination in Europe. By combining the two modes of transport, sea and air, the entire trip takes about two weeks, as opposed to four or five weeks with an all-water route, and the cost is about half that of an all-air route.

Dollar General, an extreme-value retailer, developed an interesting, low-tech approach for dealing with a challenge it faced with outbound transportation to its stores. Controlling cost and distributing merchandise efficiently to its 10,000 stores is key to maintaining its low prices and still making a profit. Each week, more than 2,000 cartons are delivered to a typical store, and 12 person-hours are required to unload a delivery truck—time the employees could have spent helping customers. Labor scheduling is a real problem because store managers have to schedule additional staff on truck delivery days and then, in some cases, the drivers cannot make deliveries at the preplanned time. In addition, many of the stores are located in urban areas that make it difficult to park delivery trucks at a convenient location for an extended time period.

To address these challenges, Dollar General invested $100 million in a delivery system called EZ store. The EZ store system involves packing merchandise for shipment to stores in easy-to-move containers called roll-tainers that serve to protect the merchandise better than regular boxes. Instead of having store staff unload the truck when it arrives, the truck drivers unload these roll-tainers on their own. A usual store receives deliveries of around 25 roll-tainers, which take a driver about 90 minutes to unload. Using the EZ store system, store employees quickly unpack the merchandise from the roll-tainers and place it on shelves. When drivers make their next delivery, they offload the filled roll-tainers and pick up the empty ones. The system has led to significant reductions in labor-hours, injuries, and employee turnover. It has also decreased the turnaround time for the truck drivers.[12]

SYSTEM DESIGN ISSUES

This section reviews the factors affecting the decisions made by retailers concerning their supply chains. These decisions involve determining what activities, if any, should be outsourced to independent firms; what merchandise, if any, should be delivered directly to the store, bypassing the DC; and how shipments directly to customers should be made.

LO4

Review the considerations in the design of supply chains.

Outsourcing Logistics

To streamline their operations and make more productive use of their assets and personnel, some retailers **outsource** supply chain functions. Many independent companies are very efficient at performing individual activities or all the supply chain activities. There are a large number of companies that can transport merchandise from the vendor to DCs or from the centers to the retailer's stores. Rather than owning warehouses to store merchandise, retailers can use **public warehouses** that are owned and operated by an independent company. Rather than outsource specific activities, retailers can use freight forwarders to arrange for the storage and shipping of their merchandise. **Freight forwarders** provide a wide range of services: tracking transportation routes, preparing export and shipping documentation, booking cargo space (or warehousing items until the cargo space is needed), negotiating the charges for and consolidating freight, and insuring the cargo or filing insurance claims as necessary.[13]

Advantages and Disadvantages of Outsourcing Supply Chain Activities

The primary benefit of outsourcing is that the independent firms can perform the activity at a lower cost and/or more efficiently than the retailer. Independent firms typically have a lower cost because they perform the activity for many retailers and thus realize scale economies. For example, independent trucking firms have more opportunities to fill their trucks on the return trip (backhaul) with merchandise for other retailers after delivering merchandise to one retailer's stores. In addition, when there are many independent firms available to undertake the activity, retailers can have the firms bid against each other to undertake the activity and thus drive down the costs.

However, when retailers outsource a supply chain activity they can no longer develop a competitive advantage based on the performance of this activity. If the retailer's competitor discovers that the retailer is significantly reducing its costs or improving its efficiency by using an independent firm, the competitor can match the performance improvement by contracting with the same provider.[14]

Pull and Push Supply Chains

Another supply chain decision retailers make is determining whether merchandise will be pushed from the DCs to the stores or pulled from the DCs to the stores. Information and merchandise flows such as those described in Exhibit 10–2 illustrate a **pull supply chain**—a supply chain in which requests for merchandise are generated at the store level on the basis of sales data captured by POS terminals. Basically, in this type of supply chain, the demand for an item pulls it through the supply chain. An alternative is a **push supply chain,** in which merchandise is allocated to stores on the basis of forecasted demand. Once a forecast is developed, specified quantities of merchandise are shipped (pushed) to DCs and stores at predetermined time intervals.

In a pull supply chain, there is less likelihood of being overstocked or out of stock because the store requests for merchandise are based on customer demand. A pull approach increases inventory turnover and is more responsive to changes in customer demand, and it becomes even more efficient than a push approach when demand is uncertain and difficult to forecast.[15]

Although generally more desirable, a pull approach is not the most effective in all situations. First, a pull approach requires a more costly and sophisticated information system to support it. Second, for some merchandise, retailers do not have the flexibility to adjust inventory levels on the basis of demand. For example, commitments must be made months in advance for fashion and private-label apparel. Because these commitments cannot be easily changed, the merchandise has to be allocated to the stores at the time the orders are formulated.

DCs versus Direct Store Delivery

As indicated in Exhibit 10–5, retailers can have merchandise shipped directly to their stores—direct store delivery (path 3)—or to their DCs (paths 1 and 2). **Direct store delivery (DSD)** is a distribution method that bypasses the retailer's DC and delivers the merchandise directly to the retailer's stores.[16] Typically, vendors offering DSD provide additional services such as assessing the store's stock levels and backroom inventory to determine the right amount needed and then have the store manager approve a replenishment order. The vendor's representative may also restock the shelves or racks, rearrange merchandise, and remove dated products.

In general, using DCs results in overall lower inventory levels because the amount of backup stock needed in a centralized DC is less than the amount of backup stock needed in all the stores served by the center. For example, if a retailer had merchandise directly shipped to its stores, each store might need to stock 10 Michael Graves toasters for a total of 500 units in the 50 stores served by a DC. By delivering products to a DC, the same level of availability could be achieved with 350 toasters (5 in each store and 100 in the DC). Because the stores get frequent deliveries from the DC, they need to carry relatively less extra merchandise as backup stock. Thus, DCs enable the retailer to carry less merchandise in individual stores resulting in lower inventory investments systemwide.

However, DSD is more efficient for the following situations:

- Products such as potato chips and bread that have low value density (cost per cubic inches) and can be easily damaged if handled through multiple checkpoints.

- Products such as milk and eggs that have a short shelf life and where freshness is important to customers.

- Products like bottled water that are costly to transport.

- Products that are supplied by vendors' warehouses that are in close proximity to high-volume retail stores.

- Suppliers, like Hallmark and American Greetings cards, that have a large assortment of low-priced merchandise that can be easily shipped in small packages to retail stores.

- Retailers that have a limited number of outlets, and therefore do not have the scale economies to build and operate DCs.

- Products like video games and fashion apparel for which speed to the market is necessary to satisfy customer demand early in its life cycle (e.g., video games need to be available for sale on their launch date).

- Products such as ice cream requiring special storage or handling that cannot easily be provided by a retailer.

Many larger vendors such as Coca-Cola, Kraft Foods, Frito-Lay, PepsiCo, and Hallmark distribute extensively through DSD. However, the rising transportation costs (e.g., higher gasoline prices) are reducing the amount of DSD merchandise.[18]

Dolly Madison's baked goods are delivered directly to the retailer's store, bypassing the DC, ensuring that customers can get the freshest merchandise.

Reverse Logistics

Reverse logistics is the process of capturing value from and/or properly disposing of merchandise returned by customers and/or stores. A reverse logistics system processes merchandise that is returned because it is damaged, has been recalled, is no longer sold to customers because its selling season has ended, the merchandise was incorrectly sent to a store or directly to a customer, the product has been discontinued, or there is excessive inventory in stores or DCs. The returned merchandise might involve returns from a customer to a retail store, from a retail store to a DC, or from a DC to a vendor. [19]

When customers return items to retail stores, the stores collect the items and send them to DCs or centralized returns centers. Sophisticated retailers enter information about each item into their information systems so that it can be used to evaluate products, vendors, and the returns process. When the product arrives at the center, the retailer needs to examine the product and decide what do with it. Some of the potential dispositions are return it to the vendor for a refund, repair and/or repackage it and sell it as new, sell it to an outlet store or broker, donate it to charity, or recycle it. In general, retailers prefer to return items to the vendor for a refund. Due to the high cost of refurbishing and transporting small quantities, some vendors negotiate with retail buyers to offer a percent of sales discount for returns and have the retailers dispose of the merchandise, either giving it to charity or throwing it away.

Reverse logistics systems are challenging. Some differences between the forward flow of merchandise, shown in Exhibit 10–5, and the reverse flow include the forms of consolidation, product quantities, the distribution patterns, and cost transparency. First, a forward process sends goods from a few DCs to a vast number of stores or customers, whereas with a reverse process, goods come from all over and must be consolidated in one or a few receiving centers. Second, the goal of the forward process is consistent quality; the reverse process exists inherently because of the lack of consistency in the products involved. Third, a distribution plan in a forward process is designed carefully and set in advance. For a reverse process, the ad hoc distribution pattern can take a variety of unpredictable patterns. Fourth, the forward process constantly seeks more cost transparency in its standardized cost structures, but such a goal is not pertinent to the reverse process, for which none of the cost-imposing processes are likely to be standardized.[21]

Two reasons more attention is being directed toward reverse logistics are the growth of sales through Internet channels and the increasing interest in environmental sustainability. First, the percentage of returned merchandise is much greater for purchases made through the Internet channel compared to the store channel. Because the percentage of merchandise returns bought through the Internet channel is as much as four times greater than for merchandise bought through the store channel, the growth in Internet sales is going to significantly increase the number of returns and the cost of processing them through the reverse logistics system.

Second, the efficiency of reverse logistics affects environmental sustainability because packaging and shipping materials are processed through the reverse logistics system. When retailers reduce transportation costs by consolidating shipments to stores and DCs and optimize the disposal of returned merchandise, they reduce harmful emissions, energy usage, and their costs. Green logistics is becoming a standard business practice.

Drop Shipping

Drop shipping, or **consumer direct fulfillment,** is a system in which retailers receive orders from customers and relay these orders to vendors; the vendors then ship the merchandise ordered directly to the customer. Such systems are especially popular among companies that need to ship products made from bulky or heavy materials (e.g., lumber, iron).[23]

From the retailer's perspective, drop shipping reduces the retailer's supply chain costs and investment because the vendor, rather than the retailer, assumes the costs and risks of supplying merchandise to customers. The vendor has to build and operate the DCs, hire and pay for employees to pick and pack individual orders, and manage inventory. Drop shipping is particularly attractive for retailers that do not have DCs capable of fulfilling individual orders from customers. However, drop shipping can lengthen delivery times and increase costs, particularly for customers who order multiple items from different vendors. In addition, retailers do not have control over an aspect of their offering that is of importance to their

REFACT

The cost of processing a return can be up to three times the cost of an outbound shipment of an item.[22]

customer—how and when orders are delivered. Finally, defining the process for handling returns is an issue.

Supply Chain for Fulfilling Catalog and Internet Orders

The DCs and supply chain and information systems for supporting catalog and Internet channels are very different from those supporting the store channel. The typical retail DC supporting a store channel is designed to receive a relatively small number of cartons from vendors and ship about the same number of cartons to its stores. In contrast, DCs supporting nonstore channels are designed to receive about the same number of cartons from vendors but ship a very large number of small packages to customers. Thus, warehouses designed to support nonstore channels are basically one large break pack area. In addition, the information system for supporting a store channel focuses on products—making sure that the right number of products are delivered to each store—while information systems supporting nonstore channels are focused on the customer—making sure that the right customer receives the right product.

Because completely different DC designs are required for supporting the different channels, when a store-based retailer adds nonstore channels, it has to outsource fulfillment of the nonstore sales, designate separate areas within the present DCs for shipments to individual consumers, build different DCs for the new channels, or fulfill orders by picking and packing merchandise in their stores.

Some retailers initially outsourced the fulfillment function when they added an Internet channel. For example, Toys "R" Us turned to Amazon for help after a disastrous holiday season when many of its customers did not receive their orders on time, creating many unhappy children and angry parents on Christmas morning. Toys "R" Us entered into a 10-year agreement with Amazon to outsource the fulfillment of its sales through nonstore channels. Even though Amazon's fulfillment capability is very efficient, over time Toys "R" Us acquired this capability and found that outsourcing its Internet channels was an impediment to creating a unified, multichannel offering. So, Toys "R" Us ultimately terminated its outsourcing contract with Amazon.[24]

Instead of building DCs for nonstore sales fulfillment, Macy's is using the backroom of its stores as impromptu shipping centers, because, as one executive noted, "We've spent the last 153 years building warehouses. We just called them stores."[25] To make use of this existing capacity, Macy's will convert nearly 300 of its more than 800 stores into fulfillment centers. These centers should facilitate inventory management; a store with too much inventory can ship the extra to the fulfillment site, which can then place the items up for sale online. Orders placed online can get filled by the nearest stores, which should reduce shipping costs and time.

Yet because filling orders by hand using inexperienced workers is relatively inefficient, there is some debate about whether retailers should operate separate DCs to deal with store and nonstore channels or use the same DCs for both. Synergies between the channels can be exploited if the same centers are used for all. For example, less inventory is needed to support distribution for all channels from one center. However, these potential synergies might be limited, and the difference between the operations of each area might cause confusion. In addition, if same-day or next-day delivery for orders placed through nonstore channels is very important to customers, retailers might develop a dedicated hub-and-spoke design for nonstore channel fulfillment. The hub-and-spoke design would have many geographically diverse smaller distribution centers supporting a large center. The smaller centers would be located closer to customers allowing for faster and cheaper shipping times for the retailer.[26]

COLLABORATION BETWEEN RETAILERS AND VENDORS IN SUPPLY CHAIN MANAGEMENT

LO5

Explain how retailers and vendors collaborate to make sure the right merchandise is available when customers are ready to buy it.

As we discussed previously, retailers' and vendors' objectives for supply chain management are to minimize investments in inventory and costs and still make sure that merchandise is available when and where customers want it. Retailing View 10.1 at the beginning of this chapter illustrated how fast-fashion specialty retailers, such as Zara, excel at coordinating their stores, designers, and production capability to achieve these objectives.

Benefits of Coordination

Supply chain efficiency dramatically improves when vendors and retailers share information and work together. By collaborating, vendors can plan their purchases of raw materials and their production processes to match the retailer's merchandise needs. Thus, vendors can make sure that the merchandise is available "just in time," when the retailer needs it, without having to stock excessive inventory in the vendor's warehouse or the retailer's DCs or stores.

When retailers and vendors do not coordinate their supply chain management activities, excess inventory builds up in the system, even if the retail sales rate for the merchandise is relatively constant. This buildup of inventory in an uncoordinated channel is called the **bullwhip effect.** The effect was first discovered by Procter & Gamble, which saw that its orders from retailers for Pampers disposable diapers were shaped like a bullwhip, with wide swings in quantity ordered, even though retail sales were relatively constant (see Exhibit 10–6). Its retailers were ordering, on average, more inventory than they really needed.

Research has found that the bullwhip effect in an uncoordinated supply chain is caused by the following factors:

- *Delays in transmitting orders and receiving merchandise.* Even when retailers can forecast sales accurately, there are delays in getting orders to the vendor and receiving those orders from the vendor. In an uncoordinated supply chain, retailers might not know how fast they can get the merchandise, and thus they order more than they need to prevent stockouts.

- *Overreacting to shortages.* When retailers find it difficult to get the merchandise they want, they begin to play the shortage game. They order more than they need to prevent stockouts, hoping they will receive a larger partial shipment. So, on average, the vendor ships more than the retailer really needs.

- *Ordering in batches.* Rather than generating a number of small orders, retailers wait and place larger orders to reduce order processing and transportation costs and take advantage of quantity discounts.[27]

EXHIBIT 10–6
Bullwhip Effect in Uncoordinated Supply Chain

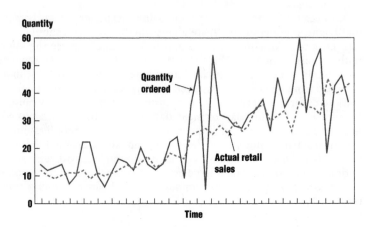

These factors cause the bullwhip effect even when sales are fairly constant. However, for many retailers, sales are not constant. They go up dramatically when retailers put merchandise on sale and during special gift-giving times of the year. These irregularities in sales heighten the bullwhip effect and the buildup of inventory in the supply chain.

Vendors and retailers have found that by working together, they can reduce the level of inventory in the supply chain and the number of stockouts in the stores. Four approaches for coordinating supply chain activities, in order of the level of collaboration, are (1) using EDI; (2) sharing information; (3) using vendor-managed inventory; and (4) employing collaborative planning, forecasting, and replenishment.

Using EDI

The use of EDI to transmit purchase order information reduces the time it takes for retailers to place orders and for vendors to acknowledge the receipt of orders and communicate delivery information about those orders. In addition, EDI facilitates the implementation of other collaborative approaches discussed in the following sections. However, the use of EDI without other collaborative approaches only addresses one factor discussed previously—the delay in transmitting and receiving orders—that causes the buildup of inventory in the supply chain.

Sharing Information

One of the major factors causing excessive inventory in the supply chain is the inability of vendors to know what the actual level of retail sales are. For instance, suppose a consumer packaged goods vendor offered discounts to retailers several times a year, hoping that the price reduction would be passed on to customers. Instead, however, the retailers purchased extra inventory and kept the extra discounts to increase their margins. Just looking at the orders it received, the vendor might think that demand for its products had increased significantly and therefore increase its production, causing an inventory buildup. To reduce this effect, vendors are using the retailer's sales data.

Sharing sales data with vendors is an important first step in improving supply chain efficiency. With the sales data, vendors can improve their sales forecasts, improve production efficiency, and reduce the need for excessive backup inventory. But additional levels of collaboration are needed to use this information effectively. The sales data reflect historical data, not what the retailer's plans are for the future. For example, the retailer might decide to delete a vendor's SKU from its assortment—a decision that clearly affects future sales. The two approaches discussed in the next sections introduce a forward-looking collaborative perspective.

Vendor-Managed Inventory

Vendor-managed inventory (VMI) is an approach for improving supply chain efficiency in which the vendor is responsible for maintaining the retailer's inventory levels. The vendor determines a **reorder point**—a level of inventory at which more merchandise is ordered. The retailer shares sales and inventory data with the vendor via EDI. When inventory drops to the order point, the vendor generates the order and delivers the merchandise.[28]

In ideal conditions, the vendor replenishes inventories in quantities that meet the retailer's immediate demand and reduce stockouts with minimal inventory. In addition to better matching retail demand to supply, VMI can reduce the vendor's and the retailer's costs. Vendor salespeople no longer need to spend time generating orders on items that are already in the stores, and their role shifts to selling new items and maintaining relationships. Retail buyers and planners no longer need to monitor inventory levels and place orders.

The use of VMI is not a new approach. Frito-Lay and other snack food, candy, and beverage vendors have used VMI combined with direct store delivery to manage the inventory of their products on supermarket shelves for a long time.

However, technological advances have increased the sophistication of VMI. The sharing of POS transaction data, for instance, allows vendors to sell merchandise on **consignment:** The vendor owns the merchandise until it is sold by the retailer, at which time the retailer pays for the merchandise. Consignment selling provides an incentive for the vendor to pick SKUs and inventory levels that will minimize inventory and generate sales. Because the vendor is bearing the financial cost of owning the inventory, retailers are more willing to allow the vendor to be responsible for determining the inventory plan and appropriate assortment for each store.

Although it is a more advanced level of collaboration than simply using EDI and sharing information, VMI has its limitations. While the vendor coordinates the supply chain for its specific products, it does not know what other actions the retailer is taking that might affect the sales of its products in the future. For example, Pepsi might not know that a supermarket will be having a big promotion in three weeks for a new beverage introduced by Coca-Cola. Without this knowledge, Pepsi would ship too much merchandise to the supermarket.

Collaborative Planning, Forecasting, and Replenishment

Collaborative planning, forecasting, and replenishment (CPFR) is the sharing of forecasts and related business information and collaborative planning between retailers and vendors to improve supply chain efficiency and product replenishment. Although retailers share sales and inventory data when using a VMI approach, the vendor remains responsible for managing the inventory. In contrast, CPFR is a more advanced form of retailer–vendor collaboration that involves sharing proprietary information such as business strategies, promotion plans, new-product developments and introductions, production schedules, and lead-time information.

A precursor to the Internet-based systems used for CPFR occurred in 1987 when Walmart and Procter & Gamble forged a partnership to control their inventory. The partnership program improves product availability, decreases inventory, and reduces costs, which Walmart passes on as savings to its customers in the form of lower prices. Retailing View 10.3 describes West Marine's CPRF collaborations with its vendors.

RADIO FREQUENCY IDENTIFICATION DEVICES

LO6

Discuss RFID and its implications for retailers.

Radio frequency identification (RFID) is a technology that allows an object or person to be identified at a distance by means of radio waves. Radio frequency identification devices are tags that transmit identifying information and are attached to individual items, shipping cartons, and containers. They then transmit data about the objects in which they are embedded. The RFID technology has two advantages over traditional bar codes. First, the devices can hold more data and update the data stored. For instance, the device can keep track of where an item has been in the supply chain and even where it is stored in a DC. Second, the data on the devices can be acquired without a visual line of sight. Thus, RFID enables the accurate, real-time tracking of every single product, from manufacturer to checkout in the store. It eliminates the manual point-and-read operations needed to get data from UPC bar codes.[29]

In 2003, Walmart announced its plan to require a few hundred suppliers to put RFID tags on full pallets and individual cases of products sent to select DCs. The roll-out started in 2005 but rapidly fizzled for a variety of reasons, including unclear cost savings for Walmart, supplier push-back on absorbing the tagging costs, and Walmart's attention being diverted to other priorities such as sustainability.

Now the RFID gold rush may be on again for two reasons. First, the value proposition and return on investment (ROI) for item-level tagging of apparel and accessories is becoming increasingly clear. Second, it appears that retailers are willing to absorb part of the cost because both retailers and vendors benefit from item-level RFID tagging. Consequently Walmart, Macy's, Marks & Spencer, Dillard's, JCPenney, and others have implemented large-scale, item-level RFID initiatives. Macy's announced that items representing about 30 percent of its total

REFACT

More than 1 million apparel items had RFID tags in 2012, and the number of tagged items is expected to grow substantially in the coming years.[30]

annual sales are being tagged. Marks & Spencer is tagging all apparel and home goods products at all of its stores.[31]

Benefits of RFID

Item-level RFID can be a win–win benefiting both retailers and vendors.

Retailer Benefits   The primary benefit of tagging individual items to retailers is to economically provide an accurate, real-time measure of item inventory levels. With these data, retailers can dramatically reduce inventory levels and stockouts.

RETAILING VIEW   West Marine's Collaboration with Its Vendors   10.3

Apparently, at one time, retailers believed that boaters liked dark, poorly organized stores and staffers who were better at telling stories than locating necessary items. We can guess that because boating supply stores were just like that for many years—at least until West Marine decided to change the rules of the game.

The founder of the company, Randy Repass, envisioned great customer service provided to boaters who could stop by a single source for all their boating needs. The vision was clearly a good one, and West Marine has grown into a chain with more than 400 North American stores. These stores, along with West Marine's catalog and Internet channels, provide everything from ropes to electronics, covering more than 50,000 SKUs.

For most boaters, the time to buy these supplies is during boating season: April through October. Unlike most retailers, which enjoy sales peaks during the holiday season, West Marine looks forward every year to the 4th of July holiday. Promotions offered frequently by suppliers also helped create substantial uncertainty in West Marine's demand predictions, which in turn led to lost sales due to supply chain inefficiencies.

To deal with these inefficiencies and demand challenges, West Marine adopted collaborative planning, forecasting, and replenishment (CPFR) programs, in conjunction with most of its key suppliers. To start, it met with its key suppliers so that together they could develop better forecasts. The result was a system that collects daily SKU-level sales, together with store-level inventory information, then generates a year-long forecast that is specific to the level of demand that day, by store and by SKU. West Marine then sends the forecast to its suppliers to help them schedule their production, and together they use the information to time their marketing and promotional events.

Because CPFR has become so integral to West Marine's merchandising and planning, it also has revised the retailer's organizational structure. Every category manager (CM) for West Marine works closely with a merchandise

West Marine was a pioneer in the use of CPFR to work with its vendors to coordinate supply their chains.

planner (MP). While the CM takes responsibility for vendor strategies and marketing links, the MP directs supply chain relationships. Together, these MPs and CMs host quarterly meetings with suppliers to update their supply chain planning, keeping the marketing, production, distribution, and transportation departments from both firms closely in the loop. In monthly meetings—to which all team members are invited—the planners also review recent CPFR results to identify any supply chain hindrances, plan new initiatives, and resolve any remaining concerns.

Sources: www.westmarine.com; Joel Wisner, Keah-Choon Tan, and G. Keong Leong, *Principles of Supply Chain Management: A Balanced Approach*, 3rd ed. (Mason, OH: Southwestern, 2011); T. Schoenherr and V. M. R. Tummala, "Best Practices for the Implementation of Supply Chain Management Initiatives," *International Journal of Logistics Systems and Management* 4, no. 4 (2008), pp. 391–410.

DISCUSSION QUESTION

What benefits and risks face West Marine as it engages in CPFR with its vendors?

This RFID chip can be embedded in merchandise to determine where the merchandise is in the supply chain.

The following situation illustrates this benefit. Assume one of GameStop's stores has just received a shipment of 10 units of the hottest new video game. The store sold 5 units and 5 units were stolen by an employee. GameStop's inventory control systems thinks there are still 5 units on the shelf at the store and thus does not send more replenishment units of the video game to the store. Customers trying to buy the game are frustrated and may think that GameStop is not a good place to buy the hottest video games. To correct this problem, GameStop needs to frequently have its employees count up the number of units on the shelf for each SKU, compare the physical count with the number of units indicated by the inventory control system, and make a correction when there is a difference. If the video games had RFID tags, each unit on the shelf would be sending out a radio signal. There would be no signals from the stolen items, and the inventory control system would have accurate, real-time data. Stockouts would be reduced, and sales associates would have more time to provide customer service instead of counting inventory.

Another benefit of item-level RFID is to reduce theft. The technology can track products throughout the supply chain and identify their locations at all times. This helps reduce theft in transportation, at DCs, or in stores.

Retailing View 10.4 describes how Lord & Taylor uses RFID tags on shoes to provide a better shopping experience as well as to reduce costs.

10.4   RETAILING VIEW   RFID at Lord & Taylor

Lord & Taylor's shoe department faced a common retail problem: It's hard to sell a product that customers can't see. In its flagship Fifth Avenue store in New York, thousands of different styles and colors of shoes are displayed every day. Sales associates try to restock the samples on the selling floor, but to identify the styles missing from each display, sales associates had to physically touch every shoe to scan its bar code. It took two to four people working about six to eight hours just to do a complete scan. Thus, it was only economically feasible to take the inventory of samples weekly. Ironically, high traffic and sales actually compounded the problem—as more shoes were sold, more display samples went missing. Days might pass with dozens of styles missing from display samples. Useful data for restocking the displays came slowly. After the scan, stores received their missing style list the next day.

To deal with this, Lord & Taylor installed a new system to put RFID chips in each shoe and collect information from the signal coming from the RFID chips. Each day before the department opened, one or two associates walked the department with handheld RFID readers to inventory the sample shoes on the floor. As soon as the inventory was complete, a missing sample report was printed from a local PC. With this report in hand, associates then located and replaced the missing samples. With the RFID system, it only took an hour to complete the scan and get the report.

The company is looking to expand its RFID program to other departments. Regional Operations Manager Rosemary Ryan says, "We are trying to figure out how we can make it work for our jewelry departments. We're also trying to pilot it in luggage this fall—that would be another easy win for us—and men's suits. Wherever we have an inventory with a

By putting RFID chips on its shoes, Lord & Taylor can get an accurate count of its merchandise in an hour, reducing both labor cost and stockouts.

lot of sizes, styles, and colors that must be constantly replenished, RFID has proven to deliver big benefits. We want to reap those benefits across our operations."

Sources: "More Sales: RFID Speeds Accurate Inventory of Display Samples," *Motorola Solutions*, 2012; "Macy's, Lowe's, Lord & Taylor Receive VICS Achievement Awards," *RIS*, May 10, 2012; and "Lord & Taylor Deploys Motorola Solution at Flagship Store in New York," *RFIDNews*, January 4, 2012.

DISCUSSION QUESTION

For what types of merchandise is using RFID systems most appropriate? Why?

Vendor Benefits   RFID is not free for suppliers. Tags are the main cost. They can add 5 to 30 cents per item shipped, depending on volumes, the type of tag, and services provided by a service bureau and/or label convertor. In addition, there are one-time costs for readers and implementation costs such as retraining staff and IT integration (depending on what the supplier is trying to accomplish). Thus per-item cost is a problem for low margin items.

When retailers' sales increase due to fewer stockouts, vendor sales also increase. In addition, there are potential process improvements that vendors can realize. Some of the more immediate and obvious ones involve using RFID for pack verification, ship verification, and ASN generation. **Pack verification** happens after a worker has packed a case or carton, usually just before sealing it. All of the RFID tags in the case are read and compared against the ship order. **Ship verification** is similar, except that it happens as cartons are loaded onto the truck or onto a pallet. This confirms again that the right items are being loaded. Using RFID provides an almost 100 percent guarantee that the ASN will always match exactly what was shipped.

For luxury items, RFID can be used to verify authenticity. However, this requires strict security and control over tags, as well as thinking through the supply chain and where in the chain authentication might best be done. Today, luxury brands are building systems and infrastructure for distributors, retailers, and end-consumers to verify the RFID tags and the authenticity of the item.[32]

SUMMARY

LO1 **Understand the strategic advantage generated by a supply chain.**

Supply chain management is a set of activities and techniques firms employ to efficiently and effectively manage the flow of merchandise from the vendors to the retailer's customers. These activities ensure that the customers are able to purchase merchandise in the desired quantities at a preferred location and appropriate time. Efficient supply chain management provides two benefits to retailers and their customers: (1) fewer stockouts and (2) tailored assortments. Supply chain management coupled with improving supply chain efficiency also has significant implications with respect to environmental sustainability.

LO2 **Describe the information and merchandise flows in a supply chain.**

A retailer's information system tracks the flow of merchandise through distribution centers to retail stores and their customers. Most communications between vendors and retailers occur via electronic data interchange over the Internet. Most multistore retailers operate their own distribution centers. Sometimes merchandise is temporarily stored at the DC; other times it just passes directly through the center from an inbound to an outbound truck. Retailers have developed data warehouses that provide them with intimate knowledge of who their customers are and what they like to buy. The data warehouses are being used to strengthen the relationships with their customers and improve the productivity of their marketing and inventory management efforts.

LO3 **Consider the activities that are undertaken in a distribution center.**

Most large retailers own and operate their own DCs. Some of the activities performed by the center are managing inbound and outbound transportation, receiving and checking merchandise shipments, storing and cross-docking merchandise, and getting merchandise floor-ready.

LO4 **Review the considerations in the design of supply chains.**

In designing their supply chain management systems, retailers make decisions about what activities to outsource; when to use a push and pull system for replenishing stores; what merchandise to cross-dock; and whether to ship merchandise to stores through a DC, use direct store delivery, or have products drop shipped to customers. The DCs and supply chain and information systems for supporting catalog and Internet channels are very different from those supporting the store channel. The importance of reverse logistics is growing because of the high returns for merchandise bought through the Internet channel and environmental sustainability issues.

288   SECTION II   Retailing Strategy

LO5 **Explain how retailers and vendors collaborate to make sure the right merchandise is available when customers are ready to buy it.**

Retailers and vendors are collaborating to improve supply chain efficiency. Electronic data interchange enables retailers to communicate electronically with their vendors. Effective collaborative approaches include information sharing, VMI, and CPFR. These approaches represent the nexus of information systems and logistics management. They reduce lead time, increase product availability, lower inventory investments, and reduce overall logistics expenses.

LO6 **Discuss RFID and its implications for retailers.**

RFID has the potential of further streamlining the supply chain. Small RFID devices are affixed to pallets, cartons, and individual items and can be used to track merchandise through the supply chain and store information, such as when an item was shipped to a DC. Most of the recent applications involve tagging individual items and focusing on reducing inventory and stockouts.

KEY TERMS

advance shipping notice
  (ASN), 272
backhaul, 268
break pack area, 275
bullwhip effect, 282
checking, 275
collaborative planning, forecasting,
  and replenishment (CPFR), 284
consignment, 284
consumer direct fulfillment, 280
cross-docked, 275
direct store delivery (DSD), 278
dispatcher, 274
distribution center (DC), 266

drop shipping, 280
electronic data interchange
  (EDI), 273
fast fashion, 270
floor-ready merchandise, 276
freight forwarders, 277
logistics, 274
outsource, 277
pack verification, 287
pick ticket, 276
point-of-sale (POS) terminal, 271
public warehouse, 277
pull supply chain, 278
push supply chain, 278

radio frequency identification
  (RFID), 284
rain check, 269
receiving, 275
reorder point, 283
reverse logistics, 279
security policy, 273
ship verification, 287
stockout, 269
supply chain management, 266
ticketing and marking, 276
universal product code (UPC), 271
vendor-managed inventory
  (VMI), 283

GET OUT AND DO IT!

1. **CONTINUING ASSIGNMENT** Interview the store manager working for the retailer you have selected for the Continuing Case assignment. Write a report that describes and evaluates the retailer's information and supply chain systems. Use this chapter as a basis for developing a set of questions to ask the manager. Some of the questions might be these: Where is the store's DC? Does the retailer use direct store delivery from vendors? How frequently are deliveries made to the store? Does the merchandise come in ready for sale? What is the store's percentage of stockouts? Does the retailer use a push or pull system? Does the store get involved in determining what merchandise is in the store and in what quantities? Does the retailer use VMI, EDI, CPFR, or RFID?

2. **INTERNET EXERCISE** Go to Barcoding Incorporated's web page at www.barcoding.com/, and

search for *retail, warehouse management,* and *RFID.* How is this company using technology to support retailers with information systems and supply chain management?

3. **INTERNET EXERCISE** Go to the home page of *RFID Journal* at www.rfidjournal.com/, and search for *supply chain* in the current issue. Summarize one of the recent articles, and explain how the key concept(s) described could make the shopping experience better for consumers and improve efficiency in the supply chain.

4. **INTERNET EXERCISE** Go to the home page of Vendor Managed Inventory at www.vendormanagedinventory.com/index.php, and answer the following questions: What is vendor-managed inventory? What are the benefits and limitations of a vendor-managed inventory approach?

DISCUSSION QUESTIONS AND PROBLEMS

1. Retail system acronyms include DSD, VMI, EDI, CPFR, and RFID. How are these terms related to one another?

2. Explain how an efficient supply chain system can increase a retailer's level of product availability and decrease its inventory investment.

3. This chapter presents some trends in logistics and information systems that benefit retailers. How do vendors benefit from these trends?

4. What type of merchandise is most likely to be cross-docked at retailers' DCs? Why is this often the case?

5. Why haven't more fashion retailers adopted an integrated supply chain system similar to Zara's?

6. Explain the differences between pull and push supply chains.

7. Consumers have five key reactions to stockouts: buy the item at another store, substitute a different brand, substitute the same brand, delay the purchase, or do not purchase the item. Consider your own purchasing behavior, and describe how various categories of merchandise would result in different reactions to a stockout.

8. Abandoned purchases as a result of stockouts can mean millions of dollars a year in lost sales. How are retailers and manufacturers using technology to reduce stockouts and improve sales?

9. What is a universal product code (UPC)? How does this code enable manufacturers, distributors, and retailers to track merchandise throughout the supply chain?

10. For what types of products is item-level RFID most beneficial for retailers?

SUGGESTED READINGS

Bardaki, Cleopatra, Panos Kourouthanassis, and Katerina Pramatari. "Deploying RFID-Enabled Services in the Retail Supply Chain: Lessons Learned toward the Internet of Things." *Information Systems Management* 29, no. 3 (2012), pp. 233–245.

Benton, W. C. *Purchasing and Supply Chain Management*, 3rd ed. New York: McGraw-Hill, 2014.

Dittmann, J. Paul. *Supply Chain Transformation: Building and Executing an Integrated Supply Chain Strategy*. New York: McGraw-Hill, 2011.

Fernie, John, and Leigh Sparks. *Logistics and Retail Management: Emerging Issues and New Challenges in the Retail Supply Chain*, 3rd ed. London: Kogan, 2009.

Finne, Sami, and Hanna Sivonen. *The Retail Value Chain: How to Gain Competitive Advantage through Efficient Consumer Response (ECR) Strategies*. London: Kogan, 2009.

Fisher, Marshall, and Ananth Raman. *The New Science of Retailing: How Analytics Are Transforming the Supply Chain and Improving Performance*. Boston: Harvard Business Press, 2010.

Haag, Stephen, and Maeve Cummings. *Management Information Systems for the Information Age*, 9th ed. New York: McGraw-Hill, 2013.

Hofer, Christian, Henry Jin, R. David Swanson, Matthew A. Waller, and Brent D. Williams. "The Impact of Key Retail Accounts on Supplier Performance: A Collaborative Perspective of Resource Dependency Theory," *Journal of Retailing*, 2012. Vol 83, number 3, September 2012, pp. 412–420.

Kauremaa, Jouni, Johanna Smaros, and Jan Holmstrom. "Patterns of Vendor-Managed Inventory: Findings from a Multiple-Case Study." *International Journal of Operations & Production Management* 29, no. 11 (2009), pp. 1109–1139.

Sari, Kazim. "On the Benefits of CPFR and VMI: A Comparative Simulation Study." *International Journal of Services and Operations Management* 6, no. 1 (2010), pp. 73–88.

Customer Relationship Management

EXECUTIVE BRIEFING
Jim Lewis, Founder and CEO,
Enhanced Retail Solutions

In 2002, after working in store management in South Florida and merchandise management at JCPenney's corporate headquarters in Plano, Texas, I decided to open my own software/consulting firm. At the time, retailers and vendors were collecting massive amounts of sales and inventory data that helped profile their customers' purchase behaviors (now referred to as "big data"), but they were not converting this data into actionable information they could use to make better decisions.

The first software applications we developed were for vendors. A number of retailers give vendors access to the POS data associated with the vendor's sales. But most vendors do not have the capability to crush this massive data describing every transaction or how to make it useful in optimizing sales and inventory at the store level. So we developed software that summarizes the vendor's performance much like the dashboard on a car. It allowed the vendor to communicate more effectively with its retail buyers and make actionable recommendations that the buyers appreciated. Soon after its introduction, many retail buyers recognized its benefits and now use the software.

While our initial activities provided vendors and retailers with a tool to access *how* well they are performing, we now are concentrating on examining *why* vendors and retailers are doing well or poorly. For example, one of our apparel clients was concerned when a large, national retail customer was going to drop their line due to low sales. When we analyzed their sales data with the retailer, we found that the client's line was selling very well in some stores and poorly in others. Using the census data we have in our database, we found that the stores that were doing well for the vendor's line were in trading areas dominated by minority consumers. We helped our client make a presentation showing that the retailer would increase its profits if it didn't stock our client's line in about half its stores but increased its assortments in the retailer's stores located in areas with a high concentration of minorities.

We are now finding that the assortment decisions can integrate with supply chain activities. When analyzing a retailer's sales pattern for an imported, private-label product line, we found that the product line sold much better on the East Coast than on the West Coast. When the retailer's supply chain sourcing people learned about this sales pattern, they changed

CHAPTER 11

the sourcing for the product line from East Asia to Mexico and saved $2 million in transportation costs—$2 million on one product line!

Store-level data is also being used to significantly improve forecasting accuracy. Advanced features in our software analyze in-stock patterns by store and update future inventory requirements accordingly. This enabled a client that supplies bed sheets to the major chains to reduce their overhead by 20 percent because they don't have to keep products as long in their warehouse.

Today most retailers collaborate with their vendors to use retail analytics to optimize their business. It certainly has been a competitive advantage for Walmart. While the techniques may be advanced, the basis for use is not—it builds on the fundamentals of retail—getting the right product at the right time to the right place in the right amount.

The business press and retailers are talking a lot about the importance of becoming more customer-centric and managing their customer relationships better. Retailers are spending millions of dollars on computer systems to collect and analyze data about their customers. With all this buzz, you would think that the customer is a popular new kid in the neighborhood. However, the customer is more like an old friend who's been taken for granted—until now.

Consider the following: Shari Ast is on her third business trip this month. She takes a cab from Boston's Logan Airport to the Ritz-Carlton, her favorite hotel in Boston. As the doorman opens the car door for her, he greets her with, "Welcome back to the Ritz-Carlton, Ms. Ast." When she goes to the registration desk, the receptionist gives her a room key. Then she goes to her room and finds just what she likes—a room with a view of the Boston Common, a single king-size bed, an extra pillow and blanket, a printer with a wireless connection for her laptop, and a basket with her favorite fruits and snacks.

The Ritz-Carlton provides personalized service for its preferred customers.

Shari Ast's experience is an example of Ritz-Carlton's customer relationship management program. **Customer relationship management (CRM)** is a business philosophy and set of strategies, programs, and systems that focuses on identifying and building relationships with a retailer's valued customers. CRM enables retailers to develop a base of loyal customers and increase its **share of wallet**—the percentage of the customers' purchases made from the retailer.

Traditionally, retailers have focused their attention on encouraging more customers to visit their stores, look through their catalogs, and visit their websites. To accomplish this objective, they have used mass-media advertising and sales promotions to attract visits from customers. This approach treats all existing and potential customers the same. They all receive the same messages and the same promotions.

Now, retailers are concentrating on developing customer loyalty and increasing share of wallet by providing more value to their best customers by using targeted, personalized merchandise, services, and promotions. Mindy Grossman, CEO of HSN, believes "it would take 10 new customers to replace one 'best' customer."[1] Her perspective is supported by research indicating that retailers are more profitable when they focus on retaining and increasing sales to their best customers rather than attempting to generate sales from new customers or less profitable existing customers.[2] In the following sections of this chapter, we discuss in more depth the objective of CRM programs and the elements of the CRM process.

THE CRM PROCESS

LO1

Describe the customer relationship management process.

The objective of the CRM process is to develop loyalty and repeat-purchase behavior among a retailer's best customers. Customer loyalty is more than having customers satisfied with a retailer and making repeat visits. For example, a customer might exclusively patronize a local supermarket because it is the only supermarket convenient to her house, but not be loyal to the supermarket. If another supermarket opened with a somewhat better offering, the customer might immediately switch to the new supermarket even though she was a repeat customer at her present supermarket.

Customer loyalty means that customers are committed to purchasing merchandise and services from the retailer and will resist the activities of competitors attempting to attract their patronage. Thus, if our preceding consumer was loyal, she would not switch to the new supermarket even though its offering was somewhat better.

Loyal customers have a bond with the retailer based on an emotional connection that is more than a just having a positive feeling about the retailer. This emotional bond is a personal connection. They feel that the retailer is a friend. Their goodwill toward the retailer encourages them to make repeat purchases and recommend it to their friends and family.

All elements in the retail mix contribute to the development of customer loyalty and repeat-purchase behavior.[3] Customer loyalty can be enhanced by creating an appealing brand image, offering exclusive merchandise, providing convenient locations, and providing an engaging shopping experience. However, personal attention and customer service are two of the most effective methods for developing loyalty. For example, many small, independent restaurants build loyalty by functioning as neighborhood cafés, where servers recognize customers by name and know their preferences. Nordstrom invites its best customers to grand-opening celebrations, pampers them during private shopping parties, and provides

EXHIBIT 11–1
The CRM Process Cycle

concierge services and free alterations. Such practices are more effective than discounts because when a retailer develops a personal connection with customers, it is difficult for any competitors to attract them away. The CRM programs and activities discussed in this chapter use information systems and customer data to personalize a retailer's offering and increase the value that its best customers receive. Personalized value also can be provided by employees in face-to-face interactions with customers. These forms of personalization are discussed in more detail in Chapter 18.

Overview of the CRM Process

Exhibit 11–1 illustrates that CRM is an iterative process that turns customer data into customer loyalty and repeat-purchase behavior through four activities: (1) collecting customer data, (2) analyzing customer data and identifying target customers, (3) developing CRM through frequent-shopper programs, and (4) implementing CRM programs.[4] The process begins with the collection and analysis of data about a retailer's customers and the identification of its best customers. The analysis translates the customer data into information and activities that offer value to these targeted customers. Then these activities are executed through personalized communications with customers. Each of the four activities in the CRM process is discussed in the following sections. Retailing View 11.1 describes the how Kroger uses customer data to facilitate its decisions.

COLLECTING CUSTOMER SHOPPING DATA

The first step in the CRM process is to construct a **customer database.** This database is part of the data warehouse described in Chapter 10. It contains all the data the firm has collected about its customers and is the foundation for subsequent CRM activities.

 LO2

Understand how customer shopping data are collected.

Customer Database

Ideally, the customer database should contain the following information:

* *Transactions.* A complete history of the purchases made by the customer, including the purchase date, the SKUs purchased, the price paid, the amount of profit, and whether the merchandise was purchased in response to a special promotion or marketing activity.

- *Customer contacts.* A record of the interactions that the customer has had with the retailer, including visits to the retailer's website, inquiries made through in-store kiosks, comments made on blogs and Facebook pages, merchandise returns, and telephone calls made to the retailer's call center, plus information about contacts initiated by the retailer, such as catalogs and e-mails sent to the customer.
- *Customer preferences.* What the customer likes, such as favorite colors, brands, fabrics, and flavors, as well as apparel sizes.
- *Descriptive information.* Demographic and psychographic data describing the customer that can be used in developing market segments.

11.1   RETAILING VIEW   Using Customer Data at Kroger

Kroger is the largest supermarket retailer in the United States, with more than $70 billion in sales. It is also the sixth largest retailer in the world. Its impressive status is largely the result of a strategic decision it made to build a competitive advantage by collecting and analyzing customer data, then to use such data to manage its customer relationships. It began working with the UK-based consulting firm Dunnhumby in 2001. Since then, the partners have developed a joint venture called Dunnhumby USA that is responsible for converting all the data that Kroger collects from its customers when they swipe loyalty cards or enter their phone numbers at the point-of-sale into viable information that can help Kroger make decisions.

Similar to most supermarkets, Kroger's primary communication tool is a weekly newspaper circular featuring sale products. Category managers nominate products to include in the circular, and space is allocated according to the importance of the product category, any special promotions offered by vendors, and the margin Kroger earns on the advertised item.

Dunnhumby USA analyzes the products that customers buy at the same time to make assortment and promotion decisions.

By analyzing which items customers purchase in each trip, Dunnhmby USA has been able to improve this method and increase the effectiveness of the weekly circular. In particular, the purchase data identified complementary products, such that they prompted the sale of other items. For example, when customers purchase sliced deli roast beef, they also tend to purchase other deli meats, cheese, mustard, mayonnaise, and a loaf of fresh rye bread. But when they buy deli turkey, they don't buy these additions. Thus, roast beef is a better candidate for the circular, because it will tend to trigger the purchase of other items.

Kroger mails 55 million loyal customer mailings to their frequent-shopper cardholders every quarter. These mailings offer promotions on products that customers normally buy, as well as on products that Kroger predicts they would like, based on its analyses of what similar customers buy. So, for instance, if Kroger can predict that a customer is part of a young family, based on the purchase of hot dogs, Kellogg's Cocoa Krispies, and a lot of animal crackers, it can provide that family with a coupon for milk.

Retailers frequently segment their market using demographic variables, such as age, income, and education,

but they are poor predictors of sales (see Chapter 4). Dunnhumby USA's analyses enable Kroger to develop a better segmentation scheme based on actual purchase behavior rather than demographics. With these analyses, Kroger can identify customer segments that have a newborn baby, like to cook, or entertain frequently. Such precise segmentation capabilities not only help Kroger appeal appropriately to customers, encouraging their loyalty, but they also enable better decisions about in-store assortments, merchandise locations, store locations, and promotional designs.

Sources: Dhruv Grewal, Michael Levy, and Britt Hackmann, "Making Loyalty Programs Sing," Working Paper, Babson College, 2013; Josh Pichler, "Firm Remakes Retailers' Knowledge of Shoppers," *The Cincinnati Enquirer*, January 31, 2013; and Josh Pichler, "DunnhumbyUSA Combs through Data to Help Retailers Reward their Most Loyal Customers," *The Cincinnati Enquirer*, January 31, 2013.

DISCUSSION QUESTION

Why is segmentation based on purchase behavior superior for encouraging customer loyalty to segmentation based on demographics?

Customer transactions are collected from a POS terminal and stored in a customer database.

Different members of the same household might also have interactions with a retailer. Thus, to get a complete view of the customer, retailers need to be able to combine individual customer data from each member of a household. For example, Richards is a family-owned apparel chain in Westport and Greenwich, Connecticut. Spouses often buy presents for each other at Richards. The chain's database keeps track of both household-level purchases and individual purchases so that sales associates can help one spouse buy a gift for the other. The database also keeps track of spending changes and habits. Anniversaries, birthdays, and even divorces and second marriages are tracked along with style, brand, size, and color preferences, hobbies, and sometimes pets' names and golf handicaps.[7]

Identifying Information

It is relatively easy for retailers to construct a database for customers using nonstore channels because these customers must provide their contact information, name and address, so that the purchases can be sent to them. It is also easy to keep track of purchases made by customers patronizing warehouse clubs because they need to present their membership cards when they make a purchase. In these cases, the identification of the customer is always linked to the transaction. When retailers issue their own credit cards, they also can collect the contact information for billing when customers apply for the card. However, identifying most customers who are making in-store transactions is more difficult because they often pay for the merchandise with a check, cash, or a third-party credit card such as Visa or MasterCard.

Five approaches that store-based retailers use to overcome this problem are to (1) ask customers for identifying information, (2) connect Internet and store purchasing data, (3) offer frequent-shopper programs, (4) use biometrics to identify customers, and (5) place RFID chips on merchandise.

Ask for Identifying Information   Some retailers have their sales associates ask customers for identifying information, such as their phone number, e-mail address, or name and home address, when they process a sale. This information is then used to link all the transactions to the customer. However, some customers may be reluctant to provide the information because they feel that the sales associates are violating their privacy.

Connect Internet and Store Purchasing Data   When customers use third-party credit cards such as Visa or MasterCard to make a purchase in a store, the retailer cannot identify the purchase by the customer. However, if the customer used the same credit card while shopping at the retailer's website and provided shipping information, the retailer could connect the credit card purchases through its store and electronic channels.

Offer Frequent-Shopper Programs   **Frequent-shopper programs,** also called **loyalty programs,** are programs that identify and provide rewards to customers who patronize a retailer. Some retailers issue customers a frequent-shopper card. In both cases, customer transaction data are automatically captured when the card is scanned at the point-of-sale terminal. Customers are enticed to enroll in these programs and provide some descriptive information about themselves by offering them discounts if they use the cards when making purchases from the retailer. These frequent-shopper programs are discussed in more depth in following section of this chapter.

Use Biometrics   Rather than asking for identifying information or having to present a frequent-shopper card, some retailers use biometrics to identify customers and provide a cardless, cashless method of payment. When retailers use **biometrics,** they are measuring human characteristics such as a person's hand geometry, fingerprints, iris, or voice. When a retailer installs a biometric system, customers can preregister their fingerprints and credit card information and pay for products by simply placing their finger for a second or two on a fingerprint scanner at the checkout POS terminal. The use of biometrics can ensure that key customer data are captured consistently. Using biometrics results in faster checkout and the ability to target promotions. In addition, customers who enroll in the program can have their fingerprint scanned when entering the store and receive a printout of personalized product discounts.

Customers benefit from the convenience of faster checkout and receipt of frequent-shopper coupons and discounts without having to carry a lot of cards in their wallets. The faster checkout also benefits retailers by reducing labor costs. The retailers can accumulate the customer information quickly and accurately. In addition, retailers are using biometric systems to reduce employee fraud and shoplifting. These systems can detect when employees have had a coworker check in or out for them and whether the person returning merchandise for cash is the same as the person who bought it, not someone who stole it from the store.[9]

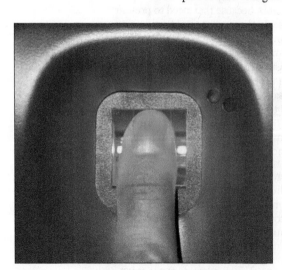

Biometrics are used to link transactions to individuals.

Place RFID Chips on Merchandise   Perhaps RFID provides the most convenient approach, from the customer's perspective, for customers to make purchases. An RFID reader in the store can acquire the customer's personal information from small devices carried by customers and RFID tags on the merchandise they want to purchase. In addition, using a global satellite tracking system, the store reader could also collect information about where the customer has been in the store.

Privacy and CRM Programs

The collection and analysis of data about customer attitudes, preferences, and shopping behaviors enables retailers to target information and promotions and provide greater value to their customers. However, many customers are concerned that retailers violate their privacy when they collect detailed personal information. Even if customers trust a retailer, they are concerned that the data may not be secure and/or may be sold to other businesses.

Privacy Concerns   There is no consensus about the definition of personal information. Some people feel that personal information is all information that is not publicly available; others include both public (e.g., driver's license, mortgage data) and private (e.g. hobbies, income) information. The degree to which consumers feel their privacy has been violated depends on:

- *Their control over their personal information when engaging in marketplace transactions.* Do they feel they can decide the amount and type of information that is collected by the retailer?
- *Their knowledge about the collection and use of personal information.* Do they know what information is being collected and how the retailer will be using it? Will the retailer be sharing the information with other parties?[10]

These concerns are particularly acute for customers using an Internet channel, because many of them do not realize the extensive amount of information that can be collected without their knowledge. This information is easily collected using cookies. **Cookies** are small files stored on a customer's computer that identify customers when they return to a website. Because of the data in cookies, customers do not have to identify themselves or use passwords every time they visit a site. However, cookies also can enable the collection of data about what pages people have viewed, other sites the people have visited, how they spend money online, and their interactions on social networking sites.

Protecting Customer Privacy   In the United States, existing consumer privacy legislation is limited to the protection of information associated with government functions and with practices in credit reporting, video rentals, banking, and health care. Thus, in the United States, the privacy of most consumer data is not protected. However, Congress is considering new legislation on consumer privacy, which is guided by three principles:[11]

- *Privacy by design.* Encourage businesses to treat consumer privacy as their "default setting," thus shifting the responsibility for privacy protection from consumers to retailers. Companies should also delete information about their customers that is no longer needed, provide reasonable security for data, limit collection of data consistent with the context of a particular transaction, and implement guidelines on how and when customer data will be eliminated.
- *Simplified consumer choice.* Develop ways that consumers can track their online activities. Specifically, they should have a simple method of turning off the ability of a firm to install a cookie that permits them to track the web pages consumers have viewed. This Do Not Track (DNT) function is similar in concept to the Do Not Call (DNC) list that consumers can join to opt-out of telemarketing calls.
- *Greater transparency.* Improve consumer understanding of how consumer data are collected through better education and information.

In response to potential government regulations, proactive U.S. retailers are attempting to self-regulate by developing privacy policies. Some retailers have appointed privacy advocates, including the creation of an executive chief privacy officer. Such appointments help ensure that privacy concerns are communicated throughout the organization, that an appropriate organizational privacy-sensitive culture is in place, and that the organization is adhering to its privacy policies.

While there are few consumer privacy regulations affecting retailers in the United States, the European Union (EU), Australia, New Zealand, and Canada have more stringent consumer privacy laws, and they are contemplating an

298   SECTION II   Retailing Strategy

increase in these restrictions. Some of the provisions of the EU directive on consumer privacy are the following:

- Businesses can collect consumer information only if they have clearly defined the purpose, such as completing the transaction.
- The purpose must be disclosed to the consumer from whom the information is being collected.
- The information can be used only for that specific purpose.
- The business can keep the information only for the stated purpose. If the business wants to use the information for another purpose, it must initiate a new collection process.
- Businesses operating in Europe can export information from the 27 EU countries only to importing countries with similar privacy policies. Thus, U.S. retailers, hotel chains, airlines, and banks cannot transfer information from Europe to the United States because the United States does not have similar privacy policies.[12]

Basically, the EU perspective is that consumers own their personal information, so retailers must get consumers to agree explicitly to share this personal information. This agreement is referred to as **opt in.** In contrast, personal information in the United States is generally viewed as being in the public domain, and retailers can use it any way they desire. American consumers must explicitly tell retailers not to use their personal information—they must explicitly **opt out.**[13]

In summary, there is growing consensus that personal information must be fairly collected; that the collection must be purposeful; and that the data should be relevant, accurate, essential to the business, subject to the rights of the owning individual, kept reasonably secure, and transferred only with the permission of the consumer. Many retailers that collect customer information have privacy policies. Retailers need to assure their customers that information about them is held securely and not passed on to other companies without the customer's permission.

REFACT

Eighty percent of U.S. consumers believe that it is important to be able to opt out of the sharing or sale of collected data.[14]

ANALYZING CUSTOMER DATA AND IDENTIFYING TARGET CUSTOMERS

LO3

Explain the methods used to analyze customer data and identify target customers.

The next step in the CRM process (see Exhibit 11–1) is to analyze the customer data and convert them into information that will help retailers develop programs for increasing the value they offer to their best customers, or those customers whose loyalty and repatronage will add significantly to the retailer's bottom line. Two objectives for analyzing the customer database are (1) identifying the retailer's best customers and (2) using analytical methods to improve decisions made by retail managers. These two objectives are discussed in this section.

Identifying the Best Customers

One of the goals of CRM is to identify and cater to the retailer's most valuable customers. Retailers often use information in their customer databases to determine how valuable each customer is to their firm. The value of a customer, called **customer lifetime value (CLV),** is the expected contribution from the customer to the retailer's profits over their entire relationship with the retailer. Retailers typically use past behaviors to forecast their CLV. To illustrate some of the factors considered in developing a measure of CLV, consider the purchase histories of two customers during the last 12 months shown here:

	December	January	February	March	April	May	June	July	August	September	October	November	Total
Shirley	$400	0	0	0	0	0	0	0	0	0	0	0	$400
Marcia	$10	$10	$25	$25	$15	$25	$40	$20	$35	$35	$50	$65	$355

Which woman has the highest CLV—that is, who would be the most valuable customer for the retailer in the future? If the retailer only considered the purchases made by the two women over the past 12 months, the retailer might conclude that Shirley is most valuable because she has bought the most merchandise during the last 12 months ($400 versus $355). But Shirley's purchase history might reflect her visit to the United States from Brazil, making a one-time purchase, and being very unlikely to patronize the retailer again. As the retailer digs deeper into the data, it might decide that Marcia is the most valuable customer because she purchases merchandise both more frequently and more recently. In addition, her monthly purchases are trending up. Even though Shirley might have bought more in the last 12 months, Marcia's purchase pattern suggests she will buy more in the future. Retailing View 11.2 illustrates the use of an **RFM analysis**—a method often used in catalog and Internet channels to determine customer segments that a retailer should target for a promotion or catalog mailing. The method uses three factors to evaluate the potential contribution of each customer segment: how *recently* the customers in the segment made a purchase, how *frequently* they make purchases, and how much *money* they have spent.

In the example, the classification of customers into these segments is based on the profitability of the customers, not sales. The use of sales to identify a retailer's best customers can be misleading. For example, airlines assign rewards in their frequent-flyer programs on the basis of miles flown. These programs provide the same rewards to customers who take low-cost, less profitable flights as to those who make a larger contribution to the airline's profit by flying first class and paying full prices. Sophisticated statistical methods are typically used to estimate the CLV for each customer, like Shirley and Marcia, based on more than their recency, frequency, and amount purchased.[15] These deeper analyses consider the gross margin from the customer's purchases and the costs associated with the purchase, such as the cost of advertising and promotions used to acquire the customers, and the cost of processing merchandise that the customer returned. For example, customers who pay full price and buy the same amount of merchandise have a higher CLV than customers who only buy items on sales. Customers who return 30 percent of the merchandise they purchase have a lower CLV than customers who rarely return merchandise.

Retail Analytics

Retailers can use data they have collected about their customers to measure each customer's CLV. In the remaining portion of this section, we explain how the availability of a customer database provides a resource that retailers can use to develop strategies and make better decisions. Retailing View 11.3 describes how the drugstore chain CVS derives insights by analyzing its extensive customer database.

Retail analytics are applications of statistical techniques and models that seek to improve retail decisions through analyses of customer data.[16] **Data mining** is an information processing method that relies on search techniques to discover new insights into the buying patterns of customers, using large databases.[17] Three of the most popular applications of data mining are market basket analysis, targeting promotions, and assortment planning.

Market Basket Analysis   In a **market basket analysis,** the data mining tools determine which products appear in the market basket that a customer purchases during a single shopping trip. This analysis can suggest where stores should place merchandise and which merchandise to promote together based on merchandise that tends to show up in the same market basket.

To perform a market basket analysis, a computer program counts the number of times two products get purchased at the same time. An often-used example of market basket analysis is the discovery by a supermarket chain that on Friday

11.2 RETAILING VIEW Illustration of RFM Analysis

The RFM analysis in Exhibit 11–2 was conducted by an apparel retailer that needed to decide to which customer segments to send its catalogs. The retailer divided its catalog channel customers into 32 segments on the basis of how many orders each customer placed during the previous year, how much merchandise the customer purchased during the past 12 months, and the last time the customer placed an order. Each segment is represented by one cell in Exhibit 11–2. For example, the customers in the upper-left cell have made a purchase within the last 2 months (recency), made one or two purchases in the last year (frequency), and spent less than $50 over the last 12 months (money). For each RFM segment, the retailer determined the percentage of customers in the segment who made a purchase from the last catalog sent to them. For example, 5 percent of the customers in the upper-left cell of Exhibit 11–2 placed an order from the last catalog sent to them. With information about the response rate and the average gross margin from orders placed by customers in each cell, the retailer can calculate the expected profit from the last catalog sent to customers in each cell. For example, if the average gross margin from orders placed by customers in the upper-left cell is $20 and the cost of sending a catalog to customers in the cell is $0.75, with a five percent

response rate the catalog would make $0.25 per customer mailed a catalog in that segment:

$20 contribution × 0.05 response rate = $1.00 expected revenue per person

$1.00 − $0.75 cost person = $0.25 expected contribution per person

Using the 32 segments in Exhibit 11–2, the retailer might develop a strategy for each segment, as shown in Exhibit 11–3. For example, the retailer might focus on building its loyalty among customers in the segments in the lower-left area but not send any more catalogs to customers in the upper-right segments, because they are not profitable.

Sources: David Gillman, "Use SPSS Statistics Direct Marketing Analysis to Gain Insight: Analyze Customer History Using RFM," October 26, 2012, ibm.com/developerworks/; Jayanthi Ranjan and Ruchi Agarwal, "Application of Segmentation in Customer Relationship Management: A Data Mining Perspective," *International Journal of Electronic Customer Relationship Management* 3, no. 4 (2009), pp. 402–414; and Ching-Hsue Cheng and You-Shyang Chen, "Classifying the Segmentation of Customer Value Via RFM Model and RS Theory." *Expert Systems with Applications* 36, no. 3 (2009), pp. 4176–4184.

DISCUSSION QUESTION

How and why would a retailer use RFM analysis?

EXHIBIT 11–2
RFM Analysis for a Catalog Retailer

		RECENCY			
Frequency	**Monetary**	**0–2 months**	**3–4 months**	**5–6 months**	**Over 6 months**
1–2	<$50	5.0%*	3.5%	1.0%	0.1%
1–2	Over $50	5.0	3.6	1.1	0.1
3–4	<$150	8.0	5.0	1.5	0.6
3–4	Over $150	8.8	5.0	1.7	0.8
5–6	<$300	10.0	6.0	2.5	1.0
5–6	Over $300	12.0	8.0	2.7	1.2
Over 6	<$450	15.0	10.0	3.5	1.8
Over 6	Over $450	16.0	11.0	4.0	2.0

*Percentage of customers in the cell who made a purchase from the last catalog mailed to them.

SOURCE: Reprinted by permission of Harvard Business School Press. Adapted from Robert Blattberg, Gary Getz, and Jacquelyn Thomas, *Customer Equity: Building and Managing Relationships as Valuable Assets* (Boston: Harvard Business School Press, 2001), p. 18. Copyright © 2001 by the Harvard Business School Publishing Corporation; all rights reserved.

EXHIBIT 11–3
RFM Target Strategies

		RECENCY			
Frequency	**Monetary**	**0–2 months**	**3–4 months**	**5–6 months**	**Over 6 months**
1–2	<$50	First-time customers		Low-value customers	
1–2	Over $50				
3–4	<$150	Early repeat customers		Defectors	
3–4	Over $150				
5–6	<$300	High-value customers		Core defectors	
5–6	Over $300				
Over 6	<$450				
Over 6	Over $450				

SOURCE: Reprinted by permission of Harvard Business School Press. Adapted from Robert Blattberg, Gary Getz, and Jacquelyn Thomas, *Customer Equity: Building and Managing Relationships as Valuable Assets* (Boston: Harvard Business School Press, 2001), p. 18. Copyright © 2001 by the Harvard Business School Publishing Corporation; all rights reserved.

evenings between 6 and 7 p.m., many market baskets, particularly those bought by men, contained both beer and baby diapers. This relationship between beer and baby diapers arises because diapers come in large packages, so wives, who do most of the household shopping, leave the diaper purchase to their husbands. When husbands buy diapers at the end of the workweek, they also want to get some beer for the weekend. When the supermarket discovered this shopping pattern, it put a premium beer display next to the diapers. Because the premium beer was so conveniently placed next to the diapers, men tend to be up-sold and buy the premium brands rather than spend time going to the beer aisle for lower-priced brands.

RETAILING VIEW   CVS Caremark Gains Useful Insights from Its Customer Database   11.3

The market intelligence group at CVS Caremark is responsible for building the firm's data warehouse and analyzing the data to develop programs and promotions that increase its share of wallet. Customers in its ExtraCare frequent-shopper program earn a percentage of their purchases back as ExtraBucks that they can use in the store during future shopping trips. The percentages earned as ExtraBucks vary by product type, from 2 percent of all in-store sales to 10 percent on beauty products. Customers also earn double ExtraBucks on more than 100 diabetes-related products and 5 ExtraBucks for every 10 prescriptions they fill. E-mails and direct mail provide them with helpful health and beauty insights, new-product information, and coupons, in addition to free merchandise when CVS Caremark has special vendor promotions. Using each member's buying habits, CVS Caremark personalizes the coupons it gives to ExtraCare program participants. With a "Send to Card" feature, it also eliminates the need for paper coupons: ExtraCare members can assign their ExtraBucks rewards and coupons directly to their loyalty cards, or else they can upload all the information to their smartphones, using the ExtraCare mobile app.

REFACT

ExtraCare, the top frequent-shopper program in the retail industry, attracts approximately 92 million active cardholders. More than 67 percent of all transactions and 82 percent of front-end sales in CVS stores feature the use of ExtraCare loyalty cards.[18]

By analyzing the buying behavior of ExtraCare customers, CVS has discovered some interesting cross-promotional opportunities. For example, about two-thirds of customers who buy toothpaste did not buy toothbrushes. To encourage them to do so, the retailer targets toothpaste consumers with special toothbrush promotions. It also uses special promotions to increase the overall size of their market baskets. For example, it offers a $4 coupon to customers whose average market basket is $15 if they reach $25 in purchases, whereas customers who normally spend $25 get a $10 coupon if they make a $50 purchase.

Beyond the store, CVS Caremark analyzes its database to tailor its assortment and location decisions to the needs of its loyal, local community. For example, it identified a segment of customers who lived in urban areas with a dearth of grocery store options. So it expanded grocery, fresh, and on-the-go food items available in stores located in the same neighborhoods.

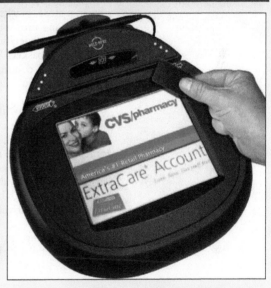

The use of data to make better decisions at CVS Caremark starts with customers scanning in their ExtraCare card.

Finally, to ensure that they never question their own loyalty, CVS Caremark is very protective of customers' privacy. Its programs are all opt-in, and it sends mailings only to customers who give it permission to do so. At times, it uses outside processing companies as agents to help print and send mailings, but these agents never receive any personal customer information beyond names and addresses. CVS Caremark commits to never granting or selling any specific information to any manufacturer or direct marketer.

Sources: www.cvs.com/ExtraCare; Greg Jacobson, "CVS Aims to Personalize Retail Experience," *Chain Drug Review*, April 23, 2012.

DISCUSSION QUESTION

How does CVS Caremark use the data it collects from its ExtraCare program?

Some other examples of how market basket analyses have revised product locations are as follows:

* Bananas are the most common item in Americans' grocery carts, so supermarkets often place bananas both in the cereal aisle and in the produce section.
* Tissues are in the paper goods aisle but also mixed in with cold medicine.
* Measuring spoons appear in the housewares section and also hang next to baking supplies, such as flour and shortening.
* Flashlights are placed in the hardware aisle and with a seasonal display of Halloween costumes.
* Snack cakes appear in the bread aisle, but they also are available next to the coffee.
* Bug spray is merchandised with hunting gear and with household cleaning supplies.

Targeting Promotions   Beyond aiding decisions about where to place products in a store, market basket analysis can help provide insights into assortment decisions and promotions. For example, retailers might discover that customers typically buy a specific brand of conditioner and shampoo at the same time (in the same market basket). With this information, the retailer might offer a special promotion on the conditioner, anticipating that customers will also buy the (higher margin) shampoo at its full price.

Assortment Planning   Managers have to make decisions about what merchandise to carry in each category. Customer data also can be mined to help with these assortment decisions. By analyzing which products the retailer's most valued customers purchase, the manager can ensure that they are available in the store at all times. For example, an analysis might discover that customers in its highest CLV segment are very loyal to a brand of gourmet mustard. However, this brand of mustard is only the tenth best seller in the retailer's mustard category across all customers. Due to its relatively low sales, the retailer might consider dropping the mustard brand from its assortment. But based on this analysis, the retailer would decide to continue offering the mustard, fearing that these high CLV customers would defect to another retailer if the gourmet brand was no longer stocked in its stores.

DEVELOPING CRM THROUGH FREQUENT-SHOPPER PROGRAMS

LO4

Outline how retailers develop their frequent-shopper programs.

As mentioned earlier, frequent-shopper programs, or loyalty programs, are marketing efforts that reward repeat buying behavior. Two objectives of these programs are to (1) to build a customer database that links customer data to their transactions and (2) to encourage repeat purchase behavior and loyalty. The implications of the first objective are discussed in a preceding section of this chapter; the implications of the second objective are reviewed in the following section.

Effectiveness of Frequent-Shopper Programs

Although frequent-shopper programs are useful for building customer databases, they are not particularly useful for building long-term customer loyalty.[19] The perceived value of these programs by consumers is low, because consumers perceive little difference among the programs offered by competing retailers. Most programs simply offer customers price discounts that are available to all customers that register for the programs. These discounts are appealing to price-conscious shoppers but not necessarily to the high CLV shoppers. In addition, competitive advantages based on frequent-shopper programs are rarely sustainable. The programs are very visible, so they can be easily duplicated by competitors. They also are very expensive in most cases.[20] A one percent price discount might cost large retailers around $100 million—and that is only after they invest up to $30 million to get the loyalty program up and running. Over time, they must continue to invest, up to $10 million annually, to maintain the program, including IT costs, marketing efforts, and training.

Finally, loyalty programs are difficult to revise or correct. Once they become part of customers' shopping experience, the retailer has to inform customers about even the smallest changes. If those changes imply that customers are losing some of the benefits of the programs, a strong negative reaction is likely, even from customers who exhibit relatively little loyalty in the first place.

Frequent-shopper programs have limited effectiveness because consumers join all of the programs offered by competing retailers.

Making Frequent-Shopper Programs More Effective

Frequent-shopper programs seek to encourage repeated purchases and develop customer loyalty. To build true loyalty, retailers need an emotional connection with consumers, as well as a sense of commitment from them. When a Starwood Hotels representative helped a frequent customer find a car when she was stranded in Chicago, then called the woman's husband to let him know she was fine, that associate ensured the traveler's loyalty.[22] Therefore, to move frequent-shopper programs beyond simple data collection and short-term sales effects, retailers might (1) create tiered rewards, (2) treat frequent shoppers as VIPs, (3) incorporate charitable activities, (4) offer choices, (5) reward all transactions, and (6) make the program transparent and simple.[23]

Offer Tiered Rewards   Many frequent-shopper programs contain cascading tier levels, such as silver, gold, and platinum. The higher the tier, the better the rewards. This reward structure provides an incentive for customers to consolidate their purchases with one retailer to reach the higher tiers. Some programs combine both discounts and points. For example, a retailer might offer a $5 discount on purchases between $100 and $149.99, $10 dollars off purchases from $150 to $249.99, and $15 off purchases of $250 or more. Then beyond $250, customers accumulate points that can be redeemed for special, unique rewards, such as a free shirt or tickets to a local baseball game.

A key requirement for a tiered program is designing tiers that consumers perceive as attainable. Frequent shoppers can calculate the tier level they can achieve with their usual spending pretty easily. They may be less inclined to shop at a retailer or participate in its frequent-shopper program if the tiers are impossibly distant. Although Neiman Marcus has a reward tier for customers who make $600,000 in annual purchases, a similar reward tier would be vastly inappropriate for a grocery store loyalty program.

Treat High CLVs as VIPs   Consumers respond to being treated as if they are someone special. Effective programs, therefore, go beyond discounts on purchases to offer unique rewards. For example, in its PowerUp Rewards program, GameStop encouraged its target customers to spend more on racing and fantasy video games by offering tickets to NASCAR races or backstage access to Comic-Con.[25] The rewards accordingly should match the retailer's target market to make customers feel really special: A private shopping night might be important for a heavy Nordstrom shopper, whereas an exclusive tour of the company's facility might be more interesting for Apple customers. These events also should be promoted in advance to encourage

REFACT

More than 17 percent of customers indicate that loyalty programs are "very influential" in their purchase decisions.[21]

REFACT

American Airlines launched the first frequent-flyer program in 1981. In 1984, Neiman Marcus launched the first frequent-shopper program by a retailer selling products.[24]

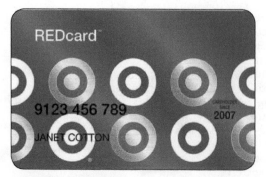

Target enhances the effectiveness of its frequent-shopper program by linking it to donations to local schools.

more customers to enroll and pursue enough points to be invited to attend the events.

Incorporate Charitable Contributions Many programs are linked to charitable causes. For example, Target donates one percent of all purchases made with its REDcard to local schools. Although these altruistic rewards can be an effective element of a frequent-shopper program, they probably should not be the focal point of the program.

Offer Choices Not all customers value the same rewards, so the most effective frequent-shopper programs offer choices. Sainsbury, a UK supermarket chain, allows customers to use their Nectar points for vouchers at a variety of retail partners. Caesars Entertainment has different programs for guests who live close to one of its properties and for customers who must fly to its casinos or resorts. It also introduced Total Rewards Member Pricing, which enables loyalty program members to get better pricing than nonmembers at Caesars property restaurants as well as the opportunity to purchase presale show tickets.[26]

Starwood Hotels (which owns the Westin, W, Sheraton, and Four Points chains, among others) maintains a program within its Starwood Preferred Guest program, called Moments, that gives point-holders chances to bid in an auction for spectacular experiences. Participants use their earned points to bid on the right to attend a variety of exclusive access events: meeting Coldplay backstage before a concert, playing golf with pro Lorena Ochoa, or meeting the chef while having dinner at the famous Per Se restaurant.[27]

Reward All Transactions To ensure that the retailer collects all customer transaction data and encourages repeat purchases, programs need to reward all purchases, not just purchases of selected merchandise or those made through certain channels (e.g., in-store versus online). Customers should gain entry to an introductory tier with nearly their first purchase, to encourage them to join. Accordingly, Sephora designates customers as Beauty Insiders the moment they sign up for a card. Once they spend $100—not much at the cosmetics counter—they qualify to receive a free sample-sized product.[28]

Make the Program Transparent and Simple Effective programs are transparent in that they make it easy for customers to keep track of their spending and available rewards. When they are both transparent and convenient, loyalty programs can quickly become integral to shoppers' consumption choices. Thus, there is an increasing use of smartphone-linked programs that let customers earn and redeem rewards through a mobile app, instead of requiring them to remember their cards or coupons. With a push of a button, shoppers can recall their point totals, how much more they need to spend to reach a desired prize, or whether they can redeem points for something great today.

When loyalty programs also are simple, their effectiveness increases even more. A program with a confusing maze of rules and regulations has little appeal to consumers. Some airlines have suffered from accusations that their confusing black-out dates and redemption rules make their loyalty programs virtually useless. Instead, simple, straightforward programs can succeed just by offering a few options consistently and dependably.

Retailing View 11.4 describes how the Neiman Marcus InCircle program goes beyond offering price discounts to building loyalty with its best customers.

RETAILING VIEW InCircle Builds Neiman-Marcus' Share of Wallet **11.4**

Neiman Marcus targets the top two percent of consumers, in terms of their income, which generally means that people in its stores are well-educated and well-traveled. These sophisticated shoppers are attracted to the retailer's InCircle frequent-shopper program, widely considered a CRM best practice.

The InCircle program is linked to the store credit card and offers six levels of benefits, based on annual purchases at Neiman Marcus. Circle 1 indicates purchases less than $2,500; the Chairman's Level means the customer has spent more than $600,000 that year.

Depending on their tier, customers receive from two to five InCircle points for every dollar charged on their credit cards. For every 10,000 points earned, the members receive a $100 gift card. In addition, they accrue other benefits, depending on their spending level: discounts on in-store dining, free alterations, store delivery, hassle-free parking, fur storage, free repair and cleaning of jewelry, engraving, shoe and handbag repair, monogramming, and discounts at salons, to name a few. Customers at the higher levels also receive some unusual rewards, such as a concierge service that will locate an item that customers have seen on TV or a fashion runway, make a reservation at an exclusive restaurant, and run errands.

InCircle members can quickly look up their point balance on the InCircle website. They receive e-mails announcing special events and notifications when they are approaching a new tier level. They also get *Entrée* magazine, a publication produced by Time Warner exclusively for Neiman Marcus. In turn, Neiman Marcus asks for feedback about how it can help improve its value for InCircle members.

Neiman Marcus' InCircle frequent-shopper program is a benchmark for other programs.

At the store level, sales associates unobtrusively gather insights about customers, using their prior purchases and behaviors in the store. Once they have struck up a relationship, the sales associates contact customers directly when a new shipment of their favorite brand has arrived, for example. The sales associates also move freely throughout the store to find whatever items their InCircle members want at the time or to encourage them to make use of the services available, such as gift wrap and travel advice.

Sources: www.incircle.com, www.neimanmarcus.com, and 10K 2012 Neiman-Marcus annual report.

REFACT

More than 35 percent of Neiman Marcus sales are to customers enrolled in the InCircle program.[29]

DISCUSSION QUESTION

What are the elements of Neiman-Marcus's InCircle program that build customer loyalty?

IMPLEMENTING CRM PROGRAMS

Having developed CRM through frequent-shopper programs, the last step in the CRM process is to implement those programs (see Exhibit 11–1).

LO5

Explain various ways to implement effective CRM programs.

Customer Pyramid

For most retailers, a relatively small number of customers account for the majority of their profits. This condition is often called the **80-20 rule**—80 percent of the sales or profits come from 20 percent of the customers. Thus, retailers could group their customers into two categories on the basis of their CLV scores. One group would be the 20 percent of the customers with the highest CLV scores, and the other group would be the rest. However, this two-segment scheme, "best" and "rest," does not consider important differences among the 80 percent of customers in the "rest" segment. Many of the customers in the "rest" category are potentially "best," or at least, good customers. A commonly used segmentation scheme divides

EXHIBIT 11–4
The Customer Pyramid

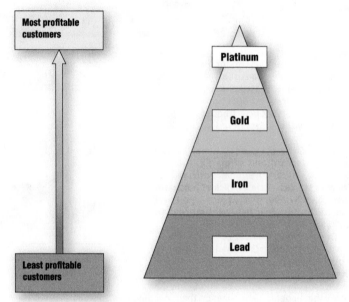

SOURCE: Valarie Zeithaml, Roland Rust, and Katherine Lemon, "The Customer Pyramid: Creating and Serving Profitable Customers," *California Management Review* 43 (Summer 2001), p. 124. Reprinted with permission.

customers into four segments, as illustrated in Exhibit 11–4, or even 10 deciles. This scheme allows retailers to develop more effective strategies for each of the segments. Different CRM programs are directed toward customers in each of the segments. Each of the four segments is described next.[30]

Platinum Segment   This segment is composed of the customers with the top 25 percent CLVs. Typically, these are the most profitable and loyal customers who, because of their loyalty, are typically not overly concerned about prices. Customers in this quartile buy a lot of the merchandise sold by the retailer and often place more value on customer service than price.

Gold Segment   The next quartile of customers, in terms of their CLVs, make up the gold segment. Even though they buy a significant amount of merchandise from the retailer, they are not as loyal as platinum customers and patronize some of the retailer's competitors. The profitability levels of the gold-tier customers are less than those of the platinum-tier customers because price plays a greater role in their decision making. An important objective of any CRM program is to provide incentives to move gold-tier customers to the platinum level.

Iron Segment   The customers in this quartile purchase a modest amount of merchandise, but their spending levels, loyalty, and profitability are not substantial enough for special treatment. Although it could be possible to move these people up to higher tiers in the pyramid, for reasons such as limited income, price sensitivity, or shared loyalties with other retailers, additional expenditures on them may not be worth it.

Lead Segment   Customers with the lowest CLVs can make a negative contribution to the firm's income. They often demand a lot of attention but do not buy much from the retailer. When they do buy from the retailer, they often buy merchandise on sale or abuse return privileges. They may even cause additional problems by complaining about the retailer to others. As a result, retailers do not direct any attention to these customers.

In the following sections, we discuss programs retailers use to retain their best customers, convert good customers into high-CLV customers, and get rid of unprofitable customers.

Customer Retention

Two approaches that retailers use to retain customers and increase the share of wallet are personalization and community.

Personalization   An important limitation of CRM strategies developed for market segments, such as a platinum segment in the customer pyramid (Exhibit 11–4), is that each segment is composed of a large number of customers who are not identical. Thus, any offering will be most appealing for only the typical customer and not as appealing to the majority of customers in the segment. For example, customers in the platinum segment with the highest CLVs might include a 25-year-old single woman whose needs are quite different from those of a 49-year-old working mother with two children.

The availability of customer-level data and analysis tools helps retailers overcome this problem and offer unique benefits and targeted messages to individual customers in a cost-effective manner. Some retailers provide unusually high-quality, personalized customer service to build and maintain the loyalty of their best customers. For example, upscale department stores such as Saks Fifth Avenue and Neiman Marcus provide wardrobe consultants for their best customers. These consultants can arrange special presentations and fittings in the store during hours when the store is not open or at the customers' offices or homes. Nordstrom holds complimentary private parties for invitees to view new clothing lines. Saks Fifth Avenue offers free fur storage, complimentary tailoring, and dinner at the captain's table on a luxury cruise line. At Andrisen Morton, a Denver men's apparel specialty retailer, salespeople occasionally contact customers directly; if the store receives a new shipment of Brioni suits, they call customers who have purchased Brioni in the past. If a customer has been relatively inactive, the associates might offer him a $100 certificate for something he has not bought in a while.

Developing retail programs for small groups or individual customers is referred to as **1-to-1 retailing.** Many small, local retailers have always practiced 1-to-1

Amazon personalizes its Internet interactions with customers by analyzing its customer database to present offerings that will be of interest to each of its customers.

retailing. They know each of their customers, greet them by name when they walk into the store, and then recommend merchandise they know the customers will like. These local store owners do not need customer databases and data mining tools because they can keep the information in their heads. But most large retail chains and their employees lack such intimate knowledge of their customers. Thus, CRM enables larger retailers to develop relationships similar to those that many small local retailers have with customers.

Another aspect of personalization is to involve the best customers in the retailer's business decisions. Some retailers ask their best customers to participate in focus groups to evaluate alternatives the retailer is considering. Loyalty increases when customers feel valued for not just the money they have spent, but for their opinions.

The personalized rewards or benefits that customers receive are based on unique information possessed by the retailer and its sales associates. This information, in the retailer's customer database, cannot be accessed or used by competitors. Thus, it provides an opportunity to develop a sustainable competitive advantage.

The effective use of this information creates the positive feedback cycle in the CRM process (see Exhibit 11–1). Increasing repeat purchases from a retailer increases the amount of data collected from the customer, which enables the retailer to provide more personalized benefits, which in turn increases the customer's purchases from the retailer.

Community   A second approach for building customer retention and loyalty is to develop a sense of community among customers. A **retail brand community** is a group of customers who are bound together by their loyalty to a retailer and the activities the retailer sponsors and undertakes. Community members identify themselves with other members and share a common interest and participation in activities related to the retailer. They also feel an obligation to attract new members of the community and help other members of the community by sharing their experiences and product knowledge. By participating in such a community, customers become more reluctant to leave the "family" of other people patronizing the retailer.[31]

The Nike stores create a sense of community by hosting running groups that meet weekly at the store for refreshments. Members who have logged more than 100 miles earn special recognition, and the Nike Plus website communicates with runners' Apple iTouches/iPhones to track their running metrics. More than half of the runners involved in Nike's program use this system, visiting the website more than four times a week.

TAG/Burger and Bar at Madison Street in Denver creates a sense of community by encouraging customers to send in original hamburger combination recipes through e-mail, Facebook, and Twitter. Every month, management chooses the best one and offers it for sale for a month. The winner gets as many as he or she wants for the month that it is featured.

Walmart solicited its community of "Walmart Moms" from among bloggers who already were writing about the challenges of modern motherhood—and the quest for savings and value. The 11 original bloggers offered high-quality content and had strong influences on their readers, leading Walmart to enlist them to share their advice and insights on "living well." Although many of the posts, hosted through Walmart's website, are specific to finding grocery bargains, the community site covers a broad range of topics, from green living to politics to health issues. The retailer does not pay the mothers and even requires them to disclose any forms of compensation they might receive (e.g., travel expenses, free products for trials). Yet, in many cases, the information they post resonates with Walmart's brand image. Furthermore, Walmart gains invaluable feedback from not only the bloggers (who now number more than 20), but also all the other moms who follow their posts. By entering into conversations with the bloggers,

Walmart supports blogs by independent bloggers to encourage a community of value-oriented moms.

posters, and commentators, Walmart builds connections with a critical target market of modern moms.[32]

Customer Conversion: Making Good Customers into Best Customers

In the context of the customer pyramid (Exhibit 11–4), increasing the sales made to good customers can be referred to as customer alchemy—converting iron and gold customers into platinum customers.[33] A way to achieve customer alchemy is through **add-on selling,** which involves offering and selling more products and services to existing customers to increase the retailer's share of wallet with these customers.

A retailer's customer database reveals opportunities for add-on selling. Many retailers use their data on customers' shopping histories to suggest products to them. For example, if a supermarket discovers that customers are buying cat food and not kitty litter, it might distribute coupons for kitty litter to the customers. These coupons could be provided to the customers when they enter the store and swipe their frequent-shopper cards, when they log on to the retailer's website, or through messages sent to the customers' mobile phones.

Amazon.com is a master at generating add-on sales through its recommendations. Personalized recommendations, based on past purchases, are made when consumers first visit the website. If they scroll down to get more information about a book, the site recommends other books that have been bought by customers who purchased the book being examined. Then a bundle of two books, the one being examined and a complementary book, is offered at a discounted price. Retailing View 11.5 describes how American Girl increases its share of wallet.

310   SECTION II   Retailing Strategy

Dealing with Unprofitable Customers

In many cases, the bottom tier of customers actually has a negative CLV. Retailers lose money on every sale they make to these customers. For example, catalog retailers have customers who repeatedly buy three or four items and return all but one of them. The cost of processing two or three returned items is much greater than the profits coming from the one item that the customer kept. Customers in the bottom tier may also be there because they stopped buying from the retailer for a period of time and then resumed patronizing the retailer. For example, customers may vanish because a competitor is offering a more attractive offer, or they are dissatisfied and then return months or years later as a new customer. The costs of their (re)acquisition make them unprofitable. The process of no longer selling to these unprofitable customers can be referred to as "getting the lead out," in terms of the customer pyramid.[34]

Approaches for getting the lead out are (1) offering less costly services to satisfy the needs of lead customers and (2) charging customers for the services they

---

11.5   RETAILING VIEW   American Girl Motivates Customers to Purchase Doll Add-Ons

When American Girl first hit the market in 1986, the limited line of dolls represented 9-year-old girls who lived at different times in history, combined with books that told each doll's story. Youthful consumers loved the 18-inch dolls and learned a little bit of history as they read about how a young girl would have lived at different points in the past. The popularity of the line encouraged the retailer to expand the associated items available, creating many opportunities for customers to buy add-on merchandise.

For example, for shoppers less interested in history than in the present, the Just Like You line features contemporary dolls. If a younger sister at home wants her own doll, American Girl offers the Bitty Baby line, with soft dolls more appropriate for 3- to 6-year olds. Across all these lines, consumers can find a wealth of accessories to buy for their dolls, including clothing, accessories, toys, and so forth.

Because the dolls and their accessories promise education and embrace diversity, millions of girls and their parents exhibit significant loyalty to American Girl. To enable them to live an American Girl life, the company released a film, *Kit Kittredge: An American Girl*. The book series also has expanded, to include six texts about each doll; really active readers also can keep up with their monthly *American Girl* magazine.

Perhaps the greatest add-on opportunity is available through the American Girl stores (currently, there are 14 throughout the United States). Families make vacations out of visits to the store. Each trip is likely to include a photo shoot of the girl and her doll; a salon visit to shape and style her doll's hair; a three-course lunch at the café, with a seat provided for her doll; and a new outfit for the doll, with a matching version for the girl. If a doll has had too many adventures and needs repairs, the store has a hospital. Such an outing can cost more than $300, but parents, after getting over the sticker shock, often indicate that they believe the experience is worth it.

American Girl increases its share of wallet with customers by offering special services like hairdressing and dining with dolls.

Community activities also have been developed around American Girl dolls. For example, local libraries host American Girl parties. The events attract dozens of girls and their dolls and feature events and discussions that are specific to the time periods that each doll represents. Service organizations even have developed American Girl fashion shows to support local charities.

Sources: www.americangirl.com; David Rosenberg, "Looking at American Girls with Their American Girls," *Slate*, January 25, 2013; Michelle Wildgen, "The Rise of American Girl Rebecca Rubin," *Forward*, January 2, 2012; and Amy Ziettlow, "Lessons From American Girl Dolls: The Divorce Generation," *The Atlantic*, January 18, 2013.

DISCUSSION QUESTION

How does American Girl help ensure that its existing customers spend more with it?

are abusing. For example, a retailer might get 70,000 daily calls, about three-quarters of which go to automated systems that cost the company less than $1 each. The remaining calls are handled by call center agents that cost $13 per call. The retailer could contact 25,000 lower-tier customers who placed a lot of calls to agents and tell them they must use the website or automated calls for simple account and price information. Each name could be flagged and routed to a special representative who would direct callers back to automated services and tell them how to use it.

Rejecting customers is a delicate business, though. Sierra Trading Post, an online retailer of apparel and outdoor equipment, has been criticized by customers who received e-mails, seemingly out of the blue, informing them they can no longer shop with the retailer because they have returned too many items. Yet, the company guarantees satisfaction and offers a full refund to any unhappy customer, regardless of how long the customer has owned a product.

SUMMARY

LO1 **Describe the customer relationship management process.**

Customer relationship management (CRM) is a business philosophy that includes a set of strategies, programs, and systems that focus on identifying and building repeat purchase behavior and loyalty with a retailer's most valued customers. Loyal customers are committed to patronizing a retailer and are not prone to switch to competitors. In addition to building loyalty by increasing customer value, CRM programs are designed to increase the share of wallet that a retailer earns from its better customers.

Customer relationship management is an iterative process that allows the retailer to encourage increased loyalty through its efforts to (1) collect customer data, (2) analyze the customer data and identify target customers, (3) develop CRM and frequent-shopper programs, and (4) implement CRM programs.

LO2 **Understand how customer shopping data are collected.**

Retailers collect extensive data about customers, which they store in their databases. To gather these data, retailers might ask for it at the point of sale, obtain it through online channels, or gather it from applications that customers submit to a loyalty program. Although it can be challenging to ensure that all collected data are accurately connected with each customer transaction, the collection and analysis of data about customer attitudes, preferences, and shopping behaviors enables retailers to closely target their promotions and provide more value to their customers.

However, many customers are concerned that retailers might violate their privacy when they collect detailed personal information. There is a growing consensus that personal information must be fairly collected, that the collection must be purposeful, and that the data should be relevant and kept reasonably secure. Anticipating increasing data privacy regulations, many retailers are working proactively to establish secure methods that can guarantee the privacy of their customers' data.

LO3 **Explain the methods used to analyze customer data and identify target customers.**

Once retailers have collected sufficient data, they must analyze them to derive actionable information. A common measure for describing shoppers is their customer lifetime value (CLV). Another method describes the recency, frequency, and monetary amount (RFM) of their purchases. More sophisticated retail analytics also include market basket analysis, which provides information about the products most commonly purchased together. Such information can inform retail decisions about which assortment to maintain in a store to appeal best to valuable customers, as well as which merchandise items to promote together to increase sales.

LO4 **Outline how retailers develop their frequent-shopper programs.**

Frequent-shopper programs serve two main purposes: (1) build a customer database that links customers to transactions and (2) encourage repeat purchase behavior and loyalty. Frequent-shopper programs can be effective for building a customer database, but they are not very useful for ensuring long-term customer loyalty. To enhance their loyalty effects, frequent-shopper programs should seek to (1) create tiered rewards, (2) treat

312 SECTION II Retailing Strategy

frequent shoppers as VIPs, (3) incorporate charitable activities, (4) offer choices, (5) reward all transactions, and (6) make the rewards program transparent and simple.

LO5 Explain various ways to implement effective CRM programs.

Using this information about customers, retailers can develop programs to build loyalty in their best customers, increase their share of wallet with better customers (e.g., convert gold customers into platinum customers), and deal with unprofitable customers (getting the lead out). Four approaches that retailers use to build loyalty and retain their better customers are (1) launch frequent-shopper programs, (2) offer special customer services, (3) personalize the services they provide, and (4) build a sense of community. To deal with unprofitable customers identified by their CRM data, retailers need to develop lower-cost approaches to serve them, or else exclude those customers altogether from the retail offer.

KEY TERMS

add-on selling, *309*

biometrics, *296*

cookies, *297*

customer database, *293*

customer lifetime value (CLV), *298*

customer loyalty, *292*

customer relationship management (CRM), *292*

data mining, *299*

80-20 rule, *305*

frequent-shopper program, *296*

loyalty program, *296*

market basket analysis, *299*

1-to-1 retailing, *307*

opt in, *298*

opt out, *298*

retail analytics, *299*

retail brand community, *308*

RFM analysis, *299*

share of wallet, *292*

GET OUT AND DO IT!

1. **CONTINUING ASSIGNMENT** Interview the store manager working for the retailer you have selected for the continuing assignment. Ask the manager if the store offers a frequent-shopper/loyalty program and how effective it is in terms of increasing the store's sales and profits. Find out why the manager has these views and what could be done to increase the effectiveness of the program. Then talk to some customers in the store. Ask them why they are or are not members. Find out how membership in the program affects their shopping behavior and relationship with the retailer.

2. **INTERNET EXERCISE** Go to the home page of a retailer that you frequent and review its privacy policy. How is this retailer protecting its customers' information? Which policies, or lack of policies, raise your concern? Why? Which policies give you comfort that your private information is being protected? Why?

3. **INTERNET EXERCISE** Go to the website of the Electronic Privacy Information Center (www.epic.org), and review the issues raised by the organization. What does this watchdog organization feel are the most important retailers' consumer privacy issues? How will these issues evolve in the future?

4. **INTERNET EXERCISE** Go to the home page of 1-800-Flowers at www.1800flowers.com, and read about the Fresh Rewards program. How does this company's CRM program help it to track its better customers, grow its business, and increase customer loyalty?

DISCUSSION QUESTIONS AND PROBLEMS

1. What is a customer relationship management (CRM) program? Describe one CRM program that you have participated in as a customer.

2. Why do retailers want to determine the lifetime value of their customers? How does past customer behavior help retailers anticipate future customer retention?

3. Why do some customers have a low or negative CLV value? What approach can retailers take with these customers to minimize their impact on the bottom line?

4. Why do customers have privacy concerns about the frequent-shopper programs that supermarkets offer,

and what can supermarkets do to minimize these concerns?

5. Why are most frequent-shopper programs ineffective in terms of building loyalty? What can be done to make them more effective?

6. Which of the following types of retailers do you think would benefit most from instituting a CRM program: (a) supermarkets, (b) banks, (c) automobile dealers, or (d) consumer electronics retailers? Why?

7. Develop a CRM program for a local store that sells apparel and gifts with your college's or university's logo. What type of information would you collect about your customers, and how would you use this information to increase the sales and profits of the store?

8. What are the different approaches retailers can use to identify customers by their transactions? What are the advantages and disadvantages of each approach?

9. A CRM program focuses on building relationships with a retailer's better customers. Some customers who do not receive the same benefits as the retailer's best customers may be upset because they are treated differently. What can retailers do to minimize this negative reaction?

10. Think of one of your favorite places to shop. How does this retailer create customer loyalty and satisfaction, encourage repeat visits, establish an emotional bond between the customer and the retailer, know the customer's preferences, and provide personal attention and memorable experiences to its best customers?

SUGGESTED READINGS

Blattberg, Robert, Edward Malthouse, and Scott Neslin. "Customer Lifetime Value: Empirical Generalizations and Some Conceptual Questions." *Journal of Interactive Marketing* 23 (May 2009), pp. 157–168.

Cox, Emmett. *Retail Analytics: The Secret Weapon.* Hoboken, NJ: Wiley, 2011.

Christopher, Martin, Adrian Payne, and David Ballantyne. *Relationship Marketing.* New York: Routledge, 2012.

Gandomi, Zolfaghari. "Profitability of Loyalty Reward Programs: An Analytical Investigation," *Omega* 41, 4 (August 2013), pp. 797–807.

Gomez, Blanca, Ana Arranz, and Jesus Cillan. "Drivers of Customer Likelihood to Join Grocery Retail Loyalty Programs. An Analysis of Reward Programs and Loyalty Cards," *Journal of Retailing and Consumer Services* 19, 5 (September 2012), pp. 492–500.

Hochman, Larry. *The Relationship Revolution: Closing the Customer Promise Gap.* Hoboken, NJ: Wiley, 2010.

Kumar, V., and Werner Reinartz. *Customer Relationship Management,* 2nd ed. New York: Springer, 2012.

Linoff, Gordon, and Michael Berry. *Data Mining Techniques: For Marketing, Sales, and Customer Relationship Management,* 3rd ed. Hoboken, NJ: Wiley, 2011.

Nguyen, Bang. "The Dark Side of Customer Relationship Management: Exploring the Underlying Reasons for Pitfalls, Exploitation and Unfairness." *Journal of Database Marketing & Customer Strategy Management* 19 (2012), pp. 56–70.

Peltier, James, Debra Zahay, and Donald Lehmann. "Organizational Learning and CRM Success: A Model for Linking Organizational Practices, Customer Data Quality, and Performance." *Journal of Interactive Marketing,* 27, 1 (2013), pp. 1–13.

Verhoef, Peter, Rajkumar Venkatesan, Leigh McAlister, Edward C. Malthouse, Manfred Krafft, and Shankar Ganesan. "CRM in Data-Rich Multichannel Retailing Environments: A Review and Future Research Directions." *Journal of Interactive Marketing,* 24, no. 2 (2010), pp. 121–137.

Retail Communication Mix

EXECUTIVE BRIEFING
Katrina Davis, Social Media and
Communications Coordinator, Body Central

Body Central is a multichannel specialty apparel retailer with more than 250 stores located in enclosed malls and lifestyle centers in the South, mid-Atlantic, and Midwest United States. Our target market is women from diverse cultural backgrounds interested in wearing the latest fashions at value prices. The presentation of our merchandise emphasizes coordinated outfits of tops, dresses, bottoms, jewelry, accessories, and shoes fits the many lifestyles of our customers—casual, club, dressy, and active. The majority of our products are priced under $30.

When I came to work at Body Central four years ago, I realized that I really enjoyed marketing communications and branding. I was an early adopter of Facebook, and social media was an attractive communication vehicle, particularly for our target market. The company created a position for me to see what returns we could get communicating with our customers using social media. Now we have 150,000 organic likes on Facebook, and we have a presence on all other major social media channels, including Twitter, Pinterest, Instagram, YouTube, and a corporate blog with new posts five days a week.

Our goal for using social media is to develop a close relationship and loyalty with customers in our target market and the bloggers they follow. You can stir up a lot of activity by running contests, but people who visit us just to participate in a contest don't

CHAPTER 15

LEARNING OBJECTIVES

LO1 Identify the traditional media elements.

LO2 Identify the new media elements.

LO3 Understand how retailers use communication programs to develop

brand images and build customer loyalty.

LO4 List the steps involved in developing a communication program.

always become loyal customers or followers. The loyalty comes when we get the customers to engage in a dialogue with us and other members of our community. In 2012, I launched Fan of the Month on our Facebook page. It encouraged Body Central shoppers to share pictures of themselves in their Body Central outfits on our Facebook wall. Each month, a new fan is chosen to have her picture posted on Facebook by Body Central and is sent a prize pack full of accessories and other merchandise. Not only does it give customers a monthly incentive to follow us, but the relationships made along the way are invaluable. It's truly rewarding to Like and comment on photos of mother/daughter shopping trips, birthdays, personal weight loss success stories, and engagements. A customer was even proposed to in one of our store locations and shared it with us on Facebook. Our store associates kept her busy in the dressing room while the fiancé-to-be picked up the ring from a jeweler in the mall.

Building relationships with bloggers and encouraging them to be part of our community really pays off. There are thousands of fashion apparel bloggers. We are contacted almost every day by a blogger looking to make a connection. I spend time building relationships with the ones that appeal to our target market. The relationship can be beneficial on both ends. We reap the benefits of having our merchandise promoted by a trusted fashion voice outside of the brand. If a blogger has a big enough following, a collaborative project can drive traffic and revenue for the brand. The bloggers can increase their reach with exposure to new potential readers on our social media platforms and benefit from the exclusivity of having a personal relationship with a brand they genuinely enjoy.

To build this dialogue and sense of community, you need to communicate regularly and address problems that might arise quickly. I check our various social media platforms at the beginning of every day and address any issues. Most of these issues can be handled with a quick send of a link or a reference to customer service.

The preceding chapters in this section on merchandise management described how retailers develop an assortment and merchandise budget plan, then buy and price the merchandise. The next step is to develop and implement a communication program that will attract customers to retail locations (whether in stores or online) and encourage them to buy the merchandise available. The communication program informs customers about the retailer, describes the merchandise and services offered, helps develop the retailer's brand, and plays a critical role in encouraging repeat visits and customer loyalty.

At the end of the twentieth century, most retail communication programs were fairly simple. Local newspaper advertising was the primary medium, and the message was typically oriented toward providing incentives—usually a special price—to motivate customers to visit the store. Today, successful retailers utilize an **integrated marketing communication program** in which they integrate a variety of communication elements to deliver a comprehensive, consistent message to all customers over time, across all elements of their retail mix and across all delivery channels. For example, Chili's Grill and Bar Restaurants uses traditional media—television, radio, and billboards. But its customers can also go to Chilis.com to find restaurant locations and place an order. It also communicates with its customers on Facebook and Twitter, but believes its most effective Internet-based communication tool is through the Chili's opt-in e-mail list.[1]

Coordination among the communication elements is critical to its success. For example, if Chili's televised advertising campaign tries to build an exciting image, based on its innovative food options and friendly customer service, while its sales promotions focus on low prices, its communication methods are not consistent. Accordingly, its customers may become confused about its image and therefore not patronize Chili's.

For any communications campaign to succeed, the retailer must deliver the right message to the right audience through the right media at the right time, with the ultimate goal of profiting from long-term customer relationships, as well as short-term sales. Reaching the right audience is becoming more difficult as the media environment grows more complicated. No single type of media is necessarily better than another. The goal of a retail communication strategy is to plan all of the elements to work together so the sum exceeds the total of the individual media parts.

We now examine the individual elements of a retail communication strategy and the way each contributes to a successful communication campaign (see Exhibit 15–1). These elements are divided into traditional and new media. Traditional media elements include mass advertising, promotions, in-store marketing, direct mail, personal selling, and public relations. The new media elements include online (e-mail, mobile, websites) and social media (YouTube, Facebook, blogs, and Twitter). These media elements vary on five dimensions: personalization, interactivity, message control, extent of information provided, and the cost per exposure.

EXHIBIT 15–1   Elements of an Integrated Marketing Communication Strategy

Media/Characteristics	Personalization	Interactivity	Message Control	Information	Cost per Exposure
Traditional Media					
• Mass advertising	None	None	High	Low	Very low
• Sales promotions	Depends	Depends	High	Low	Low
• In-store marketing/ design elements	Depends	Depends	High	Depends	Low
• Personal selling	High	High	Medium	High	Very high
• Public relations	None	None	Depends	Medium	Low
New Media					
• Online	Depends	Depends	High	High	Depends
• Social media	High	High	Depends	Depends	Low

TRADITIONAL MEDIA ELEMENTS

Retailers use various traditional media elements: mass media advertising, promotions, in-store marketing, personal selling, and public relations. Each of these five media elements and their subcategories is discussed next.

Mass Media Advertising

Advertising entails the placement of announcements and persuasive messages purchased by retailers and other organizations that seek to inform and/or persuade members of a particular target market or audience about their products, services, organizations, or ideas.[2] After automobile manufacturers, retailers are the second-largest group of national advertisers, spending more than $20 billion annually. Amazon, Apple, Best Buy, Walt Disney, McDonald's, Sears Holding, Macy's, Target, and Home Depot are among the largest advertisers.[3]

Mass advertising is typically used to generate awareness in the need recognition stage of the buying process (see Chapter 4) because of its low cost per exposure and the control retailers have over content and the timing of the communication. But it is not as effective for helping consumers search for information because the amount of information that can be transmitted is limited. By its very nature, it is impossible to personalize messages or interact directly with customers. But it is a cost-effective method for announcing sales or new-store openings. Traditionally, mass advertising has been limited to newspapers, magazines, direct mail, TV, radio, and billboards.

REFACT

On a list of the top U.S. advertisers, Amazon ranks fourth among the various retailers that appear on the list. In 2011, it spent $1.4 billion worldwide ($778 million in the United States) on advertising in various formats—largely to promote its Kindle devices.[4]

Newspapers   Retailing and newspaper advertising grew up together over the past century. But the growth in newspaper advertising by retailers has slowed recently as retailers have begun using other media. Still, 57 percent of newspapers' advertising dollars are generated by retailers.[5] In addition to displaying ads with their editorial content, newspapers distribute freestanding inserts. A **freestanding insert (FSI),** also called a **preprint,** is an advertisement printed at the retailer's expense and distributed as an insert in the newspaper. Although popular with advertisers, there are so many FSIs in some newspapers that readers can become overwhelmed. As a result, some retailers have reduced the number of FSIs they use because of the clutter and because younger readers, who may be their primary target market, don't regularly read newspapers.

Newspapers are distributed in well-defined local market areas, so they are effective for targeting specific retail markets. Newspapers also offer a quick response. There's only a short time between the deadline for receiving the advertisement and the time that the advertisement will appear. Thus, newspapers are useful for delivering messages on short notice.

Newspaper readers can go through an advertisement at their own pace and refer to the part of the advertisement when they want. But newspaper ads

When customers see this ad, it highlights the deals that are being offered at Target.

aren't effective for showing merchandise, particularly when it is important to illustrate colors, because of the poor reproduction quality.

The life of a newspaper advertisement is short because the newspaper is usually discarded after it gets read. In contrast, magazine advertising has a longer life because consumers tend to save magazines and read them several times during a week or month.

Finally, the cost of developing newspaper ads is relatively low. However, the cost of delivering the message may be high if the newspaper's circulation is much broader than the retailer's target market, requiring the retailer to pay for exposure that won't generate sales.

Magazines   Advertising in national magazines is mostly done by national retailers such as Target and The Gap. With the growth of local magazines, regional editions of national magazines, and specialized magazines, local retailers can take advantage of this medium. Many magazines either offer both a print and an online version, or have transitioned to online only. This change in the business model for some magazines from print to online (or both) enables retailers to reach potential customers at a lower cost per exposure. Retailers tend to use it for image advertising because the reproduction quality is high. Due to the lead time—the time between submitting the advertisement and publication—a major disadvantage of magazine advertising is that the timing is difficult to coordinate with special events and sales.

Direct Mail   **Direct mail** includes any brochure, catalog, advertisement, or other printed marketing material delivered directly to the consumer through the mail or a private delivery company.[6] Retailers have communicated with their customers through the mail for as long as the mail has existed. The vast majority of direct mail goes to customers or the current resident of the household on a nonpersonalized basis. With the advent of loyalty and CRM programs, retailers are now able to personalize their direct mail to all customers, to a subset of the customers according to their previous purchases, or even on a personalized basis to individual customers. Although relatively expensive on a per-customer basis (because of printing, mail costs, and a relatively low response rate), direct mail is still extensively used by many retailers because people respond favorably to personal messages.

Television   Television commercials can be placed on a national network or local station. Retailers typically use TV for image advertising, to take advantage of the high production quality and the opportunity to communicate through both visual images and sound. Television ads can also demonstrate product usage. For example, TV is an excellent medium for car, furniture, and consumer electronics dealers.

In addition to its high production costs, broadcast time for national TV advertising is expensive. **Spots,** which are ads in local markets as opposed to national ads, have relatively small audiences, but they may be economical for local retailers. To offset the high production costs, many vendors provide modular commercials in which the retailer can insert its name or a "tag" after information about the vendor's merchandise.

Radio   Many retailers use radio advertising because messages can be easily targeted to a specific segment of the market.[7] Some radio stations' audiences are highly loyal to their announcers, especially in a "talk radio" format. When these announcers promote a retailer, listeners are impressed. The cost of developing and broadcasting radio commercials is relatively low.

One disadvantage of radio advertising, however, is that listeners generally treat the radio broadcast as background, which limits the attention they give the message. Consumers must get the information from a radio commercial when it is broadcast; they cannot refer back to the advertisement for information they didn't hear or don't remember.

Sales Promotions

Sales promotions are special incentives or excitement-building programs that encourage consumers to purchase a particular product or service. Some sales promotions have become integral components of retailers' long-term customer relationship management programs, which they use to build customer loyalty. The ability to personalize messages and interact directly with customers depends on the type of sales promotion retailers use. Generally, however, sales promotions provide relatively little information. But on the positive side, the ability to control the message is high and the cost per exposure is low. The tools used in sales promotions, such as coupons, rebates, and premiums, are discussed next.

Coupons   **Coupons** offer a discount on the price of specific items when they are purchased. Coupons are issued by manufacturers and retailers in newspapers, on products, on the shelf, at the cash register, over the Internet, on mobile devices, and through the mail. Retailers use coupons because they are thought to induce customers to try products for the first time, convert first-time buyers into regular users, encourage large purchases, increase usage, and protect market share against competition. Some retailers have linked coupons directly to their loyalty programs. Using detailed consumer behavior data collected through its loyalty cards, Safeway offers very personalized bargains. If one consumer buys several of the store's private-label products, such as paper towels and glass cleaner for example, she will receive an enticing coupon for the store's private-label dishwashing detergent too. Another customer might receive a coupon for the same item, but if his behavior indicates he is less likely to buy the store brand (because he has purchased name brand paper towels in the past), that coupon will be worth much less.[9]

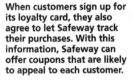

When customers sign up for its loyalty card, they also agree to let Safeway track their purchases. With this information, Safeway can offer coupons that are likely to appeal to each customer.

Rebates   **Rebates** provide another form of discounts for consumers. In this case, however, the manufacturer, instead of the retailer, issues the refund as a portion of the purchase price returned to the buyer in the form of cash. Retailers generally welcome rebates from vendors because they generate sales in the same way that coupons do, but the retailers incur no handling costs. Vendors can offer generous rebates because the likelihood that consumers will actually apply for the rebate is low because of the hassle involved in doing so. But some retailers offer "instant rebates" that can be redeemed at the point-of-purchase. Staples and Apple have simplified the rebate redemption process with "Easy Rebates" and Apple.com/promo.[11]

Premiums   A **premium** offers an item for free or at a bargain price to reward some type of behavior, such as buying, sampling, or testing. Such rewards build goodwill among consumers, who often perceive high value in them. Premiums can be distributed in a variety of ways: They can be included by the manufacturer in the product packaging, such as the toys inside cereal boxes; placed visibly on the package, such as a coupon for free milk on a box of Cheerios; handed out in the store; or delivered in the mail, such as the free perfume offers that Victoria's Secret mails to customers.

In-Store Marketing/Design Elements

Retailers and their vendors are focusing considerable attention on in-store marketing design elements and activities. As we discussed in Chapter 4, customers often make purchase decisions while in the store. So store environmental elements, such as eye-catching point-of-purchase displays, and in-store activities, such as providing merchandise samples and special events, can increase customers' time in the store and their propensity to purchase. These in-store marketing/design elements are discussed next. Chapter 17 examines other store design and visual merchandising techniques that influence customers' purchase behavior.

Point-of-Purchase Displays   **Point-of-purchase (POP) displays** are merchandise displays located at the point of purchase, such as at the checkout counter in a supermarket. Retailers have long recognized that the most valuable real estate in the store is at the POP. Customers see products like a magazine or a candy bar while they are waiting to pay for their items and impulsively purchase them. POP displays can't be personalized to each customer because the message is the same to everyone. Interactivity is low. Information content can range from minimal to high. Finally, the cost per exposure is low.

Samples   **Samples** offer potential customers the opportunity to try a product or service before they make a buying decision. Distributing samples is one of the most costly sales promotion tools, but it is also one of the most effective. Retailers of cosmetics and fragrances, as well as grocery stores, frequently employ sampling. For instance, Whole Foods provides samples of products to customers. Costco uses so many samples that customers can have an entire meal during their shopping trip. In the case of cosmetics and fragrances, sampling can be highly personal because the sales associate can easily switch to a sample a customer might want or need; but this is generally not the case for food stores because everyone typically receives the same sample. Sampling can also be highly interactive, the message can be controlled, and the information provided can be high because the sales associate

Point-of-purchase displays stimulate impulse purchases while customers are waiting to pay for their purchases.

can adapt based on the situation and the customer. Cost per exposure, however, is relatively high.

Special Events   A **special event** is a sales promotion program comprising a number of sales promotion techniques built around a seasonal, cultural, sporting, musical, or some other type of activity.[12] Special events can generate excitement and traffic to the store. Apparel and department stores do trunk shows, made-to-measure events, and fashion shows. Sporting goods stores offer demonstrations of equipment, while grocery stores might have cooking classes. Bookstores hold readings and book signings. Car dealerships can have rallies or shows of new or vintage models. Even if the sales registered during the event aren't significant, the long-term effect can be quite beneficial.

Home Depot is a proud sponsor of NASCAR.

Although it does not always take place in stores, **event sponsorship** occurs when retailers support various activities (financially or otherwise), usually in the cultural or sports and entertainment sectors. Some retailers sponsor sporting events such as the Little Caesar's Pizza Bowl in Detroit. Others buy naming rights to a sporting venue, such as Target Field, which is home to MLB's Minnesota Twins, and HSBC Arena, home to the NHL's Buffalo Sabres, or to a NASCAR car, as Home Depot has done.[13]

Special events can't be personalized, but they are highly interactive. The message and information can be controlled, and the cost per exposure is low.

Personal Selling

Personal selling is a communication process in which sales associates help customers satisfy their needs through face-to-face exchanges of information. Salespeople can personalize every message to fit the customers' needs and provide as much information as needed. It is highly interactive, and to the extent that the salespeople are well trained, the message can be controlled. Yet, the cost of communicating directly with a potential customer is quite high compared with other forms of promotion. Customers can buy many products and services without the help of a salesperson, but salespeople simplify the buying process by providing information and services that save customers time and effort. The impact of personal selling on customer service is examined further in Chapter 18.

Public Relations

Public relations (PR) involves managing communications and relationships to achieve various objectives, such as building and maintaining a positive image of the retailer, handling or heading off unfavorable stories or events, and maintaining positive relationships with the media. In many cases, public relations activities support other promotional efforts by generating "free" media attention and general goodwill. PR activities cannot be personalized and are not interactive. To the extent that the media interprets the message the way the retailer has intended and disseminates it, the message can be somewhat controlled, and the information content is modest. The cost per exposure is relatively low. The types of PR campaigns retailers use are as varied as the retailers themselves. We examine several different ways in which retailers employ public relations in their communications strategy.

Neiman Marcus and Its Christmas Catalog   The Neiman Marcus Christmas book is perhaps the nation's best-known retail catalog. Its reputation is largely due to its annual tradition of ultra-extravagant his-and-hers gifts. The unique

A recent Neiman Marcus Christmas catalog features a McLaren 12C Spider for $354,000, and his-and-hers watches, featuring scenes of Paris and Geneva, and trips to each location for $1.1 million.

merchandise generates free publicity as journalists and style watchers are astonished at what the retailer came up with each year.

The Christmas book was first distributed in 1915 as a Christmas card, inviting Neiman Marcus customers to visit the store during the holiday season. In the late 1950s, customers were asking Neiman Marcus about unique gifts and merchandise not available in the store or from other catalogs. In the 2012 Christmas book, readers came across "the most technologically advanced supercar ever," the 2013 McLaren 12C Spider, for $354,000. That price might seem like a bargain compared with the gift listed a few pages later: a set of $1.1 million, his-and-hers watches, by Van Cleef & Arpels, that featured scenes of Paris and Geneva—and came complete with trips to each location.[14] The Neiman Marcus Christmas book is mailed to 1.8 million customers and is also available on its website.

Macy's and Cause-Related Marketing   Starting in 2011, Macy's partnered with many charities in a successful **cause-related marketing campaign** (i.e., commercial activity in which businesses and charities form a partnership to market an image, product, or service for their mutual benefit). In addition to providing a benefit for society, its Shop for a Cause campaign generates a lot of publicity. The program allowed partnering charities to sell coupons, at $5 each, that gave the purchaser a 25 percent discount at Macy's on a specific day. As long as they were nonprofit organizations, charities were eligible to participate, leading to a wide range of partnerships, from Autism Speaks to The Greater Boston Food Bank to YMCAs to animal rescues to the Alliance for Lupus Research. Meanwhile, Macy's sold coupons in its stores to benefit the March of Dimes. Each charity retained all proceeds from the coupon sales, and Macy's benefited from increased sales. In 2011, the campaign raised $38 million for charity, and Macy's earned approximately $600 million in sales.[15]

Subway pays to have its products featured in nontraditional situations, such as when contestants on *The Biggest Loser* run from one restaurant to another.

Retailers and Product Placement   When retailers and vendors use **product placement,** they pay to have their product included in nontraditional situations, such as in a scene in a movie or television program.[16] The characters played by Salma Hayak and Alec Baldwin discuss, during an episode of *30 Rock*, whether McDonald's McFlurry is the best dessert in the world. On *The Big Bang Theory*, the characters frequently appear eating at Penny's workplace, The Cheesecake Factory, and Sheldon once demanded "access to The Cheesecake Factory walk-in freezer." Even in reality shows such as *The Biggest Loser*, contestants run from one Subway restaurant to the next.

NEW MEDIA ELEMENTS

Over the past decade or so, the use of newer forms of media, such as online (e.g., websites, e-mail, and mobile), and social media (e.g., YouTube, Facebook, blogs, and Twitter) has exploded. Each of these new media elements is discussed next.

LO2

Identify the new media elements.

Online Media

Websites   Retailers are increasing their emphasis on communicating with customers through their websites, which are used to build their brand images; inform customers of store locations, special events, and the availability of merchandise in local stores; and sell merchandise and services. Many retailers also devote areas of their websites to community building. These sites offer an opportunity for customers with similar interests to learn about products and services that support their hobbies and to share information with others. Visitors can also post questions seeking information and/or comments about issues, products, and services. For example, REI, an outdoor apparel and equipment retailer, offers adventure travel planning resources for hiking trips, bike tours, paddling, adventure cruises, and other trips. By doing so, REI creates a community of customers who engage in activities using the merchandise that REI sells. The community thus reinforces REI's brand image.

Many retailers encourage customers to post reviews of products they have bought or used on their websites. Research has shown that these online product reviews increase customer loyalty and provide a competitive advantage for sites that offer them.[18]

Depending on how customers use retailers' websites, they can experience a very personalized and interactive experience. The message can contain lots of information and is easily controlled. The cost per exposure is comparatively moderate because the cost of maintaining and operating a website can be expensive.

Retailers are actively using **search engine marketing (SEM)** to improve the visibility of their websites in searches. One SEM method is to use **search engine optimization (SEO)**, which is creating and adjusting website content to show up closer to the top of a **search engine results page (SERP).** These SERPs list the results that a search engine provides, in response to a user's keyword query. Thus, SEO is used to enhance unpaid or organic searches. Another SEM method is using paid search through Google's sponsored link advertising program. These results are placed above and to the right of natural or organic search results.[19]

E-mail   **E-mail** involves sending messages over the Internet to specific individuals. Retailers use e-mail to inform customers of new merchandise and special promotions, confirm the receipt of an order, and indicate when an order has been shipped. The increased use of customer databases has enabled retailers to identify and track consumers over time and across purchase situations (see Chapter 11). As a result, e-mail can be highly personal and the message very controlled. However, when the same message is delivered electronically to all recipients, e-mails more closely resemble the more impersonal medium, mass advertising. Because e-mail recipients can respond back to the retailer, it is considered an interactive medium. Finally, the cost per exposure is low.

Mobile Communications   **Mobile communications** are delivered through wireless handheld devices, such as cellular telephones, and **m-commerce** or **mobile commerce** can involve completing a transaction via the cell phone.[21] Smartphones have become far more than tools for placing calls; they offer a kind

REFACT

Despite the promise of communicating with customers and integrating promotions across various channels, only about 12 percent of retailers can access customers' online orders from within their stores. Furthermore, less than half of all retailers actually provide tailored recommendations to their customers.[17]

REFACT

According to a recent online poll, 93 percent of people would use a "Do Not Track" function if it were available on web browsers to limit intrusions on their privacy by marketers.[20]

Once Foursquare users check in at participating Walgreen's stores, they can download special deals to their phone, along with a scannable barcode.

of mobile computer with the ability to obtain sports scores, weather, music, videos, and text messages, as well as purchase merchandise. Retailers' success with mobile communications rests on apps that enable effective communications through a device with a small screen.

Retailers use applications such as Foursquare to communicate with mobile phone users and send them messages on the basis of their location, as determined by GPS technology.[22] Foursquare awards points to consumers who try out local retailers. With the GPS-based application, users also can recommend nearby retailers to friends in the area. Furthermore, the app's data analytic capabilities allow retailers to track the impact of mobile marketing campaigns.

Target uses the Shopkick app to award points to customers who walk around a store and scan products; they can redeem these points for various rewards. Other retailers use mobile channels to deliver coupons or other promotional offers, such as free shipping to customers who purchase online from the retailer while in its brick-and-mortar store. Finally, retailers might use the related location-based technology to deliver tailored, local messages to customers to drive them into their stores.

Despite the promise of mobile communications, it continues to have its drawbacks. One study found that 90 percent of U.S. survey respondents had absolutely no interest in receiving mobile ads.[23] Combining geographic location services with social media could increase crime rates;[24] for example, burglars would know how far away homeowners are from their homes.

Numerous retailers have developed applications that their consumers can use on their smartphones to access a host of services. Retailing View 15.1 highlights Staples' efforts to make things easy for their customers.

15.1 RETAILING VIEW Staples' Mobile Strategy: Reaching Customers through Smartphones

The world's largest office products company, Staples, with annual sales of approximately $25 billion, is taking an aggressive stance toward entering the mobile world. Sensing an opportunity, it is making its customers' lives easier through its mobile site and application. In 2010, the company initiated its mobile strategy by launching a mobile-optimized website to allow customers easier access on smartphones. In June 2011, it relaunched the mobile site, m.staples.com, to include product ratings and reviews, a store locator, and a store inventory search.

Also in 2011, Staples introduced a mobile application for both iPhone and Android smartphones. The app provides a streamlined version of the website, but it also supports coupon and promotion downloads. Furthermore, the app is geo-aware, such that as soon as a customer comes within a mile of a Staples store, a coupon is automatically offered.

Finally, the app allows users to build smart lists that track their supply needs and links to their Staples Rewards status (the retailer's loyalty program). By combining the smart list capability of the app with a customer's purchase history, Staples builds "virtual supply closets" for customers. The virtual supply closets combine not just customers' purchase history but also their scanned SKUs that they saved in their phones while in a store.

Sources: Christopher Hosford, "Staples' Mobile Strategy Based on Customer Convenience, Loyalty," *B to B Magazine*, March 12, 2012; Staples.com, "About Us," and "Staples Helps Small Business Owners Get Ahead in the New Year"; and Ben Stillitoe, "Staples Plans New Social Media Strategy," *Retail Gazette*, December 13, 2011.

DISCUSSION QUESTIONS

Have you used mobile apps developed by retailers? If yes, do you find them useful?

Social Media

Social media include various forms of electronic communication, which users can employ to create online communities in which they share ideas, information, their interpersonal messages, and other content (e.g., videos). Three major online facilitators of social media are YouTube, Facebook, and Twitter. As another online vehicle that encourages word-of-mouth communications, online forums enable consumers to review, communicate about, and aggregate information about products, prices, and promotions. These forums also allow users to interact among themselves (e.g., form a community).[25] Such online communities enable users to provide other like-minded consumers and retailers with their thoughts about and evaluations of a retailer's products or services.

Retailers use social media to engage their customers in proactive dialogue. When a retailer provides content in a social media website, people often begin sharing and commenting on it. The retailer then must monitor the feedback and respond if necessary—especially if the commentary is negative. For example, **sentiment mining** is a process whereby retailers can tap into a variety of online chat formats to collect consumer comments and then analyze these data to identify customers' overall attitudes and preferences for products and advertising campaigns. Scouring millions of sites by combining automated online search tools with text analysis techniques, sentiment mining yields qualitative data that provide new insights into what consumers really think. Retailers plugged into this real-time information can become more nimble, allowing for quick changes in a product rollout or a new advertising campaign. Retailing View 15.2 highlights how Dell uses the various social media analysis tools to better serve its customers.

RETAILING VIEW   Harnessing the Power of Social Media to Make Customers Happy   **15.2**

Social media has revolutionized how companies communicate with, listen to, and learn from their customers. The volume of information generated can be a powerful tool for improving all business operations, including product design, technical support, and customer service, but it is also a very daunting task simply to make sense of it all! Consistent with its image as a global leader in computing, Dell is recognized as one of the top social media brands worldwide.

The company has always valued consumer input, according to founder and CEO Michael Dell: "One of Dell's founding principles was really about listening and learning from our customers, and being able to take that feedback to improve." Dell still offers traditional online support forums, which post questions and answers for different user groups and by topic. Now, however, social media channels like Facebook and Twitter have vastly accelerated that learning curve. Dell's mobile phone app also helps users stay connected on the road.

Each of Dell's multiple, highly developed social media channels differs qualitatively. They give the company and its customers the immediacy of instant chat and conversations through Facebook, LinkedIn, Twitter, and Google+, as well as Dell's flagship blog Direct2Dell.com and a host of other blogs.

Listening and analysis—or social media monitoring—is key. It enables Dell to identify salient customer input

and trends. By teaming with social media monitor partner Salesforce Radian6, for example, Dell couples text analysis and high-volume, digital content-gathering technology methods to monitor approximately 25,000 conversations a day. In addition to customer support, the new media provide company and product news, as well as food for thought to its customers about digital business and digital life.

Dell gathers and monitors these online chats, posts responses or ideas, and engages in other discussions from its new social media listening command center. The staff includes 70 trained employees who follow and respond to social media conversations in 11 languages. All tweets, Facebook posts, and other comments that warrant a Dell response are answered within 24 hours.

Sources: Andrea Edwards, "Dell—a Top Five Social Media Brand—Looking for Fresh Ideas," *SAJE Communication*, October 12, 2011; "Introducing Dell's Social Media Command Center," Dell.com; Ed Twittel, "How Dell Really Listens to Its Customers," *ReadWriteEnterprise*, July 22, 2011; and "Social Media," Dell.com.

DISCUSSION QUESTION

Have you interacted with a retailer using one of its social media tools? If yes, was the response satisfactory?

Social media not only allow retailers to respond to unhappy customers but also to monitor trends and respond to consumer demand. Walmart uses social media to develop services and select products, such as a Christmas layaway option, by engaging with them on Facebook and Twitter.[26] Not all social media invokes positive results, though.[27] For a high-end Australian fashion boutique called Gasp, social media's power to eliminate boundaries led one of its managers to make things worse after a customer complained online of treatment she received in the store. Rather than apologizing, the manager dismissed her as unlikely to have purchased anyway, because she was "acclimated to buying from 'clothing for the masses' type retailers."[28]

As these various examples of social media indicate, they can be very personal and interactive. When the message is produced by the retailer, it can be controlled, but when customers are involved, as is the case with reviews, there is little control over the message whatsoever. Likewise, the level of information content is dependent on who is doing the communications. The cost per exposure for social media is relatively low compared to traditional media. The largest facilitators of online social media today are YouTube, Facebook, blogs, and the microblog, Twitter.

Home Depot fosters its identity with instructional do-it-yourself videos on YouTube.

YouTube On this video-sharing social media platform, users upload, share, view, and comment on videos. This medium gives retailers a chance to express themselves in a different way than they have before. A retailer such as the television home shopping company HSN, discussed in Retailing View 15.3, can broadcast its own channel, that is, a YouTube site that contains content relevant only to the company's own products.[29]

YouTube also provides an effective medium for hosting contests and posting instructional videos. Home Depot has attracted more than 18,000 subscribers and racked up more than 41 million views with an array of videos detailing new products available in stores, as well as instructional do-it-yourself videos, like "How-to Tips for Mowing Your Lawn" or "How to Repair a Toilet."[30] These videos maintain the core identity of the Home Depot brand, while also adding value for consumers, who learn useful ways to improve their homes.

Facebook This social media platform with more than 1 billion active users[31] gives companies a forum to interact with fans. Retailers have access to the same features that regular users do, including a "wall" where they can post company updates, photos, and videos or participate in a discussion board.

For Macy's, Facebook has long been a promising communication outlet, so it also became one of the first retailers to adopt the Facebook Page format. Furthermore, the Facebook timeline format has worked well in highlighting its events. Macy's has started to advertise more on Facebook, using more targeted ads to communicate with current and potential fans. Adapting along with the social media site represents just one facet in its broader plan to revamp its social media initiatives to attract more 25- to 54-year-old female consumers, along with some Gen Y fashionistas. It believes that Facebook is a great way to get the right message in front of the right people.[32]

It also provides an appealing means to target local groups of consumers for smaller retailers. For example, PCC Natural Markets in Seattle engages customers

RETAILING VIEW   YouTube and HSN   15.3

Begun as a local cable channel in 1982, Home Shopping Network (HSN) offered consumers a central location from which to buy through their televisions. As competition in this field increased, HSN tailored its communication strategy to reach more shoppers. For example, HSN.com is one of the most visited e-commerce sites. But perhaps the most powerful tool HSN has added to its communication strategy is YouTube.

By reaching 40 to 50 percent of the company's target market, YouTube gives HSN a way to interact differently with customers and further increase its share of wallet with its current customers. The video format humanizes the connection and provides additional information about products.

For consumers, YouTube offers a seamless experience. Products promoted on HSN, such as Tori Spelling's jewelry line, are available on YouTube almost immediately after they appear on television. Then, HSN marketers can use the information gathered from YouTube to target its direct mail campaigns. For example, it could send jewelry promotions to households that viewed the YouTube video clip for a necklace from the Tori Spelling Collection. Consumer responses get monitored 24/7 and measured against hourly sales goals. There's never a dull moment—it's like the CNN of shopping.

Sources: www.gstatic.com/youtube/engagement/platform/autoplay/advertise/ downloads/YouTube_InTheKnow.pdf; www.gstatic.com/youtube/engagement/

YouTube allows customers to view Tori Spelling's jewelry line almost immediately after it appears on HSN.

platform/autoplay/advertise/downloads/YouTube_BrandChannels.pdf; www.gstatic.com/youtube/engagement/platform/autoplay/advertise/ downloads/YouTube_Insight.pdf; and http://mediacommons.futureofthebook. org/imr/2010/03/24/re-branding-dynasty-tori-spellings-hsn-clips-youtube.

DISCUSSION QUESTION

Do you think accessing HSN merchandise via YouTube is useful?

in social media dialogue on Facebook about local products. To encourage participation in local events, such as its "Taste PCC: A Local Food Celebration" or "Deli Throw Down" contest, it spread vast word-of-mouth communication with minimal investment by relying on postings and tweets through Facebook and Twitter.[33]

Blogs   On a **blog (weblog)**, an individual blogger or a group of users regularly post their opinions and various topical information on a web page. The administrator of the blog can either be a retailer, an independent person or a firm. A well-received blog can communicate trends, announce special events, and create **word of mouth**, which is communication among people about an entity such as a retailer or a product or service.[34] Blogs connect customers by forming a community, allowing the company to respond directly to customers' comments, and facilitate long-term relationships between customers and the company. By their very nature, blogs are supposed to be transparent and contain authors' honest observations, which can help customers determine their trust and loyalty levels. If, however, the blog is created or sponsored by a retailer, the information may be positively biased. Also, retailers have limited control over the content posted on blog; thus the information

Retailers like PCC Natural Markets use Facebook to communicate with customers and create a sense of community.

posted can be negative or incorrect. Many retailers use blogs as part of the communication strategy. A top-ranked retailer blog is Omnivoracious, Amazon's blog, which is, naturally, about books. Dell, Apple, Sears, Best Buy, and QVC also have highly rated blogs.[35]

Twitter   In discussions of social media, Facebook and Twitter often get mentioned in the same breath, but they differ in some critical ways. Twitter is a **microblog**—a short version of a blog—in which users are limited to 140-character messages. The use of 140-character messages forces retailers to post short, timely and relevant posts. Where a retailer may use Facebook to encourage discussions of their brand, promotions, or even ask their "friends" to post videos, they are more likely to use Twitter to announce up-to-date or fast changing information to excite consumers. Twitter is actively used by both small and large retailers. Smaller retailers with limited marketing budgets love the response they can induce by sending a promotional message immediately. Before the 2013 blizzard Nemo, a local food truck tweeted at the beginning of the day, "Headed to @dumbofoodtrucks Front St & Main St! Come get Korilla before Nemo does!" allowing its customers to know both where to find them and create a sense of urgency before the storm—a huge captive audience for a local entity.[36]

Large retailers may have enough funds to mass-market through national campaigns, but Twitter provides them with a way to stay in personal touch with customers. The well-reputed Wegmans grocery store chain posts the dates and times on which it receives its produce deliveries, so customers who prize the very freshest produce can show up just as the vegetables are getting unloaded. Along with these delivery details, Wegmans tweets grower and farmer information, as well as available stock. Wegmans also uses social media to answer customer questions.

Twitter has also changed the way customers get product or service information and register praise and complaints. Whereas once customers with questions about a product or service had to call up the retailer's customer service line and sit through prerecorded voice prompts, today they can turn to Twitter to get immediate feedback. Retailers measure Twitter customer service success by the quality, accuracy, and timeliness of their response to customers' service issues.

Penske and other retailers use Twitter to address customer questions.

For example, the Penske car rental agency implemented its Twitter customer service program after spending an entire year observing how customers were using Twitter for customer service issues. In line with its findings, it trained its call-center employees to use the new technology and monitor the Twitter feed from 7:00 a.m. to 11:00 p.m. daily. Customers who tweet their car rental questions receive nearly instantaneous responses.[37]

COMMUNICATION PROGRAMS BUILD BRAND IMAGES AND CUSTOMER LOYALTY

Communication programs using the old and new media discussed in the previous sections can have both long-term and short-term effects on a retailer's business. From a long-term perspective, communications programs can be used to create and maintain a strong, differentiated image of the retailer and its store brands. This image develops customer loyalty and therefore creates a strategic advantage. Thus, brand image-building communication programs complement the objective of a retailer's CRM program discussed in Chapter 11.

LO3

Understand how retailers use communication programs to develop brand images and build customer loyalty.

On the other hand, retailers frequently use communication programs to realize the short-term objective of increasing sales during a specified time period. For example, retailers often have sales during which some or all of its merchandise is priced at a discount for a short time. Grocery stores usually place weekly ads with coupons that can be used to save money on purchases made during the week.

In this section, we discuss the role of communications programs in building **brand images**—a strategic objective. The following sections focus on the operational issues involved in developing and implementing communication programs.

Brands

A **brand** is "a name, term, design, symbol or any other feature that identifies one seller's good or service as distinct from those of other sellers."[38] In a retailing context, the name of the retailer usually serves as the brand. This type of brand informs consumers of the type of merchandise and services provided by this particular named retailer. As we discussed in Chapter 13, some retailers develop private-label brands that are exclusively sold through their channels. In some cases, private-label merchandise bears the retailer's name, such as Walgreens aspirin and Victoria's Secret lingerie. In other cases, special brand names are used, such as Walmart's Ol' Roy dog food and Sears' Die Hard batteries.

Value of Brand Image

Brands provide value to both customers and retailers. For customers, they provide information in advance about the shopping experience that they are likely to face when they patronize this retailer. They also affect customers' confidence in their decisions to buy merchandise from a retailer. Finally, brands can enhance customers' satisfaction with merchandise and services. Consumers feel different when wearing jewelry bought from Tiffany & Co. rather than Zales or when staying at a Ritz-Carlton hotel rather than a Fairfield Inn.

The value a brand image provides retailers is referred to as **brand equity**. A brand with good equity, also known as a strong brand name, influences customers'

The Ace Hardware ad on the left focuses on a short-term objective—building sales during Mother's Day. The Abt ad on the right is directed toward building Abt's brand image—a long-term objective.

decision processes, often by encouraging their repeat visits, which in turn leads to greater loyalty. In addition, strong brand names enable retailers to increase their margins because customers will tolerate higher prices. When retailers have high customer loyalty, they can engage in premium pricing and reduce their reliance on price promotions to attract customers. Brands with weaker images instead must offer lower prices and have frequent sales to maintain their market share.

Customer loyalty to brands arises from heightened awareness of the brand and beliefs and emotional ties to it. As noted in Chapter 4, retailers need to appear in a customer's consideration set, and awareness can help guarantee this presence. Retail brands such as Walmart and Target are so well known by consumers that they nearly always appear in their consideration sets. Customers also identify with specific brands. They have beliefs about the retailer's offering and have strong emotional ties to its brands. Going to Target has become a cool experience because people consider it trendy to save money and buy fashionable merchandise—including a limited collection by the haute couture designer Missoni—all at the same time and in the same store in which they grab laundry detergent.[39] These customers affectionately use the faux French pronunciation "Tar-zhay" to refer to Target. High brand awareness and strong emotional connections reduce their incentives or motivation to switch to competing retailers.

Finally, retailers with strong brand names can leverage their brands to introduce new retail concepts with only a limited amount of marketing effort. For example, The Gap has efficiently extended its brand to GapKids, gapbody, GapMaternity, and babyGap. Retailing View 15.4 outlines how J.Crew has managed to develop its own brand identity, distinct from those of its closest competitors.

Building Brand Equity

The activities that a retailer needs to undertake to build brand equity for its firm or its private-label merchandise are to create a high level of brand awareness, develop favorable associations with the brand name, and consistently reinforce the image of the brand.

Brand Awareness   **Brand awareness** refers to a potential customer's ability to recognize or recall that the brand name is a particular type of retailer or product/ service. Thus, brand awareness is the strength of the link between the brand name and the type of merchandise or service in the minds of customers.

There is a range of awareness, from aided recall to top-of-mind awareness. **Aided recall** occurs when consumers indicate they know the brand when the

RETAILING VIEW   Building the J.Crew Brand   15.4

The brand has strong name recognition: Lots of shoppers have heard of J.Crew. But in the mid-2000s, many of those shoppers heard the name and thought only "boring and preppy." When CEO Millard "Mickey" Drexler took the reins in 2003, he decided that to change J.Crew's image, he needed to appeal to customers' hearts through their fingers—that is, with the feel and look of quality clothing. By providing high-quality versions of classic clothing pieces at what it considers reasonable prices, J.Crew has been able to increase its profits, lower its debt, and expand the number of stores.

As the company promises on its website, it "partners with the finest global fabric mills and craftsmen— as well as with iconic brands such as Jack Purcell, Timex, Thomas Mason and Red Wing (to name just a few)."

J.Crew's CEO Mickey Drexler helped change the retailer's image by providing high-quality versions of classic clothing at what it considers to be reasonable prices.

Customers, therefore, come to associate the J.Crew name with high-end suppliers. But such quality comes at a price. Customers of J.Crew pay more for these brands for the promise of higher quality.

Other mall-based retailers operate at much lower price points. No one is likely to find leather shoes made by Alden at The Gap, as customers can at J.Crew. Even for seemingly similar offerings, J.Crew sets itself apart in discernible ways, such as adding hand-stitched sequins to a basic T-shirt.

Mickey Drexler also believes in allowing customers to dictate the brand image, which has resulted in the launch of uniquely female- and male-oriented lines and stores. When he received feedback indicating that women were purchasing multiple J.Crew sundresses in different colors to use as bridesmaids' gowns, he launched J. Crew bridal. The line opened its first dedicated bridal store in May 2010. Spurred by the success of its Ludlow line of men's suits, sports coats, and slacks, J.Crew opened several standalone Ludlow shops, as well as its men's-only Liquor Store in the Tribeca neighborhood of Manhattan, named after its former tenant, a liquor store. These shops carry not only Ludlow clothing, but also famous name-brand accessories. When European customers complained about

their inability to have J.Crew merchandise shipped overseas, he entered a partnership with an online retailer to make items available nearly worldwide.

Such positioning is part of what has earned Drexler the nickname "the merchant prince." Although J.Crew holds tight to its hard-earned preppy reputation, it has gained a position in customers' minds as a source of quality at reasonable prices. It also has revealed its ongoing willingness to shift as needed to meet customers' changing, demanding expectations.

Sources: Matthew Sebra, "Store Spotlight: J.Crew Opens Inaugural Ludlow Shop," *GQ*, March 1, 2012; "J.'s Crew," *The Wall Street Journal*, November 26, 2011; Tina Gaudoin, "Mickey Drexler: Retail Therapist," *The Wall Street Journal*, June 10, 2010; Meryl Gordon, "Mickey Drexler's Redemption," *New York Magazine*, May 21, 2005; and www.jcrew.com/AST/FooterNavigation/aboutus.jsp.

DISCUSSION QUESTIONS

How has your perception of J.Crew changed in recent years? Do you like the changes?

name is presented to them. **Top-of-mind awareness**, the highest level of awareness, occurs when consumers mention a specific brand name first when they are asked about the type of retailer, a merchandise category, or a type of service. For example, Container Store has a high top-of-mind awareness if most consumers respond "Container Store" when asked about retailers that sell merchandise for storing and organizing things. High top-of-mind awareness means that a retailer probably will be in the consideration set when customers decide to shop for a type of product or service.

Retailers build top-of-mind awareness by having memorable names; repeatedly exposing their names to customers through advertising, locations, and sponsorships; and using memorable symbols. Some brand names are easy to remember, such as the name Home Depot; because "Home" is in its brand name, it probably is more memorable and closely associated with home improvements than the name Lowe's.

Zara does very little advertising but has high awareness because of the large number of stores it has in great locations. Customers walk and drive by the stores, look at their artfully designed windows, and are drawn in to check out the offerings. They also know that if they don't purchase the fashionable, reasonably priced apparel when they see it in the store, it probably won't be there the next time.

Symbols involve visual images that typically are more easily recalled than words or phrases and thus are useful for building brand awareness. For example, the images of an apple with an artful "bite" missing and the golden arches enhance the ability of customers to recall the names Apple and McDonald's, respectively.

Sponsorships of well-publicized events also can provide considerable exposure to a retailer's name and increase awareness. For example, watching the Macy's

Macy's annual Thanksgiving Day parade and the accompanying publicity have built top-of-mind awareness for the retailer since 1924.

Thanksgiving parade in New York City has become a holiday tradition for many families. The Macy's brand name is exposed to tens of millions of television viewers for three hours. In addition, newspaper articles are devoted to previewing the parade and describing it afterward.

REFACT

The first Macy's Thanksgiving Day parade, held in 1924, was organized by a handful of volunteer, immigrant employees.[41]

Associations   Building awareness is only one step in developing brand equity, but the value of the brand is largely based on the associations that customers make with the brand name. **Brand associations** are anything linked to or connected with the brand name in a consumer's memory. For example, some of the associations that consumers might have with Apple are its innovative products, easy-to-use interface, Genius Bar, and unique store design, as well as specific products like the iPhone, iPad, and Mac computers. These associations can be negative as well as positive. For example, the brand Apple might also be associated with high prices. These strong associations influence consumer buying behavior. Some common associations that retailers seek to develop with their brand names are as follows:

1. *Merchandise category.* The most common association is to link the retailer to a category of merchandise. For example, Office Depot would like to have consumers associate its name with office supplies. Then, when a need for office supplies arises, consumers immediately think of Office Depot.

2. *Price/quality.* Some retailers, such as Saks Fifth Avenue, want to be associated with offering unique, high-fashion merchandise. Other retailers, such as Walmart, want associations with low prices and good value.

3. *Specific attribute or benefit.* A retailer can link its stores to attributes, such as 7-Eleven's association with providing convenience or Nordstrom's connection with offering a high level of customer service.

4. *Lifestyle or activity.* Some retailers associate their name with a specific lifestyle or activity. For example, Patagonia, a retailer offering outdoor sports equipment, is linked to an active, environmentally friendly lifestyle. Pottery Barn is associated with comfortable living in the home.

When people think of Patagonia, they think about an active, environmentally friendly lifestyle.

PLANNING THE RETAIL COMMUNICATION PROGRAM

LO4

List the steps involved in developing a communication program.

Exhibit 15–2 illustrates the four steps involved in developing and implementing a retail communication program: establish objectives, determine a budget, allocate the budget, and implement and evaluate the program. The following sections detail each of these steps.

EXHIBIT 15–2   Steps in Developing a Retail Communication Program

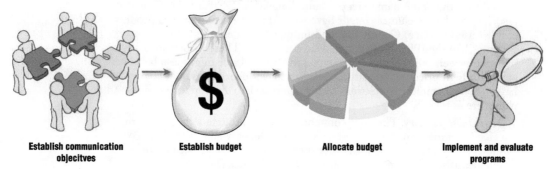

Establish communication objecitves   Establish budget   Allocate budget   Implement and evaluate programs

Establish Objectives

Retailers establish objectives for their communication programs to provide direction for people implementing the program, and a basis for evaluating its effectiveness. As discussed at the beginning of this chapter, some communication programs can have a long-term objective, such as creating or altering a retailer's brand image. Other communication programs focus on improving short-term performance, such as increasing store traffic on a specific weekend.

Although retailers' overall objective is to generate long- and short-term sales and profits, they often use communication objectives rather than sales objectives to plan and evaluate their communication programs. **Communication objectives** are specific goals related to the retail communication mix's effect on the customer's decision-making process.

Exhibit 15–3 shows some hypothetical information about customers in the target market for a Safeway supermarket. This information illustrates the goals

EXHIBIT 15–3
Communication Objectives and Stages in Consumer's Decision-Making Process

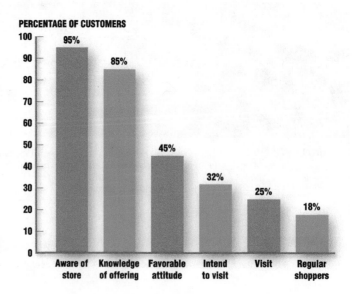

PERCENTAGE OF CUSTOMERS

- Aware of store: 95%
- Knowledge of offering: 85%
- Favorable attitude: 45%
- Intend to visit: 32%
- Visit: 25%
- Regular shoppers: 18%

related to the stages in the consumer decision-making process outlined in Chapter 4. Note that 95 percent of the customers are aware of the store (the first stage in the decision-making process) and 85 percent know the type of merchandise it sells. But only 45 percent of the customers in the target market have a favorable attitude toward the store. Thirty-two percent intend to visit the store during the next few weeks, 25 percent actually visit the store during the next two weeks, and 18 percent regularly shop at the store.

In this hypothetical example, most people know about the store and its offering. The major problem confronting Safeway is the big drop between knowledge and favorable attitudes. Thus, the store should develop a communication program with the objective of increasing the percentage of customers with a favorable attitude toward it.

To effectively implement and evaluate a communication program, its objectives must be clearly stated in quantitative terms. The target audience for the communication mix needs to be defined, along with the degree of change expected and the time period during which the change will be realized.

For example, a communication objective for a Safeway program might be to increase the percentage of customers within a five-mile radius of the store who have a favorable attitude toward the store from 45 to 55 percent within three months. This objective is clear and measurable. It indicates the task that the program should address. The people who implement the program thus know what they're supposed to accomplish.

The communication objectives and approaches used by vendors and retailers differ, and the differences can lead to conflicts. Some of these points of conflict are as follows:

- *Long-term versus short-term goals.* Most communications by vendors are directed toward building a long-term image of their products. In contrast, retailer communications typically are used to announce promotions and special sales that generate short-term revenues.

- *Product versus location.* When vendors advertise their branded products, they aren't concerned about where customers buy them as long as they buy their brands. In contrast, retailers aren't concerned about what brands customers buy as long as they buy them in their stores.

Safeway's communications objective should be to increase the number of people with a favorable attitude toward it.

- *Breadth of merchandise*. Typically, because vendors have a relatively small number of products to promote, they can devote a lot of attention to developing consistent communication programs for each brand they make. Retailers have to develop communication programs that promote a much wider range of products.

Determine the Communication Budget

The second step in developing a retail communication program is to determine a budget (see Exhibit 15–3). The economically correct method for setting the communication budget is marginal analysis (discussed shortly). Even though retailers usually don't have enough information to perform a complete marginal analysis, the method shows managers how they should approach budget-setting programs. The marginal analysis method for setting a communication budget is the approach that retailers should use when making all of their resource allocation decisions, including the number of locations in a geographic area (Chapter 8), the allocation of merchandise to stores (Chapter 13), the staffing of stores (Chapter 16), and the floor and shelf space devoted to merchandise categories (Chapter 17).

An important source of the communication budget is co-op advertising programs. A **co-op (cooperative) program** is a promotional program undertaken by a vendor and a retailer working together. The vendor pays for part of the retailer's promotion but dictates some conditions. For example, Best Buy might pay half of the expenses for ads that feature Sony digital TVs. In addition to lowering costs, co-op advertising enables a retailer to associate its name with well-known national brands and use attractive artwork created by the national brands.

A co-op advertising program with Sony provides funds for Best Buy's promotions.

Marginal Analysis Method   **Marginal analysis** is based on the economic principle that firms should increase communication expenditures as long as each additional dollar spent generates more than a dollar of additional contribution. To illustrate marginal analysis, consider Diane West, the owner and manager of a specialty store selling women's business clothing. Exhibit 15–4 shows her analysis to determine how much she should spend next year on her communication program.

For 21 different communication expense levels (column 1), West estimates her store sales (column 2), gross margin (column 3), and other expenses (columns 4 and 5). Then she calculates the contribution, excluding expenses on communications (column 6), and the profit when the communication expenses are considered (column 7). To estimate the sales generated by different levels of communications, West can simply rely on her judgment and experience, or she might analyze past

Marginal Analysis for Setting Diane West's Communication Budget   EXHIBIT 15–4

Level	Communication Expenses (1)	Sales (2)	Gross Margin Realized (3)	Rental Expense (4)	Personnel Expense (5)	Contribution before Communication Expenses (6) = (3) − (4) − (5)	Profit after Communication Expenses (7) = (6) − (1)	
1	$ 0	$240,000	$ 96,000	$44,000	$52,200	$ (200)	$ (200)	
2	5,000	280,000	112,000	48,000	53,400	10,600	5,600	
3	10,000	330,000	132,000	53,000	54,900	24,100	14,100	
4	15,000	380,000	152,000	58,000	56,400	37,600	22,600	
5	20,000	420,000	168,000	62,000	57,600	48,400	28,400	
6	25,000	460,000	184,000	66,000	58,800	59,200	34,200	
7	30,000	500,000	200,000	70,000	60,000	70,000	40,000	Last year
8	35,000	540,000	216,000	74,000	61,200	80,800	45,800	
9	40,000	570,000	228,000	77,000	62,100	88,900	48,900	
10	45,000	600,000	240,000	80,000	63,000	97,000	52,000	
11	50,000	625,000	250,000	82,500	63,750	103,750	53,750	
12	55,000	650,000	260,000	85,000	64,500	110,500	55,500	Chosen budget
13	60,000	670,000	268,000	87,000	65,100	115,900	55,900	
14	65,000	690,000	276,000	89,000	65,700	121,300	56,300	Best profit
15	70,000	705,000	282,000	90,500	66,150	125,350	55,350	
16	75,000	715,000	286,000	91,500	66,450	128,050	53,050	
17	80,000	725,000	290,000	92,500	66,750	130,750	50,750	
18	85,000	735,000	294,000	93,500	67,050	133,450	48,450	
19	90,000	745,000	298,000	94,500	67,350	136,150	46,150	
20	95,000	750,000	300,000	95,000	67,500	137,500	42,500	
21	100,000	750,000	300,000	95,000	67,500	137,500	37,500	

data to determine the relationship between communication expenses and sales. Historical data also provide information about the gross margin and other expenses as a percentage of sales.

Notice that at low levels of communication expenses, an additional $5,000 in communication expenses generates more than a $5,000 incremental contribution. For example, increasing the communication expense from $15,000 to $20,000 increases the contribution by $10,800 (or $48,400 − $37,600). When the communication expense reaches $65,000, further increases of $5,000 generate less than $5,000 in additional contributions. For example, increasing the budget from $65,000 to $70,000 generates only an additional $4,050 in contribution ($125,350 − $121,300).

In this example, West determines that the maximum profit would be generated with a communication expense budget of $65,000. But she notices that expense levels between $55,000 and $70,000 all result in about the same level of profit. Thus, West makes a conservative decision and establishes a $55,000 budget for her communication expenses.

In most cases, it's very hard to perform a marginal analysis because managers don't know the relationship between communication expenses and sales. Note that the numbers in Exhibit 15–4 are simply West's estimates, and they may not be accurate.

Sometimes retailers perform experiments to get a better idea of the relationship between communication expenses and sales. Say, for example, a catalog retailer selects several geographic areas in the United States with the same sales potential. The retailer then distributes 100,000 catalogs in the first area, 200,000 in the second area, and 300,000 in the third. Using the sales and costs for each distribution level, it could conduct an analysis like the one in Exhibit 15–4 to determine the most profitable distribution level. (Chapter 14 described the use of experiments to determine the relationship between price and sales.)

EXHIBIT 15–5
Illustration of Objective-and-Task Method for Setting a Communication Budget

Objective: Increase the percentage of target market (working women) who know of our store's location and who purchase business attire from 25 percent to 50 percent over the next 12 months.	
Task: 480, 30–second radio spots during peak commuting hours	$12,000
Task: Sign with store name near entrance to mall	4,500
Task: Display ad in the Yellow Pages	500
Objective: Increase the percentage of target market who indicate that our store is their preferred store for buying their business wardrobe from 5 percent to 15 percent in 12 months.	
Task: Develop TV campaign to improve image and run 50, 30–second commercials	$24,000
Task: Hold four "Dress for Success" seminars followed by a wine-and-cheese party	8,000
Objective: Sell merchandise remaining at end of season.	
Task: Special event	$6,000
Total budget	$55,000

Some other methods that retailers use to set communication budgets are the objective-and-task and rules-of-thumb methods, which include the affordable, percentage-of-sales, and competitive parity methods. These methods are easy to use but do not result in the optimal level of communication expenditures.

Objective-and-Task Method The **objective-and-task method** determines the budget required to undertake specific tasks to accomplish communication objectives. To use this method, the retailer first establishes a set of communication objectives and then determines the necessary tasks and their costs. The total of all costs incurred to undertake the tasks is the communication budget.

Exhibit 15–5 illustrates how Diane West could use the objective-and-task method to complement her marginal analysis. West establishes three objectives: to increase awareness of her store, to create a greater preference for her store among customers in her target market, and to promote the sale of merchandise remaining at the end of each season. The estimated communication budget she requires to achieve these objectives is $55,000.

In addition to defining her objectives and tasks, West rechecks the financial implications of the communication mix by projecting the income statement for next year using the communication budget (see Exhibit 15–6). This income statement includes an increase of $25,000 in communication expenses compared with last year. But West believes this increase in the communication budget will boost annual sales from $500,000 to $650,000. According to West's projections, the increase in communication expenses will raise store profits. The results of both the marginal analysis and the objective-and-task methods suggest a communication budget between $55,000 and $65,000.

Rule-of-Thumb Methods The previous two methods set the communication budget by estimating communication activities' effects on the firm's future sales or communication objectives. The **rule-of-thumb methods** discussed in this section use the opposite logic. They use past sales and communication activities to determine the present communication budget.[42]

EXHIBIT 15–6
Financial Implications of Increasing the Communication Budget

	Last Year	Next Year
Sales	$500,000	$ 650,000
Gross margin (realized)	200,000	260,000
Rental, maintenance, etc.	−70,000	−85,000
Personnel	−60,000	−64,500
Communications	−30,000	−55,000
Profit	$ 40,000	$ 55,500

Affordable Budgeting Method   When using the **affordable budgeting method,** retailers first forecast their sales and expenses, excluding communication expenses, during the budgeting period. The difference between the forecast sales and expenses plus the desired profit is then budgeted for the communication mix. In other words, the affordable method sets the communication budget by determining what money is available after operating costs and profits are subtracted.

The major problem with the affordable method is that it assumes that communication expenses don't stimulate sales and profit. Communication expenses are just a cost of business, like the cost of merchandise. When retailers use the affordable method, they typically cut "unnecessary" communication expenses if sales fall below the forecast rather than increasing communication expenses to increase sales.

Percentage-of-Sales Method   The **percentage-of-sales method** sets the communication budget as a fixed percentage of forecast sales. Retailers use this method to determine the communication budget by forecasting sales during the budget period and then applying a predetermined percentage to set the budget. The percentage may be the retailer's historical percentage or the average percentage used by similar retailers.

The problem with the percentage-of-sales method is that it assumes that the same percentage used in the past, or used by competitors, is appropriate for the future. Also, like the affordable method, it assumes that communication expenses don't stimulate sales and profit. Consider a retailer that hasn't opened new stores in the past but plans to open many new stores in the current year. It must create customer awareness for each of these new stores, so the communication budget should be much larger in the current year than in the past.

Using the same percentage as competitors also may be inappropriate. For example, a retailer might have better locations or brand image than its competitors. As a result, customers may already have a high awareness of the retailer's stores. Thus, the retailer may not need to spend as much on communication as competitors with poorer locations or brands.

One advantage of both the percentage-of-sales method and the affordable method for determining a communication budget is that the retailer won't spend beyond its means. Because the level of spending is determined by sales, the budget will go up only when sales go up and as the retailer generates more sales to pay for the additional communication expenses. When times are good, these methods work well because they allow the retailer to communicate more aggressively with customers. But when sales fall, communication expenses are cut, which may accelerate the sales decline.

Competitive Parity Method   Under the **competitive parity method,** the communication budget is set so that the retailer's share of its communication expenses equals its share of the market. For example, consider a sporting goods store in a small town. To use the competitive parity method, the owner-manager would first estimate the total amount spent on communication by all sporting goods retailers in town. Then the owner-manager would estimate his or her store's market share for sporting goods and multiply that market share percentage by the sporting goods stores' total advertising expenses to set the budget. Assume that the owner-manager's estimate of advertising for sporting goods by all stores is $5,000 and the estimate of his or her store's market share is 45 percent. On the basis of these estimates, the owner-manager would set the store's communication budget at $2,250 to maintain competitive parity.

Similar to the other rule-of-thumb methods, the competitive parity method doesn't allow retailers to exploit the unique opportunities or problems they confront in a market. If all competitors used this method to set communication budgets, their market shares would stay about the same over time (assuming that the retailers develop equally effective campaigns and other retail mix activities).

Allocate the Promotional Budget

After determining the size of the communication budget, the third step in the communication planning process is to allocate the budget (see Exhibit 15–2). In this step, the retailer decides how much of its budget to allocate to specific communication elements, merchandise categories, geographic regions, or long- and short-term objectives. For example, Dillard's must decide how much of its communication budget to spend in each area it has stores: Southeast, Mid-Atlantic, Southwest, Midwest, and West Coast. Michaels decides how much to allocate to merchandise associated with different crafts. The sporting goods store owner-manager must decide how much of the store's $2,250 communication budget to spend on promoting the store's image versus generating sales during the year and how much to spend on advertising and special promotions.

Research indicates that allocation decisions are more important than the decision about the amount to spend on communications.[43] In other words, retailers often can realize the same objectives by reducing the size of the communication budget but allocating it more effectively.

An easy way to make such allocation decisions is to spend about the same in each geographic region or for each merchandise category. But this allocation rule probably won't maximize profits, because it ignores the possibility that communication programs might be more effective for some merchandise categories or for some regions than for others. Another approach is to use rules of thumb, such as basing allocations on the sales level or contributions for the merchandise category.

Allocation decisions, like budget-setting decisions, should use the principles of marginal analysis. The retailer should allocate the budget to areas that will yield the greatest return. This approach for allocating a budget is sometimes referred to as the **high-assay principle.** Consider a miner who can spend his time digging on two claims. The value of the gold on one claim is assayed at $20,000 per ton, whereas the assay value on the other claim is $10,000 per ton. Should the miner spend two-thirds of his time at the first mine and one-third of his time at the other mine? Of course not! The miner should spend all of his time mining the first claim until the assay value of the ore mined drops to $10,000 a ton, at which time he can divide his time equally between the claims.

Similarly, a retailer may find that its customers have a high awareness and very favorable attitude toward its women's clothing but do not know much about its men's clothing. In this situation, a dollar spent on advertising men's clothing might generate more sales than a dollar spent on women's clothing, even though the sales of women's clothing are greater than the sales of men's clothing.

Plan, Implement, and Evaluate Communication Programs—Three Illustrations

The final stage in developing a retail communication program is its implementation and evaluation (see Exhibit 15–2). This final section of the chapter illustrates the planning and evaluation process for three communication programs: a traditional advertising campaign, a Facebook campaign, and a Google AdWords campaign by a small specialty retailer.

Advertising Campaign   Hypothetically, imagine Fabulous Fromage is a specialty import cheese shop, located just outside New York City. The store's appearance

Communicating
great products and
knowledgeable employees
help specialty import cheese
stores thrive.

combines the ambiance of a French café with the conveniences of a modern retailer; most of its merchandise is imported from France and a few other renowned cheese-making regions around the world.

Harry Owens, the owner, realizes that his communication budget is considerably less than the budget of the local Whole Foods store, which also sells gourmet cheeses. He, therefore, decides to concentrate his limited budget on a specific segment and use very creative copy and distinctive artwork in his advertising. His target market is knowledgeable, sophisticated consumers of gourmet foods and kitchenwares. His experience indicates the importance of personal selling for these seasoned shoppers because they (1) make expensive purchases but (2) seek considerable information before making their decisions. Thus, Owens spends part of his communication budget on training his sales associates.

The advertising program Owens develops emphasizes his store's distinctive image. He uses the newspaper as his major vehicle. Whereas the ads issued by Whole Foods tend to highlight price promotions on specialty cheeses, the advertising for Fabulous Fromage emphasizes French country imagery, including off-the-beaten-path scenes of French pastures and unusual art objects. This theme is also reflected in the store's atmosphere.

To evaluate his communication program, Owens needs to compare the results of his program with the objectives he has developed during the first part of the planning process. To measure his campaign's effectiveness, he conducts an inexpensive tracking study. Telephone interviews are performed periodically with a representative sample of customers in his store's trading area. Communication objectives are assessed using the following questions:

Communication Objectives	Questions
Awareness	What stores sell imported cheese?
Knowledge	Which stores would you rate outstanding on the following characteristics . . . (e.g., sales assistance)?
Attitude	On your next shopping trip for imported cheese, which store would you visit first?
Visit	Which of the following stores have you been to?

Here are the survey results for one year:

Communication Objective	Before Campaign	6 Months After	One Year After
Awareness (% mentioning store)	38%	46%	52%
Knowledge (% giving outstanding rating for sales assistance)	9	17	24
Attitude (% first choice)	13	15	19
Visit (% visited store)	8	15	19

The results show a steady increase in awareness, knowledge of the store, and choice of the store as a primary source of fine imported cheeses. This research thus provides evidence that the advertising is conveying the intended message to the target audience.

Facebook Marketing Campaign   Owens is developing a Facebook marketing campaign for a new product line he plans to import from Italy using the steps outlined in Exhibit 15–2.[44]

1. *Establish objectives.* Owens must determine the objectives he hopes to achieve through his campaign. Is it designed to increase awareness of the product line? Is he hoping more potential customers might visit and Like his Facebook page? Is his focus mainly on increasing sales of the product line? Depending on what he aims to achieve, he might focus on developing a Facebook Page, creating a Facebook App, or hosting a Facebook Event.

   As part of his objectives, he also needs to determine whom Fabulous Fromage is targeting. Facebook enables Owens to perform targeting based on location, language, education, gender, profession, age, relationship status, likes/dislikes, and friends or connections. Owens' aim is to find a big enough audience to reach those who might buy the new product line without being so big that he ends up trying to appeal to someone way outside of his target audience. A Facebook targeting example is depicted in Exhibit 15–7.

2. *Develop the budget.* Budgeting is key. Facebook allows advertisers to set a daily budget: Once the costs (usually per click) reach a certain level, the ad disappears for the rest of the day. Of course, this option can be risky if the retailer is getting great feedback, and all of a sudden, a compelling ad disappears. Therefore, similar to the campaign content, budgets demand nearly constant review. For example, if a competitor lowers its price significantly, it might be necessary to follow suit to avoid being excluded from customers' consideration sets.

3. *Allocate budget (develop the campaign).* Now that Owens knows who he is targeting and what his budget is for the campaign, the next step is to develop the communication, including the copy and images. Here again, the process is not very different from any other marketing communications campaign. There should be a call to action that is clear and compelling. Strong, eye-catching images and designs are important. And the campaign must appeal to the right customers. However, an aspect that is more critical with social media than other forms of marketing communications is that the images and messages need to be updated almost constantly. Because people expect changing content online, it would be inappropriate to run the same campaign for several months, as the shop might if it were advertising on television, for example.

2. Targeting

Location

Country: (?)   New York

- Everywhere
- By State/Province (?)
- By City (?)

Demographics

Age: (?)   24 ÷ – 35 ÷

Demographics

Age: (?)   24 ÷ – 35 ÷

- Require exact age match

Sex: (?) All   Men

Interests

Precise interests: (?)   Cooking

Switch to Broad Category Targeting (?)

Estimated Reach (?)

266,920 people

- who live in the United States
- who live within 50 miles of New York, NY
- between the ages of 24 and 35 inclusive
- who are in the category Cooking

4. *Implement and evaluate the program.* The final step is to implement and review the success of the campaign and make changes as necessary. Facebook's Ad Manager offers various metrics and reports, such as number of clicks on ads, audience demographics, and ad performance for specific time periods.

Google AdWords Campaign   Fabulous Fromage's target market is young, well-educated, men and women aged 30 to 40 years interested in food and wine. The owner's experience indicates the importance of personal selling for his sophisticated target market because the marketed customers (1) make large purchases and (2) seek information about gourmet products before making a decision. Owens has, therefore, decided to concentrate his limited budget on a specific segment and use electronic media in his IMC program to generate business through his new website.

To reach new customers, Owens is actively using search engine marketing. In particular, he is using Google AdWords, a search engine marketing tool offered by Google that allows advertisers to show up in the ad section of the search results page based on the keywords potential customers use (see the ad section in the right-hand column of the Google screen grab on the next page). Owens is also using what he has learned from his interactions with Google consultants and is rewriting content on his website to achieve search engine optimization (as we discussed earlier in the chapter). Thus, Owens is experimenting with both paid search through Google's advertising program and organic search through his revised website content.

Owens must determine the best keywords to use for his sponsored-link advertising program. Some potential customers might search using the key words, "New York Gourmet Cheese," "Imported Cheese," or other such versions. Using Google AdWords, Owens can assess the effectiveness of his

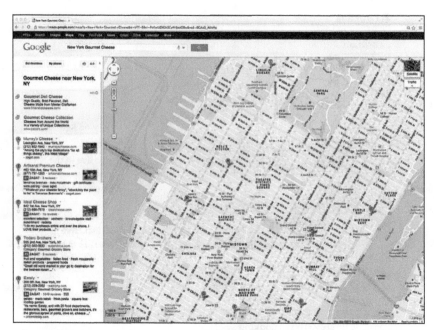

Advertisers pay Google to show up in the ad section in the right-hand column of this screen grab based on the keywords customers use in their searches.

advertising expenditures by measuring the reach, relevance, and return on advertising investment for each of the keywords that potential customers used during their Internet searches.

To estimate reach, Owens uses the number of **impressions** (the number of times the ad appears in front of the user) and the **click-through rate (CTR)**. To calculate CTR, he takes the number of times a user clicks on an ad and divides it by the number of impressions.[45] For example, if a sponsored link was delivered 100 times and 10 people clicked on it, then the number of impressions is 100, the number of clicks is 10, and the CTR would be 10 percent. The **relevance** of the ad describes how useful an ad message is to the consumer doing the search. Google provides a measure of relevance through its AdWords system using a proprietary metric known as a Quality Score.[46] The Quality Score uses multiple factors to measure the keyword's relevance to the ad text or a user's search. A high Quality Score generally implies that the keyword will result in ads that appear higher on the page, with a lower cost per click.[47] In a search for "gourmet cheese," the Fabulous Fromage ad showed up fourth, suggesting high relevance.

Using the following formula, Owens also can determine an ad's **return on advertising investment (ROAI)**:

$$ROAI = \frac{\text{Net sales} - \text{Advertising cost}}{\text{Advertising cost}}$$

For the two keyword searches in Exhibit 15–8, Owens finds how much the advertising cost him (column 3), the sales produced as a result (column 4), and the ROAI (column 6). For "New York Gourmet Cheese," the website had a lot more clicks (110) than the clicks received from "Imported Cheese" (40) (see column 2, Exhibit 15–8). Even though the sales were lower for the keywords "New York Gourmet Cheese" at $35 per day, versus $40 per day for the keywords "Imported

(1) Keyword	(2) Clicks	(3) Cost	(4) Sales	(5) Revenue − Cost (Col. 4 − Col. 3)	(6) ROAI (Col. 5/Col. 3) × 100
New York Gourmet Cheese	110	$10/day	$35/day	$25	250%
Imported Cheese	40	$25/day	$40/day	$15	60%

EXHIBIT 15–8
ROAI Assessment for Two Google AdWords

Cheese," the ROAI was much greater for the "New York Gourmet Cheese" keyword. In the future, Owens should continue using this keyword, in addition to producing others that are similar to it, in the hope that he will attain an even greater return on investment.

SUMMARY

LO1 Identify the traditional media elements.

Retailers communicate with customers using a variety of traditional media elements. These include mass media advertising, sales promotions, in-store marketing, personal selling, and public relations.

LO2 Identify the new media elements.

In the past decade or so, retailers have embraced several new media elements. The online elements include websites, e-mail, and mobile. Examples of the social media elements embraced by retailers are YouTube, Facebook, blogs, and Twitter.

LO3 Understand how retailers use communication programs to develop brand images and build customer loyalty.

An important use of communication programs is to develop strong brand images that enhance customer loyalty. Brands are very valuable to both customers and retailers because they provide information that helps enhance the shopping experience and create loyalty toward the retailer and its products and services. To enhance customers' brand image, retailers undertake communications activities that create a high level of brand awareness, develop favorable associations with the brand name, and reinforce the image of the brand.

LO4 List the steps involved in developing a communication program.

Retailers go through four steps to develop and implement their communication program: establish objectives, determine a budget, allocate the budget, and implement and evaluate the program. Marginal analysis is the most appropriate method for determining how much should be spent to accomplish the retailer's objectives because it maximizes the profits that could be generated by the communication mix. Because marginal analysis is difficult to implement, however, many retailers use rule-of-thumb methods to determine the size of the promotion budget.

KEY TERMS

advertising, *419*
affordable budgeting method, *441*
aided recall, *433*
blog (weblog), *429*
brand, *431*
brand associations, *435*
brand awareness, *433*
brand equity, *431*
brand image, *431*
cause-related marketing campaign, *424*
click through rates, *446*
communication objectives, *436*

competitive parity method, *441*
cooperative (co-op) advertising, *438*
coupons, *421*
direct mail, *420*
e-mail, *425*
event sponsorship, *423*
freestanding insert (FSI), *419*
high-assay principle, *442*
impressions, *446*
integrated marketing communication program, *418*
marginal analysis, *438*

m-commerce, *425*
microblog, *430*
mobile commerce, *425*
mobile communication, *425*
objective-and-task method, *440*
percentage-of-sales method, *441*
personal selling, *423*
point-of-purchase (POP) display, *422*
premium, *421*
preprint, *419*
product placement, *424*
public relations (PR), *423*

GET OUT AND DO IT!

1. **CONTINUING ASSIGNMENT** Evaluate the communication activities undertaken by the retailer you have selected for the continuing assignment. Describe your retailer's brand image. Briefly explain how your retailer uses each of the following elements of its communication program: direct marketing, online marketing, personal selling, sales promotions, direct mail and e-mail, mobile marketing, advertising (media used?), social media, public relations, website, and events. Do all of these elements send a consistent brand-image message to customers? Why, or why not?

2. Go to the home page for BrandZ at www.brandz.com, and click on "BrandZ Reports," then select the Top 100 Global Brands Report. On the basis of this report, list the top 20 global retail brands. In two or three paragraphs, describe what makes a strong retail brand. How were brand equity and financial performance used to measure brand value for these retailers?

3. Retailers and manufacturers deliver coupons through the Internet in addition to delivering them by mail or as inserts. Go to retailmenot.com for coupons offered over the Internet. How does this coupon distribution system compare with the other two distribution systems?

4. Trader Joe's is a gourmet grocery store offering items such as health foods, organic produce, and nutritional supplements. The company has nearly 400 stores in 37 states at which it offers more than 2,000 private-label products. Go to www.traderjoes.com, and see how the firm uses its Internet site to promote its retail stores and merchandise. Why does this retailer include recipes and a seasonal guide on its website? Does the information provided on the web page reinforce the store's upscale grocery image? Explain why or why not.

5. Go to the social media site for a retailer that you have shopped at during the last few weeks. How was social media used as an element in the retailer's communication program? What audience is being reached with social media? Is the social media message consistent or inconsistent with other communication elements? Is this a strong or weak strategy? Please explain.

6. Go to the home page for Target's Pressroom at pressroom.target.com. How does this retailer use public relations to communicate with investors and customers? Is this an effective communication tool for this retailer? Provide support for your response.

7. Go to www.facebook.com/business to see how to build pages, ads, and sponsored stories, as well as how to take advantage of mobile applications. What are some of the steps that Facebook suggests a person consider when marketing using ads?

DISCUSSION QUESTIONS AND PROBLEMS

1. How do brands benefit consumers? Retailers?

2. What are the positive and negative aspects of direct marketing from the customer's perspective?

3. What types of sales promotions have been successful with you as a consumer? Which ones have not been successful? Explain your responses.

4. What factors should be considered in dividing up the advertising budget among a store's different merchandise areas? Which of the following should receive the highest advertising budget: staple, fashion, or seasonal merchandise? Why?

5. Outline some elements in a communication program that can be used to achieve the following objectives: (a) Increase store loyalty by 20 percent. (b) Build awareness of the store by 10 percent. (c) Develop an image as a low-price retailer. How would you determine whether the communication program met each of these objectives?

6. A retailer plans to open a new store near a university. It will specialize in collegiate merchandise such as apparel, accessories, and school supplies. Consider the pros and cons of each of the following media: TV, radio, city newspaper, university newspaper, local

magazine, website, blog, and event sponsorship for this retailer to capture the university market.

7. Why do some online retailers include editorials and customer reviews along with product information on their websites? Explain how this may influence the consumer's buying behavior.

8. Assume you work for a large consumer-packaged goods firm that has learned its latest line of snack foods is moving very slowly off store shelves. Recommend a strategy for listening to what consumers are saying on blogs, review sites, and the firm's website. Describe how your strategy might provide insights into consumers' sentiments about the new product line.

9. As an intern for Dunkin' Donuts, you have been asked to develop a social media campaign for a new glazed muffin. The objective of the campaign is to increase awareness and trial of the new line of muffins. How would you go about putting such a campaign together?

SUGGESTED READINGS

Aaker, David, and Erich Joachimsthaler. *Brand Leadership: Building Assets in an Information Economy*. New York: Free Press, 2009.

Belch, George, and Michael Belch. *Advertising and Promotion: An Integrated Marketing Communications Perspective*, 9th ed. New York: McGraw-Hill, 2012.

Scott Lerman, *Building Better Brands: A Comprehensive Guide to Brand Strategy and Identity Development*, HOW Books, 2013.

Ludwig Stephan, Ko de Ruyter, Mike Friedman, Elisabeth C. Brüggen, Martin Wetzels, and Gerard Pfann. "More Than Words: The Influence of Affective Content and Linguistic Style Matches in Online Reviews on Conversion Rates." *Journal of Marketing*, 77 (January 2013), pp. 87–103.

Rapp, Adam, Lauren Bietelspacher, Dhruv Grewal, and Doug Hughes. "Understanding Social Media Effects Across Seller, Retailer, and Consumer Interactions," *Journal of the Academy of Marketing Science*, 41 (September 2013), pp. 547–66.

Sernovitz, Andy. *Word of Mouth Marketing: How Smart Companies Get People Talking*. Austin, TX: Greenleaf Press, 2012.

Smith, Ron, *Public Relations: The Basics*. New York: Routledge, 2012.

Sponder, Marshall. *Social Media Analytics: Effective Tools for Building, Interpreting, and Using Metrics*. New York: McGraw Hill, 2011.

Weaver, Jason. *Manager's Guide to Online Marketing*. New York: McGraw-Hill, 2013.

Store Layout, Design, and Visual Merchandising

EXECUTIVE BRIEFING
Fredrik Holmvik, Head of Media,
ICA Sweden

ICA is a leading Nordic retailer with more than 2,100 retailer- and company-owned stores. The company is owned by the ICA Group. ICA operates in Sweden, Norway, and the Baltic countries. It operates four store formats: ICA Nära (ICA Nearby—convenience store), ICA Supermarket, ICA Kvantum (superstore), and Maxi ICA Hypermarket (which has approximately 1,300 stores in Sweden). ICA is the largest supermarket chain in Sweden and serves more than 10 million customers per week. ICA's mission is to be the leading retailer focused on food and meals. In Sweden, ICA stores are owned by independent retailers. However, ICA (the parent organization) handles the centralized operations such as purchasing, communications, and logistics.

I am currently the head of ICA media. I have been actively working with ICA for many years, first as a consultant and now as an employee. Prior to this, I was the CEO of QB Food Tech Ltd. I have also worked as a consultant for Accenture and at Unilever in a variety of roles.

ICA has historically used a variety of traditional media (e.g., TV commercials, home flyers) and in-store paper signage to provide our customers relevant information, ranging from prices to campaigns to cooking tips. Some years ago, we introduced

digital screens and signage (what we call ICA's in-store media channel) to augment the traditional media. These screens allow us to provide relevant content, such as ICA campaigns, cooking tips, as well as vendor commercials and point-of-purchase promotions.

Our goals for these digital displays include increasing sales, improving campaign reach and effectiveness, and creating a more up-to-date image and feel for our stores. In a short time frame, we have introduced digital signage in 350 stores, covering a reach of more than 55 percent of our weekly customers. Price deals that have been advertised using our digital screens have seen sales go up by almost 100 percent. Traditional vendor advertisements drive sales as well as brand awareness. These digital displays attract consumer attention and increase their likelihood of purchasing the products being displayed. Our research shows that digital displays with moving images or films, compared to ordinary displays, double customer attention.

CHAPTER 17

LEARNING OBJECTIVES

LO1 Identify the critical issues retailers need to consider when designing a store.

LO2 List the advantages and disadvantages of alternative store layouts.

LO3 Describe how to assign store floor space to merchandise departments and categories.

LO4 Illustrate the best techniques for merchandise presentation.

LO5 Understand how retailers can create a more appealing shopping experience.

These insights have important implications for the design of stores, such as where to locate digital displays, what type of displays to use, and most importantly, what to communicate in certain departments/areas of the store. For instance, displays in the fruit and vegetable section focus on relevant communication in that area, just as displays in the bread section focus within its relevant communication range. The effectiveness of these displays varies as a function of their location in the store and the type of store. For instance, our research has shown that these digital signs can increase sales by as much as 5 percent in hypermarkets. In smaller stores, sales are also affected, and the most interesting finding here is the actual effect on being more up-to-date. The customer actually experiences a more "modern" store environment, which contributes to the overall perception of the store in a favorable way.

These digital screens also provide cost efficiencies through lower costs associated with production, printing, and getting the traditional printed material to the stores, as well as better coordination of promotions between our vendors and stores.

The environment in a store, the design of the store, and the presentation and location of merchandise in the store have significant impacts on shopping behavior. The design of a store or website attracts customers to visit the location, increases the time they spend in the store or on the site, and increases the amount of merchandise they purchase. Store design also has long-term effects on building customer loyalty toward the retailer by enhancing the retailer's brand image and providing rewarding shopping experiences that encourage repeat visits.

This chapter is part of the Store Management section because store managers are responsible for implementing the design and visual merchandising developed by specialists at the retailer's corporate headquarters. They adapt the prototype plans to the unique characteristics of their stores, then make sure the image and experience provided by the design are consistent over time. However, as discussed in this chapter, store design and visual merchandising are also elements of a retailer's communication mix and play an important role in creating and reinforcing a retailer's brand image.

The chapter begins with a discussion of store design objectives. Next, the elements of store design are discussed. The decisions about how much space to allocate to different merchandise categories and departments and where they should be located in the store are reviewed. The chapter concludes with an examination of how retailers use store design elements, such as color, lighting, and music, to enhance the customer's shopping experience.

STORE DESIGN OBJECTIVES

LO1

Identify the critical issues retailers need to consider while designing a store.

Some store design objectives are to (1) implement the retailer's strategy, (2) build loyalty by providing a rewarding shopping experience, (3) increase sales on a visit, (4) control costs, and (5) meet legal requirements.

Implement the Retail Strategy

The primary objective for store design is to implement the retailer's strategy. The design must be consistent with and reinforce the retailer's strategy by meeting the needs of the target market and building a sustainable competitive advantage. Starbucks' store designs are inspired by the Italian coffee bars that not only have great coffee, but also serve as a place to meet friends, socialize, and relax. Soft lighting, wood tables, comfortable seating, free wi-fi, and clean bathrooms make Starbucks a place where people just want to hang out and have a good cup of coffee. Retailing View 17.1 details how another innovative retailer, Apple, makes store design decisions to reinforce its overall strategy.

Build Loyalty

When customers consistently have rewarding experiences when patronizing a retailer's store and/or website, they are motivated to visit repeatedly and develop loyalty toward the retailer. Store design plays an important role in making shopping experiences rewarding. Customers seek two types of benefits when shopping—utilitarian and hedonic benefits.[1]

Store design provides **utilitarian benefits** when it enables customers to locate and purchase products in an efficient and timely manner with minimum hassle. Such utilitarian benefits are becoming increasingly important in today's time-poor society. Therefore, drugstore retailers such as CVS and Walgreens have designed their stores to include drive-through pharmacies and have invested in various technologies to augment customer convenience associated with these store design elements. They have developed mobile apps to help people refill their prescriptions; they then pick them up through the drive-through. These design elements and connected apps are further speeding up customers' shopping trips.[2]

Store design provides **hedonic benefits** by offering customers an entertaining and enjoyable shopping experience. They then want to spend more time in the store or on the website because the visit itself is rewarding. For example, Cabela's, a chain of stores catering to outdoor enthusiasts, provides an educational and entertaining experience that mixes museum-quality dioramas of wildlife on display, massive huge aquariums featuring native fish, a restaurant where diners can order wild-game sandwiches, and a shooting gallery that teaches basic shooting and

RETAILING VIEW   The Innovator Designs a Space, By and For the Geniuses   17.1

The glass cube that sits on Fifth Avenue has become nearly legendary at this point—just one more example of how Apple continually seeks new ideas to appeal to people's aesthetic and tactile senses. The cube and other visually remarkable glass entryways tell consumers that they have arrived at an Apple destination. Once they enter the light-filled spaces, Apple applies its design genius to keep them shopping happily.

Consider, for example, the Shanghai store. A glass cylinder (Apple had already done the cube in New York) rises up, seemingly from the ground. In the Hamburg, Germany, stores, the stairs to move between floors are all glass and are attached only at the top and bottom, creating a sense as if they are hanging in the air. As the architect hired to conceive of these ideas noted, "Steve [Jobs] wanted us to push the edge of technology, but it had to be comfortable for people. . . . It's an interesting challenge, how to marry the two."

Not all stores can afford a glass entryway, though. For more traditional retail spaces, such as in malls, Apple instead focuses on drawing people in by creating high ceilings, using bright but soft lighting, and placing its offerings on warm wood tables. The physical retail atmosphere helps build the communal sense initiated by its products. It also encourages and enables consumers to interact with Apple's technologically sophisticated products in a safe, inviting setting.

The layout of the stores and the products they feature also draw people further into the stores. To get to the Genius bar, they have to traverse all the way to the back of the store, walking past appealingly designed products as they do so. Even the displays of the computers are tilted at just the right angle to draw their eye.

Overall though, Apple stores reinforce the image of Apple as an innovation master. By adding unique and

The unique design of the Apple store in New York City reinforces the company's image of developing and retailing products with innovative design features.

unseen architectural elements to its flagship stores and ensuring all its stores are appealing, Apple shows just how cutting edge it remains. As the architect for the stores further noted, in lamenting Jobs's death, "Steve was a great client. . . . He would not discourage innovation that was within his vision of what Apple is or he is."

Sources: James B. Stewart, "A Genius of the Storefront, Too," *The New York Times*, October 15, 2011; Matthew Carroll, "How Retailers Can Replicate the Magic of the Apple Store . . . Online," *Forbes*, June 26, 2010; and Apple Store, www.apple.com.cn/retail/pudong/.

DISCUSSION QUESTION

How has Apple's innovative store design reinforced its innovative image?

safety lessons while also providing a fun experience. These shopping and tourism destinations draw customers from the local area certainly, but they also can attract travelers from hundreds of miles away.

Of course, few retailers can offer only utilitarian or hedonic benefits. Most need to use both routes to ensure customer loyalty. Thus, in the face of the global economic downturn, Wegmans has applied a more utilitarian look and feel in some sections, to welcome price-sensitive customers and reassure its existing shoppers that it recognizes their economic constraints.[3] The Wegmans supermarket chain explicitly designs its stores to make the chore of grocery shopping more fun: Instead of linoleum floors, harsh fluorescent lights, and narrow aisles, shoppers experience the feel of an open air market. Wegmans also offers various eat-in options, an exotic tea bar, a trail mix bar, and gourmet chef-prepared meals to take

To enhance the shopping experience, Wegmans offers gourmet chef-prepared meals to take home.

home. This unique experience for customers has helped Wegmans' 77 stores earn nearly $6 billion in sales annually.[4]

Increase Sales on Visits

A third design objective is to increase the sales made to customers on any particular visit. Store design has a substantial effect on which products customers buy, how long they stay in the store, and how much they spend during a visit. Because most consumers spend very little time and thought on shopping and selecting items in supermarkets, these purchase decisions are greatly influenced by what products customers see during their visit. What they see in turn is affected by the store layout and how the merchandise is presented. Thus, retailers attempt to design their stores in a manner that motivates unplanned purchases. As discussed later in this chapter, retailers use the cash wrap area, where people pay for merchandise, to display and therefore stimulate the sale of impulse items such as candy at a supermarket check-out terminal or jewelry at a women's apparel store.

Control Costs to Increase Profits

The fourth design objective is to control the cost of implementing the store design and maintaining the store's appearance. Although the types of lighting that Neiman Marcus shines on its expensive jewelry and crystal use more electricity and are less ecologically friendly than rows of bare fluorescent bulbs, the retailer considers such costs necessary to highlight these high-ticket items. In contrast, other retailers have embraced the notion of gaining efficiency in their energy use, as Retailing View 17.2 details.

Store designs can also affect labor costs and inventory shrinkage. Some stores are organized into isolated departments, which provides an intimate, comfortable shopping experience that can result in more sales. However, the design prevents sales associates from observing and covering adjacent departments, which makes it necessary to have at least one sales associate permanently stationed in each department to provide customer service and prevent shoplifting.

Another design consideration related to controlling cost is flexibility. Retailing is a very dynamic business. Competitors enter a market and cause existing retailers to change the mix of merchandise offered. As the merchandise mix changes, so

RETAILING VIEW   Walmart Goes Green and Lowers Its Energy Costs   17.2

In an initiative begun several years ago, Walmart continues to design new stores and retrofit older stores to ensure their energy efficiency. These stores are among the "greenest" in the world. The three main design objectives for these stores are reducing the amount of energy and other natural resources required for store operations, minimizing the raw materials used to construct each facility, and using renewable materials whenever possible.

These design elements reflect Walmart's three broad environmental goals: (1) to be supplied 100 percent by renewable energy, (2) to create zero waste, and (3) to sell products that sustain the world's resources and environment. Although such design features reduce the stores' impact on the environment, they also are expensive to build. Initial projections call for the energy used at these new stores to be 25 to 30 percent less than older stores that have not been retrofitted, reducing a store's energy costs by $500,000 annually. Such savings could increase if energy costs continue to climb.

Some of the sustainable features that have passed these steps or are currently being tested are as follows:

- A wind turbine on top of a store that produces sufficient energy to offset 5 percent of each store's electricity consumption.

- A system to collect and treat rainwater, which in turn can provide nearly all of the water required for irrigation and thus will reduce demands placed on local stormwater systems.

- The use of grass for landscaping that does not need irrigation or mowing.

- LEDs, instead of fluorescent lighting, in refrigerated cases. In cold temperatures, fluorescent lights lose life expectancy every time they are switched on and off; LEDs do not suffer from this limitation. The lights stay off until the customer opens the case. In addition to saving energy, the lights add a theatrical appeal for customers.

- A system that captures the heat generated by each building's refrigeration system, then redirects that

heat to warm the water in restroom sinks or support new radiant, floor-heating systems located beneath the entries and other areas.

Although many of these changes have been made globally, Walmart also customizes some green design choices by region:

- **Brazil:** Stores employ smart lights that dim when natural sunlight is available.

- **Mexico:** Walmart invested 640 million pesos (US$57 million) to convert a 25-acre, 50-foot deep dump into a green mall, which created 1,500 jobs. The trash produced energy through a bio-gas burning process. The green mall is now home to a Walmart supercenter, Sam's Club, Vips, and El Porton restaurants.

- **Central America:** 70 percent of stores have installed skylights to reduce lighting costs, covering approximately 15 percent of the roof space of each store.

- **China:** Walmart has begun to switch over to LED lighting throughout stores and integrated lighting controls to reduce energy usage by a target amount of 30 percent in existing stores and 40 percent in prototype stores.

- **Japan:** Prototype stores use a desiccant temperature and humidity system to reduce energy costs and CO_2 emissions.

Sources: "Taking Sustainability to New Heights," www.walmartgreeenroom/com, October 15, 2012; "No Matter the Season, Our Energy Commitment Is Always On," www.walmartgreenroonm.com, September 28, 2012; Michelle Moran, "Seeing Green," *Progressive Grocer*, March 2010, pp. 16–31; Cathy Jett, "New Design's Goal: To Cut the Clutter," *McClatchy-Tribune Business News*, October 14, 2009; and Aaron Besecker, "Walmart Store Gets Green Light," *McClatchy-Tribune Business News*, August 31, 2009.

DISCUSSION QUESTION

Are green store designs worth their cost? Why or why not?

must the space allocated to merchandise categories and the layout of the store. Thus, store designers attempt to design stores with maximum flexibility.

Flexibility is an important design consideration for college bookstores because they need to expand and contract their spaces to accommodate the large seasonal fluctuations inherent in the college-bookstore business. At the beginning of a semester, considerable space needs to be allocated to textbooks. But after the first week of the semester, the demand for textbooks decreases quickly, and space allocated to textbooks needs to be reallocated to apparel and consumer electronics. The key to providing this flexibility often lies in innovative fixture and wall systems that portion off the textbook area. **Fixtures** refer to the equipment used to display merchandise.

Legal Considerations—Americans with Disabilities Act

All store design and redesign decisions must comply with the 1990 Americans with Disabilities Act (ADA) and its 2008 amendments.[5] This law protects people with disabilities from discrimination in employment, transportation, public

The ADA has made stores more accessible for disabled consumers.

accommodations, telecommunications, and activities of state and local governments. It affects store design because the act calls for "reasonable access" to merchandise and services in retail stores built before 1993; stores built after 1993 must be fully accessible.

The act also states that retailers should not have to incur "undue burdens" to comply with ADA requirements. Although retailers are concerned about the needs of their disabled customers, they are also worried that making merchandise completely accessible to people in a wheelchair or a motorized cart will result in less space available to display merchandise and thus will reduce sales. However, providing for wider aisles and more space around fixtures can result in a more pleasant shopping experience for able-bodied as well as disabled customers.

The ADA does not clearly define critical terms such as "reasonable access," "fully accessible," or "undue burden." So the actual ADA requirements are being defined through a series of court cases in which disabled plaintiffs have filed class-action suits against retailers.[6] On the basis of these court cases, retailers are typically required to (1) provide 32-inch-wide pathways in the main aisle, to bathrooms, dressing rooms, and elevators, and around most fixtures; (2) lower most cash wraps (checkout stations) and fixtures so that they can be reached by a person in a wheelchair; (3) create disability-accessible checkout aisles; (4) provide bathrooms with handrails or grab bars; and (5) make dressing rooms fully accessible. Nor does the ADA stop at the store exit. Very clear guidelines establish the number of handicapped accessible parking spaces that stores must provide.[7] Some of these accessibility requirements are somewhat relaxed for retailers in very small spaces and during peak sales periods such as the Christmas holidays.

Design Trade-Offs

Few store designs can achieve all of these objectives, so any store design involves trade-offs among the objectives. Home Depot's traditional warehouse design can efficiently store and display a lot of merchandise with long rows of floor-to-ceiling racks, but this design is not conducive for a pleasant shopping experience.

Retailers often make trade-offs between stimulating impulse purchases and making it easy to buy products. For example, supermarkets place milk, a commonly purchased item, at the back of the store to make customers walk through the entire store, thus stimulating more impulse purchases. Realizing that some customers may want to buy only milk, Walgreens places its milk at the front of the store, enabling it to compete head-to-head with convenience stores.

The trade-off between making it easy to find merchandise and providing an interesting shopping experience is determined by the customer's shopping needs. For example, supermarket and drugstore shoppers typically focus on utilitarian benefits and want to minimize the time they spend shopping, so the design of supermarkets emphasizes the ease of locating merchandise (there are exceptions, such as Wegmans). In contrast, customers shopping for specialty goods like a computer, a home entertainment center, or furniture are more likely to spend time in the store browsing, comparing, and talking with the salesperson. Thus, specialty store retailers that offer this type of merchandise place more emphasis on providing hedonic benefits and encouraging exploration than on making it easy to find merchandise.

Another trade-off is the balance between giving customers adequate space in which to shop and productively using this scarce resource for merchandise. Customers are attracted to stores with wide aisles and fixtures whose primary purpose is to display rather than hold the merchandise. Also, shoppers do not like it when a store is so cramped that they touch one another, a phenomenon known as the "butt-brush effect."[8] However, a spacious design reduces the amount of merchandise that can be available to buy and thus may also reduce impulse purchases and the customers' chances of finding what they are looking for. But too many racks and displays in a store can cause customers to feel uncomfortable and even confused. There must be a compromise between been having a store that is too spacious and one that is overcrowded.

This section examined the various objectives retailers seek to satisfy when designing their stores. In the next section, important elements of design are explored.

STORE DESIGN ELEMENTS

Three elements in the design of stores are the (1) layout, (2) signage, and (3) feature areas. Each of these elements is discussed in this section.

L02

List the advantages and disadvantages of alternative store layouts.

Layouts

Retailers use three general types of store layout design: grid, racetrack, and free form. Each of these layouts has advantages and disadvantages.

Grid Layout   The **grid layout**, illustrated in Exhibit 17–1, has parallel aisles with merchandise on shelves on both sides of the aisles. Cash registers are located at the entrances/exits of the stores.

The grid layout is well suited for customers who are primarily interested in the utilitarian benefits offered by the store. They are not interested in the hedonic

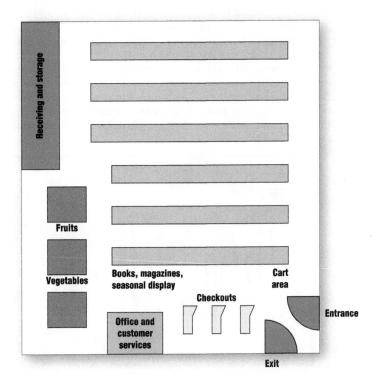

EXHIBIT 17–1
Grid Store Layout

benefits provided by a visually exciting design. They want to easily locate products they want to buy, and they make their purchases as quickly as possible. Most supermarkets and full-line discount stores use the grid layout, because this design enables their customers to easily find the product they are looking for and minimize the time spent on a shopping task that most don't enjoy.

The grid layout is also cost-efficient. There's less wasted space with the grid layout than with other layouts because the aisles are all the same width and designed to be just wide enough to accommodate shoppers and their carts. The use of high shelves for merchandise enables more merchandise to be on the sales floor compared with other layouts. Finally, because the fixtures are generally standardized, the cost of the fixtures is low.

One limitation of the grid layout, from the retailer's perspective, is that customers typically aren't exposed to all the merchandise in the store because, due to the height of the shelves, they see only products displayed in the aisle they are in. Thus the layout does not encourage unplanned purchases. Supermarket retailers overcome this limitation, to some extent, by complementing the packaged goods in the center-store grid with a racetrack of fresh, perishable merchandise categories (meat, seafood, dairy, poultry, baked goods, and produce) around the periphery of the store. Unplanned purchases are also stimulated by special displays, which are discussed later in the chapter.

In the past, supermarket retailers and consumer packaged goods manufacturers did not feel this limitation was very important. They believed that customers would be exposed to all the merchandise in the store because they would walk up and down each aisle, pushing their shopping carts. However, researchers have equipped carts with GPS locators and found that most supermarket customers enter a supermarket, turn right, go along the periphery of the store looking down the aisles, and occasionally walk down an aisle with their carts or leave the cart at the end of the aisle and walk down the aisle to select a specific item and return to the cart. A path taken by a typical customer is shown in Exhibit 17–2.[9]

Supermarket retailers and consumer packaged goods companies now recognize this problem of decreased traffic in the center core of supermarkets. Whereas the outer circumference of the store has seen some exciting improvements, such that "store perimeters have become warm, inviting, exciting, genuine and diverse," according to David Milka, director of consumer insight for S.C. Johnson, the center of the store has remained "cold, obscure, boring and non-differentiated."[10]

The answer is to get customers to spend more time in the center store. Recent research shows that the more time customers spend in stores in general, the more unplanned purchases they make.[11] One way to extend their shopping time is to make their shopping path less efficient. Thus, to expose customers to more

EXHIBIT 17–2
Example of a Traffic Pattern in a Grid Layout Supermarket

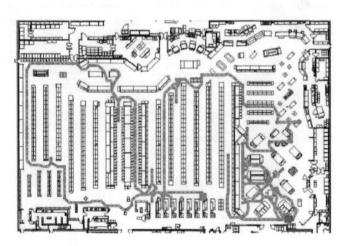

merchandise and increase their unplanned purchases in the core, supermarket retailers need to get customers to walk down more aisles. One potential approach for increasing traffic in the core would alter the straight aisles to form a zig-zag pattern. As discussed in Retailing View 17.3, IKEA uses a similar method. Another approach locates power brands—those with high awareness and market share such as Coca-Cola and Tide—and eye-attracting displays in the middle of the aisle rather than at the ends. The power brands appear from the top to the bottom, creating a swath of color that captures the attention of customers as they peek down the aisle.

RETAILING VIEW   A Hedonic Maze Filled with Utilitarian Products   17.3

IKEA stores are designed to inspire customers to weave their way through the store.

At its largest North American store in Montreal, IKEA offers 464,694 feet of functional, reasonably priced furniture, décor, and housewares. It contains various settings that showcase its products, including three full homes and approximately 50 "inspirational room settings," as well as a market hall and a restaurant that can seat 600. If you walked the entire store, you'd have completed a nearly one-mile hike.

Of course, few shoppers want to cover all that ground. Visitors looking for a new ottoman for their living room have little reason to swing through the bedroom sets. And yet, somehow, most of them wind up doing just that.

The reason is likely IKEA's distinctive, maze-like layout for its stores. Once customers enter the maze, it is difficult for them to find a specific department, or even the exit, unless they follow the path laid out for them. According to IKEA, this layout benefits customers by giving them inspiration and decorating ideas. But still the notion seems contradictory. Shouldn't a retailer make it easier for customers to find what they want?

Instead, IKEA's store flows create disorientation and directional confusion to push customers through each department. That means they spend more time in the stores and may consider more purchases. They might have stopped for an ottoman, but the bedside lamp they see in

an inspirational bedroom setting might be just the thing. In addition, customers are more likely to place appealing items in their carts for fear that they will be unable to find it again if they leave it behind. Finally, the length of time customers spend in the store makes them feel committed to the visit. If they don't pick up a few items, all that expenditure of time might seem wasted.

According to various observers, the effect is either brilliant or underhanded—or both. No one seems to leave IKEA without buying more than he or she had planned. This near-inability to stick to a shopping list seems a direct result of the carefully designed layout that causes customers to buy a number of uplanned items.

Sources: Elizabeth Tyler, "How IKEA Seduces Its Customers: By Trapping Them," *Time,* January 28, 2011; and Kathryn Blaze Carlson, "Enter the Maze: IKEA, Costco, Other Retailers Know How to Get You to Buy More," *National Post,* June 1, 2012.

DISCUSSION QUESTION

What features of IKEA and its strategy make its unique store layout appropriate for it, but not for other types of retailers?

Retailers are experimenting with creative promotional approaches to keep people shopping. For example, LocalResponse allows retailers to know what merchandise customers are talking about using social media (e.g., a tweet, Facebook update, photo on Instagram, or check-in using Foursquare) while in the store. Consequently, retailers can use the latest advances in technology to offer customers instant coupons on their mobile phones for merchandise adjacent to where they are physically located, which might entice them to find the product and buy it. Additionally, giving them an electronic coupon for merchandise located at another, potentially distant, location in the store, along with a map of where it is located, may lure them to meander through the store with the possibility that they will purchase other items along the way.

Racetrack Layout   The **racetrack layout,** also known as a **loop,** is a store layout that provides a major aisle that loops around the store to guide customer traffic around different departments within the store. Point-of-sale terminals are typically located in each department bordering the racetrack.

The racetrack layout facilitates the goal of getting customers to see the merchandise available in multiple departments and thus encourages unplanned purchasing. As customers go around the racetrack, their eyes are forced to take different viewing angles rather than looking down one aisle, as in the grid design. Low fixtures are used so that customers can see merchandise beyond the products displayed on the racetrack.

Exhibit 17–3 shows the layout of a department store. Because the store has multiple entrances, the racetrack layout places all departments on the main aisle by drawing customers through the store in a series of major and minor loops. To entice customers through the various departments, the design places some of the more

EXHIBIT 17–3   Racetrack Layout

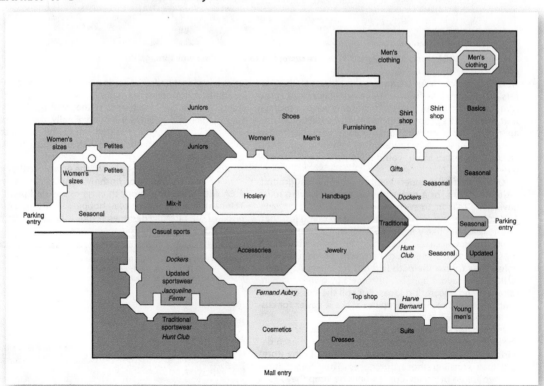

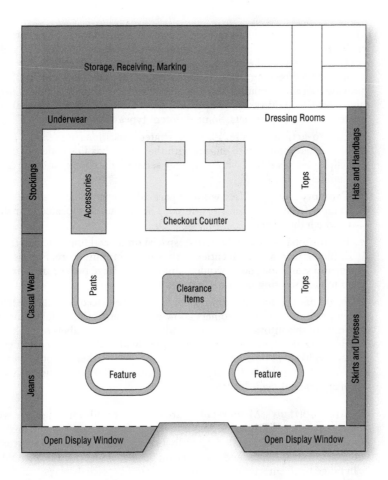

EXHIBIT 17–4
Free-Form Store
Layout

popular departments, like juniors, toward the rear of the store. The newest items also are featured on the aisles to draw customers into departments and around the loop.

The racetrack usually is wider than other aisles and defined by a change in flooring surface or color. For instance, the aisle flooring might be marblelike tile, whereas the department floors vary in material, texture, and color, depending on the desired ambience.

Free-Form Layout   A **free-form layout**, also known as **boutique layout**, arranges fixtures and aisles in an asymmetric pattern (Exhibit 17–4). It provides an intimate, relaxing environment that facilitates shopping and browsing. It appears most commonly in specialty stores or as departments within department stores. However, creating this pleasing shopping environment is costly. Because there is no well-defined traffic pattern, as there is in the racetrack and grid layouts, customers aren't naturally drawn around the store or department, and personal selling becomes more important to encourage customers to explore merchandise offered in the store. In addition, the layout reduces the amount of merchandise that can be displayed.

Signage and Graphics

Signage and graphics help customers locate specific products and departments, provide product information, and suggest items or special purchases. Graphics, such as photo panels, can reinforce a store's image. Signage is used to identify the location of merchandise categories within a store and the types of products offered in the category. The signs are hung typically from the ceiling to enhance their visibility. Frequently, icons rather than words are used to facilitate communication with customers speaking different languages. For example, a red and yellow circus tent icon identifies the area for children's toys more effectively than a black and white, worded rectangular sign. Smaller signs are used to identify sale items and provide more information about specific products. Finally, retailers may use images, such as pictures of people and places, to create moods that encourage customers to buy products. Some different types of signs are:

- **Call-to-action signage.** Placed in strategic locations in the store can convey how, where, and why to engage with the retailer via QR codes on customers' cellphones, via e-mail, short-message services, Facebook, or other digital channels.
- **Category signage.** Used within a particular department or sector of the store to identify types of products offered. They are usually located near the goods to which they refer.
- **Promotional signage.** Describes special offers and found within the store or displayed in windows to entice the customer into the store. For instance, value apparel stores for young women often display large posters in their windows of models wearing new or sale items.
- **Point-of-sale signage.** Point-of-sale signs are placed near the merchandise they refer to so that customers know its price and other detailed information. Some of this information may already be on product labels or packaging. However, point-of-sale signage can quickly identify for the customer those aspects likely to be of greater interest, such as whether the product is on sale. Walmart uses this sort of signage effectively to show customers when the price of an item has been "rolled back."

Digital Signage   Many retailers are replacing traditional signage with digital signage systems.[12] **Digital signage** includes signs whose visual content is delivered electronically through a centrally managed and controlled network, distributed to servers in stores, and displayed on flat-panel screens. The content delivered can range from entertaining video clips to simple price displays.

Digital signage provides a number of benefits over traditional static-print signage. Due to their dynamic nature, digital signs are more effective in attracting the attention of customers and helping them recall the messages displayed. Digital signage also offers the opportunity to enhance a store's environment by displaying complex graphics and videos to provide an atmosphere that customers find appealing.[13] Because the content is delivered digitally, it can easily be tailored to a store's market and remain consistent in every store, displayed at the right time and right place. Furthermore, by overcoming the time-to-message hurdle associated with traditional print signage, digital signage enables the content to be varied within and across stores at different times of the day or days of the week—without incurring the expense of printing, distributing, and installing new static signs or hiring labor to post them. If the temperatures rise, digital in-store signage might automatically advertise cold drinks; if the forecast continues to be warm and sunny, it might promote sunscreen. Of course, there is a drawback too. The initial

In-store digital displays highlight key product features and experiential elements at the point of purchase.

cost of the display devices and the system that supports the delivery of signage can be quite high.

Recent research shows customers spend $1.52 more, per trip, at grocery stores when digital displays are used. Less than $2 might not seem like that much, but the overall effect is huge in the grocery sector, with its tight margins and high volume of shoppers.[14] The effect of digital signage on sales is not limited to grocers. Lord & Taylor has added digital signage to its flagship store in Manhattan and plans to expand its use. The store reports the addition of digital signage in its fragrance department paid for itself in less than a year, and digital technology in the men's suit department led to double-digit sales increases.[15]

Feature Areas

In addition to using layout and signage, retailers can guide customers through stores and influence buying behavior through the placement of feature areas. **Feature areas** are the areas within a store that are designed to get customers' attention. They include windows, entrances, freestanding displays, mannequins, end caps, promotional aisles or areas, walls, dressing rooms, and cash wraps.

Windows   Window displays draw customers into the store and provide a visual message about the type of merchandise offered in the store and the type of image the store wants to portray. Research suggests that storefront window displays are an effective tool for building the store image, particularly with new customers who are unfamiliar with the store.[17]

Effective window displays are not easy to achieve, however, and they often demand the collaboration of a large team of designers. At The Limited, an extensive design team, led by the senior vice president of visual merchandising and store design and construction, takes several weeks, or even months, to find just the right combination of women's fashions that will attract mall shoppers strolling by the stores. Only after extensive analysis does the design team introduce their display to the stores throughout the nation.[18]

Entrances   The first impression caused by the entry area affects the customer's image of the store. Department stores typically have the cosmetics and fragrance categories at the main entrance, while grocery stores have fresh produce because these categories are visually appealing and create a sense of excitement. Whole Foods places cut flowers near the entrance to connote freshness.[19]

While the entry area plays a prominent role in creating an image, the first 10 feet of the store are often referred to as the "decompression zone," because customers are making an adjustment to the new environment: escaping from the noisy street or mall, taking off their sunglasses, closing their umbrellas, and developing a visual impression of the entire store. Customers are not prepared to evaluate merchandise or make purchase decisions in the decompression zone, so retailers try to keep this area free of merchandise, displays, and signage.[20]

Freestanding Displays   **Freestanding displays** are fixtures that are located on aisles and designed primarily to attract customers' attention and bring them into a department. These fixtures often display and store the newest, most exciting merchandise in the particular department.

Window displays need to catch the attention of the shopper and draw them into the store.

Whimsical mannequins attract the attention of children in Disney stores.

Mannequins   A **mannequin** is a life-size representation of the human body, used for displaying apparel. In the past, mannequins were often plain and boring. Twenty-first-century retailers have begun to realize that mannequins don't need to be hairless, feature-less, blindingly white, skinny space holders. They can help personify a brand, push customers to enter their stores, and perhaps even offer an ideal image that encourages shoppers to buy a little something extra that looks great on display. At the Disney Store, children are enchanted as whimsical mannequins swoop down from the ceiling or execute a perfect princess curtsy. The stylish customers moving through Ralph Lauren stores instead perceive a sense of style and sophistication, conveyed through the mannequin with a recreated face of British model Yasmin Le Bon.[21]

End Caps   **End caps** are displays located at the end of an aisle in stores using a grid layout. Due to the high visibility of end caps, sales of a product increase dramatically when that merchandise is featured on an end cap. Thus, retailers use end caps for higher-margin, impulse, and sale merchandise. In the supermarket industry, vendors often negotiate for their products to be on end-cap displays when they are offering special promotional prices.

Promotional Aisle or Area   A **promotional aisle** or **promotional area** is a space used to display merchandise that is being promoted. Drugstores, for instance, use promotional aisles to sell seasonal merchandise, such as lawn and garden products in the summer and Christmas decorations in the fall. Specialty stores and department stores tend to locate a promotional area at the back of the store or department. To get to the items on sale, customers must pass through all the full-price merchandise, which makes it more likely that something will catch their eye.

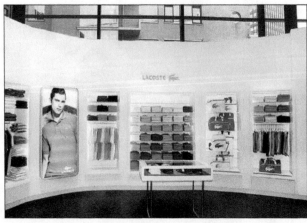

The arrangement of merchandise helps tells the story.

Walls   Because retail floor space is often limited, many retailers increase their ability to store extra stock, display merchandise, and creatively present a message by utilizing wall space. Merchandise can be stored on shelving and racks and coordinated with displays, photographs, or graphics featuring the merchandise. At the French clothier Lacoste, for instance, merchandise is displayed in bold color swaths relatively high on the wall. Not only does this allow the merchandise to "tell a story," but it also helps customers feel more comfortable because they aren't crowded by racks or by other people, and they can get a perspective on the merchandise by viewing it from a distance.

Dressing Rooms   Dressing rooms are critical spaces, where customers often decide whether to purchase an item. Large, clean, and comfortable dressing rooms put customers in the mood to buy. In recent years, retailers have even begun to compete aggressively on the basis of the quality of their dressing rooms. Old Navy has moved dressing rooms to the front of stores, so they no longer feel like "dungeons." To achieve a more refined, upscale feel, Ann Taylor stores feature chandeliers and attractive color accents in fitting rooms. Recognizing that many shoppers make trying on clothes a social event, Anthropologie has expanded the size of dressing rooms to make it easier for women to bring friends in with them. And to make the experience of waiting for a spouse trying on clothes more enjoyable, Macy's has added couches and flat-screen televisions outside dressing rooms.[23]

 Virtual dressing rooms are becoming more important and interesting to online shoppers. People cannot try on clothes displayed on a website, but the spread of webcams embedded in laptops, tablets, and desktop computers is making it possible for programmers to create "virtual dressing rooms" that could permit Internet customers to "try on" clothing and accessories, simply by standing in front of their webcams.[24]

Although technology and decor can enhance the experience of trying on clothing, some retailers are cautious about the extent to which they will use technology. The personal attention provided by sales associates remains the most effective agent for providing customer service.

Cash Wraps   **Cash wraps**, also known as **point-of-purchase (POP) counters** or **checkout areas**, are places in the store where customers can purchase merchandise. Because many customers go to these areas and wait in line to make a purchase, retailers often use them to display impulse purchase items. For example, in supermarkets, batteries, candy, gum, and magazines are often shelved at the checkout counter.

SPACE MANAGEMENT

LO3

Describe how to assign store floor space to merchandise departments and categories.

The space within stores and on the stores' shelves and fixtures is a scarce resource. Space management involves key resource decisions: (1) the allocation of store space to merchandise categories and brands,[26] (2) the location of departments or merchandise categories in the store, and (3) the size of the store.

Space Allocated to Merchandise Categories

Some factors that retailers consider when deciding how much floor or shelf space to allocate to merchandise categories and brands are (1) the productivity of the allocated space, (2) the merchandise's inventory turnover, (3) the impact on overall store sales, and (4) the display needs for the merchandise.

Space Productivity   A simple rule of thumb for allocating space is to allocate on the basis of the merchandise's sales. For example, if artificial plants represent 15 percent of the total expected sales for a hobby and craft retailer such as Michaels, then 15 percent of the store's space is allocated to artificial plants.

But as the discussion of marginal analysis for advertising allocations in Chapter 15 indicated, retailers really should allocate space to a merchandise category on the basis of its effect on the profitability of the entire store. In practice, this recommendation means that Michaels should add more space to the artificial plant section as long as the profitability of the additional space is greater that the profitability of the category from which space was taken away. In this condition, the additional space for artificial plants will increase the profitability of the entire store. However, at some point, it will be more profitable to not take away space from other categories.

Two commonly used measures of space productivity are **sales per square foot** and **sales per linear foot.** Apparel retailers that display most of their merchandise on freestanding fixtures typically measure space productivity as sales per square foot. In supermarkets, most merchandise is displayed on shelves. Because the shelves have approximately the same width, only the length, or the linear dimension sales per linear foot, is used to assess space productivity.

A more appropriate productivity measure, such as gross margin per square foot, would consider the contribution generated by the merchandise, not just the sales. Thus, if salty snacks generate $400 in gross margin per linear foot and canned soup generates only $300 per linear foot, more space should be allocated to salty snacks. However, factors other than marginal productivity need to be considered when making space allocation decisions. These factors are discussed in the next section.

In addition, retailers need to allocate space to maximize the profitability of the store, not just a particular merchandise category or department. Supermarkets often "overallocate" space to some low-profitability categories such as milk because an extensive assortment in these categories attracts customers to the store and positively affects the sales of other categories. Retailers might also overallocate space to categories purchased by their platinum customers—that is, those customers with the highest lifetime value.

Inventory Turnover   Inventory turnover affects space allocations in two ways. First, as discussed in Chapter 12, both inventory turnover and gross margin contribute to GMROI—a measure of the retailer's return on its merchandise inventory investment. Thus, merchandise categories with higher inventory turnover merit more space than merchandise categories with lower inventory turnover. Second, merchandise displayed on the shelf is depleted more quickly for items with high inventory turnover. Thus, more space needs to be allocated to this fast-selling merchandise to minimize the need to restock the shelf frequently and reduce stockouts. Many retailers, however, compensate for high inventory turnover items by assigning them more frequent deliveries so they don't take up so much space.

Display Considerations   The physical limitations of the store and its fixtures affect space allocation. Of course, store planners must provide enough merchandise to fill an entire fixture dedicated to a particular item. But in addition, a retailer might decide it wants to use a merchandise display to enhance its image. For Target to set itself apart as a source of high-quality home goods, it makes its display of private-label organic cotton sheets attractive and expansive. To really emphasize this offering, it even might overallocate space for the sheets and present a wide range of colors.

Location of Merchandise Categories and Design Elements

As discussed previously, the store layout, signage, and feature areas can guide customers through the store. The location of merchandise categories also plays a role in how customers navigate the store. By strategically placing impulse and demand/destination merchandise throughout the store, retailers increase the chances that customers will shop the entire store and that their attention will be focused on the merchandise that the retailer is most interested in selling—merchandise with a high GMROI. **Demand/destination merchandise** refers to products that customers have decided to buy before entering the store.

As customers enter the store and pass through the decompression zone, they are welcomed with introductory displays, including graphics. Once through the decompression zone, they often turn right (in Western cultures) and observe the prices and quality of the first items they encounter. This area, referred to as the "strike zone," is critical, because it creates the customer's first impression of the store's offering. Thus, retailers display some of their most compelling merchandise in the strike zone.

After passing through the strike zone, the most heavily trafficked and viewed area is the right-hand side of the store because most people turn right when come into a store. By this point in their journey through the store, customers have become accustomed to the environment, have developed a first impression, and are ready to make purchase decisions. Thus the right-hand side is a prime area for displaying high GMROI merchandise. For example, supermarkets typically locate the produce section in this area because produce appeals to the shoppers' senses. The visual/color appeal of all the different produce—bright oranges, deep reds of tomatoes and peppers, rich greens of zucchini and kale—gets a shopper's mouth watering, and the best grocery store customer is a hungry one.

Impulse Merchandise   The prime store locations for selling merchandise are heavily trafficked areas such as 10 feet beyond the entrance on the right side of the store and areas near escalators and cash wraps. In multilevel stores, a space's value decreases the farther it is from the entry-level floor. Thus, **impulse products,** or products that are purchased without planning, such as fragrances and cosmetics in department stores and magazines in supermarkets, are almost always located near the front of the store, where they're seen by everyone and may actually draw people into the store.

Demand and Promotional Merchandise Demand merchandise and promotional merchandise are often placed in the back left-hand corner of the store. Placing high-demand merchandise in this location pulls customers through the store, increasing the visibility of other products along the way. So supermarkets typically put items almost everyone buys—milk, eggs, butter, and bread—in the back left-hand corner. In department stores, children's merchandise and furniture, as well as customer service areas like beauty salons, credit offices, and photography studios, are demand or destination areas and thus located in lightly trafficked areas of the store.

The checkout counter at a supermarket is an ideal place to display merchandise typically bought on impulse.

Special Merchandise   Some merchandise categories involve a buying process that is best accomplished in a lightly trafficked area. For example, women's lingerie is typically located in a remote area to offer a more private shopping experience. Categories that require large amounts of floor space, like furniture, are often located in less desirable locations. Some categories, like curtains, need significant wall space, whereas others, like shoes, require easily accessible storage rooms.

Category Adjacencies   Retailers often put complementary categories next to each other to encourage unplanned purchases. Thus at the end of the cereal aisle, grocery shoppers often find an end cap filled with fresh bananas, and audio cables tend to hang on a display near the section featuring sound systems in an electronics store. Such displays help encourage cross-selling, as discussed in Chapter 5.

Another option is to contradict traditional placement schemes to surprise and excite shoppers. A well-known example places beer next to diapers, based on the observation that fathers making an emergency diaper run often late at night buy themselves a treat during the same trip. Consumer goods companies also hope to exploit a "halo effect" created by the fresh produce aisle in supermarkets.[27] If their

Retailers often place complementary products, such as chips and salsa, next to each other to increase unplanned purchases.

REFACT

Whereas 65 percent of men's toiletries are purchased by women, men are highly apprehensive of women's products and more likely to purchase products that are farther away from feminine-themed products.[28]

packaged goods appear next to healthy, fresh vegetables and fruit, consumers are more likely to associate those appealing traits with the manufacturers' products. But supermarkets are cautious about such moves, because the quality of the fresh produce section is a real competitive advantage. These critical trade-offs remain a constant challenge for grocers.

Location of Merchandise within a Category   As discussed in Chapter 4, most purchases in food, discount, drug, and many category specialists are either based on limited problem solving or habitual decision making. As such, retailers have a very short time, often a matter of a few seconds, to get their attention and induce them to grab an item for purchase. Retailers use a variety of rules to locate specific SKUs within a category.[29] For instance, supermarkets and drugstores typically place private-label brands to the right of national brands. Because Western consumers read from left to right, they will see the higher-priced national brand first and then see and possibly purchase the lower-priced, higher-margin private-label item on the right that looks similar to the national brand. Produce departments in grocery stores are arranged so that apples are the first item most customers see because apples are a very popular produce item and thus can best initiate a buying pattern.

Supermarkets typically display merchandise on four shelves, with the most profitable merchandise on the third shelf from the floor. The third shelf attracts the most attention because it is at eye level for adults. Merchandise that appeals to a smaller group of customers is often displayed on the top shelf because reaching for the items requires significant effort. Heavy, bulky items are stocked on the bottom shelf for safety reasons.

However, when purchase decisions are influenced by shorter consumers, positioning merchandise on the lower shelves might be more effective. For example, children may influence breakfast cereal purchases when accompanying their parents to the supermarket. Thus, the second shelf from the floor might be a prime location for the most profitable cereal brands.

Exhibit 17–5 illustrates some innovative merchandise placement options with which some grocery stores are experimenting. Specifically,

1. Place the dairy section near the front of the store so it is associated with fresh produce.
2. Place other premium products in the produce section since it makes them sell better.
3. Redesign carts to have a second shelf for fragile items and have holders for flowers and coffee.
4. Have a small milk refrigerator near the front door to better compete with convenience stores.
5. Use wood and other natural materials to induce a "farm-fresh" image.
6. Group ingredients necessary for a particular recipe, such as tomatoes, basil, and mozzarella cheese.
7. Place some organic products together and others throughout the produce section to experiment with how they sell best.
8. Bananas should go at the back of the produce department to get customers to walk through the entire department.
9. To simulate farmers' markets, add some low shelves so customers can see through the department and locate various-colored items adjacent to each other for visual appeal.

EXHIBIT 17–5
Grocery stores are experimenting in their produce departments with unconventional product placements.

Some tools that retailers use to make decisions on the positioning of items in a category are planograms, virtual-store software, and videotapes of consumers as they move through the store.

Planograms   A **planogram** is a diagram that shows how and where specific SKUs should be placed on retail shelves or displays to increase customer purchases. The locations can be illustrated using photographs, computer output, or artists' renderings. In developing the planogram, the retailer needs to make the category visually appealing, consider the manner in which customers shop (or the manner in which it would like customers to shop), and work to achieve its strategic and financial objectives. Planograms are also useful for merchandise that doesn't fit nicely on shelves in supermarkets or discount stores. Most specialty apparel retailers provide their managers with photographs and diagrams of how merchandise should be displayed. Retailing View 17.4 describes how the SAS planogramming system automated Marks & Spencer's food business.

Virtual-Store Simulation   Virtual-store simulations are another tool used to determine the effects of placing merchandise in different areas of a store and evaluating the profit potential for new items.[30] In these simulations, customers sit in front of computer screens that depict a store aisle. Retina-tracking devices record the eye movements of the customers. When the customers push forward on a handle, similar to the handle on a shopping cart, they progress down the simulated aisle. Customers can virtually reach forward, pick an item off the shelf, look at the packaging, and

Kimberly-Clark is using virtual-store software that uses a retina-tracking device to record a customer's glances. The information obtained from the software enables the retailer to get a fast read on new-product designs and displays without having to conduct real-life tests in the early stages of product development.

then place the item in the virtual cart. These virtual shopping trips allow retailers and their suppliers to develop a better understanding of how customers will respond to different planograms.

Videotaping Consumers Another research method used to assess customer reactions to planograms involves tracking customers in actual store environments. Traditionally, retailers would videotape customers' movements, but Microsoft's Kinect sensors are providing a less intrusive option. Discretely embedded in aisles, the sensors provide three-dimensional spatial recognition.

17.4 RETAILING VIEW Marks & Spencer Automates with Planograms

Marks & Spencer is a large retailer of clothing, home goods, and high-quality food products in the United Kingdom. Its food business, specializing in high-quality convenience and fresh foods, such as sandwiches and take-home dinners, occupies a prominent position in the U.K. food retailing sector.

The retailer is continuously updating its product range with new products. That process was incredibly labor-intensive: Adjusting 50 displays in 50 stores required 2,500 new, individual planograms. It took 80 to 100 full-time planogrammers to implement weekly changes in its approximately 300 stores. So, the $8.6 billion retailer worked with SAS to develop an automated planogramming system that could optimize weekly fresh-food assortments to individual stores, as well as improve product layout and customer satisfaction.

The Marks & Spencer SAS system calculates an optimal layout by determining how many shelf facings are needed for each SKU in each store. At the same time, the system maintains a consistent look but considers specific fixtures and store layouts.

By implementing automated space planning, Marks & Spencer has greatly increased the productivity of its space-planning team and gained control over store layout and product presentation. It can now do weekly plans with 20 planogrammers—and it does a much better job than before. Product placement is more efficient and uniform throughout the chain, and customers can more easily find specific products.

Such successes have driven other grocers to follow this lead. In Finland, the SOK supermarket chain is using SAS analytics to shift from 1,500 cut-and-paste planograms to store-specific versions, or around 100,000 plans to meet the needs of its 800 stores. As a further step, SOK integrates customer data gathered through its loyalty card program into the planograms. It also shares the resulting information with its suppliers to improve efficiency and supply chain planning.

Sources: Communication with SAS; and Joanna Perry, "SOK: Using Store-Specific Plans," *RetailWeek*, November 20, 2009.

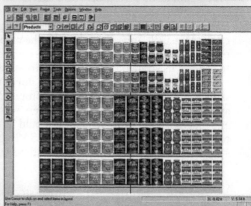

Marks & Spencer in the United Kingdom uses a planogram system developed by SAS to develop a layout that maximizes space productivity.

DISCUSSION QUESTION

Why are planograms particularly helpful for grocery retailers?

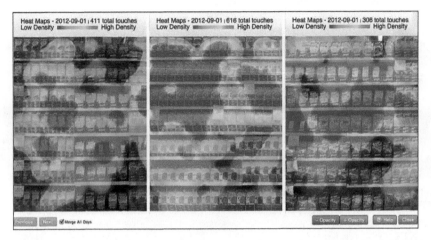

Using Microsoft Kinect sensors, firms like Shopperception create heatmaps of shopper interactions with the products (touches, pickups, and returns). The red represents the hot zones where shoppers touch the most, yellow less, and blue not at all.

Thus, retailers can unobtrusively track the amount of time people spend in front of a shelf, which products they touch or pick up, the products they return to shelves, and finally what they add to their carts to purchase.[31] The data gathered can be used to improve layouts and planograms because they can identify causes of slow-selling merchandise, such as poor shelf placement. By studying customers' movements, retailers can also learn where customers pause or move quickly or where there is congestion. This information can help them decide if the layout and merchandise placement is operating as expected, such as whether new or promoted merchandise is getting the attention it deserves.

Determining Store Size

A key space management decision is deciding how big the store should be. With the rise of online shopping and the recent recession, retailers are coming to find that bigger is not always better. Improvements in supply chain management enable stores to decrease their size but still provide sufficient inventory levels. Thus, some big-box stores are reducing their inventory on hand while also looking for other creative ways to increase their revenue. However, some of these tactics appear contradictory with the recommendations for creating an inviting atmosphere.

Stores such as Walmart and Anchor Blue simply reduced their inventory; Anchor Blue actually erected temporary walls to reduce available floor space and stopped carrying unpopular styles and sizes. Other chains, including Kmart and Home Depot, leased their unused space to other retailers, such as related small business owners and fast-food restaurants. In the longer term, most large retailers also are looking for ways to reduce store footprints. Smaller stores mean fewer SKUs available, but they also can be erected in new markets that could never support a supercenter. Small-format "Walmart Express" stores target urban markets with shops that are approximately one-third the square footage of a regular Walmart location. Staples and Office Depot similarly are opening smaller formats, between 5,000 and 8,000 square feet, to service smaller and urban trade areas.[32]

Such changes do not come easy, nor without cost. There are potentially significant benefits to retailers, though. With their smaller spaces, they likely pay less rent, can hire fewer employees and thus reduce their payroll costs, minimize inventory costs by reducing the number of SKUs, and gain access to new

Small-format "Walmart Express" stores (left) target urban markets with shops that are approximately one-third the square footage of a regular Walmart location (right).

markets. There are also negative effects of the change, and most of those focus on the customer. Customers face reduced selection, decreased comfort, and little entertainment. Smaller formats mean there is no room for communal dressing rooms, entertaining digital displays, or wide aisles that facilitate browsing. The potential outcomes suggest a broader question: Are modern consumers—time-pressured, price-sensitive, and computer-savvy—likely to embrace these new, smaller-format stores that cannot offer one-stop shopping or a seemingly unlimited selection? The promise is great for retailers that hope to entice new segments of customers, but their offer might not be enough for the average consumer.

While this section explored how retailers manage the precious and scarce resource of space in their stores, the next section looks at the "softer side" of managing a store's interior—visual merchandising.

VISUAL MERCHANDISING

LO4

Illustrate the best techniques for merchandise presentation.

Visual merchandising is the presentation of a store and its merchandise in ways that will attract the attention of potential customers. This section examines issues related to the presentation of merchandise, and the following section explores more sensory aspects of the store's environment. This section begins with a review of the fixtures used to display merchandise and then discusses some merchandise presentation techniques.

Fixtures

The primary purposes of fixtures are to efficiently hold and display merchandise. At the same time, they define areas of a store and direct traffic flow. Fixtures work in concert with other design elements, such as floor coverings and lighting, as well as the overall image of the store. For instance, in stores designed to convey a sense of tradition or history, customers automatically expect to see lots of wood rather than plastic or metal fixtures. Wood mixed with metal, acrylic, or stone changes the traditional orientation. Apparel retailers utilize the straight-rack, rounder, and four-way fixtures, while the principle fixture for most other retailers is the gondola.

The **straight rack** consists of a long pipe balanced between supports in the floor or attached to a wall (Exhibit 17–6A). Although the straight rack can hold a lot of apparel, it cannot effectively feature specific styles or colors. All the customer can see is a sleeve or a pant leg. As a result, straight racks are often found in discount and off-price apparel stores.

(A) Straight rack

EXHIBIT 17–6
Types of Fixtures

(B) Rounder

(C) Four-way

(D) Gondola

A **rounder**, also known as a **bulk fixture** or **capacity fixture**, is a round fixture that sits on a pedestal (Exhibit 17–6B). Although smaller than the straight rack, it's designed to hold a maximum amount of merchandise. Because they are easy to move and efficiently store apparel, rounders are found in most types of apparel stores. But, as with the straight rack, customers can't get a frontal view of the merchandise.

A **four-way fixture**, also known as a **feature fixture**, has two crossbars that sit perpendicularly on a pedestal (Exhibit 17–6C). This fixture holds a large amount of merchandise and allows the customer to view the entire garment. The four-way is harder to maintain properly than is the rounder or straight rack, however. All merchandise on an arm must be of a similar style and color, or the customer may become confused. Due to their superior display properties, four-way fixtures are commonly utilized by fashion-oriented apparel retailers.

A **gondola** is an island type of self-service counter with tiers of shelves, bins, or pegs. (Exhibit 17–6D). Because they are extremely versatile, they are used extensively, but not exclusively, in grocery and discount stores to display everything from canned foods to baseball gloves. Gondolas are also found displaying towels, sheets, and housewares in department stores. Folded apparel can be efficiently displayed on gondolas as well, but because the items are folded, it's even harder for customers to view apparel on gondolas than it is on straight racks.

Presentation Techniques

Some presentation techniques are idea-oriented, item and size, color, price lining, vertical merchandising, tonnage merchandising, and frontage presentation.

Idea-Oriented Presentation   Some retailers use an **idea-oriented presentation**—a method of presenting merchandise based on a specific idea or the image of the store. Individual items are grouped to show customers how the items could be used and combined. Women's blouses are often displayed with skirts and accessories to present an overall image or idea. Also, furniture stores display a combination of furniture in room settings to give customers an idea of how it would look in their homes. This approach encourages the customer to make multiple complementary purchases.

Item and Size Presentation   Probably the most common technique of organizing stock is by style or item. Discount stores, grocery stores, hardware stores, and drugstores employ this method for nearly every category of merchandise, as do many apparel retailers. When customers look for a particular type of merchandise, such as breakfast cereals, they expect to find all items in the same location. Arranging items by size is a common method of organizing many types of merchandise, from nuts and bolts to apparel. Because the customer usually knows the desired size, it's easy to locate items organized in this manner.

Color Presentation   A bold merchandising technique is organizing by color. For instance, Ralph Lauren stores often have entire collections in one color hue, all merchandised together. White House/Black Market women's apparel stores take color presentation to an extreme—most of its merchandise is black, white, or a combination of the two.

Price Lining   **Price lining** occurs when retailers offer a limited number of predetermined price points and/or price categories within another classification that are merchandised together. This approach helps customers easily find merchandise at the price they wish to pay. For instance, men's dress shirts may be organized into three groups selling for $49, $69, and $99 (see Chapter 14).

Vertical Merchandising   Another common way of organizing merchandise is **vertical merchandising.** In this approach, merchandise is presented vertically using walls and high gondolas. Customers shop much as they read a newspaper—from left to right, going down each column, top to bottom. Stores can effectively organize merchandise to follow the eye's natural movement. Retailers take advantage of this tendency in several ways. Many grocery stores put national brands at eye level and store brands on lower shelves because customers scan from eye level down. In addition, retailers often display merchandise in bold vertical bands of an item. For instance, you might see vertical columns of towels of the same color displayed in a department store or a vertical band of yellow and orange boxes of Tide detergent followed by a band of blue Cheer boxes in a supermarket.

Tonnage Merchandising   As the name implies, **tonnage merchandising** is a display technique in which large quantities of merchandise are displayed together. Customers have come to equate tonnage with low price, following the retail adage "Stock it high and let it fly." Tonnage merchandising is therefore used to enhance and reinforce a store's price image. Using this display concept, the merchandise itself is the display. The retailer hopes customers will notice the merchandise and be drawn to it. For instance, grocery stores often use an entire end of a gondola (i.e., an end cap) to display six-packs of Pepsi.

Frontal Presentation   Often, it's not possible to create effective displays and efficiently store items at the same time. But it's important to show as much of the merchandise as possible. One solution to this dilemma is the **frontal presentation,** a method of displaying merchandise in which the retailer exposes as much of the product as possible to catch the customer's eye. Book manufacturers, for instance, make great efforts to create eye-catching covers. But bookstores usually display books exposing only the spine. To create an effective display and break the monotony, book retailers often face an occasional cover out like a billboard to catch the customer's attention. A similar frontal presentation can be achieved on a rack of apparel by simply turning one item out to show the merchandise.

CREATING AN APPEALING STORE ATMOSPHERE

To provide a rewarding shopping experience, retailers go beyond presenting appealing merchandise. **Atmospherics** refers to the design of an environment by stimulation of the five senses.[33] Many retailers have discovered the subtle benefits of developing atmospherics that complement other aspects of the store design and the merchandise. Therefore, they use lighting, colors, music, scent, and even flavors to stimulate customers' perceptual and emotional responses and ultimately affect their purchase behavior. Research has shown that it is important for the atmospheric elements to work together—for example, the right music with the right scent.[34]

LO5

Understand how retailers can create a more appealing shopping experience.

Lighting

Good lighting in a store involves more than simply illuminating space. Lighting can highlight merchandise and capture a mood or feeling that enhances the store's image. Retailers also are exploring ways to save energy with technologically advanced lighting. Having the appropriate lighting positively influences customer shopping behavior.[35]

Highlighting Merchandise   A good lighting system helps create a sense of excitement in the store. At the same time, lighting must provide an accurate color rendition of the merchandise. It also allows the retailer to focus spotlights on special featured areas and items. The key determinant appears to be achieving an appropriate level of contrast, which helps attract visual attention.[36] Using lighting to focus on strategic pockets of merchandise trains shoppers' eyes on the merchandise and draws customers strategically through the store. Nike, for example, uses a lot of contrast and shadows, highlighting the merchandise but not necessarily the architecture.

Mood Creation   Retailers use lighting to set the mood for their customers. Ralph Lauren stores and boutiques in department stores use low levels of light to coordinate with their overall ambience of resembling a townhouse. Abercrombie & Fitch keeps stores purposefully dark, discouraging too many parents from entering. With their lesser concern about atmospherics, full-line discount stores, food retailers, and category specialists tend to brighter and less-expensive fluorescent lighting.

Energy-Efficient Lighting   As the price of energy soars and retailers and their customers become more energy-conscious, retailers are looking for ways to cut their energy costs and be more ecologically friendly. One obvious source of energy consumption is the lighting in a store, which makes up approximately one-third of a large store's energy costs. Light-emitting diode (LED) lighting is replacing fluorescent lighting in many stores because it reduce these costs by up to 75 percent, and they last 10 times longer than standard bulbs. Yet LEDs are more expensive initially than traditional lighting.[37]

Color

The creative use of color can enhance a retailer's image and help create a mood. Warm colors (red, gold, and yellow) produce emotional, vibrant, hot, and active responses. Thus, for sellers using online auction sites like eBay, it may be a good

Abercrombie & Fitch creates a dark environment targeted at the younger consumer.

idea to use red tones, because bidders instinctively respond with higher bids in the online auction, compared with a sale page dominated by blue hues.[38] Cool colors (white, blue, and green) have a peaceful, gentle, calming effect and appear to induce abstract thinking, leading customers to view products more favorably. Thus brick-and-mortar stores may want to use these more relaxing colors of the spectrum.[39] Although these trends are common, colors can have differential impacts, depending on various consumer traits, such as their culture (e.g., in the East, white is a color of mourning, whereas in the West, it often implies purity), their age, and their gender.

Music

Music can either add to or detract from a retailer's total atmospheric package. Most shoppers notice music playing in stores, and nearly half of them say they will leave if they do not like the selections being played.[40]

Fortunately, unlike other atmospheric elements though, music can be easily changed. For example, one retailer has a system that allows different types of music to be played at certain times of the day. It can play jazzy music in the morning when its customer base is older and adult contemporary in the afternoon for a 35-to-40-year age range customer. For its West Coast stores, it wants modern rock in the morning and Caribbean beats in the afternoon. And in Texas, it's country music all day, every day. The retailer also can "zone" music by demographics, playing more Latin music in stores that attract a higher Hispanic population.

Retailers also can use music to affect customers' behavior. Music can control the pace of store traffic, create an image, and attract or direct consumers' attention. For instance, one U.K. toy store switched from children's songs like "Baa Baa Black Sheep" to relaxed classical music and watched sales jump by 10 percent.[41] Managers realized that though children are the consumers of their products, adults are the customers. In general, slow is good. A mix of classical or otherwise soothing music encourages shoppers to slow down, relax, and take a good look at the merchandise.

Scent

Smell has a large impact on a customer's mood and emotions. In conjunction with music, it can increase customers' excitement and satisfaction with the shopping experience.[42] Customers in scented stores think they spent less time in the store than do those in unscented stores. Scents thus can improve customers' subjective shopping experience by making them feel that they are spending less time examining merchandise, waiting for sales help, or checking out.

Retailers also use different essences in different departments: baby powder in the baby store; suntan lotion in the bathing suit area; lilacs in lingerie; and cinnamon and pine scents during the holiday season.[43] Some high-end retailers, such as Saks Fifth Avenue, utilize their own unique scents, and mall shoppers can sniff out an Abercrombie & Fitch store yards away. Yet these apparel retailers are not the only ones to use this atmospheric tool. Goodwill Stores now disperse the scent of honeysuckle and sweet orange in an attempt to make its retail sites more appealing. According to a Goodwill spokesperson, "Even if the recession weren't happening, we'd be doing everything we can to create a great shopping experience. We've already taken the approach of trying to have better lighting, [a] great layout . . . this is just one more thing that we hope will help enhance the shopping environment."[44]

When New Balance spread into China, it aimed for a (Western) nostalgic sensory experience to introduce the U.S. brand. Thus, not only did the stores feature wooden floors and 1950s pop music, but they also smelled like wood and leather. Even pop singers get in on this scent action. During her California Dreaming tour, Katy Perry appealed to young fans by spreading the scent of cotton candy throughout the stadiums she played.[45]

Taste

It is a little more difficult to appeal subtly to consumers' taste buds. However, many department stores are reintroducing an old-fashioned offering to appeal to shoppers: the store restaurant. The option to grab a bite without leaving the store encourages customers to linger longer and enjoy their shopping experience more. Café SFA at Saks Fifth Avenue offers a stellar view of Rockefeller Center, while Bergdorf Goodman's BG Restaurant shows off Central Park. And for those shoppers who must have a $36 lobster club sandwich to complete their shopping expedition, Fred's at Barney's New York is the place to go.[46]

Just How Exciting Should a Store Be?

Retailers such as Cabela's, REI, Bass Pro Shops, and Barnes & Noble attempt to create an entertaining shopping environment by viewing their stores as theatrical scenes: The floor and walls constitute the stage and scenery; the lighting, fixtures, and displays are the props; and the merchandise represents the performance. This

Customers enjoying a bite between their purchases stimulates longer stays and more purchases.

creation of a theatrical experience in stores has resulted in the combination of retailing and entertainment. In contrast, retail chains such as Costco and Home Depot successfully use minimalist, warehouse-style shopping environments, but create excitement in other ways, such as giving away food samples and hosting do-it-yourself classes.

Does providing an exciting, entertaining store environment lead customers to patronize a store more frequently and spend more time and money during each visit? The answer to this question is: It depends.[47]

The impact of the store's environment depends on the customer's shopping goals. The two basic shopping goals are task completion (utilitarian), such as buying a new suit for a job interview, and recreation (hedonic), such as spending a Saturday afternoon with a friend wandering through a mall. When customers are shopping to complete a task that they view as inherently unrewarding, they prefer to be in a soothing, calming environment—a simple atmosphere with slow music, dimmer lighting, calming scents, and blue-green colors. However, when customers go shopping for fun, an inherently rewarding activity, they want to be in an exciting atmosphere—a complex environment with invigorating smells, fast tempo music, bright lighting, and red-yellow colors.

What does this mean for retailers? They must consider the typical shopping goals for their customers when designing their store environments. Grocery shopping is typically viewed as an unpleasant task, and thus supermarkets should be designed in soothing colors and use slow background music. In contrast, shopping for fashion apparel is typically viewed as fun, so an arousing environment in apparel retail outlets will have a positive impact on the shopping behavior of their customers.

The level of excitement caused by the environment might vary across the store. A consumer electronics retailer might create a low-arousal environment in the accessories area to accommodate customers who typically are task oriented when shopping for print cartridges and batteries, and it might create a high-arousal environment in the home-entertainment centers that are typically visited by more pleasure-seeking shopping customers.

Finally, retailers might vary the nature of their websites for customers depending on their shopping goals. For example, research suggests that Amazon should serve up complex, high-arousal websites with rich media to customers who indicate they are browsing but provide simpler, low-arousal sites to customers looking for a specific book.[48]

SUMMARY

LO1 Identify the critical issues retailers need to consider when designing a store.

To design a store, retailers must consider their main objectives: (1) implement their strategy, (2) influence customer buying behavior, (3) provide flexibility, (4) control design and maintenance costs, and (5) meet legal requirements. Because few store designs can achieve all of these objectives, managers make trade-offs among objectives, such as providing convenience rather than encouraging exploration or vice versa.

LO2 List the advantages and disadvantages of alternative store layouts.

Regardless of the type used, a good store layout helps customers find and purchase merchandise.

The grid design is best for stores in which customers are likely to explore the entire store, such as grocery stores and drugstores. Racetrack designs are more common in large upscale stores, such as department stores. Free-form designs are usually found in small specialty stores and within the departments at department stores.

LO3 Describe how to assign store floor space to merchandise departments and categories.

Space management involves three decisions: (1) allocating store space to merchandise categories and brands, (2) locating departments or merchandise categories in the store, and (3) determining the appropriate store size. To determine how much floor or shelf space to allocate to merchandise categories, retailers might consider the productivity of the allocated space (e.g., using sales per square foot or sales per linear foot), the merchandise's inventory turnover, its impact on store sales, and display needs. In addition, by strategically placing impulse and demand/destination merchandise throughout the store, retailers can encourage customers to shop the entire store and focus their attention on merchandise that the retailer wants to sell most.

LO4 Illustrate the best techniques for merchandise presentation.

Signage and graphics help customers locate specific products and departments, provide product information, and suggest items or special purchases. Digital signage has several advantages over traditional printed signage, but the initial fixed costs

have made its adoption slow. Feature areas are designed to get customers' attention. They include windows, entrances, freestanding displays, mannequins, end caps, promotional aisles or areas, walls, dressing rooms, and cash wraps. Finally, various types of display racks and shelving are more or less appropriate for different types of merchandise.

LO5 Understand how retailers can create a more appealing shopping experience.

Retailers employ various forms of atmospherics—lighting, colors, music, scent, and even taste—to influence shopping behaviors. The use of these atmospherics can create a calming environment for task-oriented shoppers or an exciting environment for recreational shoppers.

KEY TERMS

atmospherics, *507*
boutique layout, *493*
bulk fixture, *505*
call-to-action signage, *494*
capacity fixture, *505*
cash wrap, *497*
category signage, *494*
checkout area, *497*
demand/destination merchandise, *498*
digital signage, *494*
end cap, *496*
feature area, *495*
feature fixture, *505*
fixture, *487*

four-way fixture, *505*
free-form layout, *493*
freestanding display, *495*
frontal presentation, *506*
gondola, *505*
grid layout, *489*
hedonic benefit, *484*
idea-oriented presentation, *506*
impulse product, *499*
loop, *492*
mannequin, *496*
planogram, *501*
point-of-purchase (POP) counter, *497*
point-of-sale signage, *494*

price lining, *506*
promotional aisle, *496*
promotional area, *496*
promotional signage, *494*
racetrack layout, *492*
rounder, *505*
sales per linear foot, *497*
sales per square foot, *497*
straight rack, *504*
tonnage merchandising, *506*
utilitarian benefit, *484*
vertical merchandising, *506*
visual merchandising, *504*

GET OUT AND DO IT!

1. **CONTINUING ASSIGNMENT** Go into the physical store location of the retailer you have chosen for the continuing assignment, and evaluate the store layout, design, and visual merchandising techniques employed. Explain your answers to the following questions:
   (a) In general, are the store layout, design, and visual merchandising techniques consistent with the exterior of the store and its location?
   (b) Is the store's ambience consistent with the merchandise presented and the customer's expectations?
   (c) How do the store's layout, design, and visual merchandising support the following objectives: (1) implements the retailer's strategy, (2) builds

   loyalty, (3) increases sales, (4) controls costs, and (5) meets legal requirements?
   (d) To what extent are the store's layout, design, and merchandising techniques flexible?
   (e) How does the store utilize atmospheric elements such as color, lighting, music, and scent? Are these uses appropriate given the store's merchandise and target market?
   (f) Is the store's design environmentally friendly? If yes, please describe. If no, how could it become more "green"?
   (g) Are the fixtures consistent with the merchandise and the overall ambience of the store? Are they flexible?

(h) Evaluate the store's signage. Does it do an effective job of selling merchandise?

(i) Has the retailer used any theatrical effects to help sell merchandise?

(j) Does the store layout help draw people through the store?

(k) Has the retailer taken advantage of the opportunity to sell merchandise in feature areas?

(l) Does the store make creative use of wall space?

(m) What type of layout does the store use? Is it appropriate for the type of store? Would another type of layout be better?

(n) Ask the store manager how the profitability of space is evaluated (e.g., profit per square foot). Is there a better approach?

(o) Ask the store manager how space is assigned to merchandise. Critically evaluate the answer.

(p) Ask the store manager if planograms are used. If so, try to determine what factors are considered when putting together a planogram.

(q) Are departments in the most appropriate locations? Would you move any departments?

(r) What method(s) has the retailer used to organize merchandise? Is this the best way? Suggest any appropriate changes.

2. **INTERNET EXERCISE** Go to the home page of CoolHunters (www.thecoolhunter.net). Look at examples posted in their retail subpage. How can this information of latest trends assist with store layout, design, and visual merchandising?

3. **INTERNET EXERCISE** VMSD is the leading resource for retail designers and store display professionals, serving the retail industry since 1869 (then called Display World). Go to its web page at http://vmsd.com, and develop a list of three or four items that describe the latest trends in visual merchandising.

4. **INTERNET EXERCISE** Go to the home page of Envirosell (www.envirosell.com). How does this marketing research consulting firm support retailers by collecting consumer information to assist with store layout, design, and visual merchandising?

DISCUSSION QUESTIONS AND PROBLEMS

1. One of the fastest-growing sectors of the population is the over-60 age group. Customers in this group may have limitations in their vision, hearing, and movement. How can retailers develop store designs with this population's needs in mind?

2. Assume you have been hired as a consultant to assess a local discount store's floor plan and space productivity. Look back at Chapter 6 and decide which analytical tools and ratios you would use to assess the situation.

3. What are the different types of design that can be used in a store layout? How does the layout impact the types of fixtures used to display merchandise? Describe why some stores are more suited for a particular type of layout than others.

4. A department store is building an addition. The merchandise manager for furniture is trying to convince the vice president to allot this new space to the furniture department. The merchandise manager for men's clothing is also trying to gain the space. What points should each manager use when presenting his or her rationale?

5. As an architect for retail space, you are responsible for Americans with Disabilities Act compliance. How would you make sure that a store's retail layout both meets accessibility requirements and enables the company to reach profitability objectives?

6. What are the advantages and disadvantages of offering virtual dressing rooms from the retailers' perspective?

7. Complete the following table by briefly describing how the different retail formats could use each of the areas listed to enhance the store's image and atmosphere.

Area	Drugstore	Clothing Store	Music Store	Restaurant
Entrance				
Walls				
Windows				
Merchandise displays				
Cash wrap				

8. Reread Retailing View 17.2, "Walmart Goes Green and Lowers Its Energy Costs." Which of the environmental practices discussed do you think will be implemented by other retailers? Explain your response.

9. Reread Retailing View 17.3, "A Hedonic Maze Filled with Utilitarian Products." What do you think about IKEA's layout? Does it provide them with a competitive edge? Explain your response.

10. How can signage and graphics help both customers and retailers? Consider the following types of retail formats that you likely have visited in the past: discount store, department store, office superstore, and card and gift store. Describe which retail formats have implemented the best practices for coordinating signs and graphics with each store's image and which formats should improve this aspect of their store layout, design, and visual merchandising.

SUGGESTED READINGS

Krishna, Aradhna (Ed.). *Sensory Marketing: Research on the Sensuality of Consumers*. New York: Routledge, 2009.

Bell, Judy, and Kate Ternus. *Silent Selling: Best Practices and Effective Strategies In Visual Merchandising*, 4th ed. New York: Fairchild Publication, 2011.

Law, Derry, Christina Wong, and Joanne Yip, "How Does Visual Merchandising Affect Consumer Affective Response?: An Intimate Apparel Experience." *European Journal of Marketing*, 46 no. 1/2 (2012), pp. 112–133.

Manganari, Emmanouela E., George J. Siomkos, and Adam P. Vrechopoulos. "Store Atmosphere in Web Retailing." *European Journal of Marketing* 43 (September 2010), pp. 1140–1153.

Nordfalt, Jens. *In-Store Marketing*, 2nd ed. Sweden: Forma Magazine, 2011.

Ortinau, David J., Barry J. Babin, and Jean-Charles Chebat. "Development of New Empirical Insights in Consumer–Retailer Relationships within Online and Offline Retail Environments: Introduction to the Special Issue." *Journal of Business Research*, available electronically 2011.

Pegler, Martin. *Store Presentation and Design*, 3rd ed. New York: RSD, 2010.

Pegler, Martin. *Visual Merchandising and Display*, 6th ed. New York: Fairchild Publication, 2012.

Sorensen, Herb. *Inside the Mind of the Shopper*. Upper Saddle River, NJ: Pearson Education, 2009.

Underhill, Paco. *Why We Buy: The Science of Shopping*, 3rd ed. New York: Simon and Schuster, 2009.

Valenzuela, Ana, Priya Raghubir, and Chrissy Mitakaki. "A Shelf Space Schemas: Myth or Reality?" *Journal of Business Research*, available online, 11 January 11, 2012.

Wang, Yong Jian, Michael S. Minor, and Jie Wei. "Aesthetics and the Online Shopping Environment: Understanding Consumer Responses." *Journal of Retailing*, 87 (March 2011), pp. 46–58.